American Boarding Schools

American Boarding Schools:

A HISTORICAL STUDY

By James McLachlan

CHARLES SCRIBNER'S SONS · NEW YORK

A—8.72 (C)
SBN 684-10389-3 (cloth)
SBN 684-12963-9 (paper, SUL)

Printed in the United States of America
Library of Congress Catalog Card Number: 73-85259

For ALICE K. McLACHLAN

and J. DONALD McLACHLAN

Acknowledgments

A grant from the Committee on the Role of Education in American History made a considerable amount of the research for this book possible. In a very different form, it was submitted as a Ph.D. dissertation at Columbia University in 1966. I would like to thank my sponsor at Columbia, Richard Hofstadter, for his example, patience, and support at crucial moments, and my First Reader, Lawrence A. Cremin, for his suggestions and assistance. My debts to friends and colleagues are innumerable: I am particularly grateful to David Hall, Daniel Howe and Richard Weiss for having read and criticized the manuscript in whole or part at various stages. Joyce Crummey's assistance with the German was generous and indispensable. I owe a special debt of gratitude to George Wilson Pierson, whose detailed, concerned, and perceptive criticisms of an early version of the manuscript were of immeasurable assistance in helping me clarify my thoughts. Thomas J. Davis III of Charles Scribner's Sons has been a model of editorial patience and encouragement.

The staffs at the various schools I visited, sometimes for months, went far out of their way to smooth my path—would that more institutions were as cooperative. I am particularly grateful to Gerrish Thurber of the John Dixon Library of the Lawrenceville School. At Choate, Earle V. Leinbach and the administrative staff were most helpful. Miss Pauline Anderson, co-director of Choate's Andrew Mellon Library, shared her unique bibliographical knowledge of private schools with me, saving months of work. Rodney Armstrong and his staff at the Phillips Exeter Academy's Davis Library were unfailingly hospitable and helpful. Exeter's alumni secretary, Miss Gertrude E. Starks, gave me an awareness of the role of alumni at private schools. Exeter's treasurer, James Griswold, led me to enough primary manuscript materials to keep a battalion of historians occupied for the next decade. Conversations with St. Paul's rector, the Reverend Matthew Warren, deepened my understanding of Henry A. Coit and St. Paul's history. St. Paul's administrative vice-rector, William A. Oates, was most cooperative, as were J. Alden Manley and Mrs. Harriet Sykes of the school's Sheldon Library.

The staffs of many libraries from one end of the United States to the other made my work possible. I would like to acknowledge special thanks to the following: to the staff of Butler Library, Columbia University, for their resourcefulness in searching out the location of rare imprints; to Kimball C. Elkins of the Harvard University Archives for identifying Charles W. Eliot's marginal notations in the Schools Examination Board MSS; to Clifford K. Shipton of the American Antiquarian Society for locating the George Bancroft MSS; to the staff of the Massachusetts Historical Society for ferreting out obscure student journals; to the staff of Beinecke Library, Yale University, for their untiring help in locating apparently lost items; and to F. Garner Ranney for drawing my attention to the collections relating to the College of St. James in the Peabody Institute Library.

Los Angeles, California
March 1969

PICTURE CREDITS

1, 2, 3: Courtesy of Phillips Academy, Andover
4, 21, 22, 24, 29, 31, 33, 34: Courtesy of Phillips Exeter Academy
5, 6: Courtesy of Berne Municipal Library
7: Courtesy of Culver Pictures, Inc.
9, 14, 15, 16, 17, 18, 19, 20, 23, 25, 26, 27, 28: Courtesy of St .Paul's School
10: Courtesy of The New-York State Historical Society
11: Courtesy of The New York Public Library, Local History Room
13: Courtesy of the Maryland Historical Society
30: Courtesy of The New Hampshire Historical Society
35: Courtesy of The Groton School

Credits

The author gratefully acknowledges the permission of the following individuals and institutions to quote excerpts from the material indicated:

Letter of Charles Francis Adams, Jr.
By permission of Thomas B. Adams.
George Bancroft Papers.
By permission of the Massachusetts Historical Society.
Letter of Nicholas Murray Butler.
By permission of W. N. M. Lawrence.
Letter of John Jay Chapman.
By permission of Charles A. Chapman.
Joseph Choate Papers.
From The Manuscript Division, Library of Congress.
Eliot Papers.
By permission of Harvard University Archives.
William C. Endicott Papers.
By permission of the Massachusetts Historical Society.
Letter of Daniel Coit Gilman.
By permission of The Johns Hopkins University.
Samuel A. Green Papers.
By permission of the Massachusetts Historical Society.
Harvard College Admission Books.
By permission of Harvard University Archives.
Harvard College Papers.
By permission of Harvard University Archives.
Harvard Schools Examination Board Reports.
By permission of The Groton School, Phillips Exeter Academy, and Harvard University Archives.
Letters of Bishop William Lawrence.
By permission of the Right Reverend Frederic Lawrence.
James Mackenzie's Original Draft Plan for The Lawrenceville School, and the "Committee of Ten Folder."
By permission of the Trustees of The Lawrenceville School.

Letter of Henry Cabot Lodge.
By permission of the Honorable Henry Cabot Lodge, Jr.
Letter of Admiral Alfred Thayer Mahan.
By permission of Alfred T. Mahan.
Endicott Peabody Papers.
By permission of the Right Reverend Malcolm E. Peabody and the Harvard College Library.
Phillips Exeter Academy Archives and Collections.
By permission of the Trustees of Phillips Exeter Academy.
Jacob Riis Papers.
From The Manuscript Division, Library of Congress.
Letters of Theodore Roosevelt.
By permission of Theodore Roosevelt House, New York.
St. Paul's School Archives and Collections.
By permission of the Trustees of St. Paul's School.
Shattuck Family Papers.
By permission of Henry L. Shattuck and the Massachusetts Historical Society.
William H. Taft Papers.
From The Manuscript Division, Library of Congress.
Samuel Ward Papers.
By permission of Manuscript Division, The New York Public Library, Astor, Lenox and Tilden Foundations.
Journal of Thomas Kelah Wharton.
By permission of Manuscript Division, The New York Public Library, Astor, Lenox and Tilden Foundations.

Contents

List of Illustrations

The following illustrations lie between pages 102 and 103:

American Boarding Schools ❧

The natural school, the school we should develop and trust in, is the public school. The boarding school is an attachment to the family of those who have wealth, and it tends to turn from a nobler work the power of men's hearts and brains by the simple expedient of buying them, here with money, there with social prestige. The worst of boarding schools are ineffectual reformatories, and the best of them are scrupulously cultivated hotbeds of snobbishness and un-American class superiority. Each year new boarding schools are started, and each new one is a hindrance within narrow limits to the perception of a fact vital to education. This fact is that these costly boarding schools are in reality but a species of orphan asylum—only without the claim on our sympathies that legitimate asylums have. The parents are not dead, but selfish.

—GEORGE C. EDWARDS, in the *Educational Review,* 1902

The object of a school like this, a residential school, seems to me to be to recognize a deeper and truer principle of education [*than is possible in the public schools*]*; a residential school is . . . an attempt to establish a community, and by attempting to establish a community it recognizes this principle: that education does not consist in instruction; that it consists in instruction* plus *the processes of life which make instruction useful and valid. It recognizes the fact that the habits of the mind are of the essence of the whole process; that a mind not put to use itself is not a mind awakened and is not a mind educated. . . . A great school like this does not stop with what it does in the class room; it organizes athletics and sports of every kind, it organizes* life *from morning to night; and it does so when at its best by an intimate association of the teacher with the pupil, so that the impact of the mature mind upon the less mature will be constant and influential.*

—WOODROW WILSON, Address at the Centennial of the Lawrenceville School, 1910

Introduction

"The radical error in my case," declared Charles Francis Adams, Jr., in his autobiography, "was that I was kept at home, and brought up in an uncongenial day-school. I do not hesitate to say that these mistakes have gravely prejudiced my entire life." Things might have been very different, Adams thought, if he had been sent away to a school like England's Rugby, where he might have had his "rough edges" smoothed down.[1] Though the Adams family has never been noted for an optimistic view of either itself or the world, Charles Francis must surely have been pleased to see that his twin sons, John and Henry, had their rough edges smoothed down at Endicott Peabody's Groton School, which has often been called an American version of Thomas Arnold's Rugby.[2] In Adams's youth in the 1830s and 1840s no school that anyone would have compared with Rugby existed in the United States. By the time of his death in 1915 they dotted the Atlantic seaboard, with their heaviest concentration in Adams's own state, Massachusetts. In the twentieth century John and Henry Adams's school, Groton, could list among its alumni a president of the United States and many others prominent in government, business, and other fields.

Groton was not alone among private boarding schools in graduating alumni who played significant roles in American life. In 1941 the rector of St. Paul's School in Concord, New Hampshire, could proudly inform his trustees that one of every nineteen alumni was listed in *Who's Who in America.*[3] In 1956 *Who's Who* itself reported that a graduate of what it called the "first ten private schools" had a thirty-nine times better chance of appearing in its pages than did the average public high school graduate.[4] At mid-century one school alone—Choate, in Wallingford, Connecticut—numbered among its graduates three major national political figures: Adlai Stevenson, Chester Bowles, and John F. Kennedy. Almost unknown in Charles Francis Adam's youth, less than a century later the private preparatory schools had come to graduate leaders into American society in quantity widely disproportionate to their numbers.

Significantly, the influence of the private boarding school has even been extended into areas of the American past where it did not actually penetrate. A 1958 study of the era of Theodore Roosevelt, for instance, declared that "Roosevelt was from an old eastern patrician family of moderate wealth. . . . he attended Groton, the nearest American equivalent of the aristocratic English public schools, and then [went] to Harvard."[5] Although this sounds appropriate, when Groton was founded in 1884 Roosevelt actually was already twenty-six, a widower, and a seasoned politician.[6] Since Groton did not exist, it had to be invented.

There are many kinds of private schools: country day schools, military schools, coeducational boarding schools, and so on. The Roman Catholic church, with its extensive parochial school system, contributes the greatest number to the roster of private schools. But when "private schools" are mentioned, as often as not the first group of schools that comes to mind is apt to be that associated with the cluster of words used to describe Roosevelt and Groton—*old, eastern, patrician, aristocratic, English*—the classic northeastern boys' college preparatory schools.

These schools form a large, though at times indistinct, group of institutions. A few years ago the editor and journalist Robert Gutwillig tried to specify just *which* schools these "classic" schools were:

> At the outset, I think I should define what I mean by a prep school, for there must be at least three thousand private schools in the United States today. I am *not* speaking of three thousand schools; I am not even speaking of the approximately two hundred schools that partcipiate in the Secondary School Admission Tests program for entrance from the seventh through the twelfth grades; I *am* speaking generally of sixty boys' boarding schools in fourteen states and the District of Columbia, but more particularly of forty schools in six states and, quite candidly, only twenty-five of these schools really matter, and of these twenty-five perhaps seventeen are more central than the others, and of the seventeen a dozen at most influence the rest enormously, and several headmasters

> told me the list could really be cut to nine and, finally, there are still quite a few people who maintain that if a boy did not attend one of five or six schools, he might just as well not have gone to school at all, or worse yet, gone to public school.[7]

The seventeen schools Gutwillig finally chose as his "core" group were: St. Paul's, St. Mark's, Groton, St. George's, Kent, Middlesex, Phillips Exeter, Phillips Andover, Taft, Hotchkiss, Choate, Deerfield, Milton, Loomis, Gunnery, Lawrenceville and Hill. Other journalists have made other lists, and have encountered almost as much difficulty deciding just which schools should be included, and why.[8]

What common characteristics unite the schools mentioned so far? They are all boarding schools for boys; their major explicit aim is to prepare their students for college; and, while—like private colleges—they are all publicly incorporated nonprofit institutions, they receive their support not from the state but from private philanthropy and from tuition charges. However, "tuition-charging college preparation" is hardly an adequate enough phrase with which to categorize these schools. For generations they have been a center of controversy in discussions of American education. Their critics have labeled them "class schools" teaching little but snobbery. Their defenders have maintained that they are truly "independent" schools—bastions of liberal experimentation and leadership in contrast to the timidity, inertia and stifling bureaucratic control they attribute to the public school system.[9] In truth, very little is known about them.

Historians—academic and otherwise—have been of little help in understanding these schools. For instance, one good standard history of American education dismisses private schools as "class" schools—neatly giving them an extremely intriguing label without enlarging our understanding of them.[10] In 1903, in the only attempt yet made to write a comprehensive history of American secondary education, Elmer E. Brown noticed these schools, almost in passing. They seemed to Brown to form a distinct group, but the only way he was able to categorize them was by saying that they were a large "class of boarding schools, under various forms of control, which have been browing up in recent years."[11] Other historians have mentioned the boarding schools only glancingly—and usually disparagingly. Arthur Mann, for instance, has claimed that in the 1880s the Bostonian "descendents of the generation that had led the nation in the public school movement chose to educate their own progeny at St. Paul's and Groton, where British names, sports, and methods of instruction were aped."[12] Considering that in a representative year at St. Paul's—that of 1894–95—there were only six boys from Boston at St. Paul's, and that in its first decade (1884–93) Groton graduated all of forty-one students, this statement appears somewhat excessive.[13] Another social historian, Dixon Wecter, agrees with Mann as to the English nature of these schools. "Groton, St. Paul's, St. Mark's, and Choate," he writes, "are patterned somewhat artificially upon Eton, Harrow, and Winchester, even to the introduction of 'fives' at Groton and a modified fag system at St. Mark's, are richly significant of social Anglophilia. . . . several American critics have pointed out with dismay that our prep school tradition has neglected to borrow the British concept of public service or social obligation in the larger sense."[14]

In recent years sociologists have had something of a field day with these schools, and at least one agrees with Wecter. "Thoughtful Americans," the sociologist Digby Baltzell has written, ". . . have often compared the records of graduates of Exeter, Andover, Groton, or St. Paul's, with records of their English counterparts from schools such as Eton and Harrow. Seventeen old Etonians, for example, have been Prime Ministers of England. . . . while the statesman from the private school in America is conspicuously the exception."[15] Baltzell goes on to claim that in the late nineteenth century the New England boarding schools and some Eastern universities "became upper-class surrogate families on almost a national scale." The demand for these schools, he writes, "was the result of the same social forces which produced the national corporation, the nationally advertised brand, the national market, and an increasingly centralized government." These schools, he asserts, "serve the sociological function of differentiating the upper classes from the rest of the population." Sixteen private boarding schools in particular, Baltzell noted, "set the pace and bore the brunt of criticism received by private schools."[16] The select sixteen on Baltzell's list of schools were as follows:

1) Phillips Academy	Andover, Mass.	1778
2) Phillips Exeter Academy	Exeter, New Hampshire	1783
3) Episcopal High School	Alexandria, Virginia	1839
4) Hill School	Pottstown, Pennsylvania	1851
5) St. Paul's School	Concord, New Hampshire	1856
6) St. Mark's School	Southborough, Mass.	1865
7) Lawrenceville School	Lawrenceville, New Jersey	1883
8) Groton School	Groton, Mass.	1884
9) Woodberry Forest Sch.	Woodberry Forest, Va.	1889
10) Taft School	Watertown, Conn.	1890
11) Hotchkiss School	Lakeville, Conn.	1892
12) Choate School	Wallingford, Conn.	1896
13) St. George's School	Newport, Rhode Island	1896
14) Middlesex School	Concord, Mass.	1901
15) Deerfield Academy	Deerfield, Mass.	1903
16) Kent School	Kent, Conn.	1906

Baltzell's ideas—if not his thoroughly elitist ideology—have been extremely persuasive. For instance, in *The Power Elite* the late C. Wright Mills relied heavily on Baltzell's then still unpublished work to construct what he thought to be a model of a national ruling elite.[17] Another sociologist, G. William Domhoff, followed Baltzell in claiming that at these schools the "child learns upper-class values, upper-class manners, and most of all upper-class speech, one of the most telltale signs of class and regional origin."[18]

Journalists, historians, and sociologists, then, converge to a significant degree in their portrayals of the private preparatory school. They are creations of the late nineteenth century, they imitate English public schools, and they are "aristocratic" or "upper-class" institutions. I confess that when I began this book I shared the conventional picture. As I soon discovered, I was mistaken on all three counts.

To begin with, while most of the schools listed above were indeed founded in the late nineteenth century, they were by no means unique to that period. The late nineteenth-century schools were the heirs of traditions that took concrete institutional shape at least as early as the 1820s. They built upon a heritage of fifty or sixty years of American experience with boarding schools. Since most of the schools which embodied this heritage had disappeared by the time of the Civil War, the earlier tradition of American boarding schools has been hitherto largely overlooked. An understanding of the later schools, however, is impossible without a knowledge of their predecessors.

The notion that American private boarding schools are imitations of English public schools appears to be widely held. Historians such as Mann consider it a bad thing for American schools to have "aped" English schools. In truth, American educators would seem historically to deserve the reputation for imitativeness once ascribed to the Japanese. Over the course of the past, the American college has copied the English college, the American university has copied the German university, the American kindergarten has copied the German kindergarten, and the American public school system has copied the Prussian school system. Direct borrowing of cultural forms aside, in the case of the American boarding school the possibility always remains that similar cultural traditions and social conditions in the United States and in England produced institutions which—at least superficially—seemed alike. Part of our task will be to determine the degree to which American boarding schools were the result of native innovation or of borrowing from abroad.

Historians, of course, do not consider cultural imitation in itself necessarily bad. No one, for instance, has ever objected to the immediate imitation by Americans of Toynbee Hall, the first British settlement house. Objection to the private boarding school has not been based upon its educational merits but upon the supposition that it is somehow elitist. To Americans like George Edwards, the private boarding schools have always been a symbol of "un-American class superiority." They have represented a threat to the liberal, egalitarian, social order which—at least since the 1830s—Americans have assumed should be the natural order of things. The United States, most Americans have agreed, should be free of the law of social gravity: it should not have an upper class or a lower class—it should have only a middle class. And, all in all, Americans have come close to their hearts' desire; whether or not the United States has ever had a class structure definable by any traditional criteria is an open question.

Since the United States had no feudal past, it did not have an aristocracy. Whether or not it has had an upper class is a different matter. Perhaps there once was an American upper class; perhaps there is one today. But no historian or sociologist has ever demonstrated convincingly that one has or does exist. Elites, yes; subcultures, yes: but these are not the same things as social classes. Nor is the American boarding school the proper subject with which to begin an investigation of the problem. While the following pages will shed some light on these matters, this is not their primary concern.[19]

Classes aside, we are obviously dealing with, for the most part, the sons of rich Americans, since most of the schools we will discuss were—and are—very expensive to operate and therefore charged very high tuition fees. As recently as 1904–05 two-thirds of the adult male workers in the United States did not make even $600 a year; in 1893 St. Paul's tuition was $600, as was Groton's. And tuition was only the beginning of the expenses involved in sending a boy to one of these schools. Scholarship students aside, most of the boys at these schools were the sons of rich Americans.[20]

Rich parents did not send their sons to private boarding schools to serve "sociological functions," or to learn "upper-class values, upper-class manners, and most of all upper-class speech." If such things existed, most of the boys at these schools had probably learned them before leaving home. What they did not know of them they learned from their peers at the schools, not from their masters. What their education was to consist of and the manner in which it was to be conducted were determined not by parents or by a class but by schoolmasters. And, with one or two exceptions, most boarding school headmasters were not rich Americans, but middle-income intellectuals, moralists, or clergymen, who would have blanched at the sight of an "upper-class value," and who were the heirs of educational traditions that transcended particular social classes. For most of their history, these schools have consciously educated their students to avoid, abjure, and despise most of what are traditionally thought to be aristocratic or upper-class values and styles of life. They have worked instead to *prevent* the development of aristocratic attitudes. They have tried to inculcate their students with what are usually thought to be classically "middle-class" values: self-restraint, rigid self-control, severe frugality in personal style, and the ability to postpone immediate gratifications for larger future ends. How successful they have been in this is another matter: like all educational institutions, private boarding schools have been faced with the inherent conflict between the values that the school wishes to transmit and those that its students bring with them from their homes and communities. Whatever their latent sociological function may have been, the manifest aim of these schools has always been to educate, not the aristocrat, but something quite different—the bourgeois gentleman.

Since Plato's *Republic* philosophers have debated the nature of the good society, and thus the methods most appropriate to educate those who should rule society—the best, or true *aristoi.* For much of American history this concern was focused in discussions of the nature of the American gentleman. Since there can be only a few of the "best" at any one time, the concept of the American gentleman has been of necessity elitist. And, insofar as American boarding schools have attempted to educate American gentlemen, they have been elitist. Until quite recently, so too have been most American colleges and universities. For most of the nation's past those who attended college or university were generally (though not without considerable debate and objection) expected to form the nation's professional, technical—and to a much lesser degree—cultural, social, and political elites. The institutions that have striven towards the highest standards of their times have naturally tried to attract students prepared to their satisfaction. To a certain extent, the expansion of private boarding schools in the late nineteenth century was a response to the needs of the emerging American university.

For the greater part of human history extended formal education has been limited to a relativity few members of a particular society. Until almost yesterday most people were educated not in institutions but in various sorts of apprenticelike arrangements. Until the late Renaissance, higher education was largely concerned with the immediately utilitarian aim of training clergymen, lawyers and physicians. In the past two centuries, however, a revolution in education has occurred in the West. Educational institutions have assumed many of the functions once performed by society at large, and have responded to society's continual demands to take on new functions. No longer are most people educated informally. Instead, children, youths, and even adults are confined to educational institutions for a large part of their lives. The rationale usually given for this is that modern, technological, industrial society demands intensive and highly specialized training which can only be accomplished over a long period of time. Whether or not this is so, the result has been a mixed blessing. Kenneth Keniston, an acute commentator on contemporary society, sees in these developments the emergence of a new stage of human life, "youth," which continues today into the twenties and thirties, and "provides opportunities for intellectual, emotional and moral development that were never afforded to any large group in history." This extension of youth and concurrent attendance at an institution of higher education, Keniston argues, "tends to free [the student]—to free him from swallowing unexamined the assumptions of the past, to free him from the superstitions of his childhood, to free him to express his feelings more openly and to free him from irrational bondage to authority."[21] Perhaps. My own bias—and a major, though largely unexplicit, theme of the following pages—is that long-extended formal, institutionalized, education also has other, less happy, effects. It extends, I would argue, the period of dependency the young of any society must undergo beyond all reason. Extended dependency prevents the individual from taking up a meaningful and satisfying role in his society until an advanced age. It leaves him with a sense of sullen—and understandable—resentment towards that society. Instead of contributing to the growth of a mature sense of identity it actually inhibits such a process. In the past, this period of extended dependency was bearable for the relatively limited number of youths who underwent it. Generally, they were rewarded with positions in one of their society's elites. In part, the history of the private boarding school is the story of the beginnings of the extension of the period of institutionalized dependency for the youth of the United States.

Ours is a complex story of the constant interplay of men and ideas, institutions and society. But from the outset a few strands are clear. A major aim of the American boarding school has been to preserve the innocence of childhood into a pure and responsible maturity. At least since the 1820s many rich Americans have preferred to have their sons educated in pastoral isolation, secure from the physical and moral corruptions and temptations of an increasingly urbanized and industrialized society, in schools modeled on idealized "families" in which the child's "natural depravity" could be suppressed and his "naturally good" impulses carefully nurtured. The history of the private boarding school suggests a loose analogy to the present. Today the majority of Americans—compared with past experience—are rich. And, as the census of 1970 will probably demonstrate, the United States has become, not a nation of cities, but a nation of suburbs. Like the rich of old, a generation of Americans—isolated in their self-segregated, pastoral, suburbs—has attempted to preserve the innocence of its children into a pure and idealistic maturity. The generation that fled to the suburbs seems to have achieved this aim—though its children's explosive combination of radical innocence and radical idealism has had unexpected results. For a nation that has been recently inundated in the radical innocence and idealism of the young, the story of not dissimilar trends in the past may be of more than passing interest.[22]

Formal education in an affluent United States is no longer inherently elitist. The emergence of a "mass elite" places hitherto elite institutions in an anomalous position. The social situation and educational practices of the private boarding schools remained relatively static for the three decades after the ending of this study in the 1920s. Then, in the 1950s, the favored admission position of the alumni of the leading boarding schools vis à vis the Ivy League and other of the "best" colleges and universities began to deteriorate. Due to the immense improvement in public secondary instruction since the 1950s, institutions of higher education have been able to pick and choose from among an overwhelming number of secondary school graduates prepared to their satisfaction. No longer must the elite college or university depend upon the sometimes dull or uninterested but properly prepared youth for its students. In large part, the liberal society has been achieved: all careers are open to all talents.

Not surprisingly, as I write the private boarding schools are undergoing a season of drastic self-reassessment. Their old favored position in relation to elite universities has vanished. Except for the very, *very* rich the wealth or social connections of their students' parents is irrelevant in an increasingly affluent and meritocratic society. It will be interesting to see how the image of the American gentleman is transformed when the consumer society is completed and all the nation becomes Southern California.

In the past, the American boarding school has tried to educate its students so that they would neither drop-out nor sit-in. The gentlemanly ideal to which it has attempted to mold its students has been a conservative one. Not the reactionaly liberalism which usually calls itself conservative in the United States, but a conservatism of a more classical kind. Its nature is suggested well by his biographer's somewhat puzzled description of one boarding school alumnus, Franklin D. Roosevelt. Roosevelt, James MacGregor Burns suggests, "seems to have been a conservative by many tests." As Burns outlines them, the basic elements of the conservative tradition are:

> the organic view of society, compelling a national and social responsibility that overrides immediate class or group interest; a belief in the unity of the past, the present, and the future, and hence in the responsibility of one generation to another; a sense of the unknowable, involving a respect for the limits of man's knowledge and for traditional forms of religious worship; a recognition of the importance of personal property as forming a foundation for stable human relationships; personal qualities of gentility, or gentlemanliness, that renounce vulgarity and conspicuous display and demand sensitivity to other persons' needs and expectations; and an understanding of the fact that while not all change is reform, stability is not immobility.[23]

Burns thinks it odd that Roosevelt fits this pattern—which he considers British—so well. This conservative tradition, however, is not exclusively British; it has long been a living—though largely unexamined—American tradition, embodied particularly in certain American educational institutions, and in none more clearly than the boarding schools whose history is discussed in the following pages.

In outlining that history we will go far beyond the limits of the institutions themselves. Though we will focus on the words and actions of those most immediately concerned, our story will take us to places as disparate as Tombstone, Arizona, and Göttingen, Germany. It will involve individuals ranging in time from Lord

Byron to Booker T. Washington, from Jonathan Edwards to Phillips Brooks, from John Adams to John Kennedy. It will touch on the history of the American family, on American religion, on the American city, and on the history of the child in America. Even then it will be incomplete, something less and something more than a history of the private preparatory school.

Part I *Federalists*

Chapter I

The Gentleman and the Academy

At Harvard early in the nineteenth century the annual Phi Beta Kappa Address was a widely anticipated event, and seldom as much so as on 31 August 1809. The speaker of the day was to be Joseph Stevens Buckminster, minister to Boston's fashionable Unitarian Brattle Street Church. Only twenty-five years old, Buckminster was already considered by his contemporaries to be one of the most promising intellectual figures of the young republic. Buckminster, a short, muscular man with acquiline features, arose to speak. "The indescribable charm of his personal appearance and manner," a member of his audience recalled, "the look, the voice, the gesture and attitude, the unstudied outward expression of the inward feeling,—of these no idea can be formed by those who never heard him."[1]

Titled "On the Dangers and Duties of Men of Letters," Buckminster's address was in effect an outline for the creation of a high culture in the United States and a prescription for the role of the educated man within that culture. It was decisive in helping to define the cultural aims of a generation of Boston and Cambridge intellectuals. Out of the cultural milieu it expressed and shaped would develop a series of institutions that, by the end of the century, would give concrete form to high culture in the United States. The impulses expressed in Buckminster's speech would lead to an attempt to found great scholarly libraries, to an attempt to reshape American higher education, and, not the least, to a related effort to improve the quality of preparation for college by means of private boarding schools.

"In the usual course of national aggrandizement," Buckminster began prophetically, "it is almost certain, that those of you, who shall attain to old age, will find yourselves the citizens of an empire unparalleled in extent; but is it probable, that you will have the honour of belonging to a nation of men of letters?"* Buckminster was not at all sure. "So greatly have our habits of thinking," he said, "been disturbed by the revolutions of the last thirty years that the progress of our education, and, of course, the character of our learning, have not a little suffered." In France science had advanced and in England education had remained stable, but in the United States these decades had been ones of declension. "Here," Buckminster said,

> the French revolution, immediately succeeding our own, found the minds of men in an unsettled state, and, as you may well imagine, did not help to compose them. Our forms of education were becoming more popular and superficial; the knowledge of antiquity began to be despised; and the hard labour of learning to be dispensed with. Soon the ancient strictness of discipline disappeared; the curriculum of studies were shortened in favour of the impatience or the necessities of candidates for literary honours; the pains of application were derided, and a pernicious notion of equality was introduced, which has not only tainted our sentiments, but impaired our vigour, and crippled our literary eminence.

While the United States had much ground to recover from these cultural reverses, Buckminster did not despair; he hoped that he and his audience might live to see the dawn of an American "Augustan age." This would only come about, however, if the American scholar should not be too "tempted to turn his literary credit to the quickest account, by early making himself of consequence to the people, or rather to some of their factions." Not that the well-educated man should *not* take part in public affairs. Far from it. "There is hardly to be found a consummate statesman or warriour in a literary age," Buckminster reminded his audience, citing Alexander, Caesar, Charlemagne and Alfred the

*In the early nineteenth century, "man of letters" had somewhat the same connotation of today's "intellectual," while the phrase "literary institution" connoted "educational -cultural-intellectual" institution.

Great, "who was not himself a man of letters." The danger of a too-early entry into the public arena was balanced by the danger of not entering it at all. "There are some finely attempered spirits," said Buckminster, "who, disgusted at the grossness which belongs to the common conquests and occupations of active life, are in danger of relinquishing its real duties in the luxurious leisure of study. In the actual state of the politicks of our country, this opposite temptation has been already felt by many studious minds." The American scholar must not hide himself in his library. "Truth, truth," Buckminster exclaimed, "is indeed the ultimate object of human study; and though the pleasure of learning is often in itself a sufficient motive and reward, yet we are not to forget that we all owe something to society." American society desperately needed deeply educated and public-spirited theologians, preachers, moralists, jurists, statesmen, philosophers, historians, and poets. Not only the future of the republic, but that of Protestant Christianity, would depend upon such men. And, Buckminster added, these new Augustans might very well be educated right there in Cambridge, at Harvard—if the University received proper support. "Go to the rich," Buckminster exhorted his audience:

> and tell them of the substantial glory of literary patronage! Tell them of the Maecenases of former days! Tell them, that the spirit of commerce has always been propitious to the arts and sciences! Show them the glories of the Medici of Florence; the republican renown of Holland, once studded with splendid universities, and fruitful in great men, fostered by the rich merchants of her cities! Show them that island of the blessed [Britain], where so many rich endowments of schools and of literary institutions have mingled forever together the glories of commerce and of science! And, if this will not touch them, read the roll of the former benefactors of our university; of the Hollises and the Hancocks. These were merchants; and men too, whom posterity will never cease to honour; men, whom all the great and good spirits that have issued from this seat of learning will go and congratulate in heaven, as their benefactors![2]

"Going to the rich" was precisely what American intellectuals would do over the course of the nineteenth century. While institutions to further high culture were few and far between in 1809, a century later the United States was covered with universities, colleges, schools, museums, musical organizations, libraries, and research institutes created in large part through the patronage of the rich. But American clergymen-intellectuals (the roles were barely differentiated in Buckminster's day) not only went *to* the rich, but brought the rich—or, more properly, the children of the rich—to themselves. In schools and academies, colleges and universities, they sought to mold not only their successors, but generations of young Americans—affluent and otherwise—into a particular social and character type. The ideal they strove towards—for themselves as much as for their students—was implicit, if not directly mentioned, throughout Buckminster's address. A biographer of a close friend of Buckminster's, John Thornton Kirkland—who would become president of Harvard the following year—put it succinctly. "The character to which he proposed to form his pupils," Kirkland's biographer wrote, "was that of the Christian scholar and gentleman."[3]

The ideal of the Christian scholar and gentleman was an ancient one, and had passed through many permutations before it reached early nineteenth-century New England. In Elizabethan England the three main elements of gentility had been thought to be virtue, learning, and wealth. In the Puritan areas of Stuart and Hanoverian America, wealth had taken a fourth or fifth place to sincere Christianity as a necessary attribute of gentility. Nor in Buckminster's New England was there a necessary correlation between social status and gentility. "Gentlemen," John Adams once explained, were not "the rich or the poor, the high-born or the low-born," but "all . . .who have received a liberal education." As Edwin Cady has put it, "the *class of gentry,* representing an overt culture-pattern which had developed in response to social needs, must be distinguished carefully from the *concept of the gentleman,* a primarily covert culture-pattern extant as a system of ideal values long before the class came into being."[4] The cultural ideal was independent of the social fact. What Buckminster was suggesting in his speech was that the mercantile class be indoctrinated with the ideal of the Christian gentleman and scholar, that, in fact, unless virtue and learning co-opted wealth the

United States could not develop a high culture of its own.

Concern over the proper relation between the gentlemanly ideal and American society was not confined to the Boston-Cambridge area. Thomas Jefferson and John Adams, for example, agreed that there was such a thing as a "natural" gentleman—or, as Adams put it: "There is a natural Aristocracy among men; the grounds of which are Virtue and Talents." They agreed too that there was, both North and South, an "artificial" aristocracy, composed of certain old, prominent, families. "Our Winthrops, Winslows, Bradfords, Saltonstalls, Quincys, Chandlers, Leonards [,] Hutchinsons [,] Olivers, Sewalls," Adams wrote to Jefferson in 1813, "are precisely in the situation of your Randolphs, Carters and Burwells, and Harrisons. Some of them unpopular for the part they took in the late revolutions, but all respected for their names and connections and whenever they fall in with the popular Sentiments, are preferred, ceteris paribus to all others." Adams mistrusted anyone who held power, be he a "natural" or an "artificial" gentleman.[5] Jefferson was more optimistic. He tried to provide for rule by the natural *aristoi*—or best—through an elaborate educational system. But outside of nineteenth-century New England few American intellectuals were as successful as Buckminster in reconciling the intellectual and cultural elitism implicit in their pursuits with the social and political equalitarianism inherent in the ideals of the American Revolution. Jefferson was no exception; his educational system—an attempt to bridge the gap between the cultural ideal and the social fact—simply provided for an uneasy accommodation between the "natural" and the "artificial" aristocracies, or gentlemen.

Jefferson believed that it was the duty of the state "to provide that every citizen in it should receive an education proportional to the condition and pursuits of his life." He gave no indication of the manner in which the state would be able to guess just what a small child's "condition and pursuits" might be in adult life. After a three-year common elementary education the mass of citizens would be divided into two classes—the laboring and the learned. Then, "those destined for labor will engage in the business of agriculture, or enter into apprenticeships to such handicraft art as may be their choice; their companions, destined to the pursuits of science, will proceed to the college. . . ." The learned class—or gentlemen—Jefferson continued, could be subdivided into two sections: "1, Those who are destined for learned professions, as a means of livelihood; and 2, The wealthy, who, possessing independent portions, may aspire to share in conducting the affairs of the nation, or to live with usefulness and respect in the private ranks of life." Both branches of the learned class, Jefferson thought, should share a common general education in the higher branches of language, mathematics, and philosophy: "the wealthy to qualify them for either public or private life; the professional section will need those branches, especially, which are the basis of their future profession, and a general knowledge, of the others, as auxiliary to that, and necessary to their standing and associating with the scientific class."[6] Such a plan, Jefferson hoped, would rake "twenty of the best geniuses . . . from the rubbish annually."[7] While Jefferson managed to found the capstone of his system, the University of Virginia, he never succeeded in establishing its necessary foundations. To the north, however, in Buckminster's New England and the areas settled from it, such a system—a system which developed "natural" gentlemen and accommodated "artificial" gentlemen—already, in effect, existed.

Joseph Stevens Buckminster was the product of that system. A close examination of his career provides us with a concrete example of the manner in which education entered into the making of the early American gentleman and with a touchstone against which to compare later American educational practices. Born in 1784, he was the son of the Reverend Joseph Buckminster, minister to the Congregationalist North Church in Portsmouth, New Hampshire. His upbringing was the classic New England one of plain living and high thinking. He began studying Latin grammar at four, attended the town-maintained Latin Grammar school, and at the age of eleven was sent to the not-far-distant Phillips Exeter Academy to prepare for college. In his last quarter there he reviewed the Greek Testament, Cicero and Vergil, and read Livy's *Roman History.* He also studied Hugh Blair's *Rhetoric* and Jedidiah Morse's larger *Geography.* For spice, he found time to borrow from the Academy's library Rollin's *Ancient History, a Life of Cicero,* Kennet's *Roman Antiquities,* D'Arnay's *Private Life of the Romans,* and Boswell's *Life of Johnson.* For light amusement he read *The Spectator,* Moore's *France,* and Sir William Temple's *Essays.* He entered Harvard's sophomore class at the age of thirteen, in 1797. While Buckminster was certainly precocious, his seemingly extremely youthful age at entering college was not, as we shall see, unusual.

College was a new experience for Buckminster, and his father sent him detailed instructions for his conduct there. They were typical of the doting, stern—and almost obsessive—concern any well-educated contemporary New England Puritan father would have felt for his son:

> You are now placed in a situation, my son, in which you must exercise care for yourself and the things you have with you, without depending upon others. You have hitherto boarded in a family [at Exeter] where you have had kind female care; you must now take care of yourself. Keep every thing in order; your clothes in their place, your books in their place, and be not in so much of a hurry as to leave them in confusion and disorder. Lock your trunk and your study, when you go out. Make a little paper book and put down all your expenses. You must bear half the expenses of the room, such as candles, etc. I suppose it will be customary to have some wine in your room, to offer to strangers. I hope it is not the custom to offer scholars or classmates wine when they call; but when a gentleman or friend from out of town calls, it will be necessary. . . . I would not have you mean, nor profuse; but entirely just in your part of the expense.

The elder Buckminster's concern with Joseph's finances was well taken. Poor as the proverbial churchmouse on his ministerial salary (it never exceeded $600–$700 a year), his son's education was a heavy burden on the family's finances. Joseph found it difficult to keep himself decently clothed. On trips home to Portsmouth he had to walk much of the way in order to save on coach fares. Buckminster had a brilliant career at Harvard, graduating in 1800 at the age of sixteen. He then returned to Phillips Exeter to serve for three years as an instructor. At nineteen his wealthy relatives, the Theodore Lymans of Waltham, employed him as a tutor in their family in order to give him enough free time to pursue theological and philosophical studies on his own and with the nearby Reverend James Freeman. In 1804 he preached his first sermon and was asked to serve as minister to the wealthy congregation of Boston's Brattle Street Church. His father might well have been proud, but in fact looked upon his son's career with deep misgivings. The elder Buckminster, a graduate of theologically conservative Yale, was a sternly orthodox Trinitarian Congregationalist and had sent his son to latitudinarian Harvard with misgivings. They were well founded. In his years at Harvard, of study with Freeman, and on his own, the younger Buckminster had come under the influence of the new Unitarian doctrines then splitting the old order in New England. It was as a Unitarian that Buckminster was called to Brattle Street. His brief career there was most successful. A Christian, a scholar, and a gentleman, he was as much at ease in Europe and Boston's fashionable drawing rooms as in his pulpit and study. Seemingly without obstacle, he had moved from earnest and respectable poverty to a position of responsibility and power and on the way had become one of Adams and Jefferson's "natural" aristocrats.[8]

Buckminster's career was not unique. His older friend John Thornton Kirkland, president of Harvard, followed much the same course. Born in 1770 the son of a poor missionary on the New York frontier, Kirkland prepared for Harvard at the Phillips Academy in Andover, and after graduation returned to the college as a tutor in 1792. Genial, sociable, and witty, Kirkland was elected minister of Boston's New South Church, where, almost without their realizing it, he led his parish from Congregationalism into Unitarianism. As Samuel Eliot Morison has described this "natural" aristocrat, he embodied "the Federalist ideal of a gentleman and scholar; the best of those 'old-fashioned New England divines softening down with Arminianism,' 'good, wholesome, sound-bodied, sane-minded, cheerful-spirited men,' whom Dr. Holmes remembered affectionately among the visitors to his father's parsonage."[9] The New England system of education, formal and informal, was almost expressly designed for such boys. (Although being a minister's son helped, it was not crucial.) The free Latin Grammar school prepared the boy for the usually very inexpensive academy; the academy in turn prepared him for a frugal course at one of New England's colleges. If he was bright and industrious, the college had prepared him to enter the group of merchants, lawyers, and clergymen who in effect ruled Federalist New England.

Buckminster and Kirkland were members both of the Federalist elite and of the Anthology Society, an organization designed to promote much the same cultural values and goals as those Buckminster discussed in his speech. Styling itself, appropriately enough, "A Society of Gentlemen," the Society had its beginnings in 1804 when a Boston publishing firm requested William Emerson, minister to Boston's First Church, to assume the editorship of *The Monthly Anthology, or Magazine of Polite Literature,* an almost-moribund journal that had led a precarious existence since 1803.[10] Emerson (the father of Ralph Waldo Emerson), widely-known in greater Boston for his cultural interests, asked several friends to help him with the new venture. Fourteen Bostonians—all of the Federalist persuasion—joined Emerson in 1805 to inaugurate the Anthology Society.

For the most part, the members of the Society were "natural" gentlemen. Among the first was John Sylvester John Gardiner, rector of Episcopalian Trinity Church, an Englishman of Johnsonian bearing and wit, who had been a student of Dr. Samuel Parr, reputedly England's foremost classical scholar. He was joined by Samuel Cooper Thacher, later minister to the New South Church, and William Smith Shaw, a lawyer and bibliomaniac. It was an extraordinarily youthful group. At forty-one Gardiner, elected the first president, was the oldest, while Emerson was thirty-seven and Shaw but twenty-seven. Of the eleven additional members two were in their thirties and nine in their twenties.[11] Clergymen, lawyers, and physicians, they met weekly over suppers of woodcock or roast goose, and with "much pleasant conversation & good humour" discussed present and future contributions to their journal.

In their magazine the Anthologists sought, as Lewis Simpson has written, "to mediate for the new nation between two visions of its cultural fate: a vision of the progress of letters in America and a prospect of the barbarization of letters in America."[12] The prospect of cultural barbarization was as immediate to the Anthologists as the possibility of cultural progress. Fisher Ames, the gloomy prophet of Federalism and an idol to many Anthologists, summed up their fears: "Our country," he wrote in 1803, "is too big for union, too sordid for patriotism, too democratic for liberty. What is to become of it, he who made it best knows. Its vice will govern it, by practicing upon its folly."[13] Buckminster's 1809 address gave witness to both visions, but, like most of the Anthologists, he belonged to a younger generation than Ames, and tended more towards optimism than pessimism. The slide into a money-grubbing, democratic barbarism might be reversed, and a positive national culture created if America possessed a class of Christian gentlemen and scholars.

In an early issue, William Emerson personified the Anthologists' hopes for their journal—and, incidentally, outlined the education designed to produce the Christian gentleman and scholar. "We are daily introducing him to the acquaintance of the wise and good, and laying plans to give him an excellent education." The *Anthology*-gentleman would be "instructed in several ancient and modern languages, matriculated in two or three universities, and versed in almost every art and science." He should be associated with learned and humane societies both at home and abroad, and should "inspect the colleges, hospitals, and armies of Europe, take now and then a peep into the cabinets of princes, and get a general acquaintance with the great affairs of the political world." Scholarship, in this ideal education, was not to preempt gentility. The Anthologist's offspring, Emerson continued, should "not be destitute of the manners of a gentleman, nor a stranger to genteel amusements. He shall attend Theatres, Museums, Assemblies, Balls, &c. and whatever polite diversions the town may furnish; so that whilst he is familiar with the love of books and the wisdom of sages, his dress and conversation shall borrow mode and graces of the most polished circles in our society."[14] Few of the Anthologists had enjoyed such an education themselves; among their accomplishments was to assure that many of their descendants—intellectual *and* physical—would be educated in just this manner. The Anthologists thought that a class of Christian gentlemen and scholars, who would resist the slide into barbarism and create a national culture, might be brought about by forming institutions which would embody their cultural values and ideals; they would thereby spread these qualities in their own generation and transmit them to the next.

The most immediate result of the Anthologists' interest in founding institutions to further their cultural goals was their establishment of the Boston Atheneum in 1807. Anthologists gave parts of their own collections to the new library, and Buckminster went abroad to purchase books and to examine the

Liverpool Atheneum as a model for Boston.[15] But the Atheneum was a long-term project; closer at hand were other, ancient, well-established literary institutions—the colleges of America, particularly Harvard. It might be equally wise, Anthologists thought, to reform existing institutions as to form new ones. Despite the great number of educational institutions in America, the Anthologists felt that "the higher branches of learning, those which elevate the soul, and teach man the use of his noble faculties, droop for want of culture."

"An English school-boy," Bristol-born Anthologist Robert Hollowell Gardiner wrote, "must possess a classical knowledge, superior to what is acquired here at any period of a university education." The cause of this sorry state was twofold: first, Americans scattered their resources on scores of second-rate institutions; and second, were not willing to pay instructors enough "to maintain the rank of gentlemen." The solution was to concentrate the nation's financial and intellectual educational resources: "instead of founding new colleges and academies, publick and private liberality should be directed to institutions, already established." Some institutions might satisfy popular demands by specializing in applied technology, while a very few others—perhaps only one—should concentrate the nation's resouces in "polite literature and the higher branches of science." By offering very high salaries, the most outstanding talents in the nation might be attracted to the faculty. Ample scholarships should be provided to attract "poor lads of talents, selected from the different academies." The admission age should be raised to a level where the students were old enough "to lay aside puerilities," while "higher qualifications should be required for admittance, that their time might not be wasted, as it is now, in obtaining, what ought to have been learnt at school." Above all, "the scholars must be made gentlemen, and treated as such, that they may consider those placed over them as friends, who have an interest in their welfare, and not treat them with the indignity and petty contempt, due only to petty suspicious tyrants."[16]

While such proposals were ambitious, they were not Utopian. However, by 1812 it might have appeared that all the Anthologists' hopes would come to little. In 1811 the Society itself, plagued by financial troubles, disbanded, and in 1812 one of its central figures, Buckminster, tragically died. But most of the individuals who had composed the Society and contributed to its journal were still very much alive. The gentlemanly cultural goals supported by the Anthologists were now diffused over a far wider area than greater Boston. In particular, when Anthologist John Thornton Kirkland became president of Harvard, he followed a course much like the one proposed in the *Anthology* three years before.

In its short career the Society had attracted as members or contributors several brilliant New Englanders, including Daniel Webster, John Quincy Adams, and Benjamin Silliman. Among the younger members of this group were George Ticknor, the Society's last secretary, and Andrews Norton, later theology professor at Harvard. Kirkland counted on these younger men to raise Harvard's standards. In the decade after the *Anthology's* demise, Kirkland—directly and indirectly—encouraged and often financially supported, along the lines Emerson had sketched in 1805, the education in Europe of young men like Ticknor and Edward Everett, younger brother of Anthologist Alexander Everett. Once returned home, Kirkland and his supporters hoped, these newly minted Christian gentlemen and scholars would apply their talents to the Harvard faculty.[17]

Raising intellectual standards at Harvard, however, was no simple task, as Kirkland was well aware. "In our eagerness to create and bring forward the literary profession and make better scholars," he wrote in the *Monthly Anthology's* successor journal, the *North American Review,* in 1818, "we may attempt acquisitions beyond the market and lose our labour." But the goals, so long held by the Anthologists, seemed worth the effort. "The measure of improvement within our reach," Kirkland continued, "cannot in all cases be ascertained without trial, and we cannot say that nobody will buy what no one has offered to sell."[18] But Kirkland and other former Anthologists had realized for years that before any significant improvements in higher education could be made it would be necessary to improve drastically the quality of secondary education. "We can do nothing at Cambridge," one of Kirkland's proteges declared in 1819, "till we contrive the means of having the boys sent to us far better fitted than they are now."[19]

What was wrong with American secondary education in 1818? Just about everything, according to Joseph Green Cogswell, a

Kirkland supporter who anonymously published two articles in *Blackwood's Edinburgh Magazine* the following year. The articles in the influential British review constituted a far-ranging critique of American culture and education and must have come as a shock to many Anthologists: it was one thing for the Anthologists themselves to criticize American culture; it was a quite different matter to find fifteen years' worth of their own ideas summed up in one of those Scottish journals which they admired but unhappily found consistently denigratory towards the United States.[20] They would have been even more annoyed if they had known that the anonymous critic was not only an American but a former contributor to the *Monthly Anthology* as well.[21]

Born in Ipswich, Massachusetts, in 1786, Joseph Green Cogswell was, like Buckminster and several other Anthologists, a graduate of the Phillips Exeter Academy and Harvard. After college he studied law, first with the Anthologist idol, the conservative Federalist Fisher Ames, and then with the equally conservative Judge William Prescott, father of the historian. Deciding for a time against a legal career, he travelled to India and Europe as a supercargo on a merchant ship. In 1812 Cogswell married the well-to-do Mary Gilman, daughter of a governor of New Hampshire, and practiced law for a short time in North Carolina. His wife, however, died the following year, and the deeply depressed Cogswell spent two desultory years of retirement as a Latin tutor at Harvard. In 1815 he again resumed the travels that were to mark all but a few periods of his life and returned to Europe, this time for a stay that would last for five years.[22]

As befitted someone steeped in the judicial critical style of the Anthologists—and a former pupil of Fisher Ames—Cogswell was frankly a cultural elitist. ("The literary character of a nation," he wrote, "depends upon the degree of knowledge among the few, not upon the universal diffusion of it among the many.") He began his critique with a discussion of the American academies —"that class of schools, in which the foundation is laid for a liberal education." These academies, Cogswell explained to his British audience, "are not always exclusively classical schools; some are partly appropriated to education for the counter and the counting-room; and as far as this object goes there is no striking defect in them; it not being a very difficult matter to teach a lad to count his fingers and take care of his dollars." As far as humanistic, classical culture was concerned, however, Cogswell found the academies "totally deficient; there is not one, from Maine to Georgia which has yet sent forth a single first rate scholar; no, not one since the settlement of the country, equal even to the most ordinary of the thirty or forty, which come out every year from Schule Fforta and Meissen [famous German secondary schools.]"[23]

His articles, Cogswell told a friend, were "both bitter tho scrupulously just."[24] Bitter they were, though their justice was called into question by his countrymen back home. "We are constantly *reproached* for being so low in the scale," replied former Anthologist Sidney Willard, a Harvard faculty member, "as if it were a voluntary, and even wilful degradation." Some of Cogswell's charges, he thought, were "shameless absurdities," simply "sweeping calumnies against the characters of our young men." But, he felt obliged to admit, "the preparation made for College at some of our schools and academies is miserably defective." Willard had more than a suspicion that *Blackwood's* anonymous critic might be an American; if so, he suggested, the author should return home and do something to repair the conditions he described.[25]

Cogswell did return home, and he more than answered Willard's admonitions. In 1823 he established the Round Hill School, which repaired all of his own criticisms of the American academy and which, more than any other institution, embodied the Anthologists' cultural values. Round Hill would not only meet —and surpass—the demand of the Anthologists and the Harvard reformers for well-prepared college students, but it would educate a generation of Christian gentlemen and scholars. Moreover, it would set the pattern for the American boarding school of the nineteenth century. But there were curious lapses in Cogswell's 1819 assessment of American college preparation. Before turning to Round Hill and the fulfillment of the Federalist educational ideal we must examine more closely the traditions and forms of secondary education with which Cogswell and the Anthologists were most familiar.

Cogswell discussed only one form of education by which a boy might be prepared for college. However, in late eighteenth- and early nineteenth-century United States there were at least five others, which he oddly ignored. These methods ranged from "private" to "public" instruction, with Cogswell's target, the academy, perhaps the most "public"—and ubiquitous—of all. (When men of the late eighteenth and early nineteenth centuries used these terms in connection with education, more often than not they meant them in their traditional, literal senses. Thus, "private education" suggested individual instruction, or education *in private,* while "public education" signified group instruction, or education *in public.*[26]) First, in apprenticelike fashion a boy might be privately tutored by his local minister in the rather minimal amounts of Latin, Greek, and mathematics required to enter college, or he might live with a more-distant minister's family for a year or so while the same process was carried on. Through the early nineteenth century this was probably the most common form of college preparation in the North.[27] Second, a family might hire a private tutor to live with them and prepare their sons for college. This practice was particularly common among well-to-do families in the South.[28]

The third form of college preparation, verging almost on the institutional, was available only to families which lived in or near a good-sized town or city. As social and economic life in the American colonies had grown more complex in the eighteenth century, a system—perhaps too elaborate a word for essentially ad hoc arrangements—of private day schools had developed. The curriculum of the private (in the sense we have used the term they were literally "public") grammar schools was decided by the needs of the local community and the interests and capabilities of the private schoolmaster. While an individual school might or might not prepare students for college, typically the private grammar schools offered two types of education—"academical" and "useful." "Academical" education included Latin, Greek, logic, rhetoric, English grammar, sometimes mathematics, natural philosophy, and astronomy, and thus might ready a boy for college. The "useful" course might include almost anything—bookkeeping, surveying, navigation, gauging, mensuration, and shorthand were among the subjects often offered. The private grammar shool thus met two needs: it could provide a broad classical education and sometimes preparation for college, and it supplied vocational instruction to meet the needs of a growing commercial society in which the European system of craft or skill training by apprenticeship had apparently never taken deep or widespread root. But private schools never achieved permanent institutional form. Typically the schoolmaster was a young man fresh from college, out to find a place for himself in the world. For most, teaching was only a two- or three-year stop before going on to a more lucrative and respected occupation.[29] Also, there were apparently a very few scattered and short-lived private boarding schools in the South, but no records to speak of have survived of them.[30]

The Latin Grammar school, the fourth form of college preparation available to Americans, was also the most ancient. In order to assure their society of a well-educated and steady supply of religious and civil leaders, in the seventeenth century many New England towns had been required by law to support schools that would train boys in enough Latin, Greek and mathematics to enter college. The Latin Grammar school was never a popular institution, and did not escape the disruption the Revolution brought to all areas of American life. Burdened with debts from the war the citizens of the new nation sought to reduce public expenditures in all possible ways. To many, "aristocratic" college-preparation seemed a field particularly amenable to budget cutting. In the 1780s and 1790s all the New England states reduced their support for education. By 1800 the state-financed Latin Grammar school was a dying institution. Shortly after Cogswell wrote, in 1824, even in Massachusetts, the cradle of the tax-supported Latin Grammar school, only seven towns still required their maintenance.[31] Buckminster's 1809 complaints of educational declension—and the Anthologists' fears of a slide into democratic barbarization—had not been too far from the mark.

The fifth form of college preparation not considered by Cogswell was established by American colleges themselves. Everywhere in the United States except in New Hampshire, Massachusetts, Rhode Island, Connecticut, and New Jersey, until well into the nineteenth century many American colleges maintained their own preparatory "departments" in order to assure themselves of a continual supply of students prepared to their satisfaction. Princeton, Columbia, and the University of Pennsylvania had such departments in the eighteenth century. While in other areas of the nation this method of college preparation would linger on well into the 1800s, in the first half of the century the more ambitious northeastern colleges came to rely more and more on outside institutions and individuals for prospective students. They looked first to Cogswell's main concern, the American academy.[32]

While nineteenth-century Americans interested in secondary education used the academy as their standard of praise or blame, today it is almost forgotten. But when Cogswell wrote, most Americans who continued their education beyond the elementary subjects or wished to prepare for college did so at an academy. The first incorporated academy, the Phillips Academy in Andover, Massachusetts, received its charter in 1780; between the Revolution and the turn of the century at least fifty-two such institutions were successfully established in New England alone. By 1830 there were almost a thousand incorporated (and thousands more unincorporated) academies in the United States, and by 1850, the crest of the academy movement, about six thousand existed.[33]

The origins of the academy are obscure; it may have grown from suggestions of Benjamin Franklin, from readings of John Milton, or it may have been inspired by the example of the academies established by English Nonconformists across the Atlantic.[34] In any case, the first two significant academies, the Phillips Academy at Andover and the Phillips Exeter Academy—both attended by so many of the Anthologists—seem to have been inspired in a general way by the Great Awakening, the religious revival that swept the American colonies in the 1740s. The Awakening sparked an intense interest in secular and humanitarian philanthropies, both within and without the churches.[35] In New England in 1742, for instance, Jonathan Edwards, one of the movement's major figures, suggested that along with domestic missions and other charities wealthy Americans might establish and support "schools, in poor towns and villages, which might . . . not only . . . bring up children in common learning, but also might very much tend to their conviction and conversion, and being trained up in vital piety; and doubtless something might be done in this way, in old towns, and more populous places, that might have a great tendency to the flourishing of religion in the rising generation."[36]

We can, perhaps, hear echoes of Edward's plea for domestic

missions in a 1762 letter of John Phillips, a successful merchant of Exeter, New Hampshire, who had been deeply influenced by the Awakening. Noting the retirement of his brother Samuel, of Andover, Massachusetts, from public life, Phillips wrote him that "you now have more leisure to employ your thoughts and cares upon the very important proposal you made, of a united effort in our family, for doing some special service for God."[37] John Phillips had noticed in a Boston newspaper the announcement of a missionary society recently formed to convert and educate the American Indians. "Our parents," he reminded his brother, "designed and educated us to serve Christ personally in the work of the ministry; our time has been otherwise employed; our other labors by his blessing succeeded. May our God have the fruits of them. . . ." The specific object of Phillips's charity turned out to be a school founded by Eleazar Wheelock in Lebanon, Connecticut, for the education of Indians. Phillips gave 100 to the school, and followed this with other gifts when it moved to New Hampshire and became Dartmouth College. The Phillips brothers continued to make donations to various causes and institutions throughout the 1760s and 1770s. Their charities, though worthy, might well have continued to be undirected but for the religious and educational interests of Samuel Phillips's son.

Samuel Phillips, Jr., was the individual most responsible for founding the Phillips academies at Andover, Massachusetts, and Exeter, New Hampshire, and thus for giving initial impetus to the academy movement in America. He was born in his father's new mansion at North Andover in 1752, the only one of seven children to reach maturity. Until the previous generation most Phillipses were Puritan divines. Samuel Phillips, Sr. (1715–90), and his two brothers, John Phillips of Exeter (1719–95) and William Phillips of Boston (1722–1804), were all intended for the ministry by their clergyman father. Instead, they accumulated substantial fortunes in business, married well, and played significant roles in the affairs of their Commonwealths. But the Puritan heritage of duty and moral earnestness remained; it was in this atmosphere that Samuel, Jr., grew up, sickly, bookish, and solitary, in the North Andover mansion. In 1765 he was sent to the Dummer School, a new institution at South Byfield, Massachusetts.

The Dummer School had opened only two years before, in 1763. It was established under the terms of the will of William

Dummer (1677–1761), onetime acting governor of Massachusetts, who left his house and farm at Byfield for its support. Five freeholders of Byfield were to select a master for the school, who would in turn be removable only by the Overseers of Harvard. They chose Samuel Moody, who educated over five hundred boys before his retirement in 1790. One of the very few attempts ever made in the American colonies to support a secondary school through the common English method of endowments in land, Dummer made considerable provision for scholarship (or "charity") students. With his "aristocratic" background, Samuel Phillips felt decidedly ambivalent about many of these students. Though only a minority of the students went on to college, all received a classical education, including Phillips, who entered Harvard in 1767.[38]

After a distinguished undergraduate career Phillips graduated from college in 1771. In 1773 he was married and was also elected to succeed his father as town clerk and treasurer of Andover. The following year he headed a town committee to enforce the Non-Importation Agreements, and in the next year, at only twenty-one won election as a delegate to the revolutionary Provincial Congress. In the turbulent 1775–76 session of the Congress Phillips made a sound reputation as a Speaker, conferred with George Washington on the defense of Boston, and was responsible for moving the Harvard library from Cambridge to safety at Andover.

Phillips's most important contribution to the patriot cause, however, was in the supply of ammunition to the continental armies. Early in the war the American forces found themselves plagued with a shortage of gunpowder. In January 1776 Phillips proposed to build a powder mill, with funds of his own and a government subsidy, at Andover. The legislature agreed, and in May the mill, with Phillips in charge and an old classmate from the Dummer School, Eliphalet Pearson, as chemist, began deliveries to the army.[39]

In the years before the Revolution, many Americans were obsessed with fears of corruption—political, social, and otherwise—in England and in the colonies. British politicians and their appointees in America, many thought, were engaged in a conspiracy to reduce the colonies to the status of Asiatic despotisms.[40] Samuel Phillips seems to have shared such fears, for unlike his conservative father and uncle, he was a strong supporter of colonial rights. "Let this truth be indelibly engraved on our breasts," he had written as early as 1770 in an undergraduate essay on *Liberty,* "that we cannot be happy without we are free. . . . The cause requires our utmost vigilance; we should watch against every encroachment, and with all the fortitude of *calm, intrepid resolution* oppose them. . . . Unborn generations," he continued, in classical periods "will either bless us for our activity and magnanimity, or curse us for our sloth and pusillanimity."[41]

Six years later, on the eve of the Revolution, Phillip's fears for his country had become even more intense. "Observations have been made upon the various irregularities which are daily appearing," he complained, probably in 1776, "the very frequent instances of the decay of virtue, public and private, the prevalence of public and private vice, the amazing change in the tempers, dispositions, and conduct of people in this country within these thirty years." What was the cause of this distressing state of affairs? "The trouble," Phillips explained, "is owing to the neglect of good instruction. Upon the sound education of children depends the comfort or grief of parents, the welfare or disorder of the community, the glory or ruin of the state. The present public ignorance gives rise to a fear of events the most dreadful. . . ." While in the midst of actively supporting a political revolution, Phillips apparently recoiled from any suggestions of social disorder. "What method can be taken?" to repair this distressing state of affairs, he asked. Like so many Americans after him, Phillips turned to an educational institution for his solution:

> Let then a public building be erected for the purpose, and the children sent, be supported and continued there for a certain term, *say from the age of seven to fourteen.* One of the best of men can be found to take command, who shall proportion his attention to the various branches of education according to their importance, who shall make it his chief concern to see to the regulation of the *morals* of the pupils, and attentively and vigorously to guard them against the first dawnings of depraved nature. He shall instruct them in the several relations they sustain to God, their parents, the public, and their

neighbors, and make their whole course of education one continued lecture on all that is great and good.

From such an institution as this what a surprising change might be reasonably expected. Instead of the present degeneracy which has increased upon us with such rapidity, what blessings may we not look for. We have more reason to hope for success from such labors than from those of *priest and magistrate* united. How great an advantage has the teacher in exerting his influence upon his pupils so early in life and keeping them away from bad examples, as was done in Mr. Moody's [Dummer] school, although it was attended with more difficulty there on account of *collections* [i.e., students] *from every quarter* than it would be here. When we consider that this plan had such success among the ancients, what may we not expect from it when joined to the advantages of the Christian religion? Among the thirty to whom I have mentioned the plan, I have not heard one dissentient voice, but have received vastly higher approbation than I had reason to expect.

Such, then, was Phillip's prescription for the good society: political revolution would be supported to preserve liberty and to avoid corruption, while the traditional social and religious order would be regenerated through education. Phillips's initial plans for his academy were among the earliest examples of what, over the next three decades, would become the commonplace American belief that formal education was a basic necessity if the new Republican social order was to be ensured. "Must so glorious a plan fail for want of money," he asked, "when there are so many to whom it would be a relief to part with some of it?"[42]

Phillips had surprisingly little difficulty implementing his plans. His father and his uncle John of Exeter were enthusiastic; they seem to have been waiting for just such an opportunity to dispose of their fortunes. By the beginning of 1777 land in Andover for the new school had been purchased and a building was under way. The next task was to secure a suitable master for the school. In all his discussion to the academy Phillips had had one person in mind for his position, his old friend Eliphalet Pearson, who soon agreed to serve as the Academy's first "Preceptor" at 80 a year.

Phillips's initial intentions in founding his academy were

thoroughly within the Puritan educational tradition. His "conversion" was the central religious experience in the life of the New England Puritan of the seventeenth or eighteenth centuries. Of it he asked what twentieth-century Americans might ask of psychoanalysis: personal rebirth. To the orthodox Calvinist, man was a sinful, lost, wretched creature. He could only be redeemed from this miserable state when he was brought to realize—usually through the invocation of feelings of terror, guilt, and worthlessness—his condition and his utter dependence upon the will of God. Faith in Christ might then bring his redemption; he would be "converted," or spiritually reborn. The result of the conversion experience was very often a complete realignment of the individual's psychic economy, an amazing release of energy, and gain in self-confidence.[43] For the devout Puritan, as Edmund Morgan has noted, "the main business of education was to prepare children for conversion by teaching them the doctrines and moral precepts of Christianity. . . . The ultimate purpose of education was salvation."[44] As it had been in the seventeenth century, as it was for Jonathan Edwards, this was Phillips's major educational goal. "The object in educating youth," he advised Pearson, "ought to be to qualify young persons as ornaments, as blessings, and as comforts in the vineyard of the Lord." Moreover, the religious instruction of the academy was intended to be of the strictly orthodox variety of Calvinism. The Master was advised to impress upon the pupils the doctrines of "the fall of Man—the Depravity of Human Nature—the Necessity of Atonement." The students were to be particularly warned of "the erroneous and dangerous doctrine of justification by our own merit." Coupled with his remarks on the New England ministry, it seems more than possible that Phillips intended his academy to be a sort of junior divinity school, possibly to stand as a conservative bulwark of orthodoxy against the winds of Unitarianism then just beginning to sweep New England.[45]

When it came to the academy's curriculum Phillips's conservatism was decidedly radical. "I think our general plan of educating youth is injudicious, unnatural, and absurd," he told Pearson. "As soon as an infant is capable of muttering English, he is put to his accidence [i.e., Latin grammar]. In the Latin, youths fall back upon something that has been dead these hundred years and never will exist again. . . . In it they study months without one new idea. . . . It is a pity that the best six years of youth should be spent in studying heathen writers." To preserve religious and social orthodoxy, Phillips was apparently ready to jettison the whole tradition of Protestant humanism, which for almost three hundred years had been based squarely on the study of the Greek and Latin classics. Pearson, however, soon persuaded Phillips of the virtues of Latin. When the academy finally opened, its curriculum did not differ markedly from the Latin Grammar school's.[46]

Phillip's ideas on the social status of the students his academy would serve were also conservative, and were based upon his own experiences with "charity" students at the Dummer School. Phillips wanted no such students in his own school:

> There are, no doubt, a great number of respectable wealthy parents who would be glad to have their children educated, and cheerfully be at the expense, but they find so great danger of their morals being totally corrupted [by poor charity students] that they are utterly deterred therefrom. This great difficulty being removed, there is reason to believe that the school would always be as full as conveniency would admit of, and certainly the happiness of such a child (a rich one) is of as great consequence as that of a poor child, his opportunity of doing good greater. His disinterestedness is a great argument in favor of his honest intentions in following the profession of a minister, that he does it from principles, and not from *a lucrative view;* but [charity] scholars must purse this; they speak because they are hired to; it is their living, say the scoffers.[47]

However, by the time the Massachusetts legislature incorporated the academy in 1780, little trace of Phillips's initial intentions in founding his academy remained:

> And in order to prevent the smallest perversion of the true intent of this Foundation [the Constitution of the Academy reads], it is again declared that the *first* and *principal* object of this Institution is the promotion of true Piety and Virtue; the *second* instruction in the English, Latin, and Greek languages, together with writing, arithmetic, music, and the art of speak-

ing; the *third,* practical geometry, logic and geography; and the *fourth* such other of the liberal arts and sciences or languages as opportunity and ability may hereafter admit and as the trustees shall direct.[48]

Eliphalet Pearson's advice apparently prevailed: Andover—at least for its first thirty years—did not become a junior divinity school, its curriculum was the traditional classical one, and it was not limited to the sons of the rich—"charity" scholars were provided for early. Samuel Phillips's original intention of founding a conservative divinity school would not be fulfilled until 1809, when the Phillips family would be instrumental in establishing the Andover Theological Seminary.

The Phillips Academy opened its doors on 20 April 1778, well before its actual incorporation. It was the era before developmental psychology, and thus before the rigid segregation of children by age group. Therefore, in medieval fashion, the ages of the pupils at Andover varied enormously. The youngest, Josiah Quincy (a nephew of the Phillips brothers, later mayor of Boston and president of Harvard), was only six years old; in class he sat next to thirty-year-old James Anderson of Londonderry, New Hampshire. The Academy obviously met a long-felt need; starting with thirteen students, by the end of the year it had fifty-one.[49]

The Phillipses hoped that their Academy might set an example. "Earnestly wishing that this Institution may grow and flourish," the Andover Constitution reads, "that the advantages of it may be extensive and lasting, that its usefulness may be so manifest as to lead the way to other establishments on the same principles. . . ." The first response to this hope came from within the Phillips family itself. John Phillips of Exeter, who had been so generous to the Andover school, shortly decided to found an academy in his own town. The Phillips Exeter Academy was incorporated in 1781 and opened in 1783; it met with the same success as its sister school at Andover. The Phillipses endowed both academies liberally; their gifts to teach school amounted to over $100,000. Exeter and Andover remained the wealthiest secondary schools in the United States until well after the Civil War.[50]

Andover's Constitution stipulated that control of the

Academy was to be vested in a self-perpetuating board of seven to thirteen Protestant trustees, a majority of whom were never to be residents of Andover. The first board consisted of four clergymen and eight laymen (including Pearson, who was later ordained a minister) distinguished in commerce, farming, law and politics.[51]

The device of incorporation lifted from the Phillips academies the dependence upon the too-often transient single teacher that had afflicted most private secondary schools of the colonial period. The incorporated board of trustees ensured the permanence and continuity of the institution. In this, the model was probably the organization developed by the colonial colleges. Richard Hofstadter has described that organization as "the presence on the board of clergymen either in equal numbers to laymen or in predominant strength; a denominational affiliation of some kind; but hospitality to matriculants of other sects; the centrality, in the institution's governance and development, of the strong president; the essential independence . . . from either control or support by the state."[52]

The corporate form of organization would become the norm for the academy movement. Americans of the eighteenth and early nineteenth century did not necessarily consider corporations "private" organizations. They assumed that "the general intent, the purpose, of all corporation was for better government, either general or special." The corporation was a device long familiar to Americans. "The corporate mechanism for applying the power of the government to special areas," Oscar and Mary Handlin have pointed out, "was not peculiar to nor original with . . . America."[53] Massachusetts, after all, had begun as a chartered trading company. After independence Massachusetts and other new states entered on a conscious policy of incorporating groups of individuals whose activities were thought to promote the general welfare in areas of endeavor where the state had neither experience nor funds to expend. Since academies would certainly promote education, a socially desirable objective, the state incorporated them—as it incorporated the Massachusetts Medical Society, the American Academy of Arts and Sciences, or as the United States Congress would incorporate the Bank of North America in 1782. Not until the Dartmouth College case in 1819 did a sharp legal distinction between the powers of the public and private sectors begin to take shape. Before the Civil War the device of incorporation allowed states to give encouragement, exercise some control, and sometimes give direct aid to the thousands of academies almost spontaneously organized by education-hungry Americans from one end of the nation to the other.

The curricula of the two Phillips academies were not the same. Under Pearson's influence, Andover remained a college preparatory school, offering only the subjects required for entrance to the colleges—Latin, Greek, and mathematics—along with intensive religious instruction and a smattering of history. The curriculum at Phillips Exeter, however, was organized on the plan that would be followed by most later academies. Much on the lines of the private English grammar schools of the colonial period, it was divided into two "departments"—the "Course of Preparation for College" and the "English Department." The latter course offered at one time or another English grammar, geography, geometry, trigonometry, logic, chemistry, United States and modern history, astronomy, moral and political philosophy, and French and Spanish. All this was provided at relatively low cost: Andover's tuition was $2.50 a quarter in 1780, Exeter's $12.00 a year in 1812.[54] On top of these charges, however, students had to cover the costs of their room and board, which averaged about $1.50 a week in the New England academies of the early nineteenth century.[55]

Within a few years of the founding of Andover and Exeter other academies were established throughout the United States. Most followed a common pattern, somewhat more state and secularly oriented than that of the colonial colleges, which Robert Middlekauff succinctly describes as "a government vested in laymen established by a charter issued by the state, a financial status dependent upon both public and private contributions, and a curriculum more or less classical."[56] The impetus for founding academies came from a multitude of sources: from private individuals, from town meetings, from state legislatures, and from religious groups, to suggest only a few.[57] Most, nowhere near as well endowed as the Phillips academies, depended primarily upon tuition for financial support. This, however, was supplemented by grants of land from the states, by lotteries, by sales of stock, and by private and public gifts. Characteristically, incorporated academies were controlled by a board of trustees composed of the "better sort" of men of a particular area—lawyers, physicians, landholders, and clergymen; the far larger number of unincorporated academies followed much the same pattern.

Requirements for admission to academies varied widely; they accepted students ranging in age from nine to at least thirty. Scholastically, ability to read and write seems to have been the general minimal standard for admission. Morally, most schools would probably have agreed with the 1819 "Rules and Regulations" of the Richmond Academy in Georgia. They stated that "no Youth can be admitted to this Academy who is known to be habitually immoral."[58]

The academy's predominance as the characteristic institution affording a secondary education to Americans was to be much shorter than the Latin Grammar school's had been. In New England (and probably elsewhere) the peak years of growth for the academy, measured by the number incorporated, began at just about the same time that Cogswell made his criticisms of the institution—between 1821 and 1840.[59] After this period the academy first went into a slow, then a rapid decline. The institution that replaced it, as characteristic of its age as the academy was of the early republic, was the public high school. By the middle of the nineteenth century the academy was beginning to be considered more and more as a *private* institution, one that no longer promoted the general welfare and was therefore no longer entitled to state encouragement or support.

Whatever the academy's ultimate fate, in its years of predominance it also constituted, like all schools, a social system. Historians of education have generally assumed that academies "were typically boarding schools rather than day schools."[60] If one defines a boarding school as an institution at which students live in dormitories supervised and regulated by a faculty, precisely the opposite would seem to have been typical. Students at many academies, unless native to the town in which they were located, boarded with private families located within convenient distance of the institution's buildings.[61] The only "residential schools" to speak of in America at the time of the founding of the Phillips academies were the American colleges; the idea of boarding students was almost exclusively connected with higher education.[62] At Phillips Andover, for example, no dormitories were constructed for fifty years after the school's founding. Until then, students lodged with "respectable" citizens of the town—including, in the early years, Samuel Phillips himself.[63] When Joseph Buckminster went to Exeter in 1796, he boarded with a family; not until 1855 did Phillips Exeter build a dormitory—and it accommodated only 42 boys. Another dormitory was not constructed until 1893.[64] Deerfield Academy in Massachusetts opened in 1799 with 269 pupils; not until ten years later was the Academy itself able to board students—and even then it provided only twelve rooms.[65]

John Phillips hoped that academies might promote "true Piety and Virtue"; the Deerfield trustees directed that "the preceptors and ushers, besides teaching the arts and sciences, should instill into the minds of the pupils moral and Christian principles, and form in them habits of virtue and the love of piety."[66] Such objectives, however, were difficult to achieve; students were not under the direct control of academy authorities except during actual attendance at class or at other academy exercises. Otherwise, they were left much to their own devices—which might be something less than "virtuous and pious." Trustees' minutes are filled with innumerable discussions and regulations concerning the conduct of boarding houses and the students who lived in them. For instance, the Richmond Academy in Georgia declared in 1819 that the "following immoralities" would be "liable to the animadversion of the teachers [:] Profane swearing, lying, theft, drunkenness, Sabbath breaking, Cock-fighting, Gambling, obscene language, or conduct of any kind, quarrelling, fighting, [and] frequenting vicious company."[67] Such minuteness of regulation would hardly have been necessary in a boarding school; some of the strictures would not have been needed at all.

Discipline, however—or the maintenance of certain norms of behavior—was not lacking among most academy students. "Boys were very rarely suspended or expelled," an 1833 alumnus of Phillips Exeter recalled of his schooldays. "They boarded in good families in the town and were under good influences. They were treated as members of the family and subject to its discipline. If there was trouble in the house, the head of the family usually settled it without carrying it to the faculty."[68] What was true of Exeter, New Hampshire, in this respect, was probably true to one degree or another of many of the towns and villages in the United States in which academies were located: the whole community served as an extension of the academy. In effect, the *community* was a school, transmitting informally its own culture to the students as surely as formal knowledge was being transmitted to them in the few hours a day they spent in classes.

Such close integration of school and society presupposed a relatively stable, homogeneous society. A family that sent its children to an academy assumed, in effect, that the communities and families in which its children would live could be counted upon to share the same values as itself and that therefore the child would not be exposed to "contaminating" influences. The academy, neither a boarding school nor a day school, would serve the child as a bridge between his own parents and society at large, a sort of halfway house between the family and the world, where, while being introduced to a broader tradition of knowledge, he would still be subject to the traditional discipline of the family and the small community.

Or so, ideally, it must have seemed. By 1819, however, critics of the academy were no longer sure that the institution could properly fulfill new cultural goals. It could "teach a lad to count his fingers and take care of his dollars," Joseph Green Cogswell —himself a graduate of Exeter—had said, but little else. "It would not be unreasonable to say," Cogswell added, "that a boy in America, who is put to learn the ancient languages, loses his whole time, from the moment he begins the Latin Accidence, till he takes his bachelor's degree." The fault was due, Cogswell said, in best Anthologist fashion, to "the instructors of the classic schools in America; they are mere language masters, not scholars." Academy teachers simply prepared students to meet the already low college entrance requirements without awakening their love of learning or teaching them how to think. This could in part be ascribed, Cogswell thought, to a fault endemic to American culture. "The object of learning is misunderstood in America," he wrote, "or rather, it is valued only as far as it is practically useful . . . all kinds of knowledge, that are not to be turned to immediate account, are either totally neglected, or very imperfectly cultivated." To this typically Federalist critique of American education Cogswell added one more stroke—a criticism of the academy as a social system. A "great defect in the system," he complained, "is the practice of leaving boys too much to themselves. They live separate from their masters, who know nothing of the use, which they make of their time, except when they are collected in the school-rooms; and being but about seven hours of the day, the residue of it is, of course, spent in idleness."[69]

The gist of Cogswell's criticisms of the American academy was simple; it summed up a generation of the Anthologists' critique of American culture and education. A high culture in the United States equal to Europe's would have to be based upon a class of Christian scholars and gentlemen. Institutions were needed to give direction and continuity to these nationalistic cultural goals. In particular, the American academy was not educating the Christian scholars and gentlemen needed to raise the standards of American higher education and American culture as a whole.

Some new means of producing Christian scholars and gentlemen—"natural" or "artificial"—must be found. The question for Cogswell's generation was where. In his articles Cogswell had written approvingly of European secondary schools, particularly those of Germany. It was there that the Anthologists would seek new educational forms which might embody and further the cultural goals they strove to impress upon the new nation.

Chapter II

The Search for New Educational Forms

"If we are not yet in possession of the best practical methods of instruction employed in Europe," declared the *North American Review* in 1819, "we can, surely, by diligent inquiry learn them, and then proceed to apply them ourselves." Americans should not let petty feelings of nationalism interfere: "the people of America must do as other nations have done; as in ancient times the Romans did, when they sent to Greece for their instructers; and, as at the present day the less learned nations of Europe do, when they hold out inducements to able professors from their more learned neighbours to come and reside among them."[1] This was precisely the course Thomas Jefferson had followed in 1794 when he tried to persuade the faculty of the University of Geneva to emigrate to the United States.[2] But rather than import Europeans, in the early nineteenth century Americans usually traveled to Europe themselves to investigate the newest cultural and educational practices. Joseph Buckminster's 1807 examination of the Liverpool Atheneum was among the earliest of these ventures. Over the next few decades he was followed by one traveler after another, some still well known today, some forgotten—John Griscom, William Woodbridge, Calvin Stowe, Henry Barnard, Horace Mann—the list could be extended almost indefinitely. Through their letters, reports, and translations they familiarized a generation of Americans with the latest in contemporary European educational thought and practice. As the writer in the *North American Review* had hoped, Americans would learn much from Europe—but in their own way. Each educational idea or practice would suffer a sea-change as it crossed the Atlantic, turning into something that would often be unrecognizable in its country of origin. Not the least among them was the private boarding school.[3]

President Kirkland and others who hoped to raise Harvard to true university status and fulfill the Anthologists' cultural goals supported—always in spirit and often financially—the European education of Buckminster's successors—George Ticknor, Edward Everett, George Bancroft, and Joseph Green Cogswell. Returning home heady with new ideas, this generation would attempt to bring the United States abreast of the latest development in European culture, from which the new nation had been in some respects isolated by the wars of the French Revolution.

To Europeans in the early nineteenth century Americans were still rare and curious creatures, noble savages from a pure, uncorrupted land, trailing—hopefully—clouds of republican virtue. "You are the advance guard of the human race—you are the future of the world," Madame de Staël exclaimed to the young Anthologist George Ticknor.[4] Americans did not disagree. All doors but the most reactionary were opened to them: Joseph Green Cogswell, like Ticknor, Everett, and Bancroft, met most of the outstanding liberal intellectual and artistic figures of the day. He pursued his interest in mineralogy and made a careful study of principles of organization of the University of Göttingen's library. He dined with Madame de Staël, achieved intimacy with the Bonapartes, and became a close friend of Goethe, to whom, as George Bancroft said, Cogswell always remained the "lieber Mann."[5]

"It is time," Cogswell told George Ticknor in 1816, "for Cambridge to take a rank above a mere preparatory school, and to do this she must call to her aid all the talents she can command."[6] Cogswell himself attempted to enlist Europe's best talents and experience in the cause. A few months before the publication of his critique of American culture and the American academy in *Blackwood's,* he went directly to the fountainhead of the newest in European educational theory and practice—he made a "long visit" to the school of Johann Heinrich Pestalozzi at Yverdun, in Switzerland.[7]

In the early nineteenth century Johann Heinrich Pestalozzi stood in much the same relation to education in the Western world as John Dewey would in the twentieth century. In one way or another, much of the educational thought and practice of figures as seemingly disparate as Dewey himself, Maria Montessori, or A. S. Neill can be traced back to the world of Pestalozzi and his immediate disciples—particularly Phillip Emmanuel von Fellenberg (1771–1844), Johann Friedrich Herbart (1776–1841), and Friedrich Foebel (1782–1852). Though disagreeing on many points, by their writings and practical example, these men gave the Western world a new philosophy of education from which we are still drawing.[8]

Born in Zurich in 1746, a member of a patrician Swiss family which had fallen upon hard times, when Cogswell met him in 1818 Pestalozzi was an almost legendary figure. His most influential book, *Leonard and Gertrude,* had been published in 1782, almost forty years earlier. With its successor, *How Gertrude Teaches Her Children,* it had long since passed into the mainstream of European educational thought.

The most immediate source of the young Pestalozzi's ideas was a figure whom the conservative, Federalist, Cogswell must have viewed with a critical eye—Jean Jacques Rousseau. Society, said Rousseau, was corrupt, incapable of reforming itself. Children, however, were a fount of natural goodness. If one would reform society, begin therefore with the child and the natural education of the child. Most of Rousseau's ideas on education were presented to the world in his didactic novel of 1762, *Émile.* Abstracted from the novel, Rousseau's ideas were, briefly: (1) the family is the basic educational institution; (2) the child is not a static being but goes through successive stages of growth—treatment of the child should acknowledge these different stages and not treat him like a miniature adult; (3) certain aspects of education, such as religious and moral training, should be postponed until the individual is capable of absorbing them; (4) socialization of the individual should begin in adolescence, not childhood; (5) the basic responsibility in teaching is to provide an environment which will *attract* the child to education; (6) children should be treated humanely, not controlled through threats of punishments or promises of rewards; (7) the child should be encouraged toward self-education; (8) one learns best by doing; and (9) the best teachers are those who have a thorough knowledge of the child and his environment. The seeming banality of these ideas is one indication of their impact; for late eighteenth- and early nineteenth-century education they were little short of revolutionary.[9]

Émile was a Utopian novel, the story of a young artistocrat educated "naturally" on an isolated estate. Pestalozzi, however, critically adapted Rousseau's ideas, developed them further, and ultimately put them into practice with groups of children rather than individuals. In *Leonard and Gertrude,* a didactic pedagogical novel on the lines of *Émile,* Pestalozzi emphasized heavily the primary importance of the home as an educational environment. The school, he said, should be directly modeled on the home. The best teacher, he thought, was the child's mother, since the mother was the first to engage the child's emotions and thus lay the foundations for his moral and intellectual life. In the second work Pestalozzi tried to develop a systematic pedagogical psychology based on the ideas of the first. The development of the child, he thought, recapitulates the development of the race; it was like the gradual, organic growth of a plant, and it needed the same natural, changing type of nurture one would give a plant. Education, he wrote:

> is like the art of the gardener under whose care a thousand trees blossom and grow. He contributes nothing to their actual growth; the principle of growth lies in the trees themselves. He plants and waters, but God gives the increase. . . . So with the educator: he imparts no single power to men. He only watches lest any external force should injure or disturb. He takes care that development runs its course in accordance with its own laws.[10]

Intellectual development was based on the idea of "number, form, and language" as the "elementary means of instruction, because the whole sum of external properties of any object is comprised in its outline and its number, and brought home to consciousness through language." Educational practice, then, should be based on three principles:

1. To teach children to look upon every object that is brought before them as a unit; that is, as separated from those with which it seems connected.

2. To teach them the form of every object: that is, its *size* and *proportions*.

3. As soon as possible to make them acquainted with all the words and names descriptive of objects known to them.[11]

Such a program would encourage the natural growth of accuracy and clarity of thinking, a natural progression from the simple to the complex. It could also logically lead to the idea of a school as a prepared environment, as it did with Pestolozzi's more mystical follower, Friedrich Froebel.[12] If only the "natural goodness" within the child was to be developed, then the surrounding world had to be controlled very carefully to assure that only "naturally good" influences reached the child. Such ideas, of course, might be adapted to any sort of educational program, liberal or conservative.

Pestalozzi's ideas were, in a way, a revolt against the printed book. The only way a child can begin to learn, he said, is through the direct experience of the senses—through seeing, hearing, smelling, tasting, feeling, and doing.[13] Cultivate the natural, inborn faculties of the child, do not impose from without. Therefore, present the child with natural objects, not with the abstractions found in books; and introduce exercise and manual training as a normal part of the curriculum, a part that will exercise naturally the faculties of the child. Also, since natural distinctions existed between men, the development of social classes was inevitable. One must not, however, put artificial emphasis on class education, Pestalozzi thought: one should encourage members of all social groups to develop to their full potential.

The child's moral and religious development capped Pestalozzi's educational system. The love first felt for the mother—or the "heart"—was the mediator between the mind and the hand. By cultivating the heart, he believed, one encouraged the child's moral feelings, or his relations to others, and his religious feelings, or his relations with God. The ultimate product of such an education would be men and women developed to their fullest potential, as Nature and Nature's God had intended them to be.

Unlike Rousseau, Pestalozzi had the opportunity to put his ideas into practice: first, at Neuhof in Switzerland from 1774 to 1779, later at Burgdorf from 1799 to 1805, and finally, from 1805 to his death in 1825 at Yverdun, where Cogswell visited him. Pestalozzi's primary interest was in the alleviation of the condition of the poor. The wars of the French Revolution had left many destitute, orphaned children in Switzerland. It was largely with such children that Pestalozzi worked, though after 1805 fee-paying middle-class children were admitted to his school at Yverdun. There he experimented with methods of teaching children "naturally." His efforts attracted widespread attention; from every part of Europe and America students and visitors came to study and observe his methods.

The Anthologists were not unfamiliar with Rousseau's ideas on education, nor with Pestalozzi's reputation. While finding Rouseau's *Émile* "marked by the illuminating touches and the original conceptions of genius," they felt that as a system of education it was "more conspicuous for its singularity than its truth." If a system of education based on Rousseau's ideas were widely adopted, they thought, it "would keep the human species in a state of permanency between light and darkness, between savage barbarity and civilized refinement. It would counteract the moral and physical improvement of man, the progress of knowledge, and the productiveness of industry."[14] Since the "state of savage barbarity" was precisely the future the Anthologists hoped American culture could be prevented from attaining, Rousseau could offer them little practical advice.

On Pestalozzi, the Anthologists were initially more sanguine. Rumors of his "peculiar mode of instruction" had drifted across the Atlantic, along with the claim that Pestalozzi gave his students "the accomplishments of gentlemen, as well as the knowledge of scholars." They had an opportunity to sample Pestalozzi's ideas and methods in 1808, when Joseph Neef, a disciple of Pestalozzi who had emigrated to the United States, published the first American exposition of the Swiss educator's ideas.[15] In a lengthy review, which appeared in the *Monthly Anthology* late in 1809, Robert Hallowell Gardiner made a fair and balanced assessment of Neef's plan of education. To begin with, Gardiner found the tone of the work offensive: Neef, he wrote, "is anxious to decry every other system but his own, and to represent all other instructers as ignorant, designing, pedagogues, who with a few hard words deceive the publick and pass themselves off for learned." In general, Gardiner found Neef's methods and ideas pretentious and ignorant. However, he did concede that "amidst the nonsense of this work we discover many useful notions." Gardiner was particularly intrigued by Pestalozzi's method of giving religious instruction to young children, and of teaching children how to do mental arithmetic. He objected most to Neef's denigration of the classics—in fact, of the whole human past—and to Neef's claim that his basic ideas "followed Nature," since his plan was "not to teach his pupils anything, but to make them discover everything for themselves."

"We should not have detained our readers so long upon a work of so little merit," Gardiner explained, "had it not been for the reputation of Pestalozzi, whose system Mr. Neef pretends to have embraced." Neef, Gardiner concluded, "appears to have studied Rousseau so ardently as to have embraced all his wild notions. But Rousseau wrote at a time when education appeared in its worst form; and in combating the false notions which then prevailed, he was led by the ardour of his mind into the opposite extremes. Mr. Neef has not the same apology." In dismissing Neef, Gardiner in effect dismissed Pestalozzi, for Neef's work was a fairly accurate exposition of the latter's ideas. A Pestalozzian education, it seemed, could not produce the Anthologists' cultural ideal, the Christian gentleman and scholar.[16]

A large part of Pestalozzi's reputation rested on his work with the children of the poor. In addition to his wish to improve Harvard, Joseph Green Cogswell was concerned with the children in the factories just beginning to appear in New England. Such establishments, he felt, made the children "just as completely machines as the spindles they manage." Cogswell's visit to Yverdun was due in part to his own interest in the education of the poor, in part to requests from his friend Elisha Ticknor (George's father), who hoped that Pestalozzi's school might offer some hints on an agricultural school the elder Ticknor hoped to establish for the children of the poor in Massachusetts.[17] But by 28 May 1818, when Cogswell visited Yverdun, Pestalozzi was almost senile. Never a good manager of either finances or adults, his schools had always been torn by internal dissensions.[18] Cogswell examined the institution and its collection of minerals, but jotted down in his diary: "bad order—no obedience in scholars."[19] Over a year later, on 28 October 1819, Cogswell made a second visit to Yverdun and found the situation even worse. "A painful visit it was to me," he wrote to a friend at home, "to see this good old man and real philanthropist going broken-hearted to his grave, for broken-hearted he must be, in contemplating the ruined state of the institution which he has been laboring his whole life to establish." Although Cogswell found Pestalozzi's methods interesting, he had major, typically Anthologist reservations about them. "My regrets," he explained, "are more for himself than for the public, for I do not believe his system carried to the extent he does, is the true method of storing the mind with knowledge. It would exclude memory altogether as a medium of instructing, and make use of reason alone, which is absurd."[20] Educators in Cogswell's tradition would still be making the same complaint about progressive education a hundred years later.

Cogswell's disappointment with Pestalozzi's Yverdun did not lead him to abandon his investigation of new educational experiments. Between his visits to Pestalozzi he twice visited another Swiss experimental school, as famous and perhaps even more influential than Yverdun—the complex of schools of Emmanuel von Fellenberg, a former disciple of Pestalozzi, at Hofwyl, near Berne. On his first visit to Yverdun Cogswell had found Pestalozzi filled with "hatred and envy of Fellenberg."[21] The feelings were understandable. Visitors to Fellenberg's schools, a biographer of Pestalozzi has written, "were more favorably impressed by Hofwyl than Yverdun. There was there a younger man in full control of his establishment, able to maintain order, discipline, and success. . . . They did not realize that the principles underlying this enterprise were originally Pestalozzi's."[22]

His father a senator of the republic of Berne, his mother the daughter of a famous Dutch admiral, Emmanuel von Fellenberg was born a member of the Swiss aristocracy. Brought up partially by a tutor (Albert Rengger, a friend of Pestalozzi, who later became Minister of the Interior of the Swiss Republic) at his father's castle of Wildenstein, Fellenberg's early years were spent in a manner somewhat like Rousseau's Émile. At the age of sixteen he left his home and spent the next ten years wandering about Switzerland, Germany, and France, studying and investigating the condition of the peasantry. He saw a society wracked with antagonisms, threatened by revolution in France, a society in which one class seemed irrevocably pitted against the other. In 1799, three years after his return to Switzerland, he resolved to find a remedy—largely through a system of education based on agriculture. With the considerable fortune left by his father, he purchased the estate of Hofwyl near Berne and outlined his life's plan:[23]

> Born as I am one of the aristocracy of Switzerland, let me show myself worthy of pre-eminence by deserving it. I will place every distinction of rank, which is inconsistent with the welfare of my fellow creatures, upon the altar of my country, and embrace a profession "despised and neglected of men". . . . All that I wish is "peace on earth and goodwill towards men." *I will turn schoolmaster*—a somewhat bold resolve, when one considers the general contempt in which that important office is held.[24]

No "contempt" was directed towards Fellenberg; his experiments were an unmitigated success. "Hofwyl," the American educator Henry Barnard wrote in 1854, had "attracted more attention, and exerted a wider influence than any one institution in Europe or America" over the preceding fifty years. More than one hundred reports on the school were published.[25] Between about 1810 and 1840 Hofwyl was besieged by interested visitors from every part of Europe and America, who returned home eager to put into effect its practices and to spread the theories they were based upon. Their influence on the development of education in the Western world was immense: the schools of Prussia, teacher training throughout Europe and America, the physical education movement, the organization of the nineteenth-century curriculum throughout the West, the spread of state systems of common schools in Europe and the United States, the manual and industrial training movement, the revival of sectarian education—all can be traced, at least in part, directly back to the work of Fellenberg, Pestalozzi, and their followers.

Fellenberg's Hofwyl has been remembered largely as the progenitor of agricultural, manual and industrial education. To Hofwyl, a historian of this movement has claimed, can be "traced much of our present system of employing the industrial occupations as a means of education in institutions for the care of orphaned or delinquent children or for children of Indians or Negroes."[26] But there was much more to Hofwyl than the training of the poor or outcaste. Hofwyl was the practical expression of Fellenberg's view of European society, a view which had been shaped by the upheavals of the French Revolution and Napoleonic Wars.

In 1818, the same year in which Cogswell visited Hofwyl, Fellenberg explained clearly the ideological basis of his school to another young American educator then touring Europe, John Griscom. "He seated me on a sofa," Griscom reported:

> and entered upon an explanation of the principles of his establishment, and the particular views of education, which had induced him to engage in it. He considers society as divisible into three distinct parts; the higher (comprehending the noble and the wealthy,) the middling, and the poor. The greatest defects of education, he supposed to exist in the two extreme classes. That these distinctions or classes among men, would always prevail, in every civilized country, he believed to be incontrovertible; and, of course, any attempt to break down the distinction, would be fruitless. It is, therefore, of consequence that they should be each educated in a manner conformable to their situations, but both in such a way, as to develop, to the highest extent, the best faculties of their nature; and, while it preserves the proper relation between them, it should, at the same time, encourage the feelings of kindliness and sympathy on the one part, and of respect on the other. This, he thought, could be effected upon no plan, so effectually, as by bringing them up side by side, so that they should have each other constantly in view, without any necessity of mixing or associating. The rich, by observing the industry, the skill, and the importance of the laboring classes, would learn to entertain just sentiments respecting them, and the poor, by feeling and experiencing the kindly influences of the rich, would regard them as benefactors.[27]

Fellenberg's Hofwyl was the institutional expression of these social views. It was not one school, but a complex of institutions, the most prominent of which at the time of Cogswell's visits were a farm and trade school for the lower classes and an academy for the upper class.[28] It was, in other words, an institute of social reconciliation and control, a school in which the social order was considered fixed, "without, however," as Fellenberg himself said in best bourgeois, Napoleonic fashion, "barring to superior talents, or genius, a career, where it may unfold itself with distinction, and acquire new treasures for the human race."[29] It would instill in a dissolute aristocracy a sense of social concern, while it would raise a brutalized peasantry to a sense of their own human, albeit passive, dignity.

While Fellenberg's work for the education of the poor, the object of Cogswell's initial interest, is generally still familiar, his academy for the upper classes has been almost completely forgotten. However, at the time, the academy attracted as much attention as the other parts of Hofwyl. Its most characteristic feature, one English observer noted, "lies in making instruction serve in the education of the rich, as the earning of their livelihood does in that of the poor: namely, as the principal means of education. It is less an object, to store the memory of the pupil with a variety of information, than to lead him to labour at constructing the fabric of his own education; and thus render him a valuable directing light to all around him."[30]

On his first visit to Hofwyl Cogswell was somewhat suspicious of the whole enterprise. "It was a noble effort and has already produced great good," he said. However, he felt that "when a little longer experiment shall have cleared it of some of its theoretic excellences, but practical defects, it will produce still greater, and very probably be one means of operating a real reformation of society."[31] By 1820, shortly after Cogswell visited it, the upper-class academy had about one hundred students, drawn from the nobility and gentry of several European countries, and a faculty of thirty professors. It was an extremely expensive institution: the tuition ranged between £100 and £300.[32] There was little or no intercourse between the students at the schools for the rich and the poor. "We did not see much" of the latter, Robert Dale Owen, the Scottish-American reformer, who entered Hofwyl in 1818, recalled. "But there was the kindest feeling between our college and their school; and I never saw a happier-looking set of children than they."[33] The results of this system, according to William Woodbridge, another American visitor to Hofwyl, was that "at the same time that [the poor students] became accustomed to living in view of splendour and luxury, without desiring or hoping to partake them, they learn to recognize the inferiority of their rank without being degraded by it; while the pupils of the higher classes acquire by this connection the habit of treating their inferiors with kindness and deference."[34]

The broader aim of Fellenberg's academy, as Woodbridge explained it, was *"to develop all the faculties of our nature, physical, intellectual, and moral, and to endeavour to train and unite them into one harmonious system, which shall form the most perfect character of which the individual is susceptible; and thus prepare him for every period, and every sphere of action to which he may be called."*[35] In this Fellenberg was expressing "faculty psychology," the conception of human nature current in both Europe and America for most of the nineteenth century. While different philosophers and educators might enumerate or subdivide the different "faculties" almost ad infinitum, most were agreed that the primary aim of education was to train, or *discipline,* the faculties.[36]

To Cogswell, as to most American educators of the day, Fellenberg's insistence on the development of the physical faculties must have seemed somewhat novel. At Hofwyl each student—as both John Locke and Pestalozzi had advised—was given a garden plot to cultivate as his own, in order to encourage "foresight, labour, and perseverance." For the same reasons, a carpenter shop was provided. The students engaged in the new system of German gymnastic exercises and were provided with fencing lessons, a riding school, and a swimming-bath. They also made, in small groups, annual "pedestrian journies" about the Swiss countryside.[37]

The cultivation of the physical faculties was thoroughly integrated with the cultivation of the intellectual. "The great art of educating," Fellenberg said, "consists in knowing how to occupy every moment of life in well-directed and useful activity of the youthful powers, in order that, so far as possible, nothing evil may find room to develop itself."[38] Students were provided with elaborate individual schedules which accounted for every minute of their day. No class lasted more than an hour, and study was interspersed with periods of exercise and play. Subjects which required the "greatest intellectual effort" were taught in the mornings, when the mind was thought to be freshest, while the afternoons were "devoted to writing, drawing, music, and the lighter branches of study."[39]

Hofwyl's academic curriculum was not limited to the classics and mathematics, as were those of most contemporary American academies or English "public" schools. It included, a former student remembered, "the study of the Greek, Latin, French, and German languages, the last of which was the language of the college; history, natural philosophy, chemistry, mechanics; mathematics, a thorough course, embracing the highest branches; drawing, in the senior class, from busts and models; music, vocal and instrumental. . . ."[40] Whenever practicable, Fellenberg, following the ideas of the educational philosopher Johann Herbart, began his students with the study of Greek.[41] (The rationale was that stages in the curriculum should correspond to historical evolution.[42]) In the teaching of mathematics and the sciences, particularly with the beginning students, a modified form of Pestalozzian sense impressions, direct observation, and mental gymnastics was employed.[43]

Above all, it was to the cultivation of the last of the three faculties that Fellenberg devoted his efforts. A report on Hofwyl to the Czar of Russia stated that it was "to the moral character of his pupils that M. de Fellenberg's principal, and most assiduous care is constantly directed; and uprightness of character is the quality which he most highly values. . . ." Character was to be formed by "none of the ordinary methods of encouragement, or of control." Instead,

> there is neither first nor last; neither rewards nor medals, nor any humiliating punishments. Instead of the ordinary incentives of emulation or fear, it is customary for the tutors, who are constantly with the children, to make a recapitulation, in their presence, of the principal subjects of praise or blame, which their conduct happens to have presented; the firm and gentle tone of the tutor, and the truly paternal feeling, which inspire their exhortations and admonitions, make a deep impression on the minds of the children.[44]

This system resulted in a strong community feeling between masters and students, based on the students' carefully nurtured belief "that their adoptive father and his assistants, have no object so much at heart as their virtue and happiness."[45] Cultivation of such personal feelings, it was hoped, would lead to the higher religious sentiments. "In our situation as educators and teachers," Fellenberg explained, "the most sacred duties of parents devolve upon us: we should therefore seek to present our pupils, in our efforts for their happiness, the same image of the disinterested, benevolent, and unvarying parental care of Divine Providence."[46] Formal religious instruction, however, was not ignored at Hofwyl: there were morning and evening readings from religious writings; students studied basic Scripture and on Sundays attended churches of the Catholic, Protestant, or Orthodox denominations.[47]

While on his first visit to Hofwyl Cogswell was somewhat suspicious of its "philanthropy," on his second he was nothing less than enchanted. Of the students he wrote:

> they had the happiness to be placed for their education in a school, the head of which was rather a father than a master to them. I saw a thousand proofs of the sentiments they entertain towards each other, and nothing could resemble more a tender and solicitous parent, surrounded by a family of obedient and affectionate children. There was the greatest equality and at the same time the greatest respect, a respect of the heart I mean, not of fear; instructors and pupils walked arm in arm together, played together at the same table, and all without any danger to their reciprocal rights; how delightful it must be to govern, where love is the principle of obedience.[48]

Cogswell had gone to Hofwyl to inspect the education of the poor, and had become entranced with the education of the rich. His fascination with Hofwyl and Fellenberg's ideas was understandable. Along with New England and Scotland, Fellenberg's Switzerland was an area of the world where the old Calvinist intellectual traditions—tempered by the Enlightenment and romanticism—still ran strong. Cogswell was an inheritor of the New England Calvinist tradition, albeit in its much-modified form of early nineteenth-century Harvard Unitarianism. As Edmund Morgan has pointed out, if the conscientious seventeenth-century Puritan parent "listened to his religious advisers, he employed bodily punishment only as a last resort; for the ministers who wrote and spoke on the subject almost always counseled their readers and listeners to win children to holiness by kindness rather than try to force them to it by severity."[49] Without suggesting an international Calvinist conspiracy, one can guess that Cogswell—who had an amazingly thorough knowledge of seventeenth- and eighteenth-century Puritan theology and literature—would find a certain congruence between his own inherited traditions and Fellenberg's ideas and practices. Hofwyl must have seemed to him the perfect institutional adaptation of ancient New England educational traditions and values to nineteenth-century social conditions. Fellenberg's faculty psychology, with all its educational implications and moral goals, was already familiar to Cogswell. It was taught at Cogswell's Harvard as one application of Scottish "common sense" philosophy, the reigning American academic philosophy in the years between the Revolution and the Civil War.[50] In Fellenberg's Hofwyl Cogswell had discovered the institutional embodiment of many of the Anthologists' cultural and educational values: it was an institution that demonstrably educated Christian gentlemen and scholars.

Cogswell was not the only representative of the *Anthology* tradition and of Harvard to examine the latest in European educational thought and practice. Also exploring European culture at the same time was Cogswell's young friend, George Bancroft. Born in Worcester, Massachusetts, in 1800, Bancroft was the son of Aaron Bancroft, one of the leaders of the Unitarian revolt against the established church in Massachusetts, president of the American Unitarian Association from 1825 to 1836, biographer of George Washington, and a Contributing Member of the Anthology Society. Raised in the Anthologists' intellectual milieu, Bancroft's early career had been remarkably similar to Joseph Buckminster's. Bancroft entered the Phillips Exeter Academy in 1811. The cost of board with a private family and the tuition fee of three dollars a term was a strain on the Bancroft family's finances; in his two years at Exeter George could not once afford to make the trip home to Worcester.[51] In 1813, as young as the century, Bancroft entered Harvard with the class of 1817. A brilliant student, he attracted the attention of President Kirkland and of Andrews Norton, Dexter Professor of Sacred Literature. In 1815 Kirkland had sent Edward Everett to Europe to fit himself for the post of professor of classics at Harvard. On his return

Everett had fulfilled his promise, and the reports of Ticknor, then still abroad, looked promising. So, in 1818 it was announced that Bancroft, supplied with funds from "Madame Mary Saltonstall's donation," would be sent to the University of Göttingen in Germany for a few years " 'to perfect his knowledge in the ancient languages. . . .' "[52]

At Göttingen Bancroft studied diligently—sixteen hours a day in his first months there. "One thing at least is certain," he told Andrews Norton, "the strange sort of life I lead here will teach me to bear solitude well; and being no friend to cities I sometimes think with pleasure of the comforts of a life in the country." Although Bancroft respected and enjoyed the high quality of the professors' lectures at Göttingen, he found the Germans scholars, but not gentlemen. "The people here are too cold and unsocial," he told Kirkland, "too fond of writing books and too incapable of conversing, having more than enough of courtesy, and almost nothing of actual hospitality. . . . I consider their vast erudition with astonishment; yet it lies as a dead weight on society. The men of letters are for the most part ill bred; many of them are altogether without manners."[53]

After almost two years at Göttingen Bancroft departed for a winter's study at the University of Berlin, which had been founded only eleven years before, in 1809. "I took a philosophical course with Hegel," he reported to Edward Everett, "but I thought it lost time to listen to his display of unintelligible words." Hegel aside, Bancroft found Berlin and its university far more congenial than Göttingen. He was particularly attracted—as teacher, preacher, and friend—to the philosopher Friedrich Schleiermacher, with whom he took a course of lectures on the "science of education." In letters to family, friends, and acquaintances, he sang Schleiermacher's praises. "He abounds in wit and is inimitable in Satyre," Bancroft wrote home, "yet he has a perfectly good heart, is generous and obliging—I think him to be acknowledged the greatest pulpit orator in Germany."[54]

While Bancroft was unsure of precisely which career he would take up on his return to the United States, President Kirkland had more than tentative plans for his protege. Early in Bancroft's stay in Europe, Kirkland gently suggested that a future other than the ministry might be in store for him on his return home. "I suppose," he wrote Bancroft, "a gentleman eminently qualified to set up a High School with all that [detail?] of particular and effective instruction which is practiced in Germany would be in great consideration and request here." Other friends of Harvard reinforced Kirkland's suggestion; Bancroft was receptive. "The idea, *which you suggest,* of establishing a high school," he replied to Kirkland, "appears to open a fine field for being useful. I would gladly be instrumental in the good cause of improving our institutions of education, it is our schools which cry out most loudly for reformation. To expect to devote the *whole* of my life to the duties of a school is not a very pleasing prospect. On my return I shall, however, be still very young, and could not perhaps in any way do more good than by embracing this scheme for a few years." If he followed Kirkland's scheme, Bancroft suggested, it would be necessary for him to spend a week or two studying closely some of the best schools in Germany, and, if possible, some English and Scottish schools as well.[55]

Pursuing Kirkland's plan when he arrived in Berlin in the fall of 1820, besides taking Schleiermacher's course, Bancroft examined the schools of the city. It was an exciting time to be investigating Prussian education. In a nationalistic response to the humiliating defeats of the Napoleonic Wars, over the preceding decade Prussia had completely reorganized its schools and universities and had, in effect, created the foundations of a state system of education. Bancroft visited not only the public schools of Berlin, but private ones as well. One school in particular he found especially interesting and described it thus to a correspondent at home:

> Ten young men, animated by the eloquence and patriotism of Fichte, formed a plan some years ago of establishing a school after the new principles. Each of them chose a particular branch, in which he was to perfect himself, and which he was afterwards to teach. Three of them went in the meantime to live with Pestalozzi and become acquainted with his principles from the man himself. . . . I find it quite instructive to observe their institution from time to time; they know how to unite gymnastic exercises, music and the sciences; and this is the mode of education which Plato has extolled as the perfection of the art. In this way I have excellent means of becoming

> acquainted with the old and the new ways of teaching in Germany. . . .[56]

Bancroft did not limit his investigations of German education to Berlin. During his stay in Europe he had in his charge Frederick Hedge, son of Professor Levi Hedge of Harvard. Responsible for finding a suitable school for the difficult young Hedge, after two mistakes Bancroft finally placed him in one of Germany's oldest and most famous boarding schools—Schulpforta, near Naumberg in Prussian Saxony. "By its antiquity, its beauty, its wealth, its celebrity," write Matthew Arnold in 1865, Schulpforta was "entitled to vie with the most renowned English schools." Actually, in 1821 Schulpforta was far superior to any contemporary English school. An ancient monastery, it had been secularized and then turned into a school in 1543. When Bancroft placed Frederick Hedge there, Schulpforta was under the headmastership of the great classical scholar Ilgen, who in his reign brought the school abreast of the newest educational ideas while preserving its tradition of excellence in classical studies. In a twelve-page, closely written letter to Professor Hedge, Bancroft described every conceivable aspect of the school, from the kitchens to the curriculum, from the faculty to the students' schedules. Schulpforta was, he concluded, "in fact a little world in itself"—a perfect educational environment.[57]

Bancroft left Berlin in February 1821 to make a leisurely trip about Europe which lasted almost a year and a half. He visited Goethe for a second time, dropped in on lectures at the University of Heidelberg, and spent three months in Paris where he was introduced about by Washington Irving and Alexander von Humboldt. In September 1821 he began a six weeks walking tour of Switzerland and then turned south to Italy where he met, among other famous figures of the day, Princess Pauline Borghese and Lord Byron.[58] The dry and dull years at Göttingen slipped quickly away; Bancroft's letters and journals during his Swiss tour were written in the worst style of effusive Romantic nature-worship. However, during his Italian trip he paused to write in his journal a summary of his ideas on education:

> In reflecting on establishing a school on a large foundation, it appears to me that something new might be undertaken with usefulness and advantage. 1. Greek should be the

first language taught. . . . 2. Natural History should be taught: it quickens all the powers, and creates the faculty of accurate observation. Even in the town schools so much of natural history as relates to the plants of husbandry and weeds which torment the farmer, ought to be taught simply but thoroughly to every boy, and most of all to the poorest—whose lot it is to till the earth. 3. Emulation must be most carefully avoided, excepting the general and mutual desire of excelling in virtue. No one ought to be rewarded at the expense of another, and even where there is nothing but prizes, they who fail of gaining them, may have been impeded by the nature of their talents and not by their own want of exertion. 4. Corporal punishments must be abolished as degrading the individual, who receives them, and as encouraging the base passions of fear and deception. 5. Classes must be formed according to the characters and capacities of each individual boy. 6. Country schoolmasters might be formed with little expense by annexing to the school an institution for orphans, to be educated for schoolmasters. Of these the best might be chosen for a learned discipline, and be fitted for taking care of academies. 7. Eventually a vast printing establishment might be annexed to the school.[59]

These plans are obviously an amalgam of what Bancroft had learned from Schleiermacher and had seen himself at the schools of Berlin and Schulpforta. Although there is no evidence that he ever visited Pestalozzi's or Fellenberg's institutions, their influence on Bancroft's thought is evident in his downgrading of emulation and his concern with the education of the poor and orphans, and the training of teachers.[60] Although he never managed, as he had hoped, to investigate any English or Scottish schools, when Bancroft sailed for the United States on 12 June 1822, he was thoroughly familiar not only with the latest in continental educational theory but with the best of traditional and innovative educational practice as well.[61]

Cogswell's and Bancroft's observations of continental schools came at the end of a long series of developments in European education. Hofwyl, Schulpforta, and other boarding schools were the institutional embodiments of profound changes in European thought. "This extension of the boarding-school system in the later eighteenth and early nineteenth century," the French historian Philippe Ariès has observed, "was . . . a general phenomenon, to be found in Frederick the Great's Prussia as in the England of the public schools. The English public schools became exclusively boarding schools, and this circumstance distinguished them from the grammar schools, which were attended by day-boys from the surrounding district, as were the French colleges." (Or, Ariès might have added, as were the American academies.) Ariès explains what he calls the "claustration" of the child thus:

> The development of the boarding-system after the end of the eighteenth century bears witness to a different concept of childhood and its place in society. Henceforth there would be an attempt to separate childhood from the other ages of society: it would be considered important—at least in the middle class—to shut childhood off in a world apart, the world of the boarding-school. The school was substituted for society in which all the ages were mingled together; it was called upon to mold children on the pattern of an ideal human type.

Earlier, this molding of the child to a type had "been expected not so much from *school* as from the *society* from which the child and the young man had not been excluded."[62] Ariès's discussion concerns mainly continental Europe, and perhaps his generalizations hold completely true for that area. Americans, however, had been familiar since the seventeenth century with boarding schools designed to mold students to an ideal human type—the American colleges. Granted that American college students were probably a bit older than the secondary boarding school students Ariès was concerned with, much of what Cogswell and Bancroft observed in Europe must have seemed oddly familiar to them. And, in the 1820s, after they returned home, they would see those profound changes which Ariès mentions in the very conception of the nature of the child. They would see, too, profound objective changes in social and economic conditions in the United States, changes that would make the notion of sending comparatively young children away to boarding school very attractive to many American parents.

"It is true," Cogswell could write two years after he left the

United States in 1815, "that we have no overgrown cities, and no crowded population, and the means of subsistence are within the reach of every industrious healthy individual."[63] However, what had been true in 1815 was no longer true when Cogswell returned in the 1820s. The spirit of the changes he would experience was well summed up by the American father who wrote thus to his little son in 1825: "When you again behold your birthplace you will discover that the fathers of Boston Boys have not been idlers in the absence of their sons, and that the youth in training must be very industrious to secure advance in this age of improvement."[64] Those would be the two key words of the new age —*industry* and *improvement:* the population would not only move westward to open up new, rich lands, but towards an even stranger frontier—that of the industrial city. After the War of 1812 the United States entered on a great transformation of its economy. This quickening in economic growth, the first step on the road to industrialization, was reflected in drastic changes in the American social order. By the late 1840s more than half the population of Massachusetts and Rhode Island was urbanized, while between 1820 and 1860 the urban population of the nation as a whole multiplied eleven times. Where in 1790 only one-twentieth of the population could be classified as city-dwellers, by 1860 the census counted one-fifth of the population as urban.[65]

In the longer-settled sections of the nation, along the Atlantic seaboard and particularly in the Northeast to which Bancroft and Cogswell were returning, these developments were accompanied by great changes in the social order. The westward movement drained off much of the native population of many old towns and villages. Industrialization created a new class of landless workers that the traditional village and town social order was hard put to accommodate; at the same time it filled the suddenly expanding cities with a seemingly rootless population. In the 1830s, moreover, the great tide of nineteenth-century European immigrants —at first largely from Germany and Ireland—began to reach American shores. Some agricultural towns and villages found themselves shrinking, while those in which a mill or factory was built were filled with landless, and very often foreign, workers, who shared little of the traditional culture. The burgeoning cities faced even more acute problems. As early as 1815 Boston had begun to develop a class of urban poor; in the same year New

Yorkers could find the beginnings of the slums of the lower East Side.[66] Urban growth and urban decay began at the same moment.

The Massachusetts Cogswell and Bancroft had left in the 1810s seemed built on stable economic, social, and intellectual foundations. The Massachusetts to which they returned in the 1820s would begin to overturn the old Federalist order. An elitist, agricultural, and commercial society would be replaced by a democratic, industrial, and technological one. Saturated in romantic ideas about the educational virtues of nature, Cogswell and Bancroft would see the city rapidly encroach on the countryside. They had ransacked Europe for new cultural forms in which to embody the Harvard reformers' and Anthologists' goals. A question they faced on their return was the continuing relevance of those goals or of the very notion of the Christian gentleman and scholar to an American society in rapid flux.

Chapter III

The School in the Garden: Round Hill and the Federalist Educational Ideal

Cogswell and Bancroft found the return to their homeland far more trying than the adjustment to Europe had been. Their attempts to put into practice the ideas they had absorbed in Europe would be rebuffed again and again in Boston and Cambridge. Finally, they would flee from the city to the country. There, in great Nature's garden, they would found the Round Hill School, which would embody the newest in European educational practice, a generation's cultural aims, and would set the basic standard for the American boarding school of the nineteenth century.

Despite all his thought about education and investigations of schools, a few months before his return home Bancroft changed his mind about his future career: he would become not a schoolmaster, but a clergyman. He received encouragement from his father, who apparently hoped that George would follow in his own footsteps—not however in Boston, but in New York City. "Nothing could be more congenial to my feelings than to do what I can for liberal Christianity, in a place like that," Bancroft wrote. "I should never wish to become a clergyman in Boston; I dread it's [*sic*] dangerous climate, which is most dangerous for those who are obliged to speak in public, unprotected against it's [*sic*]destroying might. New York is farther to the South, is capitally situated for frequent and easy communication with Europe: and in a large city and vast state like that there would be a wider scope for literary exertions."[1] Eventually, Bancroft would spend much of his life in New York, but it was a long trip; over the next few months his fears about Boston would be confirmed a hundred times over.

"You indulge in a sarcasm upon Boston," Cogswell had accused Bancroft soon after his arrival in Europe. "I cannot allow this; it is downright heresy and comes within a hair of the unpardonable sin. Above all things," Cogswell warned the younger man, "be careful of speaking scornfully of things at home, when you write, I assure you, there is no forgiveness for such offenses."[2] Bancroft followed Cogswell's advice. His letters home contained no invidious comparisons between Boston and Europe. Unfortunately, Bancroft was not as careful in his person as he had been in his letters. Before his return to Massachusetts Andrews Norton had carefully reminded him of Boston's conservative temper: "Our state of society is such as to require an extraordinary degree of attention to manners, in order that one may be respectable and useful," he advised Bancroft. "There is no place, I believe, where anything *outré* or *bizarre* (if I may use two French words at once) is observed with a keener perception of ridicule, or tends more to the disadvantage of him in whom it is discovered." However, intoxicated with his stays in France and Italy, Bancroft proceeded to be both outré and bizarre when, clad in velvet trousers, he greeted Norton on his return with kisses on both cheeks—a most un-Bostonian custom.[3]

The reunion with Norton—long one of Bancroft's closest advisers—was an unmitigated disaster. Norton was appalled at the changes Europe had wrought in Bancroft and after a few days refused to receive him in his home. "You have done me great injustice in the estimate, which you have made of my manners and feelings," cried Bancroft, full of injured innocence. "I do not expect to be a popular tutor, because I intend to require more than has been usual; but if I become a ridiculous one, or if I do not as a clergyman show myself worthy of honour and love, I will concede that your forebodings and your opinion were just."[4] Norton's forebodings, unfortunately, proved to be, if not just, accurate: Bancroft became an unpopular tutor at Harvard and an unhonored clergyman.

Since Bancroft could not find a pulpit of his own immediately upon his return, President Kirkland offered him the post of Greek Tutor. Bancroft immediately introduced the teaching methods with which he had become familiar abroad. "I have divided the class into five parts," he explained to a friend, "taking into consideration talent, disposition to learn, general character and fondness for and previous knowledge of Greek. Each class or division pursues its studies independently of the other."[5] For Harvard, where heretofore classes had been divided only alphabetically and had droned through recitation sessions, this was a pedagogical revolution—and a fiercely resisted one. The students thought Bancroft a Prussian drillmaster and made him the butt of endless pranks. And, since he managed to teach as much Greek in one year as Harvard students had been accustomed to learn in three, Bancroft won the animosity not only of his classes but of less ambitious faculty members as well. Preaching went no better. On the strength of his European education and his father's prestige, Bancroft was invited to speak from various Massachusetts pulpits. Bancroft was a Transcendentalist before his time; his sermons, couched in the loftiest terms of German idealism and in a style that was a heady compound of Young Werther, Childe Harold, and New England, passed over the heads of his somewhat disconcerted listeners.[6] By April 1823 Bancroft could complain—with some justice—that "the year of return, which should have been perfectly happy and cheerful for me, has been the most wretched of my life."[7]

Bancroft's difficulties were not entirely due to his personality or teaching methods: the year 1822–23 was the occasion of the "Great Rebellion" on the part of Harvard's senior class. Throughout its career the class of 1823 had followed a course of mischief, dissipation, and riot. After almost two days of tumults in May 1823—and several years provocation—the college administration expelled forty-three of the seventy members of the class. Most of these students did not receive their degrees for eighteen to fifty-seven years after their proper commencement. Fifteen never received degrees at all, and one student, John Adams—son and grandson of presidents of the United States—

was only awarded his degree posthumously.[8] Despite all the Anthologists' hopes and President Kirkland's efforts, it seemed that neither Christianity, gentility, nor scholarship were being well served in Cambridge.

As Kirkland and his supporters were only too well aware, the Harvard of his day was more college—or even secondary school—than university. What was true of Harvard in this respect was true of most other American colleges of the time. In 1818 President Jeremiah Day of Yale drew up a succinct outline of the traditional collegiate ideal—the ideal that Kirkland and the Anthologists were attempting to redefine, but to which most contemporary Americans would have subscribed. For his first three years the Yale student studied Latin, Greek, mathematics, and a little natural science. In his senior year he was exposed to a hodgepodge of moral philosophy, theology, natural science, and so forth. The student did not study particular subjects so much as particular *books.* In 1818 Day reported that the freshman class "have received Webber's Arithmetic, Adams' Roman Antiquities, five books of Homer, Algebra, the 1st Vol. of Morse's Geography, and Murray's English Grammar." Such a year-long program was minimal, to say the least: in his last quarter at Phillips Exeter Joseph Buckminster had covered five times the amount of material prescribed in the Yale freshman's curriculum.

While each of the four Yale classes attended specialized lectures given by the various permanent professors, most of the instruction in the college was carried on by the tutors, who were recent outstanding graduates, little older than the students themselves. The dependence upon tutors was justified, Day wrote, because the discipline of the college was meant "to be of the paternal kind," rather than one of "threatenings and punishments." Ideally, at least, the theory of *in loco parentis* was fully carried out in practice. "To render the discipline by influence effectual," Day wrote:

> it is necessary that the *character* of each student be thoroughly understood, and that their *confidence* and affection should be secured. These objects are here attained in *this* way. When a class enters college, it is divided into two parts, and each division is put under the charge of a Tutor. He generally

continues with them three years, if he remains in office so long. He is the Tutor not of a *language* or of a *science,* but of a class, or a division. He meets them, three times a day. He becomes thoroughly acquainted with their characters. He speaks of them as *his;* and considers himself as in a degree *responsible* for their good conduct. A mutual attachment is formed between them. He gains from them an affectionate confidence; which could hardly be expected, where each student has half a dozen different instructers; and each instructer half a dozen different sets of pupils, in the course of a week. It is principally through the Tutors, that the Faculty influence the students.

Tutors, then, were not only responsible for most of the instruction, but for the discipline as well. They lived with the students, visited each student's room every day, and were counted upon to nip impending disorders in the bud.[9] Considering the age of the American college student, such a system was probably appropriate. In 1819 the average age of the Harvard freshman class was only sixteen and a half, while in 1826 two-thirds of Yale's freshmen were sixteen years old or younger.[10] The tutors continued to live with the Yale students and did not specialize in particular subjects until 1830. At Harvard, however, the tutors had been allowed to specialize in one subject as early as 1767; by 1789 a Harvard undergraduate "who treated his tutor as a friend was looked down upon as a 'fisherman,' ["brown-nose" would be one twentieth-century equivalent] and the tutors regarded the undergraduates as inmates in a reformatory."[11] Insofar as Harvard and Yale were representative, the American college was, in effect, a boarding school for adolescents. In such a situation the heavy emphasis on the colleges' role *in loco parentis* was understandable.

This situation was precisely the one that Robert Hallowell Gardiner had criticized in the *Monthly Anthology* in 1807.[12] Unless one raised the age of college students, the Anthologists thought, one could not begin to create a university. And, although the age of the American collegian was gradually raised through the first half of the nineteenth century (by 1851 two-thirds of Yale's freshman class was seventeen or older), the process was a slow one.[13]

In the meantime, the ancient collegiate ideal was being questioned from at least two sides: from those who questioned its efficacy in practice, and from those who considered it intellectually moribund. At Harvard the most vociferous critic was Bancroft and Cogswell's friend, the young former Anthologist George Ticknor. In 1819 Ticknor had returned from several years study at the University of Göttingen, determined to turn the Anthologists' ideas and the practices he had observed in Europe into reality at Harvard.

Since 1810 President Kirkland had made many steps towards moving Harvard to true university status. Fifteen professorships, for instance, were added to the college during his years of leadership. However, in 1820 most of the instruction in the college was still carried on under the antique recitation system in which a student sat and memorized part of a prescribed book, then rose and regurgitated it to his tutor. As one member of the class of 1829 remembered, "the teacher was there, not to teach, but to give marks to each student. . . . Pencil in hand, he listened in silence to the student's translation or solution of a problem, and having affixed the proper number to his name, went on to the next."[14] The various professors acted more as prestigious appendages than integral parts of the college's curriculum. Juniors and seniors listened to the professors' lectures, but whether they learned anything or not was an open question. The lectures, George Ticknor complained, were "attended by whole classes, whether the individual members were prepared for such instruction or not; no notes were taken; and a law passed a few years since, requiring examinations, was not executed. The lectures were simply read, and then the students dismissed."[15]

Added to the poor teaching on the part of the Harvard faculty was what seemed to be a decline on the part of the students' morals. Ticknor learned that "undergraduates were playing billiards at Lechmere Point, drinking brandy in the morning at the Marlboro Hotel in Boston, and contracting venereal disease by consorting with women of ill repute."[16] What was to be done? In 1821 Ticknor presented his criticisms and suggestions to Judge William Prescott, Cogswell's old mentor and a member of the Harvard Corporation:

> If we can ever have a University at Cambridge, which shall lead the intellectual character of the country, it can be I ap-

prehend only when the present college shall have been settled into a thorough and well-disciplined high school, where the young men of the country shall be carefully prepared to begin their professional studies; and where in Medicine, Law, and Theology, sufficient inducements shall have been collected around and within the college, aided by regular courses of instruction in the high branches of general learning and science, to keep Graduates there two years at least, and probably three. As, however, we are not arrived at this desirable condition, and cannot very soon hope to arrive there, the first thing to be done, in order to satisfy the reasonable demands of the community, is, to take measures to make the college a well-disciplined high school, in which the knowledge preparatory to a professional education, shall be taught thoroughly, and the habits and character of the young men fitted for the further intellectual exertions to which they are destined.[17]

For all practical purposes Ticknor's suggestions were ignored. President Kirkland was irritated, and the Corporation found that most of the faculty resented what they considered Ticknor's meddling. Only after 1824 would unexpected events force the authorities to reexamine Ticknor's call for reform—which would then be restated on a far more extensive scale than his relatively modest suggestions of 1821.

While Kirkland's temporizing and coolness towards plans for reform at Harvard must have seemed particularly disappointing to Ticknor, they were hardly less so for Cogswell and Bancroft. But the year 1822–23 had not been a completely black one for Bancroft. Tutoring and preaching might be going badly, but by December he had other plans afoot. "Shall I tell you a plan of mine?" he asked his friend Samuel Eliot:

It is still a great secret: nobody knows aught of it at home except Mr. Everett, Mr. Ticknor and Dr. Kirkland, who may have told it to Mr. Lowell, who may have told it to dozens. I have considered the nature of high schools, grammar-schools, Gymnasia and the like. I have consulted the books, which treat of education: I have reflected on the *means* and *end* of education. Now I am going to turn *schoolmaster*. . . . Mr. Cogswell has seen so much of the world, that he knows it and

> its folly: he will join me in my scheme: we will together establish a school, the end of which is to be the moral and intellectual maturity of the mind of each boy we take charge of; and the means are to be first and foremost *instruction in the classics.* . . . We will live retired from the clamours of scandal and the disputes of the irresolute. We will delight ourselves with the letters, and instead of warring against the corporation and contending with scandalous reports, we will train up a few minds to virtue and honour. . . .[18]

"It is my misery to have lived on charity, while abroad," Bancroft complained to a friend a few months later, ". . . bitter enough is the taste of it in my belly."[19] A school of his own would give him both financial independence and the opportunity to put some of his ideas about education into practice.

While not as stormy as Bancroft's, Cogswell's career in Cambridge had been equally unsatisfying. He diligently rearranged the Harvard Library on the plan of Göttingen's but received little support from the authorities. Cogswell hoped to create a great scholarly library, while the Corporation simply wanted to service undergraduates—a function which, Cogswell complained, "might as well be pursued by any shop boy from a circulating library." By autumn 1822 Cogswell was growing restless. "I have been doubting for a long while," he told President Kirkland, "if it were not wrong for me to be here; my views of education differ too much from yours and from the gentlemen of the corporation, to allow my efforts for the advancement of the institution ever to be successful."[20] An institution of their own would provide not only a solution for Cogswell's and Bancroft's personal situations but perhaps a remedy for some of the ills that were besetting Harvard as well. A supply of well-prepared students would enable Kirkland, Ticknor, and Everett to raise the standards of instruction in the college and might also lead to improvements in college discipline. The suggestions Kirkland, Everett, and others had made to Bancroft over the preceding three or four years had finally come to fruition.

The first thing to do was to find a location for the school. In the spring of 1823, after deciding against a site in the South (considered initially because so many southern students went North for their education), Cogswell and Bancroft selected

Round Hill, near Northampton, Massachusetts, as the site for their proposed school. Cogswell described it thus:

> About half a mile from the village of Northampton, on the brow of a beautiful hill, overlooking the Connecticut, and the rich plain through which it flows, and the fine picturesque hills which form its banks, we found two houses to be let for a very small rent, and, as all the circumstances connected with the situation were exactly to our minds, we concluded, at once to begin our experiment there. Accordingly we have engaged the houses from September, and expect to enter upon our new duties the first of September.[21]

Northampton was not quite the Alps, but it would do; Cogswell and Bancroft had taken Fellenberg's example of the benign moral influence of a rural environment to heart. Indeed, their bucolic location was one of the major points they stressed in advertising the school. "Among the ancient and modern writers on education," they declared in their *Prospectus,* "there is but one voice respecting the grateful and salutary influence, exercised by the beauties of scenery on the mind, and many of the eminent schools in Europe are hardly less celebrated for their site, than for their literary excellence."[22] It was, after all, the age of romantic appreciation of Nature; at almost the same time Bancroft and Cogswell were enthusing over Round Hill's landscape, Thomas Cole was making the walking and sketching trip that would inaugurate the Hudson River School and a whole new era of American art.

Having selected the site, Cogswell and Bancroft's next task was to attract the interest of parents of prospective students. In June 1823 they published their *Prospectus,* which clearly outlined the principles they planned to follow at Round Hill. They would be satisfied, they wrote, if they could "assist in forming a few of the rising generation to be somewhat more virtuous, more intelligent and more happy than they would otherwise have been." Their methods of instilling virtue, intelligence, and happiness, they thought, might "in some degree be novel":

> If we would attempt [they wrote] to form the characters as well as to cultivate the minds of the young, we must be able

> to control all their occupations. For this reason we intend to have them under the same roof with ourselves, and we become responsible for their manners, habits and morals, no less than for their progress in useful knowledge. . . .
>
> The institution, which we purpose to establish, is designed to furnish occupation for those years, which in France are spent at a *Collége,* and in Germany at a *Gymnasium.* A boy, who has completed his ninth year, is old enough to commence his regular studies, and to delay them longer would be to waste precious time, and . . . the period, when good habits are most easily formed.[23]

They would refuse, they said, to accept any boys over twelve years of age; they felt that boys older than that would already have been to other schools and have been exposed to and corrupted by other methods. "The habits of study," they explained, "which we would form, differ essentially from those which now prevail; and we hope to produce mental activity from other motives than *fear* and *emulation.*"[24] What were these novel "other motives" by which they would inspire their students? Round Hill would constitute a family, said Cogswell and Bancroft. "We must, on receiving the charge of . . . [the students], be to them as parents. And hence the methods of discipline and government must be parental . . . we shall endeavour to govern by persuasion and persevering kindness."[25]

Round Hill's curriculum, they promised, would "educate not for an ideal world, but for the world as it is. We would make not laborious students only, but faithful and useful citizens." Towards this end they outlined a curriculum that was essentially a combination of the classical and English courses of contemporary academies. It was to consist of English, the classics, modern languages, mathematics, science, history, and geography. The elements were not novel, but the combination was. Round Hill's curriculum could be taken either as a college preparatory or a terminal course of study; it would prepare a boy for either Harvard or Yale, State or Wall streets.[26]

Not all coercion was to be done away with at Round Hill. "As the fear of God is the most sacred principle of action," Cogswell and Bancroft declared, "there is none which should be developed with more care." Though not mentioning any one particular sect, they promised that Round Hill students would begin and close each day with "devotional exercises" and would regularly attend formal religious services.

Intellectual and moral instruction were not all that Bancroft and Cogswell proposed to offer at their school; they believed that a sound program of education should also include regular physical exercise. Cogswell, in his articles on American education, had complained that academy students when not in class spent their time dissipating; at Round Hill he promised instead to "appropriate regularly a portion of each day to healthful sports and gymnastics"—a distinctly novel prospect for an American educational institution at that time.[27]

To many Americans of the 1820s Cogswell and Bancroft's ideas and proposals must have seemed somewhat radical. Until well into the 1830s, Bernard Wishy has discovered, most American writers on child nurture depicted the child as a naturally depraved sinner who required strict discipline and intensive early religious training if he was to be rescued from his innate evilness.[28] Mrs. Arthur T. Lyman, one of Cogswell and Bancroft's Northampton neighbors, expressed a not uncommon suspicion of their school when she wrote that she had "misgivings in regard to the efficacy of their plan, though I have done everything to cultivate faith that anyone could. The idea of a number of children being educated without rewards or punishments, I can hardly believe possible; because it bears no analogy to any system, human or divine, that I am acquainted with. The Almighty has seen fit in his providence to keep up a system of chastisements from which the best of his creatures are not exempt."[29] Mrs. Lyman's doubts represented the conventional view of children's education that prevailed in the 1820s. But whatever some might think, Cogswell and Bancroft were hardly radical; they did not, like Rousseau or Pestalozzi, consider the child naturally "good"—they just did not consider children quite as depraved, or human nature basically so unmalleable, as most conventional thinkers of the time did. And, when put into actual practice, their ideas would appear considerably more ambiguous than they seemed on paper.

Despite their high tuition fee of $300 a year ($125 more than the estimated cost of Harvard at the same time), the two proprietors had little difficulty filling the places in their as yet unproved school. Round Hill opened on 1 October 1823 with fifteen boarding and ten day students. The school quickly attracted favorable attention from the press. And from Virginia the aged Thomas Jefferson sent his endorsement: "This will certainly prove a great blessing to the individuals who can obtain access to it," he wrote. "The only ground of regret is the small extent of its scale, in the few who can have its advantages it will lay a solid foundation of virtue as well as of learning."[30]

Round Hill's initial success was probably helped also by events occuring back in Cambridge and Boston. As Samuel Eliot Morison has described the situation, "the Federalist party had been permanently unhorsed, public clamor against the College for student disorder, high cost of education, aristocracy, Unitarianism, etc., was loud and widespread, and the Republican [i.e., Democratic] legislature" refused to renew the $10,000 annual state grant which Harvard had received over the preceding ten years. A substantial portion of the state grant had been used to defray the tuition ($55 a year) and expenses of poor students; with this source of aid cut off, within four years the total number of undergraduates declined from about three hundred to two hundred. After almost two centuries Harvard had ceased to be, for all intents and purposes, a "public" institution.[31]

To the west in Northampton, Bancroft must have felt a certain irony in his situation. Less than a year before, his friend Samuel Eliot had written from Paris that he was "sorry that our public institution [i.e., Harvard] is to lose the benefit of your talents and exertions at a time when talents and exertions are so much needed."[32] Now Harvard would turn to Bancroft and Cogswell for assistance. Shortly before the Massachusetts legislature cut off its subsidy to the University, the Harvard Corporation made the unprecedented move of extending to Cogswell and Bancroft a mortgage of $8,000 to make up the $12,000 they needed to purchase Round Hill's site and buildings.[33] Harvard would be repaid more than amply: of the 291 students who attended Round Hill between 1823 and 1831, at least 50 would go on to Harvard.[34] Harvard's old role as a quasipublic institution had been undermined by the legislature. Controlled by Unitarians, it was facing a " 'Don't send your son to Harvard' " campaign on the part of orthodox Calvinists. For a time, Round Hill would provide the besieged college with at least one sure source of well-prepared students.[35]

There was further irony in the situation. The Great Rebellion and the withdrawal of state support gave George Ticknor the opportunity to call for a full-scale reorganization of Harvard. No longer would he be satisfied with making it "a well-disciplined high school"; he would press now for changes "with the purpose of opening the College and making it a University." Here was the chance to make a "beneficial compromise" between the American college and the "most liberal conception that would be demanded by one of the merely free and philosophical Universities of Europe." Round Hill might not only supply the college with students sufficiently prepared to meet a more advanced curriculum and more demanding standards of instruction, but it would even serve to a degree as a working model of Ticknor's plans for reform.[36]

In its rigor the daily schedule that Cogswell and Bancroft devised for Round Hill bore little resemblance to any other contemporary American school. It appears to have been modeled on the schedules used at Fellenberg's Hofwyl and in some of the German schools that Bancroft had observed. In an enthusiastic article on "The School at Northampton," *The United States Literary Gazette* of February 1825 described the routine at Round Hill: The students arose at six, dressed in the school uniform (blue grey coat and trousers, light blue waistcoat), and attended religious services, at which the prayers of the Episcopal Church were used, at six-thirty. They spent the time from six-thirty to seven-fifty in their rooms studying and then went outdoors for ten minutes of calisthenics. After a hearty breakfast at eight, they spent the half hour from eight-thirty to nine on the playfield at archery, balancing, tumbling, and other games. Classes were held from nine until noon, when the students had their main meal of the day. At one there was another half-hour of exercise, and then it was back to the classroom from two until five, after which they were released for another half-hour of games and the evening meal between five-thirty and six. After supper they practiced their French until eight, and at eight-fifteen, after another short session of religious devotions, they went to bed.[37] Round Hill's schedule certainly answered one of Cogswell's major complaints about the American academies: as Bancroft could truthfully tell his sister, "we are minute men. . . . From morning until night there is not a moment which has not its business."[38] Nature might be the great teacher, but the seeds of natural depravity were given little chance to sprout.

If Round Hill's schedule was rigorous for the students, it was no less so for the faculty. In the first year the entire burden of the school fell upon the proprietors and one other instructor. The teaching system adopted at Round Hill was particularly demanding of the instructors, since it led them to function almost as private tutors. Here the proprietors developed to its extreme the system that Bancroft had unsuccessfully tried to introduce at Harvard. No classes were formed; instead, each student was assigned a book which the instructor thought equal to his knowledge. The student was allowed to prepare as much material as he wished and was expected to report to the teacher whenever he felt ready to recite. When he was ready, he was questioned closely by the teacher; if he failed, he was sent back to continue until he had mastered the lesson. "The advantage of . . . [Round Hill's] system," John Spencer Bassett has suggested, "was that no boy studied with reference to the progress of another boy [i.e., no emulation], and while he was allowed full opportunity to learn all that his interest prompted him to learn, he came to esteem excellence in his studies for its own value."[39] There was nothing particularly revolutionary in such methods—the framework was still that of the recitation system. But the spirit that informed the old system was new: no more lockstep progress for each class through a rigidly prescribed curriculum, no more forcing of the student into a Procrustean bed of rote memorization and regurgitation. The spirit was that of the new currents of romantic educational thought that Cogswell and Bancroft had become familiar with in Germany and Switzerland.

As the students increased in number, the curriculum was expanded and the faculty enlarged. "Our course is essentially a preparatory one," Cogswell and Bancroft explained to President Day of Yale,

> preparatory not to entering college, but to entering on the higher pursuits of letters and the study of the professions. It

> embraces some things, which are not usually introduced into a collegiate course; in the Latin and Greek languages it provides means for advancing further, than it would comport with the character of our colleges to require of all. On the other hand in experimental science we do little, though all the branches of the exact mathematics are taught as extensively as in any college in the country.[40]

Round Hill's particular excellence lay in the study of languages. After only about three years there, one student reported home that, besides studying history with Bancroft and English with Cogswell, he was reading—presumably in the original—Wieland's *Oberon,* Juvenal's *Sixth Satire,* Aeschylus's *Seven Against Thebes,* Sophocles' *Philoctetes,* and Cervantes's *Don Quixote.* ("There is to be sure some wit in it," he said of the last, "and a great many things to excite laughter but as far as I have read I do not think I should ever kill myself laughing at it.")[41]

Besides Cogswell and Bancroft, by 1826 ten other instructors were teaching at Round Hill. George Ticknor called the faculty the "ablest body of instructors in the country." They were paid $500 a year—a very generous salary for teachers at the time—with a prospect of a raise to $600. In fulfillment of their promise to unite systematically for the first time in America intellectual and physical education, Cogswell and Bancroft imported from Germany Charles Beck, a disciple of Friedrich Jahn, the father of the Turner gymnastics movement. (Round Hill's was the first outdoor gymnasium in the United States.) Native-born teachers taught French, Spanish, Italian, and German. Among the faculty were Cornelius C. Felton, a future president of Harvard, and Francis Grund, a German who would later write two brilliant commentaries on the United States. "If academic dignities are to count on of any avail," Cogswell and Bancroft could claim with justifiable pride, "we and those connected with us have obtained the honors of American Colleges, or of the most respected Universities of the continent of Europe; some of us have both. There are among us four at least, who would be acknowledged as having the right to instruct and lecture publicly or privately at any of the regularly constituted universities of Germany." The quality and breadth of Round Hill's instruction surpassed not only that of any other secondary school in the nation, but probably that of most contemporary colleges.[42]

Cogswell and Bancroft had promised to employ a new type of discipline at Round Hill. "The methods of discipline and government must be parental," they had said; they would govern by "persuasion and persevering kindness," not by threats and coercion. "It will not be much more arduous to maintain good moral discipline in our institution," they promised, "than it is to preserve order in a large and well-regulated family."[43] It was. In December 1826 a minor instance of defiance resulted in the immediate expulsion of at least one of the older students.[44] However, for the most part Cogswell and Bancroft's seemingly overly-optimistic scheme of discipline was the one actually used in practice. For instance, thirteen-year-old George C. Shattuck, Jr., reported this incident to his father: "Yesterday afternoon," he wrote:

> I went to find out where the tavern was which the boys went to [.] I found it and went in, one of boys were with me and when I was going way Mr. Cogswell came in, he sent me home, afterwards sent for me to come into the counting room, scolded me some [,] told me that he should not punish me, but I must promise him not to go out of bounds again. I promised him I would not. He told me that the reason he did not punish me was because he never before had reason to find fault with me. I am sorry I went there. I went out of curiosity to find out where it was.

Although this particular episode so disturbed George's doting father that he almost withdrew his son from Round Hill, Cogswell's firm yet gentle and persuasive handling of the incident appears to have been typical of Round Hill's "familial" discipline and government.[45]

While many factors entered into Round Hill's initial success, one of the most significant must certainly have been its resemblance to a familiar institution—the American college. There was little in Cogswell and Bancroft's disciplinary program that an American college president of the 1820s would not have liked to introduce into his own institution. Their heavy emphases on "familial" government, on their own roles *in loco parentis,* were almost identical with Jeremiah Day's rather idealized description of Yale in 1818. However, both Day's Yale and Kirkland's Harvard were meeting considerable difficulty in maintaining the ancient communal ideal of the Anglo-American college. Youths at American colleges could not be as effectively isolated from society and moulded to a particular character type as could children at Round Hill. The specialization demanded by the nineteenth-century explosion of knowledge and the slow transformation of the college into the university perhaps inevitably led to a breakdown in the older ideal of the college as a joint communal enterprise embracing several age groups. The more the American college educated scholars, the less it educated gentlemen. Cogswell and Bancroft's promise to have the students "under the same roof with ourselves" went far towards restoring the old collegiate ideal—but with a younger group of students. They were thoroughly within the Puritan educational tradition, but theirs was a Puritanism tempered by the Enlightenment and romanticism.

While Cogswell and Bancroft certainly benefited from American familiarity with the collegiate ideal (and obviously were influenced by it themselves), the most immediate model for their school would seem to have been Emmanuel von Fellenberg's Hofwyl.[46] A happy—and unexpected—congruence between Swiss and New England educational traditions provided Cogswell and Bancroft with the working educational forms in which they could embody the Anthologists' cultural values. The similarities are striking: at both Round Hill and Hofwyl every moment of the students' day was determined by an elaborate schedule—"we manage our boys by keeping them employed," said Bancroft. The curricula of both schools were almost identical (Bancroft even followed the Herbartian practice of beginning some students with Greek).[47] At Round Hill, as at Hofwyl, students were provided with their own garden plots and given lumber for carpentry projects. The latest in the new German gymnastic exercises was used at both schools, and the students at each were provided with a riding school and a swimming-bath. The students at Hofwyl made annual "pedestrian journies" about the Swiss countryside; those at Round Hill made an "annual journey" to places as far afield as Saybrook, Connecticut.[48] Perhaps most significant was the similarity in the ethos of both schools: so far as possible, each avoided the use of emulation, of conventional rewards and punishments, in their discipline, with the purpose of encouraging individual growth. This was to be accomplished by parental government, according to the conception of both institutions as idealized families. "How delightful it must be to govern," Cogswell had exclaimed of Hofwyl, "where love is the principle of obedience." At Round Hill he discovered for himself how delightful it could be.[49]

In the 1820s and 1830s Americans were becoming familiar with the work of Pestalozzi and Fellenberg by means other than direct observation. Beginning in the early 1820s many books and articles either reprinting parts of their original writings or giving firsthand accounts of their practices appeared in the United States.[50] Their ideas eventually formed much of the ideological base for the writings and activities of American educators such as William Woodbridge, James Carter, Edward A. Sheldon, Henry Barnard, Horace Mann, William Torrey Harris and John Dewey. However, in 1823 when Cogswell and Bancroft published their *Prospectus,* they could still be considered pioneers in adapting European educational ideas and practices to American purposes and conditions.[51]

If Cogswell, Bancroft, and many other Americans copied or adapted various elements of Fellenberg's complex of schools, no American appears *explicitly* to have adopted Fellenberg's hierarchical conception of society as naturally divided into three fixed classes—"the higher (comprehending the noble and the wealthy), the middling, and the poor"—or to have gone on to the conclusion that each class "should be educated in a manner conformable to their situations." And neither Round Hill nor any of the American Fellenberg academies were institutions where poor students were meant, as William Woodbridge had written of Hofwyl, to "become accustomed to living in view of splendour and luxury, without desiring or hoping to partake them," and thus to "learn to recognize the inferiority of their rank without being degraded by it; while the pupils of the higher classes acquire by this connection the habit of treating their inferiors with kindness and deference."[52] Fellenberg could assume that adjustments in the educational system—essentially, the accommodation of a few bright bourgeois—would be sufficient to assure the maintenance of the traditional social order and an organic society. But Americans faced a related problem: if not rule by an hereditary aristocracy, then by whom?

The question had been debated since the earliest days of the republic. John Adams and Thomas Jefferson favored rule by the "natural," as opposed to the "artificial," aristocracy. Jefferson's scheme for producing this "natural" aristocracy was strikingly similar to Fellenberg's educational plans (Jefferson was probably familiar with Fellenberg's work) and was just as thoroughly elitist.[53] Culturally as well as socially the New England Federalists who clustered about the *Monthly Anthology* were also elitists. They too believed that American society and culture should be ruled and shaped by an elite of Christian gentlemen and scholars. Their problem, like Jefferson's, was to discover how to produce such a group. One obvious way was through "literary" institutions such as Harvard or Round Hill. "Natural" aristocrats themselves, they hoped to persuade the "artificial" aristocracy of the virtues of their own values and goals, to bridge the gap between the cultural ideal of the Christian gentleman and scholar and the social reality of an increasingly aggressive, materialistic, and capitalistic social order. While Cogswell was both a cultural *and* social elitist, the younger Bancroft was considerably more liberal; he actively supported the development of a public common school system.[54] But he also believed that the Christian gentleman and scholar should have a strong—perhaps decisive—voice among the nation's governors. On an early trip to Washington he found Andrew Jackson, the first president obviously destitute of traditional high culture, to be "deficient in knowledge, and consequently liable to become the dupe of artful knaves." The "political brawlers" of the nation did not want a "man of great integrity" as president. "They know that he would frown upon their schemes. An imbecile old man may be their dupe."[55] At which point the conspicuously well-educated Bancroft entered upon an active public career. The Christian gentleman and scholar in politics, he would work to repair the deficiencies of knowledge among the political brawlers and imbecile old men of the Democratic party.

In Adams and Jefferson's lexicon, Cogswell and Bancroft would probably have been considered "natural" aristocrats; to Round Hill they attracted the nation's "artificial" aristocracy, the nearest American equivalent to Hofwyl's upper-class clientele.

"They will have their full number of scholars to begin with, picked from a much larger number," one of their supporters informed another shortly before the school opened, "so as to suit themselves as to age and other abilities, and taken from the best families of the country to give them a reputation,—such as Mr. Otis, W. Sullivan, George Lyman, Prime of New York, etc., etc."[56] Students came from every part of the United States and from abroad. Of the 291 who attended the school between 1823 and 1831 adout 40 percent came from New England, 30 percent from the South, and 18 percent from the Middle States.[57] The states sending the largest numbers of students were Massachusetts, New York, and South Carolina. As one of Round Hill's alumni later recalled, Cogswell and Bancroft's "prospectus drew, like a magnet, boys from Maine to Georgia, sons of parents the most cultivated and wealthy the country could then boast."[58]

In the 1820s the main bases of America's "artificial" aristocracy were still landownership, commerce, and, to a lesser extent, the professions. It was precisely from such wealthy and firmly established families that Round Hill drew most of its students. The names of many great merchant families of the North, landed families of the South, and pioneers in industrialization appear on its list of alumni. For example, from Massachusetts came Thomas C. Amory, Thomas G. Appleton, Henry W. Bellows, William Ellery Channing, II, John Murray Forbes, William C. Gorham, William Lawrence, Robert T. S. Lowell, Benjamin E. Morse, Lathrop J. Motley [*sic*], Theodore Sedgwick, and Charles S. Storrow; from Maine, Robert H. and F. Tudor Gardiner; from New York, James and William Brevoort, William E. Howland, Philip Kearney, Robert L. Livingston, Herman and Thomas Newbold, Alexander van Rensselaer, William Wadsworth, and Samuel, Henry, and Marion Ward; from Virginia, Bernard and William Carter; from South Carolina, William Habersham, D. Hayward Hamilton, Robert Hayne, T. Pinckney Huger, Ralph S. Izard, Keating S. Laurens, and T. Pinckney Middleton. Tom Appleton was indeed correct when he pointed out that his classmates had been "sons of parents the most cultivated and wealthy the country could then boast"; a list of Round Hill's alumni is almost a living register of John Adams's artificial aristocracy. Moreover, these families did not disappear over the course of the nineteenth century. In 1903, eighty years after Round Hill's founding, one of Bancroft's biographers would be struck by the fact that "the very names of the pupils might be mistaken for the boys now at one of the existing schools drawing chiefly upon Boston or New York."[59]

The continental character of Round Hill's students raises an interesting question: why, in an era of difficult and dangerous transportation, would a well-to-do family send its small sons halfway across North America from a place like Charleston or New Orleans to be educated in Northampton? Why, in fact, send one's children away from home at all? The answer is simple, though somewhat surprising. The practice of sending one's children—even at very tender age—to be raised and educated with others was not an eighteenth- or nineteenth-century innovation. It was in fact a very ancient European, and particularly English, custom. A late fifteenth-century Italian traveler to England, for instance, observed that:

> The want of affection in the English is strongly manifested towards their children; for after having kept them at home till they arrive at the age of seven or nine years at the utmost, they put them out, both males and females, to hard service in the houses of other people, binding them generally for another seven or nine years. And these are called apprentices, and during that time they perform all the most menial offices; and few are born who are exempted from this fate, for everyone however rich he may be, sends away his children into the homes of others, whilst he, in return, receives those of strangers into his own.[60]

Although this custom had all but died out among the English aristocracy by the seventeenth century,[61] it apparently survived in the new world. "Puritan children were frequently brought up in other families than their own even when there was no apparent educational advantage involved," the somewhat puzzled Edmund Morgan has observed. "Almost every surviving correspondence of seventeenth-century New England gives evidence that the custom existed." Morgan has also noted that this practice was common in the colonial South. "The children of gentlemen," he writes, "were frequently placed as servants in the families of other gentlemen."[62] In fact, hundreds of Southern colonial planting families sent their children even farther away—across the Atlantic to England to be raised and educated.[63] TheFrench historian Philippe Ariès has suggested that "this way of life was probably common in the West during the Middle Ages. . . . Children were not kept at home: they were sent to another house, with or without a contract, to live there and start their life there, or to learn the good manners of a knight, or a trade, or even to go to school and learn Latin."[64] As we have seen, this was precisely the situation that existed in American academy-towns until well into the nineteenth century.[65] It implies conceptions of the child, the family, and the community very different from those of the late-nineteenth and twentieth centuries. Such a situation suggests that children were thought capable of playing a full part in the society about them, that it was not necessary to "protect" them, to separate them from adults or older or younger children. Contemporaries in the 1780s would have seen little anomaly in six-year-old Josiah Quincy sitting next to a thirty-year-old man in the schoolroom at Phillips Andover, nor in the Yale freshman class of 1826 which ranged in age from fourteen to twenty-three years.[66] "The Tudor educational system was characterized by a total lack of stratification by age," Lawrence Stone has observed. In the sixteenth century ". . . boys of widely varying ages were assembled together to pursue the same courses of study."[67] Such medieval patterns lingered on long in colonial America.

Philippe Ariès attributed the claustration of children in boarding schools at the end of the eighteenth and beginning of the nineteenth centuries to a profound change in the conception of the nature of the child.[68] Such a change would become apparent in the United States in the 1830s.[69] The difficulty with Ariès's notion is that neither the Anthologists nor Cogswell and Bancroft seem to have held a particularly novel conception of the child and his nature. Moreover, the goal of educating Christian gentlemen and scholars was hardly a nineteenth-century innovation. On close examination, however, there was one outstanding motive in particular for sending a boy to Round Hill. The father of one student summed it up well: "No principle in human nature," Dr. George C. Shattuck of Boston wrote to a friend, "is half so strong and steady in its operation as the love of liberty, and the restraints on personal liberty in the city to young children are . . . severe in connection with the debilitating influence of a tainted atmosphere, which is the [evil] of the city."[70] Round Hill was established at a time of unprecedented urban growth; as early as the 1820s, the burgeoning American city seemed morally and physically polluted; it was no place in which to raise children. Or so George Shattuck and many other American parents seem to have felt. In the United States in 1820 there were only eleven cities with a population of over 10,000: of the 101 students at Round Hill in April 1829, 72—or 71 percent—came from ten of those eleven cities. If the definition of an urban area is stretched a bit to include Savannah, Natchez, and Wilmington, fully 85 percent of Round Hill's students in 1829 were city boys.[71] So far as Round Hill was concerned, sentiments such as Shattuck's seem to have been shared by many other well-to-do American urbanites. And such sentiments were persistent. "So long as people dwell in great cities," one prep school headmaster wrote in 1925, over a hundred years after Round Hill's founding, "where the atmosphere, physical and moral, is in large measure unwholesome, at least for young people, so long the boarding schools will continue to minister to the children of those who can afford to send them out of the towns."[72] In the century after 1823 such mistrust of the city as an environment for children would remain one of the most consistent themes in the founding of American boarding schools. Insofar as the United States was concerned, the nineteenth century claustration of the child in boarding schools seems to have been due as much to urbanization as to changes in the idea of the child. Perhaps the same is true of Europe as well.

Elements other than mistrust of the city entered into Round Hill's attractiveness to parents. As Ariès wrote of European boarding schools, one of Cogswell and Bancroft's primary goals at Round Hill was "to mold children on the pattern of an ideal human type."[73] The reason "of most consequence" for his being at Round Hill, one student recognized, was "that of morals, and of learning how to acquire a character and ever after to support it."[74] The "character" in question was that of the Federalist ideal, the Christian gentleman and scholar. Round Hill's program could hardly have been better calculated to produce that ideal: it promised to develop all the faculties of the child—intellectual, moral, and physical—to the utmost. It promised, to use an anachronistic phrase, to develop "the whole child." The Anthologists recognized this and gave the school their full support. Some, like Robert Hallowell Gardiner, sent their sons (F. Tudor and Robert Hallowell, Jr.); others, like Andrews Norton and George Ticknor, lent financial and moral support. And despite the tension between the proprietors and the administration, Harvard made every effort to assure Round Hill's success. Many Round Hill parents seem to have felt that Christian gentlemen and scholars could not be developed at a contemporary academy where children boarded with miscellaneous nearby families and, presumably, joined in the life of the larger community. Looking back years later at his father's motives in sending him to Round Hill, George Shattuck remembered that in his childhood "there were . . . academies where the instruction in Latin, Greek, and mathematics was very thorough. The boys boarded in private houses and went to school to study and recite. But Mr. Cogswell's object was not merely to train the intellectual faculties and to supply the mind with knowledge. He wished to train the physical and moral faculties, and in order to do this he must live with the boys and have them constantly under observation and care."[75] In the United States as in Europe, many wealthy parents appear to have felt that education—in the broadest sense of the word—could no longer be left to society at large, but should better be entrusted to the controlled environment of the boarding school. The prohibition at Round Hill against leaving the institution's grounds without special permission, the uniform clothing (which made the student instantly recognizable if he did leave), effectively—and safely—isolated the child from the society about him.

Unlike the student at an academy, the boy at Round Hill lived a rigidly controlled life confined almost completely to his peers and to the faculty—he lived, in effect, within a unique subculture. He brought, however, his own needs and patterns of conduct with him. "When I came here I was pleased with the novelty of it," Sam Ward of Jamaica, Long Island, wrote his father. "I never had before been joined with so large a number of boys; I mean (when I say joined) to say, not that, I had never been at so large a school before, (for Jamaica was much larger) but I never had been in the same *community,* in the same *fellowship,* and *family* with so many. I did not know anything scarcely of Boys' customs, games, and plays, then, or at most, not one quarter so much as I do now."[76] Despite having his brothers Henry and Marion as fellow students, Sam was desperately homesick for his family in New York—for his parents, his sisters, his grandfathers, his aunts, and presumably the servants, too. He was in a very different company, fellowship, or family, at Round Hill, one confined to his peers and masters. And his peers were not from Jamaica, but from places as far distant as New Orleans, Charleston, Philadelphia, or Boston, and were members of families "the most cultivated and wealthy the country could then boast." The "Boys' customs" were their customs. At the same time that Cogswell and Bancroft were trying to educate Christian gentlemen and scholars, Round Hill was forging a common national subculture among the sons of many rich urban Americans. The associations formed in childhood at Round Hill would lead to many intermarriages among wealthy families from one end of the country to the other.

Cogswell and Bancroft's activities did not go unnoticed back in Cambridge. Between 1823 and 1825 George Ticknor and his friends on the Harvard Corporation tried to introduce to Harvard many of the changes that Cogswell and Bancroft were employing so successfully at Round Hill. The division of classes by proficiency—which Bancroft had tried unsuccessfully to use during his term as Greek tutor—was introduced, along with the division of the college into academic departments. Students were required to wear uniform clothing; the undergraduate who wenched in Boston or gambled at Lechmere Point would now be instantly recognizable. But outside of his own department, Ticknor's reforms came to little. There was opposition from the faculty, and President Kirkland straddled every fence in sight. In effect, a generation's dreams for Harvard ended in 1828 with the resignation of President Kirkland. The constant turmoil of the preceding few years had revealed incredible clerical and financial mismanagement on the genial but sloppy president's part. Although Cogswell was among those considered for the presidency, it finally went to Josiah Quincy, former mayor of Boston and also a former member of the Anthology Society. Quincy put the administration and finances of the college in order, but while he supported Ticknor in his own department, the college sank back into older curricular and teaching ways. And within six years Round Hill itself would no longer exist. The Anthologists' dream of turning Harvard into a compromise between an American college and a German university languished until Ticknor's nephew, Charles Eliot, became president in 1869.

The possible failure of the Anthologists' program was not unforeseen. "In our eagerness to create and bring forward the literary profession and make better scholars," Kirkland had written in 1818, "we may attempt acquisitions beyond the market and lose our labour." The intervening decade had not only shown that "nobody would buy what Harvard had to sell," but that Harvard was rather inept at production.[77] The course of American education over the next four decades would be set not in Cambridge, but in New Haven. In 1828 President Day of Yale and Professor James Kingsley published a report on the conduct of the college (with which, incidentally, most of the Harvard faculty would have agreed) that became the model for scores of other American colleges. Essentially an expanded version of Day's report of 1818, the gist of the 1828 report was that the old forms and goals of collegiate education should be retained: the aim of higher education was to discipline, or train, the students' faculties and to furnish their minds with basic factual knowledge in the traditional communal and paternalistic setting.[78] The Yale Report was realistic; if nothing else Harvard's experience over the preceding decade had shown that Americans as yet lacked the capacity, finances, or wish to support a university on the European model. For the next two generations the American college would remain, at its best, a "well-disciplined high school." And that was no small achievement in a developing nation. The Anthologists would turn their attention to other cultural institutions: George Ticknor established the Boston Public Library in the 1850s, and Cogswell was largely responsible for establishing the nucleus of the great New York Public Library in the 1840s.[79]

Inevitably, the failure to reform Harvard had effects on Cogswell and Bancroft's efforts at Round Hill. Part of their early success was dependent—despite the protestations to the contrary in their *Prospectus*—on preparing older boys for college. "Round Hill," wrote G. H. Bode, a faculty member whom Cogswell and Bancroft had persuaded to emigrate from Germany, "could establish a sound and solid system [of liberal education], if it were independent of the colleges, but it is not. . . . It was a great mistake to admit boys trained and drilled after the common manner, which had become an inveterate habit to them, to their

15th or 16th year, in order to fit them for college in a very short time. I objected and resisted, but could effect nothing, because the promise was given to fit them."[80] By 1827 most of these older students were preparing to leave Round Hill.[81] The question arose of where to send the boys who were going to colleges other than Harvard, and with it the question of where Round Hill's curriculum and methods would fit into the wider structure of American higher education. After clearing the way with the former Anthologist, professor Benjamin Silliman, Cogswell and Bancroft inquired of President Day of Yale as to the college's entrance requirements. It was here that they expected to find a real stumbling block. "We wish for an assurance," they wrote, "that you will be satisfied with the requisite knowledge of the *subjects,* and be indifferent as to the books, out of which candidates for admission have got it; that you will expect, not that a boy shall have read precisely this or that work in Latin or Greek, but have acquired a sufficient amount of knowledge of those languages, and, if you please, have read a certain amount of books, without deciding absolutely what those shall be." Since both American secondary and higher education at the time was chained to the memorization of certain prescribed texts, Cogswell and Bancroft's rather defensive insistence on the primacy of subjects over books is understandable. Yale was apparently amenable to this novel college preparation and accepted at least four students from Round Hill.[82]

One other problem arose in connection with the admission of Round Hill's students to colleges. They had received an extraordinarily thorough education in Northampton and were prepared to enter the junior or even senior classes of the average college. The colleges, however, demanded of the students, as Cogswell and Bancroft put it, "a free equal to the tuition up to their standing." In other words, a Round Hill alumnus who entered the junior class would have to pay tuition not only for his junior and senior years but for his freshman and sophomore years as well. Even affluent parents might very well rebel at paying, in effect, twice for their sons' education. For the less affluent, it made certain colleges out of the question. Despite vigorous arguments, Cogswell and Bancroft were unable to persuade Yale of the justice of their point here: so far as Yale was concerned, Round Hill students would pay the full four-year tuition. Cogswell and Bancroft accepted the ruling resignedly. "There is one case," they wrote President Day, "in which the law will operate with great severity. It is that of a young person, whose father is high among the Episcopal Clergy, but by no means affluent."[83] So, not only did Cogswell and Bancroft have difficulty resolving their curricular and teaching practices with the colleges, but administrative and financial conflicts were evident as well.

With the older boys prepared for college, in 1827–28 Cogswell and Bancroft apparently decided to return to their original plan and concentrate on the sustained education of children from a younger age group and to break their *immediate* ties to the colleges.[84] It was perhaps inevitable. With President Kirkland's almost forced resignation and the diminution of George Ticknor's influence at Harvard, much of the force of the impetus for educational reform which had originally inspired Round Hill lessened. Cogswell and Bancroft had been in advance of their age. "If we would transfer to our country the successful practice of older ones," Bancroft had written during Round Hill's early years, "it cannot be done by timid imitation. Our national institutions, our political principles, our whole condition and wants differ so much from those of Europe, that, whatever assistance we may draw from the other continent, each foreign system must be nationalized, before it can be successfully adopted."[85] And, unfortunately, Round Hill was never to be "nationalized," never to fit snugly into the American academic system of the 1820s and 1830s.

Cogswell and Bancroft had succeeded in recreating in America one of the better German *Gymnasien,* with all their high standards. In Germany the students would have proceeded directly from a *Gymnasium* like Round Hill to a university or professional school. In fact, only a successful university graduate *could* be admitted to a profession in Germany. In America, however, there were no true universities in the 1820s and 1830s, let alone rigorous professional standards. By European standards, the colleges were little more than glorified *Gymnasien* that offered a curriculum hardly more advanced than Round Hill's; dominated as the American academic system was by the college, Round Hill could not be integrated within it. As an institution Round Hill was at least one, and perhaps two, generations early on the American academic scene—an unassimilable foreign element in the structure of American education. American colleges would long attempt to do, in Bancroft's words, "what never can be done jointly and well, at once to impart elementary instruction and to teach the sciences and professions."[86]

Other more immediate and personal reasons, however, entered into Round Hill's ultimate failure. Bancroft, from the beginning, had planned on spending only a few years as a schoolmaster.[87] He was never particularly satisfied in this role, nor were his students satisfied with him. In his years at Round Hill he wrote textbooks, translated books from the German, wrote many magazine articles and began to dabble in politics. After his marriage in 1827 to Sarah Dwight, daughter of a wealthy Springfield family with far-flung business holdings, his interest in schoolmastering grew less and less. In 1830 Cogswell finally proposed that he take over full administrative and financial responsibility for the school, while Bancroft, if he wished, would continue to teach some.[88] Bancroft agreed; he severed his connections with Round Hill in 1831, and, with a sense of relief, applied his talents to the reorganization of his wife's family's banking interests in Ohio. The Round Hill years dwindled quickly into Bancroft's past. Within a decade he would be known to all the world as the first important historian of the United States, a powerful figure in the Democratic party, and ultimately, as one of the nation's foremost men of letters, statesmen, and diplomats. But even on the broad stage of public affairs Bancroft's preoccupation with the Anthologists' cultural values remained strong. In 1845, while serving as President Polk's secretary of the navy, he established still another school behind the back of a reluctant Congress. The United States Naval Academy at Annapolis, however, was designed not to educate Christian gentlemen and scholars but simply *officers* and gentlemen.[89]

Cogswell, now the sole proprietor, had always been the emotional center of the school; it was he, not Bancroft, who left the deepest impression in the minds of Round Hill's alumni. Cogswell was the perfect romantic schoolmaster: "He was the organizer, manager, and father of the community," one of his students recalled in later years. "His department especially was that of moral and affectionate influence, besides which he was head farmer, builder, gardener and treasurer of the place."[90] Cogswell was many things, but definitely not a good businessman. Despite the incorporation of the school and the purchase of stock by several prominent Americans, he found himself sinking deeper and deeper into debt as he tried to maintain the school's standards.[91] The immediate motives for Cogswell's decision to close Round Hill are elusive, but it seems safe to say that he was both a poor administrator and was growing tired of the constant necessity to raise funds for the school. Prospects looked brighter for Cogswell in the South. An indifferent Harvard would soon have to look elsewhere for well-prepared students.[92] After unsuccessfully offering to sell Round Hill to Henry Wadsworth Longfellow, Cogswell closed it in 1834. He then took up the direction of a newly founded secondary school in Raleigh, North Carolina, The Episcopal School—which was, curiously enough, a sort of institutional "grandchild" of his own Round Hill.[93]

Cogswell's move to the South was significant. Among Round Hill's stockholders was Senator Daniel Webster of Massachusetts; among its students was a boy from South Carolina named Robert Hayne.[94] After the sectional tension aroused by the acrimonious debates between Webster and Senator Robert Hayne of South Carolina in 1830, perhaps no northern school which drew as heavily from the South as did Round Hill could have maintained its national character. But the South—and the southern gentleman—held a strong appeal for Cogswell. "Every one knows," he had written of the English-educated gentleman of Charleston in 1819, "what an influence they have had upon the society of that place—what an elegance, and grace, and polish, they have given to its manners, and what a charm there is about themselves: they are men, who would have been the companions of Atticus, had they lived at Rome in the Augustan age."[95]

The South and its cavaliers, however, proved to be somewhat less charming in actuality than in Cogswell's imagination. "The salvation of our land depends upon the education of our Southern youths," Cogswell wrote home shortly after taking up his new post; "their notions are extravagant beyond all that we can conceive of, and our government is gone if their opinions go on unchecked." The pall of slavery permeated everything:

> Of all the curses here [Cogswell said], there is none to compare with that of slavery, it pollutes and poisons every relation

> of society. . . . Can much be hoped for the rising generation if they are to be raised among such beings? . . . Little or nothing can be done in the most important part of education, the formation of character and the fixing of good moral principles and habits, while such a portion of the community is in so degraded and wretched a condition.

After less than two years in Raleigh Cogswell fled northwards. "The whole spell of my life is broken," he wrote, "the word South, which used to signify, to my imagination, nothing but soft breezes, beautiful flowers and warm hearts, has lost its power to charm."[96] No longer could the Federalist ideal of a unified nation shaped by a gentlemanly cultural elite bridge the growing gap between North and South. Over the next two or three decades many southern boys would be educated in institutions far more appropriate to a violent and hierarchical society than Round Hill—the military academies that sprang up everywhere in the South in the 1830s, 1840s, and 1850s.[97] Cogswell would spend most of the rest of his life among the mercantile gentry of New York City. Future generations of Christian gentlemen and scholars would be educated in the boarding schools of the Yankee North rather than in the military academies of the cavalier South.

The image of Round Hill never faded away completely; many of the social conditions that had contributed to its initial success only intensified over succeeding decades. Scores of its alumni would treasure its memory and seek for their sons an education which would recreate the brief golden day of their own and the republic's youth.

1. SAMUEL PHILLIPS, ESQ. (1715–1790).

2. SAMUEL PHILLIPS, JR. (1752–1802).

3. ANDOVER HILL IN 1786. THE PHILLIPS MANSION IS ON THE LEFT, THE ACADEMY BUILDING ON THE RIGHT.

PHILLIPS EXETER ACADEMY.

Sept. 1841

"NO scholar shall enjoy the privileges of this Institution, who shall board in any family not licensed by the Trustees." [*Constitution.*]

Therefore heads of families, who take students to board, are expected and required to maintain good order in their houses, to exercise a parental watchfulness over their boarders, and to report to the Instructers any instances of disorderly or immoral conduct, that may occur. They are also required to see, that such students as may be members of their families are punctually at home during study hours in the evening, and that they seasonably retire to rest.

Study hours in the evening, during the fall and winter Terms, are from seven until nine.

It being required of students constantly to spend Saturday evenings at their lodgings, and to engage in no employment inconsistent with holy time, and that the Sabbath be religiously observed, it is confidently expected that those, who take students to board, will see that these regulations are particularly attended to.

Agreeably to vote of the Trustees no scholar under the age of 21, is permitted to incur expense on credit, unless authorized by his parent, guardian, their agent or one of the Instructers ; and it is the opinion of the Trustees, that parents and guardians ought not to discharge debts contracted without this formality.

No student under the age of 21, after having taken lodgings, shall be permitted to exchange them without permission, first obtained from the Principal, or in his absence, from the senior Instructer present.

Gideon L. Soule

~~BENJAMIN ABBOT~~, *Principal.*

4. REGULATIONS OF A TYPICAL ACADEMY. IN EFFECT, THE COMMUNITY SERVED AS AN EXTENSION OF THE SCHOOL.

5. EMMANUEL VON FELLENBERG (1771–1844).

6. FELLENBERG'S ACADEMY FOR THE UPPER CLASS AT HOFWYL.

7. GEORGE BANCROFT.

8. JOSEPH GREEN COGSWELL IN LATER YEAR

9. THE ROUND HILL SCHOOL.

10. WILLIAM AUGUSTUS MUHLENBERG IN LATER YEARS.

11. THE FLUSHING INSTITUTE, AFTER MUHLENBERG HAD LEFT IT.

12. THE REVEREND JOHN B. KERFO
ABOUT 1840.

From the collections of the Maryland Historical Soci

13. THE COLLEGE AND GRAMMAR SCHOOL OF ST. JAMES.

14. DR. GEORGE CHEYNE SHATTUCK, JR., ST. PAUL'S FOUNDER, IN THE 1860S.

15. HENRY AUGUSTUS COIT, ST. PAUL'S FIRST RECTOR.

16. THE ORIGINAL ST. PAUL'S SCHOOL IN THE EARLY 1860S—FORMERLY GEORGE SHATTUCK'S COUNTRY HOME.

17. A STEREOPTICON VIEW OF ST. PAUL'S, CIRCA 1870S.

18. AN EARLY DORMITORY AT ST. PAUL'S.

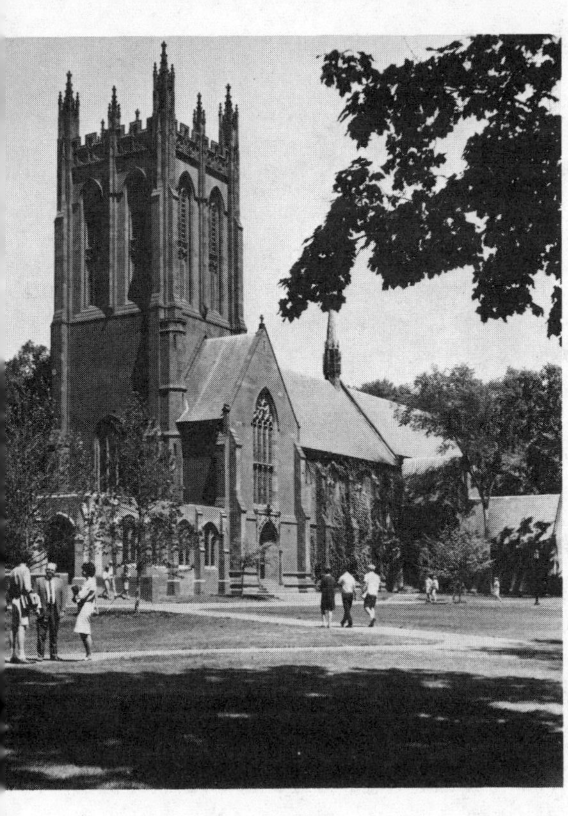

19. THE CHAPEL,
ST. PAUL'S SCHOOL (1884–1894).
HENRY VAUGHAN, ARCHITECT.

20. INTERIOR OF THE CHAPEL, ST. PAUL'S SCHOOL.

Not all the time was spent in classes . . .

21. A CLASSROOM AT PHILLIPS EXETER IN THE 1880S.

. . . students had time to cut up . . .

22. AN EXETER BOARDING HOUSE IN THE 1880S—BOOTH TARKINGTON WIELDS THE SWORD.

. . . to cultivate the physical faculties . . .

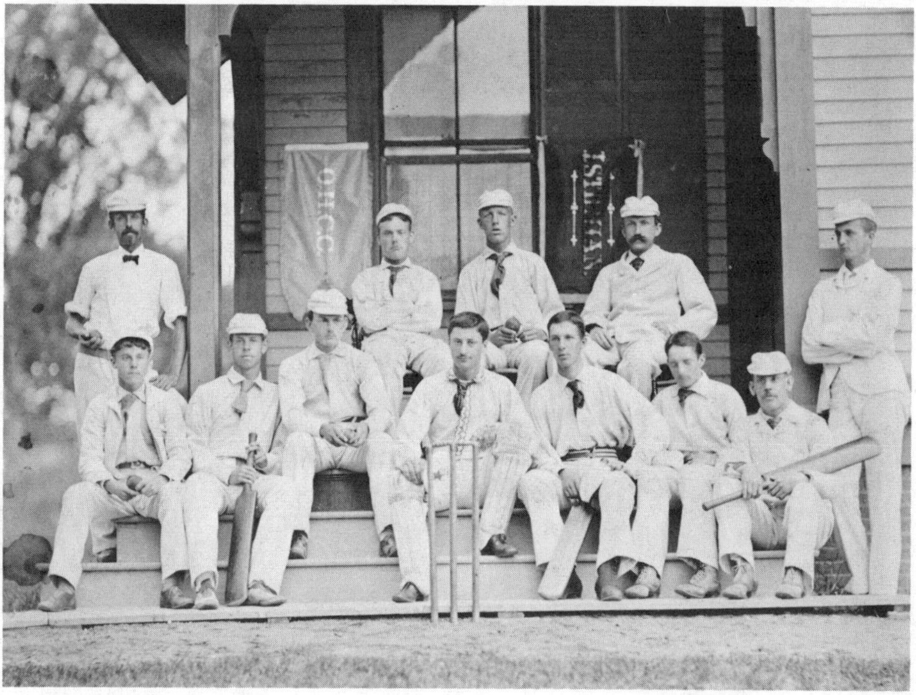

23. ST. PAUL'S CRICKET ELEVEN, 1880.

. . . especially football . . .

24. A FOOTBALL SCRIMMAGE AT PHILLIPS EXETER, ABOUT 1903.

. . . to involve themselves with important public issues . . .

25. A MOCK POLITICAL RALLY AT PROGRESSIVE ST. PAUL'S, 1912.

. . . to cultivate the gentler arts . . .

26. BANJOE CLUB AT ST. PAUL'S, 1891.

. . . to aspire to dramatic heights . . .

27. STUDENT ACTORS AT ST. PAUL'S.

. . . or just to loaf around.

28. SNAPSHOTS OF STUDENT LIFE AT ST. PAUL'S IN THE 1890s.

From the 1790s to the 1850s this was the sole building at Phillips Exeter . . .

29. THE SECOND ACADEMY BUILDING, PHILLIPS EXETER, 1794–1870.

. . . students boarded around the simple town of Exeter . . .

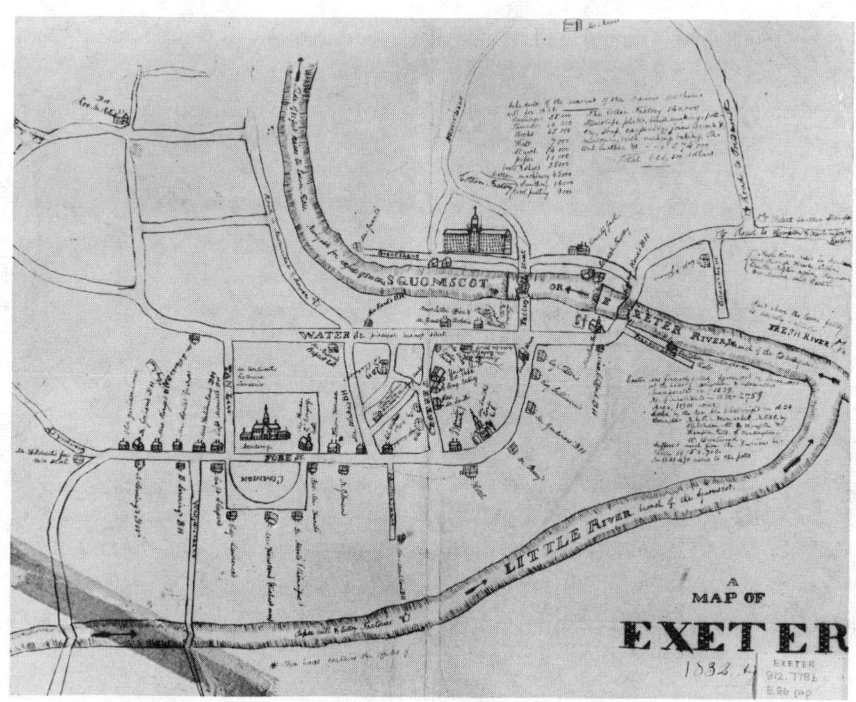

30. MAP OF EXETER, NEW HAMPSHIRE, IN 1832.

. . . only a few could be accommodated in Abbott Hall, the Academy's first dormitory, constructed in 1855 . . .

31. ABBOTT HALL IN 1909.

. . . but by the 1880s the town of Exeter was becoming more complex . . .

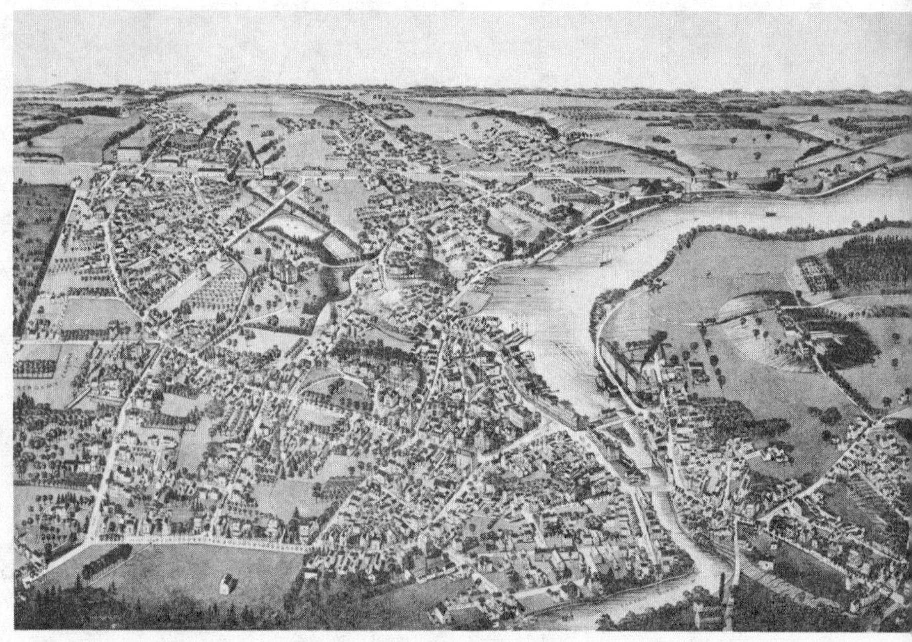

32. 1884 MAP OF EXETER.

. . . students became scattered from one end of the town to the other . . .

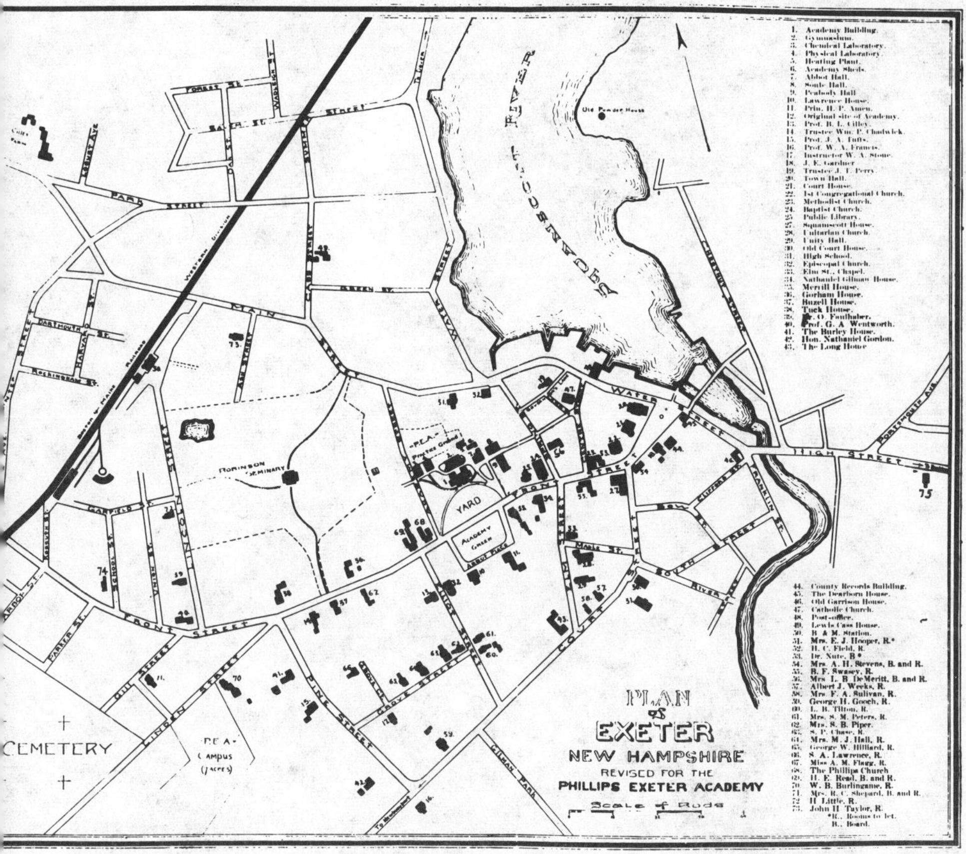

33. LOCATION OF EXETER BOARDING HOUSES, 1897.

. . . and by 1916, the Academy was turned into a small world unto itself.

34. THE PHILLIPS EXETER ACADEMY ABOUT 1916.

35. ENDICOTT PEABODY, BY JOHN SINGER SARGENT.

36. THE SCHOOLHOUSE, GROTON. PEABODY AND STEARNS, ARCHITECTS.

Part II *Victorians*

Chapter IV

The Church, the City, and the Child: The Flushing Institute

"Aristocratical and free-thinking," one of Round Hill's alumni called it when he graduated.[1] "Aristocratical" its successors would be, but never "free-thinking." There were still several students at Round Hill when Cogswell closed its doors for the last time in 1834. Leaving to become principal of a new Episcopal school in the South, Cogswell apparently advised parents to send their sons to another new Episcopal school, the Flushing Institute on Long Island, which had been founded just six years before by William Augustus Muhlenberg, a young Episcopal clergyman from Pennsylvania.[2] It was a natural choice, for the Flushing Institute was based on the same principles as Round Hill. "The general features of the system," a young instructor at the Institute discovered shortly after his arrival, "both moral and educational, were taken from the famous institution of M. Fellenberg, at Berne in Switzerland—whose views our excellent Principal had fully espoused, and elaborated in his establishment with great success."[3]

Like Round Hill, the Flushing Institute had a relatively short life; but, also like Round Hill, it exerted an influence far out of proportion to its immediate achievements. Contemporary and later Episcopalian schools and colleges, an historian of Episcopal education has remarked, "Turned to Muhlenberg for a successful method of impregnating education with Christian principles."[4] It was Muhlenberg, another Episcopal historian wrote, "who first started and made successful, with the success which has been the fruitful germ of all its rich after-growth, the church school."[5] While they hardly slighted Christianity, Cogswell and Bancroft's main objective at Round Hill was the development of gentlemen and scholars. But the metamorphosis of the boarding school into the Episcopal church school necessarily implied a shift in priority of goals. While Muhlenberg and his successors would continue to strive to educate Christian gentlemen and scholars, they would emphasize much more strongly the Christian elements of the ideal type. Missing too from Muhlenberg's thought was the fear of a slide into cultural barbarism, the suspicious pessimism of the Federalists. It was replaced by the optimistic, evangelistic spirit of the massive revival of organized Protestantism that left so deep an imprint upon the middle years of the nineteenth century in the United States—the movement called the Second Great Awakening or the Protestant Counter-Reformation.[6]

William Augustus Muhlenberg was a product of that revival—but of the extremely muted form it would take within the Protestant Episcopal church. Muhlenberg's career embraced an amazing range of aspects of American religious life in the nineteenth century. Aside from his educational work, he was also a writer of widely popular hymns, the rector of an influential and experimenting church (the Church of the Holy Communion in New York City), the founder of the first Episcopal religious order for women in the United States, the founder of the church hospital (St. Lukes's, in New York), the real progenitor of Episcopal social work, a widely followed innovator in Episcopalian ritual, and the founder of St. Johnsland, a utopian colony for the aged. Yet, this imaginative, lively, and sometimes controversial figure has attained only an obscure place in American religious history.[7]

Muhlenberg was born in Philadelphia in 1796, the son of Henry William Muhlenberg, a well-to-do wine merchant and member of a distinguished Pennsylvania family. Muhlenberg's father died in 1807, when William was only eleven. He grew up within his mother's prosperous, upper-middle-class family, of German background but English-speaking. (Muhlenberg, curiously, never mentioned his father's rather well-known family until late in life.) He attended the Philadelphia Academy, run by Dr.

James Abercrombie, assistant to William White, Episcopal bishop of Pennsylvania. Despite its name, the academy seems to have been more an elementary than a secondary school. Abercrombie emphasized religious instruction a good deal more than was customary at the time. Perhaps because of this influence Muhlenberg decided upon graduation to become a minister. He went from Abercrombie's school to the University of Pennsylvania Grammar School—a conventional academy—and graduated from the university itself in 1815. In his years there both institutions were under heavy Episcopal influence, and Muhlenberg left the university still determined to become a minister.[8]

Since there were no Episcopal theological seminaries in the United States in 1815, Muhlenberg, after consultation with Bishop White, "read" for the ministry with the Reverend Jackson Kemper. He was ordained a deacon in 1817 and spent the next three years as the bishop's assistant. They were vigorous years; Muhlenberg founded the first Sunday school in the area, started Bible classes and made innovations in the direction of more elaborate music, ritual, and organization in the church.

Although Muhlenberg was a member of a small denomination (there were, for instance, 2,600,000 Methodists in 1830, while here were only 240,000 Episcopalians[9]), it was a denomination whose members had an influence far out of proportion to their numbers. The few Episcopal clergymen in Philadelphia were wealthy and socially prominent. "A peculiarity about all of them," a contemporary wrote, "was that had they not been clergymen, they would, from their family, manner, etc., have been leaders in society."[10] It was only natural, then, that when Muhlenberg was made co-rector in 1820 of St. James Church in Lancaster, Pennsylvania—the second largest city in the state and the heart of rich farming country—he should find among his parishioners the most prominent and prosperous members of the community, and that he should quickly assume an important role in the affairs of the area.[11]

Besides starting a Sunday school and attempting to found a library, Muhlenberg also sat on the Board of Controllers of the First School District of Pennsylvania and served as secretary of the Lancaster Public School Board. As secretary Muhlenberg in effect ran the Lancaster public school. Instruction at the school, confusingly enough, was given according to the plan of Joseph

Lancaster, the English educator whose theories were sweeping the United States in the 1820s. Under the Lancasterian—or Monitorial—system, the schoolmaster taught the older students who in turn taught the others. This made it possible for one teacher to handle a large number of students and kept the expense of operating a school down—an aim close to the hearts of all Americans. Muhlenberg would later adapt the system to his own ends.[12]

Deeply absorbed in religious and educational affairs in Lancaster, Muhlenberg's thoughts increasingly turned to ways in which his two predominant interests might be combined. In 1824 he considered starting some sort of boarding school—possibly to be run by a clergyman—in Lancaster. He might, he thought, attract students between the ages of thirteen and eighteen, the years "when habits are acquired, sentiments adopted, and the character of the man is formed."[13] The plan, however, never came to fruition. An abortive love affair intervened, and in 1826 Muhlenberg resigned his pulpit in Lancaster, determined to voyage to Europe in order to make a study of European schools.

Muhlenberg never reached Europe. Instead, his trip stopped far short of its destination—in Flushing, Long Island. On arriving in New York City Muhlenberg found that his ship was delayed; he also received a plea to "supply"—or serve as temporary minister—at St. George's Parish in Flushing, an hour's boat trip from New York. Flushing, cut off by marshes from the city, was a pleasant village of about two thousand, whose principal enterprise was tree nurseries. Muhlenberg must have found it congenial, for on the first of July 1827 he was elected rector by the vestry of St. George's. But there again his thoughts returned to his two preoccupations—education and the furtherance of the work of the Episcopal church. Late the following year he resigned his rectorship, this time with a fully developed plan for combining both interests in a new institution to be founded nearby, the Flushing Institute.[14]

Both of Muhlenberg's major interests, education and the Episcopal church, were in a state of reorganization and expansion in the 1820s. Most American religious denominations suffered disruption during the revolutionary years, but none as seriously as the Episcopalian. Identified as closely as the church was with Great Britain, the breach with the mother country inevitably left it weak, disorganized, and demoralized. For the Episcopal church, the years between 1789 and 1811 were ones of slow recuperation, of sinking roots deep in the soil of the new nation. But by 1811 recovery was almost complete: the church, its body reorganized and its spirit stirring, was ready once again to look outward. It was in the years between 1811 and 1830 that the church, as an Episcopal historian has written, "attained the relative position among American religious groups which it has held ever since, not only in respect to numbers, but as to the character and location of its members as well, for by 1830 it had already become predominantly an urban and upper-class denomination."[15]

The first half of the nineteenth century was a period of vigorous growth and increased influence for all Protestant denominations in America. The main technique by which this was achieved was the religious revival. Beginning in the West early in the century, after 1840 the religious revival meeting enjoyed two decades of immense popularity in the East. The sometimes uproarious camp meetings of the frontier gave way to the more decorous prayer meetings of the cities.[16] The religious aim of the nineteenth century's revival was much the same as the seventeenth century's preparation and conversion experience—spiritual rebirth leading to an active and committed Christian life. Though in a way the revivals supplied an instant conversion experience, they were by no means all whoops and hollers or long hours on the "anxious bench" of penitence. Revivalism, in Timothy Smith's definition, was simply "the use of special efforts to secure conversions amidst excited group emotions."[17] This was a method to which the larger number of American Protestant denominations could subscribe. Some denominations, however, while hoping for conversions, held aloof from such emotional methods, particularly the Unitarians and the Episcopalians. Not, however, *all* Episcopalians. There had always been tension within the church; by the 1840s it was split into two distinct parties, the evangelical and the High Church. The Oxford Movement and the Tractarian Controversy of the 1840s aroused fears of a mass exodus to Rome and intensified the split. In a paragraph that summarizes volumes of church history, Timothy Smith has described the situation thus:

Differences between the two groups lay not so much in their observance of liturgy and sacraments or their respect for episcopal powers as in the way in which they regarded these matters. As the church's historian put it sixty years ago, evangelicals emphasized the individual reception of grace: High-churchmen, the institutional administration of grace. "The watchword of the one was experience; that of the other, authority." To the former group, then, sacraments and ritual liturgy were simply means to inspire the believer to live in vital, spiritual relation to his Lord. To the other, they were significant for their own sake, objective channels of grace. The Low Church emphasis on experience led them to approve affiilation with other Christians in evangelistic endeavors, as well as to introduce prayer meetings, extemporaneous exhortation, and, in some cases, seasons of revival into their program of worship. Laymen inevitably found a larger place of usefulness under their banner. Conversely, admirers of the Oxford Movement feared religious enthusiasm, opposed all measures of gospel work other than those which the liturgy allowed, and considered their church a divine institution rather than a voluntary association. They were, by definition, sectarian and conservative.[18]

Muhlenberg attempted, not unsuccessfully, to straddle both positions. His strong aesthetic sense, his love of ritual, ceremony, and formal organization, naturally attracted him to the High Church party, while his intense desire to win converts to the church, his deep interest in the social problems of the day, and his emphasis on personal religious experience led him to sympathize with the evangelical wing of the church. Quite logically, therefore, he styled himself an "Evangelical Catholic"—a position which did not endear him to the more inflexible members of either party and perhaps accounts for some of his historical neglect.[19]

Whatever their differences, both High and Low Church Episcopalians shared with other Protestant denominations a wish to extend and make permanent their influence. These means, more often than not, included the establishment of a denomination's own educational institutions. The views of the Methodists, expressed at the 1832 Indiana Conference of the church, are representative of almost all contemporary Protestant denominations:

> When we examine the state of the literary institutions of our country, we find a majority of them are in the hands of other denominations, so that our people are unwilling (and we think properly so) to send their sons to those institutions. Therefore we think it very desirable to have an institution under our own control from which we can exclude all doctrines which we deem dangerous; though at the same time we do not wish to make it so sectarian as to exclude or in the smallest degree repel the sons of our fellow citizens from the same.[20]

Other denominations agreed wholeheartedly; between the Revolution and the Civil War at least 516 colleges and universities were founded in the United States (though only 104 survived), the majority of them under sectarian auspices.[21] Most of these institutions were probably inferior to the better academies of the time. But however low their standards, minimal their facilities, and narrow their intellectual outlook, they did provide Protestant "Counter-reformers" an institutional bulwark against deism, skepticism, rationalism, and general "immorality."[22]

Episcopalians were relatively laggard in founding their own educational institutions. Although there had long been a statutory provision requiring the president of Columbia College to be an Episcopalian, it was not truly an Episcopal institution; the first Episcopal college, Geneva (now Hobart) College, did not open until 1824. Muhlenberg himself had to "read" for the ministry; Episcopalians did not have a theological seminary of their own until 1822, when the General Theological Seminary began classes in New York City.[23] Before the 1820s Episcopal secondary schools were almost as scarce as institutions of higher learning. There were a few academies run by Episcopalians—like James Abercrombie's in Philadelphia which Muhlenberg had attended as a child—but no school in which religion deeply informed the institution's organization, curriculum, or daily life.[24]

Muhlenberg's extensive activities in educational affairs in the early 1820s and his deep interest in the advancement of the church came together in his plan for a new Episcopal school, the Flushing Institute, which he published in 1828.[25] It was the logical outcome of his experience, of long thought, and of the educational ferment in which Episcopalians, as well as other Protestants, were involved at the time. Muhlenberg actually had no need to travel to Europe; though we unfortunately lack direct evidence concerning the exact books he read, on the evidence of his writings over the following few years we can safely say that he was thoroughly familiar with the work of Fellenberg and had saturated himself in current European educational thought. Moreover, he had as an immediate model for his Institute the still-successful Round Hill, and perhaps the direct counsel of Cogswell as well.[26]

Muhlenberg's plans for the Institute apparently began to take shape shortly after he took up his duties at St. George's. In July 1827 his old friend and mentor, the Reverend Jackson Kemper, asked him for advice on setting up a church school in Philadelphia. Muhlenberg's reply gives some indication of the direction in which his thoughts were tending:

> An ordinary day school . . . would be of little service to the church compared with what would arise from a boarding school under proper regulations. Discipline is as important as a branch of education as instruction—there can be little of the latter of a religious nature in a day school. . . .
>
> I am still so full of my own project that in the ways of education I cannot think of anything else—When my institute succeeds I will do everything in my power to form schools on the same plan wherever practicable. I would willingly be a missionary on the subject of education. But first I wish to establish a model school—my scheme is an extensive one—but I fear to unravel the whole lest you think me visionary. . . .[27]

While the notion of a boarding school was novel enough for the time, underlying it was an intensely evangelical impulse: what Muhlenberg really hoped to do was to start a comprehensive Episcopal institution which would combine secondary, higher, and theological education under one roof—a sort of three-stage vertical seminary. Some years later he outlined this ideal school, which he had been striving towards when he began the Flushing Institute. What he would most like to do, he said, was to:

> . . . get the Church to endow an Institution which shall do the same service for the Church that West Point is doing for the Army. My idea of *"Cadets of the Church,"* I am sure, is the true one. *We shall never cope with Rome until we have a disciplined body of men ready to go at the word of command wherever they are sent. We should have a religious order of "Brothers of Obedience."*[28]

Muhlenberg would eventually attempt to make the Flushing Institute such a school, but meanwhile his plans were confined simply to secondary education. His plan of education was, he thought, among Protestants of the time, somewhat novel. There could be no such thing as non-sectarian teaching of Christianity; as he said, "Cristianity could not be taught in the abstract," but only in the way it was professed by some particular church. "On this subject," he pointed out, "the Roman Catholics are consistent. Their faith is sedulously interwoven with their Education—hence the secret of their constancy in its profession."[29]

Contemporary education, Muhlenberg thought, was too narrowly confined to its intellectual and physical aspects, while "moral" education was sadly neglected. With what kind of moral education, he asked, did most educational institutions provide their students? "Let the fact that pious parents regard the academic term of their children, as a period full of danger, be the answer to the question." Contemporary educators made their greatest error, he wrote, in giving "to literary or scientific education, a rank and a consequence which are denied to Moral Education. The liberal arts are not to be undervalued. . . . But since the interests of virtue are everlasting and essential to human happiness, they demand the first care in whatever affects the character of the rising generation."[30]

By "moral education" Muhlenberg meant not only religious education but also what Bancroft and Cogswell might have called "character education." He spelled his notions out in eight "leading principles":

> 1. Moral Education must be based on Christianity.
> 2. The Bible must be the subject of systematic instruction.
> 3. Moral discipline should as far as possible be preventative.

> 4. Proper Physical Education is a powerful auxiliary to moral discipline.
>
> 5. Reproof and admonition should for the most part be administered in private.
>
> 6. Corrective discipline should be chosen, and regulated with a view to the implanting of principle.
>
> 7. Rewards like punishments should have reference to the cherishing of principle.
>
> 8. Moral government should be mild and affectionate, yet steady and uniform.[31]

The final purpose, the desirable end of these maxims was, in Muhlenberg's words, that *"the pupil must be made to perceive that the law of God is the law of the school."*[32] As with the Puritans or the Phillips family, for Muhlenberg the ultimate aim of education was the religious one of salvation.

On the second phase of his program, "Intellectual Education," Muhlenberg offered "but one or two observations . . . since there are here less pretensions to reformation." In language almost identical with that of the Yale Report of 1828 (which was published a few months after Muhlenberg's work, in January 1829), he declared that his main principles would be, first, that "the ancient languages are the best groundwork of liberal learning"; and second, that "the art of study should be taught."[33] The Institute, in other words, would discipline and furnish its students' minds in the traditional manner. The third part of his program would be "Physical Education," whose importance, he noted, was "finally beginning to be duly estimated. . . . Exercise, diet, and habits conducive to health," he declared, "are legitimate objects of Education, and may easily be regulated when the school constitutes the household." The implication should have been obvious to his contemporaries: students' health could not be properly looked after in the average academy, which did *not* "constitute a household."

Aside from religious education, Muhlenberg placed the greatest stress in his prospectus on the claim that his Institute would be run as a *family;* the image of the school as family was emphasized and reemphasized throughout. To put his principles of moral, intellectual, and physical education into practice, he promised to "form a household, . . . consisting of the Principal, the Governess, the teachers, the Tutors, and the Pupils."[34]

What possible similarity, one might well ask, could a boarding school for young boys bear to a family or household? So far as the actual organization of the institution went, the answer would have to be, very little. But Muhlenberg's insistence that his Institute would be governed as a family was more than rhetoric: between 1800 and the Civil War the image of the family became one of the major controlling metaphors in American social thought and popular culture. In fact, as late as the twentieth century, prep school headmasters would still be echoing Muhlenberg's claim that their institutions were operated as families. In discussing the family, as with the gentleman, we must distinguish between the cultural ideal and the social fact, between the *concept of the family* and the actual *composition of the family* in nineteenth-century America. Of the former we know a great deal, of the latter very little.

In seventeenth-century Puritan thought the family was conceived of as the first society and as the basic unit of all later societies. After the Fall the family alone was not enough to cope with man's evil nature; states, therefore, were established. Paradise lost, God entered into a covenant with man which promised salvation in return for faith. The covenant was made not only with individuals, however, but with families, states, and the church. The family became the basic model for church and state. "The essence of the social order," in Puritan thought, Edmund Morgan has written, "lay in the superiority of husband over wife, parents over children, and masters over servants in the family, ministers and elders over congregation in the church, rulers over subjects in the state. A child might possess superior talents and ability to his father, but within the family his father remained superior. A church member might be the richest man in the community, but his pastor held authority over him in the church. In each relationship God had ordained that one party be the superior, the other inferior."[35] It was a patriarchical, authoritarian solution to the perennial quest for social order.

By the nineteenth century covenant theology had long since been rejected by many descendants of the Puritans. In the thought of Harvard's moral philosophers, for example, society was not conceived as a covenanted, *voluntary* association, but as an organic unit, made up like the human body of interdependent parts, each necessary to the proper functioning of the whole. The family, however, remained central to the thought of the Unitarian moral philosophers and those of other denominations as well. American moral philosophy was based on the Scottish common sense philosophy of the eighteenth century; the family and clan held a central place in the Scottish philosophers' political theory.[36] Anglican Bishop Butler and Edmund Burke—both of whom deeply influenced Unitarians and Episcopalians—similarly held that the family, not the individual, was the basic unit of society. Once covenant theology had been rejected, the family thus could not help but fall under peculiar scrutiny. "Harvard Unitarians," Daniel Howe has observed, "were prone to see both the church and the state as large families. . . . The welfare of both . . . was dependent on the cultivation of the domestic virtues and the maintenance of the integrity of the family."[37] The same observation could be extended to Episcopalians.

As in high thought, so in popular American romantic culture: the family, now often called the Home, was expected to bear the burden of cultivating too all those "domestic virtues"—affection, love, obedience, and so forth—on which the future of the republic depended. In poetry, in didactic novels like Catharine Maria Sedgwick's *Home* (1835), in the innumerable gift books that provided a sure index to popular values and taste, the bourgeois family—and the mother in particular—was admonished to take on a new educational role, the conscious cultivation of the moral faculties.[38] The family and the home were painted as a secluded refuge from a society which was daily growing less Christian, more competitive, and more confusing.

In the light of all this it is hardly surprising that many Americans conceived of institutions—particularly schools—as idealized families, or that Muhlenberg would claim his students would be "children of a family regulated solely with a view to their improvement, in religion, learning, and manners."[39] Only if the family and the virtues it was thought peculiarly well suited to nurture could be sustained would social dissolution be halted and an organic society maintained. The boarding school was one manifestation of this quest for stability.

Although 99 percent male institutions, boarding schools did not ignore the role of the woman and the mother, so important in romantic educational thought. If the school was truly to fulfill the familial image, women obviously had to occupy a conspicuous spot in the organization. In nineteenth- and twentieth-century boarding schools the headmaster's wife typically assumed the role of a hyperidealized "mother" of the institution, the quintessence of female purity and unreachable moral superiority. While this role must surely have been almost unbearably trying for many of these women, in school histories they are invariably portrayed as the "ministering angel" heroine prominent in nineteenth-century popular fiction. At Round Hill Bancroft's sister Jane filled the role until she married one of the faculty; at the Flushing Institute it would be occupied by Muhlenberg's own mother. But notwithstanding the presence of women and the invocation of familial images, the boys' boarding school was an aggressively male oasis in an increasingly feminized culture, a nineteenth-century embodiment of older, patriarchical, and authoritarian familial patterns and values. In this, as in other respects, it resembled the greater number of antebellum Amerian colleges.

Muhlenberg's debt to the colleges as a model was evident not only in his typically nineteenth-century elaboration and intensification of the school's role *in loco parentis,* but in his use of tutors. The tutor was the principal medium of instruction in the early nineteenth-century college. But to this traditional role Muhlenberg added a new twist: at the Flushing Institute tutors would offer "a modified system of mutual instruction." Muhlenberg had adapted his experience in Pennsylvania with the Lancasterian system to new ends. Tutors were to be advanced students, over seventeen, who would receive free education, room, and board in return for their services. They would live in dormitories with the pupils; this would be especially useful, Muhlenberg claimed, in language almost identical to that of President Day's 1818 Report on Yale, "in communicating a right tone of feeling to the young community, in nipping disorder in the bud, and in applying those maxims of Moral Education which have been detailed." There is a certain confusion about the actual age of the students Muhlenberg expected to be dealing with. In his plans of 1824 he had implied that the students would be between thirteen and eighteen.[40] Muhlenberg made this quite clear in later years when he wrote of the college which he ultimately added to the Institute. "The age of collegians," he declared, "is the very period of life when they most need the discretionary guidance of parents and governors, and when no written laws are sufficient to regulate their conduct. From fourteen to eighteen is the most critical period of human life."[41] From very fragmentary evidence, the age of students at the Institute seems to have ranged from about nine to sixteen. Again, as at Round Hill, the goals of the collegiate reformers were being fulfilled—but with children rather than late adolescents or youths.

Although his plan was an ambitious one, Muhlenberg had surprisingly little difficulty implementing it. The Flushing Institute was organized in the manner of most contemporary academies: in January 1827 it was incorporated by eight Long Islanders and a board of five trustees was chosen. The Institute was almost exclusively a local, Flushing affair; all but one of the trustees were vestrymen of Muhlenberg's church, St. George's. Like the trustees of other academies of the time they were leading citizens of the area—prosperous merchants and professional men. To raise funds to build the Institute the trustees issued 260 shares of stock at fifty dollars a share. Eventually there were thirty-five stockholders in the corporation, none of whom owned more than 20 shares. Besides Muhlenberg, among the stockholders, were most of his relations, several old friends from Lancaster, and various Episcopal clergymen. The only direct, formal connection between the Flushing Institute and the Episcopal church was Muhlenberg himself. Muhlenberg promoted the Institute vigorously: he wrote all the bishops in the church, most of the prominent Episcopal clergymen in the country, and scores of old friends and acquaintances. The cornerstone for the Institute was laid in the summer of 1827, and in December of 1828 it opened its doors to its first pupils.[42]

The Institute's tuition, like Round Hill's, was high for the time —$250 (later raised to $300), which covered all expenses except books, stationery, and instruction in French and instrumental music.[43] Despite this the school met with immediate success. In the sixteen years of its existence the Flushing Institute would draw most of its students from the Middle Atlantic states—particularly New York and Pennsylvania—and from much the same group of wealthy and cultivated urban families that sent their sons to Round Hill.[44]

One of Muhlenberg's prime appeals was to parents' fears of the many possible deleterious effects of the city on their sons.

Not only did the city threaten the child's health (and the American city of the 1830s was a very unhealthy place indeed)[45]—it posed an even greater threat to the child's morals. Muhlenberg used the *Journal of the Institute at Flushing*—apparently meant to be read more by the parents than the students—in a clever manner to enhance the appeal of the Institute. A typical issue, for instance—that of May 1833—carried a long essay reprinted from the *Sunday School Journal* on "Juvenile Vice in Our Cities," which described in horrified detail a school in Boston, a so-called "gymnasium." This gymnasium was in reality "a den of intemperance and gaming"; boys of fifteen or so made up half the customers of the place, in which the air was "foul with tobacco and liquors." Aside from "drinking, bowling, and swearing," the main activity was gambling. The customers bet on cock fights and on a "gaming-table" which was fixed so that the houe won five out of six games. Even on Sundays these debaucheries continued until four o'clock in the morning. So, the article concluded, were American youth being corrupted—and not only in Boston. If the horrified reader did not at this point heave a grateful sigh of relief that his sons were safely protected at Flushing from the wiles of the wicked city, Muhlenberg drove the moral home with his next two selections: "A Hymn at Sunset," and a poem about the best romantic teacher of them all—"A Mother Teaching Her Child to Pray."

Muhlenberg's voice was only one of a mounting chorus warning of urban evils that swelled throughout the 1830s, 1840s and 1850s as American cities grew eleven times over—and were filled not only with native farm boys but with foreigners from abroad. A new class of juvenile delinquents was appearing in the larger towns and cities of the nation, declared the New England reformer Edward Everett Hale. It was a class of:

> piratical, adventurous, unprincipled boys and girls—who earn their own living, or steal it; who are therefore free from the control of their parents, because they contribute the assessments to the family means, which cannot be dispensed with. At an alarm of fire, or on the public reception of a hero, or at the parade of a military company, such young adventurers may be seen in remarkable throngs, rendering no assistance where assistance is needed; thwarting and confounding po-

> licemen and marshals; and compelling the least attentive observer to ask what is to become of them and the State, of which they shall be the men and women.[46]

What would be called in the twentieth century a "delinquent subculture of youth" was being created in American cities; society was losing control of its children. "Go to the cafes and restaurants of any city," one observer wrote:

> and look at the mere boys who swagger up to the bar, and toss off their glasses with such indifference, and swear, and smoke and gamble with all the shameless hardihood of veterans in vice; or reckon the number of boys that are found nightly at the enginehouse, the circus, the theatre, the billiard-rooms, and the bowling-alley, listening to the teachings, and gazing at the sights that are there nightly presented; hearing the boasting tales of vicious exploits with which the frequenters of such places are entertained, until they long to emulate their vile achievements. Remember, then, the temptations that low pot-houses and groggeries, and yet viler dens, are constantly holding out to those who seek cheap indulgences and excitements, and can it be wondered at, that, if boys are allowed to spend their evenings and their Sabbaths away from home, and beyond parental oversight, they should be corrupted? Could it be otherwise, without a miracle?[47]

What was the cause of this distressing state of affairs? Edward Everett Hale had a perceptive answer—industrialization, urbanization, and the consequent change in educational forms:

> The old system of apprenticeship offered to every child who had not a father training him, a master to whom that duty fell. And in the customs of life of the smaller towns and more scattered society, there were not the dangers, which in crowded neighborhoods, flow from indiscriminate charity. The older system of manufacture, therefore, and simpler habits of life, did not feel the necessity which we feel of distinguishing crime among children from the crimes of adults.[48]

Industrialization and urbanization were not only corrupting children in cities, contemporaries feared—they were splintering the organic nature of society itself, dividing the United States into two nations, the rich and the poor. By 1848 Horace Mann could fearfully point to "poverty" on the one hand and "profusion" on the other as the two most ominous trends in American social development.[49] One way by which anarchy might be avoided, the organic nature of society maintained, and children preserved from corruption, many reformers hoped, was by instituting a public education system to get the children off the streets and into schools where the community could exercise some control over them. "I want to see," said one supporter of the public school movement in 1839:

> the children of the rich and the poor sit down side by side on equal terms, as members of one family—a great brotherhood—deeming no one distinguished above the rest but the best scholar and the best boy—giving free and equal play to their affections, at a time of life when lasting friendships are often formed, and worldliness and pride and envy have not yet alienated heart from heart.[50]

Elementary public schools, naturally, came first. But with the founding in Boston in 1821 of the English Classical School (later the English High School), a solution to the problem of extending secondary education to many children without sending them to a distant academy was discovered. The high school offered much the same course of studies as the "English" branch in contemporary academies. The objectives of the Boston High School were, in the words of Josiah Quincy, mayor of Boston in the 1820s, "to enable the mercantile and mechanical classes to obtain an education for those children whom their parents wished to qualify for active life, and thus relieve them from the necessity of incurring the expense incident to private academies."[51] Within a few years other towns and cities had founded similar schools, and by 1860 there were probably several hundred public high schools, mainly in the Northeast and Midwest.[52]

The trustees of the Phillips Exeter Academy recognized the trend towards state-supported secondary education as early as 1848, when they decided to discontinue their English department. The original purpose of the department, they felt, had been met by the "multiplication of English Academies and High

Schools." Not one student in the past seven years had finished the English Course. "Those students," the trustees found, "whose bad habits, or want of capacity prevent their success in the Latin, usually desire to finish their Academic Course in the Eng[lish] Room. In this way, the Eng[lish] Room is liable to be filled up with the idle and stupid." The trustees recommended, therefore, that the Academy concentrate on the "instruction of young men of talents and promise, in a thorough Classical Course of study including, as heretofore, all those mathematical and other English branches belonging to such a course. . . ."[53] They decided, in other words, to concentrate on preparing students to meet the college entrance requirements.

The public high school did not fully displace the academy until well after the Civil War. Although high schools gradually added "classical" courses to their curricula, a majority of college students still prepared in the academies.[54] But the course of future developments in secondary education was becoming clear by the 1850s. An academy like Exeter, with its large endowment, could sustain itself as a college preparatory school. Most academies, however, were largely dependent on tuition fees; with competition from free public secondary schools most either quietly collapsed, were taken over by towns and cities as local public high schools, or were upgraded into normal schools and colleges.[55]

By the 1840s and 1850s the drift towards state-controlled and financed education was unmistakeable; the American people, as one student has observed, had "defined their political consensus in terms of popular liberty and public education."[56] Social control over children, the restoration of order, would be accomplished through local primary and secondary schools rather than in distant institutions.

Some educational reformers, however, hoped to institute a full-scale system of state boarding schools. "State schools," the Scottish-American reformer Robert Dale Owen wrote in 1830, drawing on his own experience at Fellenberg's Hofwyl, "to be republican, efficient, and acceptable to all, must receive the children, not for six hours a day, but altogether; must feed them, clothe them, lodge them; must direct not their studies only, but their occupations and amusements; must care for them until their education is completed, and then only abandon them to the world, as useful, intelligent, virtuous citizens."[57] Such wholesale application of egalitarian and communitarian principles to education met with violently mixed reactions. Public schools, most educational reformers felt, should indeed transmit a common culture to all Americans; but at the same time the bourgeois family must be maintained, children must not be separated from their parents. As late as 1866 the principal of a Massachusetts academy could ruefully point out that "the grand argument against the academical system of middle schools and against colleges as well is, that pupils must not be domiciliated [*sic*] away from the supervision of tutorial governors and teachers. It is assumed that there is 'no place like home'. . . ."[58] "No place like home," that is, for the majority of middle-income Americans. What was happening to many of the children of the rich and the poor, those two groups that the reformers had hoped to see within one common family, was quite another story.

One solution to the problem presented by the children of the urban poor was characteristic of the age—place them in a special institution, separate them from the subculture of urban delinquency. So, in 1824, the House of Refuge for Children was founded in New York City; in 1826 a group of citizens organized a House of Refuge in Philadelphia; and in 1828 Boston established the House of Reformation for Juvenile Offenders. By 1860 there were over a hundred such institutions. Like Round Hill or the Flushing Institute, they were boarding schools for mainly city children. They were meant, however, not to educate Christian gentlemen and scholars but frugal and industrious workers. They seem to have been quite successful educationally—not at training happy workers but at transmitting the subculture of poverty and crime. It was estimated at one point that graduates from the Houses of Refuge made up 29 percent of the adult prison population.[59]

Like the reform school, the boarding school was a completely controlled environment, carefully isolated from society in order to assure the development of a particular character and social type. It was here, Muhlenberg thought, that contemporary colleges failed. To make clear the advantages of the "family" boarding school in contrast to conventional academies and colleges, early in 1833 Muhlenberg ran a series of articles in the *Journal of the Institute at Flushing* on "The College System and Its Evils." (Ostensibly by "A Parent," they bear strong traces of Muhlenberg's style and ideas; authorship aside, they are a good index to the values Muhlenberg emphasized in attracting parents' attention to his school.) What happens, the writer asked, when a youth leaves "the sanctuary of his Christian home" for college? He enters a society of striplings like himself, and most likely falls among bad companions. "It is a premature severance of the ties of domestic affection. Nature avenges every disturbance of her economy. She does so here." What were the results of such "alienation and exposure"?:

> The son visits home after a year at college. The delighted parent exclaims, "How much more of the man. What ease of manners. What readiness in conversation!" I grant the gain, but must also reckon the loss. Has he retained his former frankness of behavior? Does the blush of modesty still glow instinctively on his cheek? Is he still satisfied with the society of home? Are his evenings still spent at the fire side? Has he no secrets to withhold from his parents? May his mother and sisters know everything? The boy has leaped into the would-be man. He apes the importance if not the vices of manhood, and lays aside as childish things the very ornaments of youth.

Somehow, the questions seem more appropriate of a young *girl* returning from college than a young *boy:* the appeal here is obviously to mothers. To underline this, the next article in the series, on "the further bad influences of colleges," lists first that "maternal influence is weakened." Other unfortunate results of higher education were "a want of respectful deference for superiors," a "spirit of insubordination," and the "adoption of low standards of morality."

In a curious way, the Flushing Institute's description of the effects of college life on American boys parallels the description of American children by contemporary foreign travelers in the United States. In particular, British travelers to America between 1845 and 1935, Richard Rapson has discovered, left a very clear picture—"with near unanimity they found the children detestable."[60] Earlier, in the 1820s and 1830s, many commented, like the English reformer Harriet Martineau, on "that freedom of manners in children of which so much complaint has been made by observers." Miss Martineau's reaction to the freedom granted

American children was favorable; she found "the independence and fearlessness of children a . . . perpetual charm to [her] eyes."[61] However, the reaction of the acidulous Mrs. Frances Trollope was probably more common: "I have conversed with many American ladies," she snapped, "on the total want of discipline and subjection which I observed universally among children of all ages, and I never found any who did not both acknowledge and deplore the truth of the remark."[62] Even a relatively liberal American educator could, after a tour of English schools, remark that "*a sense of order* was tenfold and an hundredfold greater among English than American boys."[63] "Order," "subjection," and "discipline" are here juxtaposed to "freedom" and "disorder" as desirable qualities in children. If the observers were correct, it would seem that American children maintained until well into the nineteenth century many of those qualities of maturity and self-reliance which Philippe Ariès attributes to all children in the Middle Ages.[64] The young American was still a person; he had not yet been turned into a dependent child or adolescent. By sealing them off from society, the boarding school would effectively hasten the process of transforming the young into adolescents. This could be done *either* within the nineteenth-century bourgeois family or in an institution modeled on the family. "My model of discipline," the writer in the Flushing *Journal* declared, "is the good old family government of our forefathers."

A family indeed the Flushing Institute apparently was. We catch an intimate glimpse of it from Thomas Wharton, a young English artist who arrived there in November 1832 with the grandiloquent title of "Professor of the Arts of Design and Descriptive Geometry." Soon after his trip to Flushing from New York City, Wharton wrote:

> I found myself fully established in my new home, surrounded by intelligent, well-educated and gentlemanly companions, and ready to enter upon my new duties and studies with alacrity. There were about 60 or 70 students, and a finer set of boys it would be hard to find, or under more complete, and at the same time paternal discipline—in fact—the "Institute" composed one large family, with Mr. Muhlenberg, the Principal, at its head, and the several Professors and Instruc-

> tors, many of them very young men educated in the Institution, were more like elder brothers and companions of the pupils than the austere taskmasters who usually fill those responsible parts—all seemed to look up to Mr. Muhlenberg with affection and reverence—and I never saw a scholastic establishment where a firm and methodical system of control was more happily blended with the strictest regard to the happiness and improvement of the inmates.[65]

Student life at the Institute, in fact, followed almost the same idyllic course that Muhlenberg had planned. He used much the same regimen as the one Cogswell and Bancroft had established so successfully at Round Hill: every second of the inmate's day was carefully planned. Isolated from New York City by the marshes and Long Island Sound, the pupils studied in the morning and in the afternoon and evening exercised on their playing fields or in the gymnasium, swam at Whitestone beach or played in the nearby woods and fields. They formed boating clubs and made excursions on the Sound; or they worked in their individual vegetable gardens as did students at Hofwyl and Round Hill.[66]

Within their perfectly controlled environment, the students' nurture was carried on along typical romantic lines: the development of the individual boy was stressed, not the integration of the child with his peers. Students, Muhlenberg wrote in his 1828 prospectus, should value things for their own sake, not because of the rewards or punishments associated with them. Emulation among students had more detrimental than beneficial effects: it usually led to "jealousies, contentions, and abundance of mischief." It might have a place in education for "the world," but Muhlenberg had "some difficulty in finding its place in the school of Jesus." However, he sadly concluded, "it is indigenous to the soil of our fallen nature."[67] After two years experience in running the Institute, however, Muhlenberg's grudging 1828 acceptance of emulation changed to a complete rejection of the principle. The Institute, he wrote in 1830, now avoided emulation like the plague; as a spur to study it appealed instead to the pupils' "sense of duty, and motives of a congenial kind." Muhlenberg's rationale for avoiding competition is worth quoting at some length:

> [Emulation] . . . operates successfully only on the gifted few, while it leaves the many, of moderate talents, to despair; serving rather to create a few brilliant stars, than to diffuse a general and steady light. Let the Christian youth be animated to exertion by having frequently set before him the consequence of industry in future respectability—the reasonable expectations of parents and friends—the part he will be called upon to act in life—above all, his bounded duty to cultivate whatever talents the Creator has entrusted to him. . . . It cannot be doubted, that mental energy thus aroused, is attended with an influence far more propitious to usefulness, honour, and happiness in life than when it is the product of the vanity, self-conceit, or petty rivalry, that is too often dignified with the name of honourable emulation.[68]

In his promotional literature of the following year, 1831, Muhlenberg was even more pointed in his condemnation of emulation:

> The means of getting the students to study are as important as the end because of the benefit that the means have on moral character. The effect, however, of exclusively Christian Discipline in a seminary of learning . . . is not so much to make one or two prodigies as to increase the average quantum of industry; to raise the standard of proficiency among the many of moderate abilities rather than to multiply the opportunities of distinction for the gifted few.[69]

"Why," Muhlenberg asked, "should a boy grow double over the conjugation of verbs, to which neither argument nor punishment can compel his attention, and then be dismissed as a blockhead; when, had he been directed to some department of natural science, to the arts, or even to practical mechanics, he might have won the distinction of a lad of talent." Look to the abilities of each student, Muhlenberg advised in best romantic fashion; do not attempt to impose the same traditional program on all children:

> *There is too much aim at present to make mere intellectual men.* Our seminaries look more than they ought to the learned professions as the future sphere of their alumni. Almost every par-

> ent whose circumstances allow him to indulge the idea, looks forward to his son figuring at the Bar, lecturing among the Faculty, or holding forth in the Pulpit; and the prevalent notions of Education tend to encourage the absurdity. . . . we want practical men. Men of information and principle in all walks of society. We want intelligent *merchants and manufacturers* as well as lawyers and doctors. Sensible and pious laymen, as well as learned and orthodox clergymen. To furnish these, Education must be loosed from the trammels of the monastery, and be girded as a handmaid to the practical spirit of the age.[70]

In the age of improvement higher education was to be extended beyond the traditional professions to the new leaders of American society.[71] But in Muhlenberg's words there was too the intimation that it would offer a curriculum based not on the traditional classical humanism of the Renaissance, but on something more "practical," or on something even possibly anti-intellectual. In one respect, however, Muhlenberg ran counter to the "practical" spirit of the age. Jacksonian America was ferociously competitive, the scene of a wild scramble by petty capitalist entrepreneurs to grab their share of the national pie. At the Flushing Institute, however, there was to be no emulation—or competition; individualistic striving was to be denied on the basis of Christian egalitarianism. But despite his condemnations of emulation, Muhlenberg could not stand that strongly against the currents of his age. Each month, in the pages of the school journal, coded tables of the students' ranking in class and conduct were published. The key to the code identifying the pupils was kept secret, Muhlenberg said: it was known only to the teachers, the students, and their parents.[72] In this rather backward way were romantic educational ideas accommodated to Jacksonian America.

One of Muhlenberg's major motives in establishing the Flushing Institute was the evangelical one—his wish to advance the fortunes of the Episcopal church. In the long run this aim met with only limited success, but while the Institute remained in existence Muhlenberg did manage to saturate it in a religious atmosphere. At the Institute he introduced services far more elaborate in the way of music, vestments, ritual, and symbolism than anything to which most American Episcopalians of the time were accustomed. It was the aesthetic elements of religion that left a particularly deep impression on his students; Muhlenberg's practices would later be adopted not only at other church schools but in ordinary Episcopal parishes throughout the country.[73] A typical Sunday at the Institute might be like that of 20 January 1833, when in the morning, Thomas Wharton recorded in his Journal, "Mr. Muhlenberg preached an excellent discourse on 'Death' and in the afternoon read a tract contrasting the last moments of the infidel 'Hume' with those of the eminent Dr. Finley of Princeton, N.J."[74] However, aside from brief morning and evening prayer readings and the services at the times of the great holy days of the year, Muhlenberg did not force formal religion on his students. *"So great,"* he wrote a former student, *"is my dread* [of the stultifying effects] of frequent and long public *services upon children that is my chief objection to choristers chanting the service daily."*[75]

Another of Muhlenberg's main aims had been either to influence young men towards the ministry or actually train them for it. In this he had only limited success. While several Episcopal clergymen and laymen prominent later in the century were educated at Flushing, Muhlenberg finally decided that because of the social class a church school, of necessity, had to draw upon for support, its students could not provide likely material for the priesthood. "A church school," he ruefully advised a former student, "is not a garden to raise weeds in; but alas! as long as church schools can receive only the children of the rich, they will be raising crops of weeds. You can only do your best by rooting out the most noxious."[76]

If in some ways the Institute represented a frustration of the broader evangelical impulse for Muhlenberg, in others it allowed for its complete fulfillment. Like most Episcopalians Muhlenberg abjured the emotional revival meeting as a means of induce religious conversion; he relied instead on the individual suasion of each child to bring about the same end. "There can be no doubt," Daniel Howe has observed, "that the formation of Christian character was the Boston Unitarian substitute for the Puritan conversion experience." If Muhlenberg was representative, somewhat the same observation could be made of Episcopalians. The full force of emotional, sentimental Victorian religiosity was brought to bear on the child at the Flushing Institute:

> A boy was rarely any length of time in his [Muhlenberg's] presence without being drawn almost magnetically to his side, and then one kind arm would go up and around the youth's neck, and the other hand, perhaps, be laid upon his head, in that benediction which he had a way of his own of thus expressing; or else, according to another habit peculiar to him, he passed through and through the boy's hair, as though seeing what he was made of.
>
> At one time, accidentally coming upon him, while thus drawing a boy to his heart, these words were heard, "Say, Down, devil! down, devil!" The youth with kindled eye and glowing cheek was looking up into the master's face, always at such times fullest of that heavenly light which the painter Huntingdon has called his "evangelic look," and it was plain the younger was receiving gratefully from the elder the counsel he needed for the conquest of some dominant bad habit.[77]

The twentieth century would be too ready to draw all the wrong inferences from such scenes: it was actually only one not unusual incident in the great Victorian drama, in which, as Walter Houghton has observed, "the Christian life became in literal fact a life of constant struggle—both to resist temptation and to master the desires of the ego."[78] The emotional moral earnestness which suffused the Institute was far distant from the "aristocratical and free-thinking" spirit that had informed Round Hill. "Christian nurture" leading to conversion and commitment had replaced Cogswell and Bancroft's modestly pessimistic Federalist aim of educating "a few of the rising generation to be somewhat more virtuous, more intelligent and more happy than they would otherwise have been."

By 1836 the Institute had proved itself a very successful financial venture. Muhlenberg now looked beyond the Institute for the fulfillment of the evangelical impulse: He dreamed of founding an Episcopal college which would train young men for the ministry and for missionary work. He set about raising money for the college and bought a site of about one hundred acres for it near the entrance to Flushing Bay on the East River. He wished to abandon the Institute at this point, but the pleas of his students' parents decided him to combine both the old and the new schools in one institution, to be called St. Paul's College and Grammar School.

While the combination of secondary and higher education in one institution would have avoided Cogswell and Bancroft's problem in meshing Round Hill's program with that of the colleges, the new enterprise was destined to fail miserably. The Panic of 1837 intervened; many of Muhlenberg's supporters were unable to make good their pledges of financial support, and the new institution lived out its life in temporary buildings. Worse, due to lack of sufficient financial backing, the New York State Board of Regents refused to give the college degree-granting powers. Added to this Muhlenberg apparently was unable to impose proper discipline among the now widely differing age groups at St. Paul's. His interest in the college and its grammar school began to fade; in 1846 he left the school to take up the rectorship of the Church of the Holy Communion in New York City, and to begin what was probably the more important phase of his life's work—the amelioration of the problems of urbanization. Like so many other private schools, the Flushing Institute, although incorporated, had been essentially a one-man operation. Without Muhlenberg's firm hand and wide social connections, it soon collapsed.[79]

The idea of the church school did not die with St. Paul's College and Grammar School. One of Muhlenberg's main hopes had been to establish a model school which other churchmen might copy. Here he was more successful. His work at Flushing attracted considerable attention among Episcopalians; in the 1830s at least five other church schools—in New Jersey, Vermont, South Carolina, Missouri, and North Carolina—were founded in direct imitation of the Flushing Institute. (It was the North Carolina school which Cogswell became principal of after leaving Round Hill. The bishop of North Carolina hoped to establish a school like the Flushing Institute, and who better to run it than the man who had started the school the Institute was patterned on?) All of these schools, however, failed—most of them in the Panic of 1837.[80] By the late 1840s only one school was still in existence where the institutional forms and educational practices initiated and developed by Cogswell, Bancroft, and Muhlenberg were still maintained—the College and Grammar

School of St. James, near Hagerstown, Maryland.

St. James was founded in 1842 through the efforts of Episcopal laymen in Hagerstown and of William R. Whittingham, bishop of the Protestant Episcopal church in Maryland.[81] Bishop Whittingham first asked Muhlenberg to serve as the head of the proposed school, but he preferred to remain in New York. As rector for the new school he sent instead the Reverend John Barrett Kerfoot, one of his favorite pupils, whom he had brought with him as a tutor when he moved from Lancaster to Flushing.[82] With much difficulty, Bishop Whittingham and the Hagerstown laymen raised enough money to purchase Fountain Rock, a magnificent, isolated mansion with twenty acres of grounds near Hagerstown, as the home for the new school.[83]

Under Kerfoot the college and its preparatory school were an almost immediate success. "The sin of our first parents," said Bishop Whittingham at the school's opening, "was an attempt to attain intellectual growth in defiance of the will of GOD."[84] To repair this fault, Kerfoot, following Muhlenberg's example to the literal letter, combined thorough religious instruction and suasion with the traditional secular education. Kerfoot made no prentensions whatsoever to originality. "St. James' Hall," he wrote in an early draft of a promotional circular, "is designed to be in every respect modelled after St. Paul's College and Grammar School. The course of studies, the mode of religious instruction, the discipline and, as far as possible the arrangements of the latter Institution will be adopted. Those who are desirous of more detailed information than can here be given of the plan proposed for the Hall, are referred to the published statements of 'The studies and discipline of St. Paul's College and Grammar School.' " In what had become the main tradition of the American boarding school, St. James's would be a "family" institution:

> The discipline aimed at will be that of a Christian Household. The instructors and students will reside together as one family, regulated in all its arrangements with a view to improvement in morals, manners and learning. The pupils will not have separate apartments, but prepare their recitations in a common study, and sleep in one dormitory under the charge of an instructor. The constant aim of the discipline will be to bring the pupils as much as possible under the

> personal influence of the instructors. Hence they will leave the grounds only when permitted, and then always in company with some one or more of the instructors or prefects, in whose company all their recreations and amusements will be conducted. The ordinary means of correction will be private and public admonitions, denial of amusement, additional tasks, confinement, etc. These, of course, must vary with character and circumstances, and can only be specified so far as to say that they will always be adapted to the education of the conscience and the heart.[85]

Like Round Hill and the Flushing Institute, then, St. James's would be the complete romantic boarding school: an isolated community, sheltered from the corrupting outside world, a controlled environment, carefully designed to nurture Christian character through the family system of intimate contact between children and adults. A system more different from that of contemporary academies is difficult to imagine.

Kerfoot recruited a small, largely northern, faculty, and soon attracted students from well-to-do families from every part of the South. The largest single group came from Baltimore, then one of the most rapidly expanding cities on the Atlantic seaboard. By 1848 St. James had 98 students, and by 1857, 117. When the college closed its session in June 1861, shortly after the beginning of the Civil War, it had almost 175 students. But that October only 16 returned. The student body had been overwhelmingly southern, and those of the pupils who were old enough loyally joined the Confederate army.[86] Kerfoot and his staff, however, were determined to keep the grammar school and college operating, and opened the October 1862 session with between 40 and 50 students. It proved to be a losing venture. The school was on the main lines of both Union and Confederate armies—the battles of South Mountain, Antietam, and Gettysburg were fought nearby—and suffered constant depredations from troops of both sides. In reprisal for the Union's arrest of a Virginia clergyman, General Jubal Early captured Kerfoot and his assistant, the Reverend Joseph Howland Coit, in 1864—and it proved impossible to keep St. James's open. Regretfully, it was closed and abandoned.[87]

To a remarkable degree Muhlenberg's writings of the 1820s

and 1830s were an anticipation of the thought of a Congregational minister of Hartford, Connecticut, Horace Bushnell. In 1846 Bushnell published his influential *Views of Christian Nurture,* a work which summed up in formal fashion many of the concerns of Muhlenberg and his generation. Distressed by revivalistic emotionalism, the transitory quality of its effects, and his own inability to inspire conversions among his wealthy congregation in this manner, Bushnell turned instead, like Muhlenberg, to the gradual Christian nurture of the plastic, impressionable child to achieve the same ends. The child's character would be formed in his first school—the Christian family and home. Within the walls of the secluded Christian home, by loving example the child would gradually absorb the firm foundations of Christian faith and character. As much a call for the regeneration of the family as a tract on child rearing. Bushnell's book envisioned a reconstituted church composed of such ideal families.

While most of Muhlenberg's values and goals paralleled Bushnell's, the former went one step beyond in his thought. For him, Christian nurture could be carried out not just in a Christian *home,* but in an *institution* modeled on a Christian home. Muhlenberg's institutionalization of Christian nurture allowed him—and other Episcopalians—to succeed where Bushnell's hopes remained simply rhetoric. The working institution provided the link between rhetoric and reality, between ideas and society, which Bushnell failed to bridge. What Barbara Cross has called Bushnell's "dream of sequestered innocence" could not be realized in the average family, Christian or otherwise.[88] It was fulfilled to a remarkable degree, however, in sequestered family boarding schools like St. James's or the Flushing Institute.

There was irony in Muhlenberg's very success. That the family boarding school should become the preferred school for the sons of America's emerging urban elites had hardly been his intention. But given the prevailing image of the child, the moral and physical character of America's burgeoning cities, the expense of running such a school, and the social composition of the Episcopal church, the outcome was perhaps inevitable.

While at Round Hill the primary stress had been upon developing both the scholarly and gentlemanly elements of the Christian gentleman and scholar, Muhlenberg shifted the emphasis heavily towards the cultivation of the specifically Christian element in the ideal type. In the future, however, the various elements of the cultural ideal would be brought into a new balance —at yet another school named St. Paul's.

After the closing of St. James's, Kerfoot went on to become, briefly, president of Trinity College in Hartford, Connecticut, and in 1865 was selected the first Episcopal bishop of Pittsburgh. His assistant, Joseph Howland Coit, accompanied by some other faculty members, made his way to the ten-year-old St. Paul's School in Concord, New Hampshire, where his older brother was serving as the school's first rector. Round Hill's Federalist legacy and the evangelical impulse represented by Muhlenberg's Institute would be united in Concord to form the classic boarding school of Victorian America—an institution which would, in turn, serve as the basic model for the private prep school of the Progressive era.

Chapter V

The Federalist Heritage and the Evangelical Impulse: The Founding of St. Paul's School

"As I watched your efforts to-day," Bishop Phillips Brooks told the students of St. Paul's School one Founder's Day in the 1890s, "and you called to one another across the field, I heard many of the names great in American history. It is only worth while to have ancestors who have served their country well, if out of the pride of birth you win high-minded reasons and desires to follow nobly where they led so well."[1] The founder honored that day, Dr. George Cheyne Shattuck of Boston, would certainly have agreed with Brooks's views and have felt a certain ambivalent pleasure with his observations on the student body. It was almost what he had planned back in 1854 when he first thought, as he wrote almost forty years later, of establishing "a school the principal but not the only object of which is to educate the sons of wealthy inhabitants of large cities."[2]

Founded in 1855 by an alumnus of Round Hill, staffed by men educated at the Flushing Institute and the College of St. James, St. Paul's School in Concord, New Hampshire, became the most influential model—accepted, rejected, but impossible to ignore—for the scores of private boarding schools founded in the decades after the Civil War. The perfect institutional embodiment of Victorian ideas of the child, education, and religion, St.

Paul's brought together in a new fashion the heritages of Muhlenberg and of Cogswell and Bancroft.

St. Paul's founder, George C. Shattuck, Jr., was one of those nineteenth-century Boston Brahmins whose lives seem to have been a solid series of unspectacular successes and unpretentious philanthropies. He was born in 1813, the son of George Cheyne Shattuck, a prominent and wealthy physician, "thoroughly steeped in benevolence," as the son's memorialist described him.[3] He went to a local private school, to the Boston Latin School for three years, and then, at the age of twelve, to Cogswell and Bancroft's Round Hill.

We have already seen something of Shattuck's years at Round Hill, and of his father's almost obsessive concern with his son. The concern was understandable. While going through the manuscripts of nineteenth-century Americans, one is struck again and again by the truly appalling rate of child mortality. The wealthy Shattuck family suffered here as other American families of the time suffered: George was the only one of six children to reach maturity. In letter after letter the elder Shattuck addressed his boy as "My dear, my *only* son." The junior Shattuck later recalled that "a principal reason for the change . . . [from the Boston Latin School to Round Hill was] the advantage of a country life."[4] He received an extraordinarily good education at Round Hill: he entered Harvard with advanced standing in the sophomore class and graduated in 1831 after only two years there.

The father's intense concern with his son did not cease with the boy's entry to college. The elder Shattuck constantly solicited the opinions of Harvard faculty members about George's abilities and prospects. George's "standing is among the *ten* highest," President Josiah Quincy finally informed the father on a note of exasperation. "This is enough to gratify the wishes of any parent—and beyond this I do not deem it wise ever to inform."[5] Other Harvard faculty members were more communicative. Their assessments of the youth were remarkably perceptive: a description of George Shattuck's character at the age of seventeen would serve for a description at the age of seventy. He is "singularly guileless and unsophisticated," said instructor Timothy Walker. "I have never seen him greatly moved in any way. Neither very much elated, nor very much depressed. . . . He is not what we call sanguine and ardent, but cool, staid and saturnine." George, wrote Cornelius C. Felton, formerly a teacher at Round Hill and later president of Harvard, "is as yet an amiable, studious, high-principled young man—and entirely free from the affectations and follies that are so common among young gentlemen of fortune. His character is so well-established, that I think no apprehensions need be entertained by his friends of any deviation from the path of honorable industry, virtuous purposes, and high intellectual pursuits."[6] Felton was foresighted, for such would be the course of Shattuck's life.

From childhood on Shattuck hoped to become a physician like his father; the father objected—fearing his son was not strong enough to endure the rigors of a medical career—but finally relented. For a student in the years before professional medical schools became common, Shattuck's medical education was broad and cosmopolitan. In his first year of study he "read" medicine with Dr. Benjamin Lincoln of Burlington, Vermont; in his second he attended the Harvard Medical School and worked with his father; in the third he studied under the professor of anatomy and surgery at Bowdoin College. (He somehow found time, during a vacation, to accompany John James Audubon on a naturalizing expedition to Newfoundland and Labrador.) He then toured most of the United States east of the Mississippi, stopping in city after city to hear lectures at various medical schools. Next, he went to Europe, where he studied for three years in Paris, Vienna, Munich, London, Edinburgh, Dublin, and Paris again. He returned home in 1840, a very well prepared young physician indeed.

Fulfilling his extensive preparation and confounding his father's fears, Shattuck's career was long and distinguished. For thirty-six years he was a visiting physician at Massachusetts General Hospital, but his major interest was in teaching medicine. From 1855 to 1859 he was professor of clinical medicine, and from 1859 to 1873 professor of the theory and practice of medicine at the Harvard Medical School. For many of these years he also served as Dean of the Medical Faculty and was responsible for the reorganization and modernization of the Medical School. And, on the side, he maintained a free dispensary near his home in Boston for the poor of the North End.

Marriage in 1840 to Anne Henrietta Brune of Baltimore, the

sister of two of his classmates at Round Hill, brought Shattuck a new and engrossing interest—the Episcopal church. Mrs. Shattuck was Episcopalian, and during the early years of their marriage Shattuck's interest in the church grew stronger and stronger. He became friendly with Bishop Whittingham of Maryland and also with Muhlenberg's former student, the Reverend John B. Kerfoot, then head of the College and Grammar School of St. James, where Mrs. Shattuck's younger brother was a student. He lectured on medicine at St. James and spent many weeks visiting there. He then left the Congregationalism he had been reared in and was baptized into the Episcopal church by Kerfoot in the chapel of St. James.[7]

Typical of the convert, Shattuck threw himself into Episcopal activities with an evangelical fervor surpassing that of most birthright Episcopalians; by the time of his death his biographer could call him "the foremost layman in the Church." He was a member of almost every society in his diocese, a delegate to every diocesan and general convention of the church, a trustee of the General Theological Seminary and other institutions, and an extremely generous contributor to church causes. (He was a communicant of the Church of the Advent in Boston, and one Sunday left in the collection box as his offering a check for $20,000.)

George Shattuck's conversion to Episcopalianism was typical of many other rich New Englanders of the time. Indeed, a recent analyst of American society has claimed that half of the "Very Rich" people in the United States appear to be Episcopalians.[8] Outside of New England, this seems to have been true at least since the beginnings of the republic. By the time of the American Revolution, an Episcopal historian has noted somewhat ruefully, the Church had "acquired something of that quality of 'upper-classness' which has handicapped its work in this country ever since."[9] However, in the early years of the nineteenth century in New England, where so many church schools would ultimately be founded, the Congregational church and its Unitarian offspring were still—literally and figuratively—the "established" churches among the rich. But over the course of the century they lost their favored places, and, by the time of the Gilded Age, it seemed almost odd for a rich New Englander to be anything but an Episcopalian.

One patrician New Englander's Unitarianism troubled his twentieth-century biographer's sense of social propriety. "By his personal appearance he should have been a prominent member of some congregation of High Church Episcopalians," John T. Morse wrote of Colonel Henry Lee of Massachusetts. Morse had an explanation for Lee's eccentric Unitarianism. "In excuse for this shortcoming on his part," he wrote, "it must be remembered that in his early days [Lee was born in 1817] churches of [the Episcopal] creed were as yet without the cachet of fashionable society in Boston, and with his family connections he could not be otherwise than a Unitarian . . . he used to allege that any New Englander who was not a Unitarian must have some defect in his intellectual make-up. He himself was a church-goer, and should be described as a devout man, at least as far as devotion goes among Unitarians. . . ."[10]

Lee's Unitarianism was hardly, of course, exceptionable among rich New Englanders. Nevertheless, in the first half of the nineteenth century Episcopalianism began to make definite inroads among rich Congregationalist New Englanders, just as it had done among rich Pennsylvania Quakers fifty years before.[11] The once-despised Episcopal church grew remarkably in New England in these years. In Massachusetts, for example, while there were only thirteen Episcopal churches in 1811, by 1839 there were thirty-eight; in Rhode Island, only four in 1811, and by 1839, seventeen. In the other New England states the proportional increase followed much the same pattern.[12] "To be an Episcopalian," Congregationalist Yale's *New Englander* magazine sneered by 1845, is "respectable . . . very respectable . . . , and it introduces one into good society."[13]

"The writer," George Shattuck once recalled, "was educated a congregationalist & the division of this body into orthodox & unitarian was taking place in his early days."[14] While Shattuck himself moved directly from Congregationalism to Episcopalianism, many others made a detour into Unitarianism. The conversion from Unitarianism to Episcopalianism of William Brooks, a wealthy Bostonian and father of the famous Episcopal bishop Phillips Brooks, exemplifies the drift of many rich New England families towards Canterbury.[15] In 1839 Brooks's wife, Mary Ann (a granddaughter of the sternly Calvinistic Samuel Phillips of Andover), grew dissatisfied with the "preaching of her

[Unitarian] relation Dr. Frothingham." Consequently, the Brookses became communicants of St. Paul's Episcopal Church. "For myself," Brooks confided wistfully in his Journal, "I feel myself attached to the Unitarian Church, having been brought up in that doctrine; but at the same time I cannot say I have no such repugnance to the Orthodox [i.e., Congregational] sect as many have. . . . Being, therefore . . . indifferent, I have given up my inclinations and prejudices for my old place of worship to gratify that of my wife. Certain it is that women make religion more a matter of conscience and the heart than men do."[16]

Brooks was probably right. An Episcopal writer, complaining in the 1930s of the "present paucity of male attendants at our services," dates the feminization of the church back to these same years "in the nineteenth century [when] this preponderance began to assume alarming proportions."[17] The trend was particularly marked in the Evangelical wing of the church. Episcopalianism did not require the emotional upheaval of revivalistic conversions; suffused with romantic Victorian sentimentalism, it consciously cultivated the tender, aesthetic faculties. And not only in Boston. "In New York and Connecticut," Barbara Cross has observed, "the Episcopalians criticized the drabness of revivalistic religion, its sacrifice of social amenities, its neglect of baptism, the church, and the family."[18] Its appeal to the more affluent citizens of an increasingly affluent nation was understandable.

With George Shattuck, as with many other Episcopalians, the evangelical impulse took a curious inward turn. Rather than depend on the instant conversion of the revival, Episcopalians typically founded institutions that drew individuals together in organic units which allowed for the gradual Christian nurture of the child. Shattuck's impulse to found St. Paul's School began with his desire to see that his sons received an education comparable in excellence to his own at Round Hill. Shattuck had an intense love of nature (perhaps a legacy of his years at Round Hill) and particularly of his family's charming summer estate at Millville, just outside Concord, New Hampshire, to which he escaped whenever possible. In the early fall of 1854, after spending some time there, he seriously considered leaving his two sons at the estate for the winter, rather than bringing them back to the city.[19] His father's death a short time later left him the possessor of a considerable fortune and enabled him to go far beyond his initial thought of having the boys tutored at his estate.[20] "When the writer," he later said of himself, "was in search of a school for his own children he did not find any in New England where he was disposed to put them. He had a country home in a healthy and beautiful spot, and as his boys must go away from home to school, he thought it well to try to start a school there." What was wrong with New England's many academies? To answer this, Shattuck looked back to his own childhood education. His words are worth repeating:

> There were academies . . . where the instruction in Latin, Greek, and mathematics was very thorough. The boys boarded in private houses and went to the school to study and recite. But Mr. Cogswell's object [at Round Hill] was not merely to train the intellectual faculties and to supply the mind with knowledge. He wished to train the physical and moral faculties, and in order to do this he must live with the boys and have them constantly under observation and care.

Academies were not boarding schools; only in a boarding school could the child be moulded, through gentle Christian nurture, into the complete Christian gentleman and scholar.

Towards the end of his life Shattuck wrote an account of what he remembered of his motives and experiences in founding St. Paul's. What preoccupied the old man most was not the school he had actually founded and seen grow to success, but his own memories of Round Hill. And what he remembered most vividly of Round Hill was its physical setting and equipment. But to the memory of Round Hill another element had been added—Shattuck's own experience in Episcopalian affairs. The story is best told in his own words:

> Having had experience & opportunities for observation in Church organizations as well as in schools, I was convinced of the Christian religion as the important factor in training and disciplining boys & men [.] . . . When in the course of time the duty came to find schools for my own children, the observation & experience of early days was fresh in my mind[.] I looked about carefully, sought advice and information from

> many friends and did not succeed in finding a school coming up to my ideal. I had a beautiful & healthy country home, but my boys could only be there for a few weeks in the year. I had a place with all the natural advantages for physical health & training. I had learned of the efforts of Dr. Muhlenberg to establish a school at College Point. I had spent weeks at the college of St. James, was intimate with the masters & had a special friendship with Dr. Kerfoot the Rector of the college, & he pointed out the present Rector of St. Pauls as preeminently the one most likely to succeed in a most difficult undertaking[.][22]

As at Round Hill, the natural setting was magnificent: "Green fields and trees, stream and ponds," said Shattuck in a classic expression of romantic, Transcendentalist nature-worship, "beautiful scenery, flowers, and minerals, are educators. The things which are seen are very valuable, and may be used to teach of Him who made them, and thus of things unseen. Religious teaching and training for beings such as we are is all important. The things of this world are engrossing; but boys ought to be trained not only for this life, but so as to enter into and enjoy eternal and unseen realities."[23] Or rather, eternal and unseen *Episcopalian* realities. Although Shattuck wrote that "the school was not intended to be sectarian," he contradicted himself in almost the next sentence. "The object," of the school, he wrote, "was to develop what was good in boys, to discourage & check what was evil[,] to train & educate all their powers mental physical moral, & the Episcopal Church was selected as that most likely to accomplish these objects."[24] St. Paul's was intended to be, quite simply, Round Hill in Episcopal dress.

Establishing St. Paul's proved to be far more difficult and taxing in reality than it eventually seemed to have been in Shattuck's memory. Shattuck's memories of Round Hill and his experience with St. James's could provide only a rough outline for embodying his ideas in a working institution. To accomplish this, he had necessarily to work with others; in this process his ideas would undergo modification. Shattuck first proposed his idea for the school to Carleton Chase, the Episcopal bishop of New Hampshire. Chase, a hearty, energetic, old man who managed to raise a large family on a salary of only $600 a year, was enthusiastic.[25] "A better location could not be found in the Diocese or elsewhere," he happily wrote Shattuck. It was the perfect place at which to fulfill the Victorian ideal of the child's secluded innocence. "It is a truly beautiful spot, locally viewed. It is in the right part of this Diocese, and in the right part of Concord,—is just far enough from the city—has a sufficiently easy access to the Rail Road, is not in the midst of an evil neighborhood (and so must be a community by itself) and is moreover surrounded by a natural scenery of a most pleasing character."[26] The bishop agreeing, Shattuck set about choosing a group of trustees for his school. The nine men he selected, all personal friends and Episcopalians, were, like the trustees of contemporary academies, as distinguished a group as he could find: the Reverend Horatio Southgate, rector of Shattuck's Church of the Advent in Boston; the Reverend Newton E. Marble, rector of St. Paul's Church in Concord; Nathaniel V. Baker, secretary of state of New Hampshire; William F. Otis, a prominent Bostonian; Isaac F. Redfield, chief justice of the Vermont Supreme Court; Matthew Harvey, chief justice of the New Hampshire Supreme Court; Jacob Carter, a prominent citizen of Concord; William E. Coale, a Boston physician and very active Episcopal layman; and Henry M. Parker, a prominent Boston lawyer. It was a thoughtfully selected group, well chosen to advance the fortunes of any institution. With the later additions of Bishop Chase and Judge Samuel H. Huntington of Connecticut, the first trustees included three clergymen, three important public officials, a lawyer, a physician, and two prominent Episcopal laymen. Shattuck himself declined to serve on the board but was present at most of its meetings. His suggestions were usually followed.[27]

The next step was the all-important one of finding a headmaster (or "rector," as the head of St. Paul's would be styled) for the school. On this man above all else the success or failure of the proposed school would rest, as Round Hill had depended upon Cogswell, the Flushing Institute on Muhlenberg, and St. James's on Kerfoot. When he thought back to his own school days, Shattuck recalled the pervading influence of Cogswell at Round Hill; everything, he said, "depends on the rector or head master of a boarding school and his power of winning the confidence, respect, and affection of the pupils. . . ."[28] The rector himself would have to be the embodiment of the age's educational ideal, a paragon of altruism. "Money making," Shattuck wrote, "should not be an object in starting or carrying on a school. A school master should look for his main reward in the world to come & not to comfort reputation or wealth in this world . . . [he] should have crucified his own will & cultivated an intense love of the Lord & Master with a burning zeal for his service if he expects to be successful in fitting boys so to live in this world as to be benefactors to their race. . . ."[29] Shattuck wanted, he remembered years later, St. Paul's to be:

> large, attracting students from all parts of a large country, with various dispositions, talents, and requirements, many of them lacking the wholesome stimulus of prospective want. To mould such into a harmonious community, to inspire it with sentiments of truth, honor, and loyalty to God and man, is no slight task, and success in it can only be expected from one who has learned to subordinate his own interest and preferences to a higher power.[30]

In effect, Shattuck was seeking the perfect missionary as his school's first rector; for him, the evangelical impulse would be fulfilled not on the frontier or in the city, but in an isolated institution. In his efforts to locate the ideal schoolmaster he investigated or interviewed at least fifteen, and probably many more, individuals. In his search he was aided principally by Bishop Chase and by Judge Huntington, whom the bishop described as "one of your hearty, sound sort of men, who, when they take hold of a thing, are apt to shake out its folds and give it a thorough inspection." Huntington in turn regarded Chase as "very safe *and* judicious," but warned Shattuck of his own unfortunate "experience as to recommendations of Clergymen of brother Clergymen."[31]

Huntington's son and Shattuck's oldest boy, George, were students together at a school near Hartford run by a Mr. Seymour. Huntington, therefore, was particularly sympathetic and understanding of the type of man Shattuck hoped to find to head the new school and offered to do anything he could to assist. "I want very much," he assured Shattuck:

> to see your school established, and that it should be a model for other schools in our Country. The great difficulty will be to obtain the right sort of a man to place at the head of it—a man who shall combine in himself the character of a gentleman a scholar and a Christian—and to this shall add aptness in teaching and whose daily life, in his most familiar intercourse with boys shall be the effectual admonition to the indolent and wayward[.]
>
> I am fully aware, how rare such men are. Still I would postpone the opening of school even a year, rather than to begin it with a teacher who did not come pretty nearly to the standard which I have briefly indicated.[32]

The standard could not be met: it proved extraordinarily difficult to discover a man who combined with intense evangelical fervor the Federalist idea of the Christian gentleman and scholar. The opening of the school was postponed for over a year while the search for a suitable rector was slowly and sometimes discouragingly prosecuted. The very failure to find the right type of man gives some indication of the novelty for the time of the kind of school Shattuck hoped to establish.

After several false starts, Shattuck and Huntington turned to a consideration of Mr. Seymour, the master of the school their sons were attending.[33] On close examination, unfortunately, Mr. Seymour seemed to be the very antithesis of the ideal Victorian schoolmaster: "One strong fact meets us both in looking at . . . [Mr. Seymour's] school," Huntington observed to Shattuck in a letter steeped in romantic educational values:

> and it is one that speaks a language that cannot be mistaken —that our sons are not attached to Mr. Seymour[,] that they have not indeed much respect for him. It is unnecessary for me to point out to you the evil influence of this single fact upon the character of a boy. I hope he will improve in this particular. It is much easier to govern boys by the rod than by love, one is a merely mechanical operation, while the other requires a high moral effort and a most consistent deportment in all things. . . . I cannot express to you how important I consider this feature in a teacher[']s character[.] You have seen no doubt fathers who ruled their families by fear rather

than love. Not but that a fond father must not *not* sometimes punish, and even severely. But he can do that with kindness, and by it inspire love and respect. A teacher must not depend upon arbitrary rules alone to govern a school—or upon the excitement of emulation *between* boys to promote scholarship. It may do very well for a few of the best scholars—the brightest boys—but it may be totally destructive to boys who have good minds naturally but are not quite as quick as some others. I have written these views to Mr. Seymour.[34]

Bishop Chase too was unhappy about the prospect of Seymour as rector. His son knew Seymour, he wrote, and thought that "he is a good scholar, but is boorish in his manners, and seems to care little for the *sauviter in modo.* This corresponds with the impression received by yourself. Now he ought to mind his maners at any rate—whether he engages in our work or not. A young man of talent, who lacks refinement without knowing it, may be mended. But a man who is coarse out of a contempt for refinement and for conventional forms, is not worth schooling. . . ."[35] Scholarship was not enough; for all concerned with the search it seemed just as important to meet the gentlemanly ideal.

Meanwhile, Shattuck grew more anxious and discouraged. His original plan, he told Huntington, was for the trustees to take "the responsibility of choosing the rector. I will," he promised, "do what I can to find candidates." A good candidate, however, was hard to find. "We have done everything in our power for a year to find a better man [than Seymour]," Shattuck complained. "To do the best in our power, such is the limit of responsibility. Sinful and frail men are all that are to be had. We may know the faults of some, and others may appear better, because we do not know them. The boys do not like Mr. S. but I can not get at anything about him which can not be altered. He probably will never be the perfect gentleman that I wish he were. . . . I can imagine a very much better man, I do not know where to find one that can be had." By this point, Shattuck was grasping at straws: "Do you know Professor A. P. Barnard late of the University of Alabama who was a candidate for the Presidency of St. John's College at Annapolis?" he asked Huntington. Was Barnard an Episcopalian? After all, "a zealous churchman whose hobby is education, might be very glad of such a post as we can offer."[36]

On 5 and 6 September 1855, almost a year after Shattuck had first thought of founding his school, the corporation held its first meetings at what was to be St. Paul's site, Shattuck's home near Concord. Shattuck and his wife deeded the estate—over fifty acres of land, including the large house, a grist mill, a saw mill, and millers' and farmers' cottages—to the corporation on three conditions: first, that the property was never to be mortgaged for debts, loans, or any other purpose; second, that the members of the corporation should always be communicants of the Protestant Episcopal church; and last, that religious education at the school should always be in accord with the doctrines, discipline, and worship of the church. Shattuck intended these gifts to be only a beginning; he planned to pour money continually into the school in its early years as needs and opportunities should arise.

Organizational affairs disposed of, the corporation proceeded to elect one Roger S. Howard, a promising discovery of the bishop of Maine, as St. Paul's rector.[37] But Mr. Howard was subject to depressions and declined. "Well—it is as it is," Bishop Chase consoled Shattuck, "and I do not know that we have cause to regret, that we tried him. It may be for the best."[38]

For the best it was. Shattuck had heard from Kerfoot of a young Clergyman engaged in missionary work in upstate New York, Henry Augustus Coit. Coit had been a pupil of Muhlenberg's at the Flushing Institute and had studied and taught briefly at St. James's. Shattuck suggested that Bishop Chase inquire of Coit's father, Joseph Howland Coit, Sr., an Episcopal clergyman, of his son's suitability for the rectorship. Chase was doubtful, for Coit was only twenty-five years old. "It struck me," he said, "that he must be too young—that he could hardly have experience and weight of character equal to the demands of so important a post." But he would trust the judgment of the father, "a plain, honest, downright, jolly man, [who] . . . will, I think, give an impartial opinion."[39]

The senior Coit's testimonial for his son was accepted with surprising alacrity. " 'His *money gumption* has never been tested,' " the father wrote Chase, " 'but with his common sense, prudence, economy and strict integrity, I think that he would have no difficulty in financeering.' " Accordingly, an executive committee of the corporation met on October 11 and selected from a list of candidates Henry Augustus Coit as rector of St. Paul's, subject to approval by the whole board of trustees. "What do you think of our selection," Marble asked the founder. "Does it meet with your views and wishes?" After meeting young Coit early in November, Shattuck was not at all sure. Bishop Chase reassured him: "The modesty and self distrust are by no means indicative of a want of proper qualifications—rather the contrary. I do not like your bold, self-assured men, who lay claim to all manner of qualifications, and before whom ordinary and wary judgements have to keep silence or else consent to be overborne with words."[40] Apparenly Shattuck thought that on balance Coit was the best candidate for the rectorship; late in November Coit began to make preparations for opening the school the following spring. The trustee ratified the decisions of the executive committee and Shattuck by formally electing Coit the rector of St. Paul's School on 15 January 1856.[41]

The intense effort and thought which Shattuck, Huntington, and everyone else concerned with the founding of St. Paul's put into achieving their educational ideal was reminiscent of Shattuck's father's own almost obsessive concern with his son's education. Edmund Morgan's observation that seventeenth-century Puritans and Virginians sent their children away to be educated because "they were afraid of spoiling them by too great affection" seems even more appropriate for the Victorian age.[42] St. Paul's brought together the Federalist goal of molding the child to the image of the Christian gentleman and scholar and the evangelical impulse of bringing about the conversion of the child through gentle Christian nurture. The basic models and intellectual inspiration for Round Hill, the Flushing Institute, and the College of St. James had been a combination of the American college, Swiss and German schools, and romantic ideas about education. In initial conception St. Paul's was based directly on its American predecessors. However, almost immediately after the school opened, a new ingredient was added to the mixture.

When St. Paul's opened with three pupils in April 1856, George Shattuck was not there, but on a long European trip. During the voyage he looked in on many other schools, from Scotland to Italy. The several private secondary schools he visited in England particularly struck him and fired his ambition for his own infant institution. "When I looked at those schools," he told Judge Huntington, "at their handsome and convenient buildings their extensive grounds their libraries pictures works of art how boys are surrounded there with objects to enlarge their minds to elevate and refine their tastes I felt how much we have to do in America how far behind we are!"[43] Shattuck, as always, was overly impressed by physical surroundings; if he had examined what was actually going on within those buildings he would have discovered that Americans in this respect were not particularly "far behind" British schools.

The American prep school is often thought to have been modeled directly on the great public schools of England.[44] However, as is probably clear by now, its inspiration came from many different and often conflicting motives and traditions, and its immediate organizational models were American, Swiss, and German institutions. Of the British public schools we have heard little or nothing—and not because Americans were unaware of their existence.[45] Considering the great reputation the public schools of England achieved in the nineteenth century, their lack of influence on American education before the Civil War seems at first more than a little puzzling.

The explanation is actually quite simple. Neither Cogswell nor Bancroft could have taken the English public schools as models; both Muhlenberg and Kerfoot eventually visited English schools but remained distinctly unimpressed; Shattuck himslf admired the plants, and the plants alone, of English schools. Before the 1860s an American educator would no more have thought of taking the English public schools as model educational institutions than an American penologist would have taken Newgate prison or an American jurist the Old Bailey as models.

At the beginning of the ninteenth century English education was at one of its lowest states—the universities moribund, secondary education so diverse that no generalization abut it is possible.[46] Suffice to say that it reflected the aristocratic nature of the society of Regency England: graceful and brutal, charming and dissolute. Scattered across England were scores of endowed, incorporated grammar schools, some dating from the Middle Ages, which had been founded over the centuries by men "who varied in social rank from kings and bishops to retired sea-captains or shop-keepers."[47] Since they educated children in groups and were incorporated and not owned by individuals, they were called "public schools." Like American academies, they were run by self-perpetuating boards of trustees. Most of the schools were small, insignificant, and academically mediocre. Contemporaries took "the excellence of Eton, Winchester, Rugby and one or two London schools . . . for granted," T. W. Bamford has observed. "The rest were usually passed over in silence."[48]

Among these schools seven in particular catered to the children of the upper-middle and upper classes—Winchester, Eton, Harrow, Shrewsbury, Westminster, Rugby, and Charterhouse. None of these schools had been meant originally to educate the children of the rich, but, as early as the middle of the seventeenth century they were admitting more and more fee-paying children of the upper classes, at the expense of nonpaying charity—or "endowment"—scholars. By the early nineteenth century they were filled largely with upperclass boys, though by no means all—and perhaps not even a majority—of upper-middle- and upper-class boys attended these schools.[49] By the 1840s this process was complete. An American traveler, on visiting one of the schools, "felt it strange that gentlemen's sons should engross, as they do, the gratuitous provision of the pious dead for the poor." However, "the headmaster assured us [Muhlenberg and Kerfoot] that they did not violate the purpose of the founder, and, of course we were too polite to say what we thought, it may be erroneously, to the contrary."[50]

General opinion notwithstanding, it was not the purpose of these schools in the early nineteenth century to produce Christian gentlemen trained for public service to the Empire: the battle of Waterloo was not won on the playing fields of Eton, if only for the reason that at the time those who fought at Waterloo would have attended Eton, the school had no playing fields. Nor were they, anymore than were contemporary American academies, boarding schools. For the most part only charity students lived in the schools' buildings—usually primitive barracks in which over seventy boys might be locked into a cold, barren room at eight in the evening, to be let out sometime the next morning. The more affluent students—the majority—boarded, as in American academy-towns, in private lodgings, which were frequently quite opulent. There they led lives often completely independent of the school authorities. They fished, hunted, played pick-up games (organized athletics did not as yet exist), and in general led a free, independent—and very often dissolute—life which reflected the style of their Regency elders. Nor was the schools' primary goal to prepare boys for the universities—in the late 1850s and early 1860s only a third of the students at Oxford and a fifth of the students at Cambridge came from the "great seven" public schools.[51] A boy might get a very good classical education at one of these schools, but it had to be acquired much on his own initiative.

What discipline there was was maintained by flogging. On 30 June 1832 Dr. Keate, the headmaster of Eton, managed to flog eighty boys in the space of a single evening. The older boys were responsible for the discipline of the younger, who acted as the older boys' servants—or "fagged" for them. The twentieth-century meaning of the word "fag" also suggests—correctly—that other services were required. Reading over the literature of the period, one is often reduced to the somewhat lurid impression that when Regency students were sober enough they spent most of their time either beating or raping one another.[52]

By the 1850s, however, when George Shattuck first visited these schools, all this was beginning to change. As the industrial revolution progressed, a new, soberer, moralizing air began to be felt. The middle-class, evangelical outlook which had informed the society of New England from its beginnings now began to pervade all levels of the society of old England; the great Victorian *embourgeoisement* was under way. In the English public schools the change is usually dated to the 1828 election of Thomas Arnold to be headmaster of Rugby. A product of the nineteenth-century Anglican revival (like his contemporary, Muhlenberg), the intensely evangelical Arnold managed to infuse Rugby with something of his own spirit through rigorous discipline and example. In effect, he turned the older boys into a missionary corps for the younger, charged with maintaining discipline throughout the whole school. In his fourteen years as headmaster Rugby was an extended revival meeting; though some of his students suffered nervous breakdowns from the moral intensity of the place, and others became intolerable prigs, the standards of morals, discipline and scholarship were improved.

Arnold had little direct effect on other schools (and surprisingly little effect on the formal organization of Rugby itself) during his lifetime. Ironically, he had more influence on education dead than alive. With the publication in 1857 of Thomas Hughes's tremendously popular *Tom Brown's School Days,* a highly idealized picture of life at Rugby under Arnold, and the subsequent publication in the 1870s of Arthur Stanley's biography, Arnold was transformed into the archetype of the Victorian headmaster. In the versions of Hughes and Stanley, Arnold would serve as an inspiration and model for scores of English and American schoolmasters of the later nineteenth century. By the time of the American Civil War it seemed that the public schools might be salvageable, that they might not only produce gentlemen, but *Christian* gentlemen.[53] It was just at this moment that George Shattuck happened to visit them.

Probably much more important than Thomas Arnold, both for the reform of the English public schools and as an example for American educators, was another English headmaster, Edward Thring of Uppingham.[54] Thring was born in 1821, the younger son of the rector and sole landed proprietor of the parish of Alford in Somersetshire. He attended Eton (which he reacted against all his life) and King's College, Cambridge, where he distinguished himself as a scholar and took holy orders. As a younger son he could expect little inheritance; he had to plan on making a living for himself. In 1853, after failing to be chosen headmaster of Durham, he was elected instead to be headmaster of Uppingham School.

Uppingham had been founded and endowed by an obscure country clergyman in 1584; it had remained an obscure local grammar school for 270 years. When Thring became headmaster, at almost the same time George Shattuck was founding St. Paul's School in America, Uppingham had about twenty-five students, a master's house, an inadequate Elizabethan schoolroom, one master with two assistants, and an uninterested board of trustees. When Thring died in 1887, it was one of the great public schools of England; Thring himself "was the only English schoolmaster of . . . [his] generation widely and popularly known by name."[55]

At Uppingham Thring introduced the "cottage system"—he replaced the barrackslike student life he had known at Eton with houses limited to a master and thirty boys. He set the class size at a maximum of twenty to twenty-five boys. (Arnold's reforms at Rugby had only managed to reduce classes from two hundred to one hundred.) He built the first school gymnasium in England and introduced shopwork, singing, and other activities as an integral part of the school's life. He created, in other words, a school which resembled Round Hill, the Flushing Institute, or the College of St. James far more than contemporary English public schools: Uppingham was as much influenced by romantic educational ideas as were Round Hill and Flushing. Thring's two main educational principles, for instance, were obvious expressions of romanticism: "First," he wrote in 1875, "the necessity that every boy, be he clever or stupid, must have proper individual attention paid to him. If he has not, the boy who has not, so far as he is neglected, is not at school. Secondly, that proper machinery for work, proper tools of all sorts, are at least as necessary in making a boy take a given shape, as in making a deal box."[56] Thring's "given shape" was the same as Arnold's, and the one American schoolmasters would also try to mold—the Christian gentleman and scholar.

Thring's influence in America and other English-speaking nations was enormous, not only through his own writings,[57] but through Edward Parkin's still very interesting biography, which is so detailed as to be almost a how-to-do-it book on establishing a school. An American situation analogous to Thring's accomplishments at Uppingham would have been the transformation of an obscure American academy into a nationally-known boarding school. This was precisely what Frank Boyden did when he became principal of an academy in Deerfield, Massachusetts, in 1903.[58] And the Phillips Exeter Academy—though hardly obscure—was to undergo a similar transformation in the 1890s. In both nations similar conditions and traditions produced similar results: the English public schools and the American private preparatory schools were both creations of the nineteenth century.

If the most influential, Thring was only one of many headmasters and Uppingham only one of the many new public schools that began to rise to challenge the "great seven" in the 1840s and 1850s. "Between the accession of Queen Victoria and 1869," T. W. Bamford has noted, "no less than thirty-one classical boarding schools were founded, and this figure does not include independent day schools or old endowed grammar schools which had acquired new energy and life."[59] Besides Uppingham, old grammar schools such as Tonbridge, Felsted, Sherborne, Oundle, Bromsgrove, Repton, and Durham were reinvigorated, and completely new ones, like Marlborough, Rossall, Lancing, Brighton, Epsom, and Wellington were founded after 1837. The reasons for the sudden explosion in the number of public schools were the same in the case of one of the earliest of the new schools, Cheltenham, founded in 1840, as for the other schools listed above: the swift growth of a large middle and upper-middle class in Britain. An historian of Cheltenham's description of its background would serve for most of these schools:

> The difficulty experienced by gentlemen in the middle class of society, and even of a higher grade, in obtaining a superior education for their sons at a reasonable rate, had long been felt and acknowledged. . . . It was not every gentleman, although he might have enjoyed the privilege himself, who could afford to place his son at Eton or Harrow. It was also beginning to be thought that those celebrated seats of learning were not turning out such eminent scholars as heretofore, and that if ever they possessed exclusive advantages for imparting a sound classical education, the privilege was now shared by younger competitors . . . studies for the competitive examinations [i.e., the civil service] and for the army, were more or less neglected. . . .[60]

The English public schools would grow and flourish over the rest of the nineteenth century. By the 1870s and 1880s they were even beginning to develop their own peculiar ethos—the cult of "manliness"—which was particularly well suited to prepare boys for service to the Empire (a development which would have surprised and distressed Thomas Arnold and the educators of his generation). As Britain, now the most powerful nation in the world, entered the full tide of her Imperial glory, her example could not help but influence other nations. In particular, the style of life of the English upper class set the standards for the upper classes of France, Germany, Italy, and for rich Americans as well. Whether the export of nannies, tweeds, scotch, and fox hunting made any deep impact on other cultures is questionable. Nevertheless, in the United States in the late nineteenth century a cult of what Lord Bryce called "Anglomania" developed among many rich Americans. The British accent pervaded all areas of American high culture, from architecture to literature. It seemed to some—like George Edwards—that it pervaded American boarding schools as well. But so far as boarding schools were concerned, with one or two exceptions (which will be discussed below) the British accent remained just that—an accent. St. Paul's for instance, adopted the British locution "form" for an academic "class"; any other direct imitation of English practice is difficult to find.

St. Paul's first rector, Henry Augustus Coit, was well aware of the differences between St. Paul's and English schools. "Neither the great English public school nor the German gymnasium," he wrote in words startlingly reminiscent of George Bancroft, "would suit us here." An American school, Coit continued, could not be "an imitation however good, of what cannot be reproduced on this side of the Atlantic—a great English public school. We cannot have Rugby, or Eton, or Harrow here, if we would. . . . This is not saying that we are above learning from England, or Germany, or any other nation, what is best in its educational work, or that we are starting out for ourselves regardless of the rich harvests of the past."[61] Most American educators probably would have agreed. And, in Coit's particular past, the most familiar examples were Round Hill, the Flushing Institute, and the College of St. James.

Coit started out with very little in 1856. As Shattuck later remembered, he and the trustees told Coit: " 'You have possession of land and buildings, but we can not promise you a salary, and you must derive your support from the fees of the scholars.' " It was not much to begin with—uncertain finances and a lonely, isolated house. But the long, sometimes uncertain search by Shattuck and his trustees for the perfect schoolmaster proved to be completely justified. When Henry Coit died forty years later, in 1895, he was acclaimed a major force in American education, a sort of American version of Arnold of Rugby, the very pattern and epitome of the American headmaster of the Victorian age. "He has given to American teachers," the trustees of the Groton School, founded almost thirty years after St. Paul's, declared in formal resolutions, "especially those in Church schools, a great and noble ideal of their office. Through the influence of his leadership other schools have been founded, and to his memory Groton turns with deep gratitude."[62] Shattuck had laid the foundations; it was up to Coit to rear the superstructure. In doing so, he created in St. Paul's the perfect institutional embodiment of the Victorian educational ideal.

Chapter VI

Innocence and Isolation: St. Paul's and the Victorian Educational Ideal

"Applications were made for all available accommodations" at the new school from the beginning, Henry Coit's brother Joseph later recalled, "and the boys received in the first months, as well as those for whom places were sought, belonged to families of excellent social position, and the favor and approval of these families were elements of future success."[1] George Shattuck's fellow alumni from Round Hill responded enthusiastically to the opportunity to send their sons and grandsons to an Episcopalian Round Hill. We know, for instance, the family names of 291 Round Hill alumni. Of these, 136 came from the North—New England, New York, and Pennsylvania. Among them, they had 108 different family names (many were brothers or cousins). Fully 75 of these same family names, or almost 70 percent, would appear on St. Paul's alumni lists between 1856 and 1914. This proportion is too high to be ascribed to coincidence. Round Hill's alumni appear to have been more than nostalgic; like George Shattuck, they wanted their sons to be given the same type of education they had received. Cogswell, Bancroft, and Muhlenberg had securely fixed the family boarding academy as the ideal school for their sons in the minds of scores of rich Americans.

As early as June 1856, Bishop Chase wrote Shattuck that

though the country was in a "bad state"—agitated over "the Sumner outrage, and Kansas affairs"—things at St. Paul's were proceeding in a much happier manner. "I have lately made a visit to St. Paul's School," he reported, "and am able to assure your confidence in the most strong and unhesitating terms. If I am not greatly deceived, and am any judge whatever in such matters, we have reason to rejoice and bless God, that our choice fell on this gentleman. He is truly . . . a most accomplished man. After his fine taste and scholarship, I was delighted to observe his practical wisdom. No one could have supposed he had been a housekeeper but two months—so *au fait* was he in every part of the business and so judiciously thoughtful of the demands of all occasions. He had six boys and had engaged six more. The boys, dear fellows, were 'as happy as the day am long.' . . . It would do your heart good to look in on the establishment."[2]

Advertisements, placed in at least four Episcopal publications, did not seem to be needed. Despite the high tuition of $300 a year (which, as Bishop Chase protested, put the school out of reach of "men of moderate means"[3]) there were 12 boys at the school by June of 1856. Five years later the school had 48 boys and 4 masters, and, on its tenth anniversary in 1866, 73 boys and 8 masters. When Coit died in 1895, St. Paul's had a faculty of 36 and its student body had grown to 345.[4] Throughout these years one of the crucial factors differentiating the family boarding school from contemporary academies—a very low faculty-student ratio—was maintained. It was, for instance, 1:12 in 1856, 1:12 in 1861, 1:9 in 1866, 1:12½ in 1876, and 1:9 ½ in 1895.[5]

In its earliest years St. Paul's drew students largely from Massachusetts, but by 1867 the future pattern of the geographical distribution of its student body was clearly forecast. Of the 86 students at the school in the session of 1866–67 over one-third (29) came from New York State, slightly less than a quarter (18) came from Massachusetts, and about a fifth (14) from Pennsylvania. Over the years the proportion of students from the Middle Atlantic states would grow larger and larger. By the session of 1890–91, for instance, of a total enrollment of 304 over a third (102) were from New York, and of these half (52) were from New York City alone. The next largest contingents were the 46 students from Pennsylvania (half from Philadelphia), and the 35 students from Massachusetts (only 13 from Boston). After the first few years there were no students at all from Concord: Coit early sealed St. Paul's off from the world around it.[6] As Owen Wister, an early Philadelphia graduate of St. Paul's recalled, "New England influence was as absent from the precepts as fish balls from the cuisine."[7] St. Paul's, in other words, situated in pastoral, rural New England, quickly became a school for the sons of rich city dwellers of the Middle Atlantic states.

St. Paul's success was in no small measure due to the stream of gifts and funds George Shattuck showered upon the school in its early years. Some were comparatively modest, as when a teacher reported that "this morning were opened some boxes which Dr. Shattuck had purchased in Paris, containing specimens in Natural History. There were stuffed animals and birds and reptiles, entomological and geological specimens, Fossils and in fact almost everything desirable in a cabinet of Nat'l History."[8] His later contributions to the school were more substantial: in 1858 he built a wing on the original building, gave $12,000 for the building and furnishing of a school chapel and in 1859 gave the school a gymnasium and bowling alley. In 1860 he contributed $5,000 more for enlarging buildings.[9] By February of 1862 Coit could write to Shattuck that "owing to your past kindness and liberality, the school I think, with proper management will require no more pecuniary aid, but I trust as time goes on, your interest will not diminish in a work which will always owe much the larger part of any measure of success it may attain to yourself."[10] Shattuck's interest, however, increased rather than diminished. That August he gave the school over $20,000 worth of stock in various New England manufacturing concerns to finance scholarships and to make necessary additions. In 1868 he gave another $8,000 to enlarge the chapel—on whose capacity the size of the student body would depend—to accommodate 330 persons.[11]

Despite Shattuck's continuing help and interest in the school, St. Paul's was uniquely the creation of Henry Augustus Coit—of his experience, his ideals, and his personality. His success was early and widely recognized. In 1863 Columbia College awarded him an honorary doctorate (he was ever-afterwards "Dr. Coit"), in 1867 he was elected to—and declined—the presidency of Trinity College, and in 1871 he followed the same course when he was offered the presidency of Hobart College. "I often wish," the president of the fledgling Johns Hopkins University wrote him in 1876, "that I could have an opportunity to tell you what good words I hear of your school, in all parts of the land." And when in the 1870s George William Curtis and Edwin L. Godkin, editors respectively of the two house organs of well-to-do college-educated Americans of the later nineteenth century, the New York *Nation* and *Harper's Weekly,* asked to enroll their sons at St. Paul's, Coit could be sure indeed that St. Paul's was securely established.[12]

"Coit is a curious man," Phillips Brooks once commented to a graduate of St. Paul's, paying the extrovert's somewhat backhanded compliment to the introvert. "He came as straight from the twelfth century as John Brown from the Old Testament," a former student recalled. For almost forty years Henry Coit *was* St. Paul's School; his image was engraved so heavily on the minds of generations of students that twenty-five years after his death "he lived so deep in men of forty and fifty that his formidable shape would appear to them in their dreams."[13] Coit's success, one of his memorialists wrote, was based squarely on his belief "that the Christian religion, backed by home influences and the manly compulsions of physical sports, is all that is necessary for the proper training of the young."[14] All these comments give witness to Henry Coit's impact; none do him or his achievements justice. Coit was above all an American Victorian; he could have existed at no other time or place.

Coit was born in 1830, the first of the eight children of Joseph Howland Coit, an Episcopal clergyman. Throughout the seventeenth and eighteenth centuries the Coits had been a steady and sometimes prominent Connecticut family. Towards the end of the eighteenth century, Henry's grandfather, Levi Coit, like so many other New England youths of the time, migrated to New York City. There he prospered as a merchant and stockbroker and married Lydia Howland, daughter of a great merchant family of New England origin. Levi Coit's oldest son, Henry Augustus, followed in his father's footsteps and joined August Belmont in business. His younger son, Joseph Howland, after graduating from Columbia College entered Princeton Theological Seminary intending to become a Presbyterian minister. His studies led him instead into the Episcopal church. Henry Coit was raised in Plattsburgh, New York, where his father held a parish for most of his life. His conversion and commitment to a deep Christian faith occurred as a child, when, in a state of considerable agitation about his spiriual condition, he first received the sacred communion bread and wine from his father's hands.

Because Henry was the eldest, considerable attention was spent on his education. The already serious and reserved child was sent to Muhlenberg's Flushing Institute, where, peculiarly susceptible to the evangelical tone of the school because of his background and nature, he seems to have adopted Muhlenberg as a second father and model. "Dr. Muhlenberg is an evangelical high churchman," he wrote home. "I observed Wesley's Hymns on his table, and a good many works on Christian education, church music, and architecture on his shelves." Muhlenberg's role as the father of his school made a deep impact on the young Coit. "Dr. Muhlenberg's character is inestimable," he told his parents. "He sympathizes and enters into the boys' feelings."

Following in Muhlenberg's footsteps, after graduating from the Institute Coit attended the University of Pennsylvania. He spent a year as a tutor at Kerfoot's College of St. James and then returned to Philadelphia to "read" for the ministry with the Reverend Richard Newton. Again following Muhlenberg's career, Coit became a master in a parish school in Lancaster, Pennsylvania, until his ordination, after which he briefly assisted his father and then served as a missionary in upstate New York. The week before he took up his duties at Concord he married Mary Bowman Wheeler, daughter of a prominent Philadelphia family.[15]

Like so many Victorians, Henry Coit was an exceedingly odd and complex man. With Coit one always has the impression of tremendous tension, of a personality held together only by the utmost exercise of the will. But whatever storms raged within, Coit's exterior was bland to the point of diffidence. (As a young man his appearance was almost girlishly handsome; he bore a disconcerting resemblance to the young Rimbaud.) He was never truly at ease with adults, and seems to have felt secure only with children (though one has doubts even of this). "He was shy when he met parents," one of his students recalled, "few of them ever saw the true man at his full stature, as he was in the pulpit, or on Thursday evening in the schoolroom, or at times in his study, dealing with a difficult case."[16] Coit's shyness, in fact, had almost prevented him from being offered the rectorship of St. Paul's. Bishop Chase had described the first impression Coit made to Judge Huntington thus: "There is one thing I must regret in Mr. Coit . . . ," he had said. "That is a want of easy volubility in speech. It is sometimes painful to witness the difficulty with which he satisfies himself in regard to the precise words in which he shall express himself. But I shall hope, as he is yet a young man, he will get the better of this, as he becomes more familiar with his position." As Chase hoped, as soon as Coit was established within his own isolated domain at St. Paul's, the impediment vanished. "Mrs. Shattuck," Chase reported to Shattuck the following month, "will remember our conversation touching Mr. Coit's hesitation in speech—how we regretted it. Pray, tell her we would not think of it now. It is all gone—or, nothing is observable. I spent a day at . . . [St. Paul's] and unfailingly found him on all proper subjects animated, fluent, and very intelligent."[17]

Over the years, as the school grew Coit retreated into a curious kind of personal isolation. He seemed to be not simply unworldly, but almost other worldly. Faculty and students thought him "a man of another kind, a sort of angel."[18] To another alumnus he "seemed unaware of the United States, and the President, and all others in authority, save when the Episcopal service obliged him to pray for them on Sunday mornings."[19] Coit felt, as he once wrote an alumnus, that "the evil one and the sinful flesh are in wait on every side to drag us down."[20] He tried, not unsuccessfully, to banish both the flesh and the devil from himself and from his school.

Coit was not, of course, a saint. There were times when even his rigid self-control could break down. The offender would then feel a flash of wounding sarcasm. Coit could be provoked to an unreasonable degree by extremely unlikely incidents—particularly those involving the loss of self-control in others. ("To think of those delicate little features relaxed in drunkenness," he commented of a recent graduate's arrest on a collegiate drinking spree.[21]) One small boy at St. Paul's, for instance, received a hamper of food from home, gorged himself and vomited during the night. The next day Coit was heard by eavesdroppers delivering the following tirade: "You will pack your trunk immediately. The carriage has been ordered to take you to the train. Your parents are expecting you. *Dirty little pigs like you shall not stay at this school.*"[22] But such incidents were rare; if Coit demanded high standards of self-control in others, he maintained even higher ones himself.

Coit was well aware of his unique role as an institutionalized Victorian paterfamilias. "I sit there [in the school chapel] as a sort of embodiment of their [the students'] consciences," he once remarked.[23] And that was precisely his role at St. Paul's—he functioned as the superego of the institution. "The training of conscience," he said, "is the highest part of education."[24] Coit himself served as a model conscience for the students, and for not a few of the faculty members as well. It is no wonder that he was appearing in the dreams of alumni twenty-five years after his death. The conscience, however, was only one aspect of a particular character-type which St. Paul's was designed to produce. "The majority of right-minded parents," Coit wrote, "are more anxious that their boys should be gentlemen than scholars or successful businessmen."[25] The difficulty lay in determining just what it meant to be an American gentleman in the Victorian age.

Contemporaries were surer of what a gentleman was *not* than of what a gentleman was. The terms of the problem were stated well in 1874 in a novel written by another Episcopal clergyman, Robert Lowell. Older brother of James Russell Lowell, an alumnus of Round Hill, and sometime poet, Lowell served as the second rector of St. Mark's School founded in 1865 in Southborough, Massachusetts. *Anthony Brade,* his novel, was set at a thinly disguised school called "St. Bartholomew's" in the town of Eastham. The main theme of the novel concerned the qualities which went to compose the American gentleman. Only a few times in the novel, however, was the theme made explicit. One of those instances reads thus (a group of students are talking around a bonfire):

> "All boys are gentlemen, ain't they?" [Hutchins] asked; but, as objections were beginning of a sudden to rise from every side, he changed the form of his expression, and limited its generalization: "All *our* fellahs, I mean, of course. What do you say, Wilkins?" he said, appealing to the largish small boy, who was ready and waiting to speak.
>
> Here many hands poked the pieces of wood and brands together, and several mouths puffed up flames.

"To be sure, all Bartlemas fellows are gentlemen," said the boy who had been called upon, and whose features and complexion perhaps imperfectly satisfied Remsen's requirements; for he had a smooth skin and soft hair, if not the very expressive eyes which made part of Remsen's catalogue of gentlemenly qualities. "Every rich man's son's a gentleman, ain't he?" he asked a little doubtfully; for, in truth, the question was a deep-going one, and these boys were groping among the elements of things.

"Not without you give him an education, an' *make* a gentleman of him," said Tom Hutchins; "and not always then."

Remsen was inclined to go further than this:—

"I know they used to say that anybody couldn't be a gentleman if his father and grandfather wasn't one too." . . .

"*My* fathers and grandfathers," said Wilkins, glad of so large an audience, "were all gentlemen." This he said with much satisfaction, and with that kindliness, and that condescension, and that easiness to be propitiated, which mild people show who are secure in the enjoyment of a privilege which cannot be shared by others.

"Your father used to make real good clo'es, I know," said Hutchins; "but"—

"But he didn't make 'em himself: his men made 'em," said the scion of a noble stock. "He had ever so many men."

Wilkins' gentility was allowed to stand where he put it.[26]

"The five pillars of aristocracy," John Adams had written almost seventy years before, "are beauty, wealth, birth, genius, and virtue."[27] Lowell rejected most of these criteria as defining attributes of the ideal American gentleman: to be a gentleman did not depend upon beauty, upon birth, upon social status, or upon wealth. It might have something to do with education—but this was left unclear. Lowell demonstrated in the rest of the novel that to him true gentility depended upon the last of Adams's criteria —personal virtue. Henry Coit would have agreed wholeheartedly. The discipline of his ideal school, he wrote, "will be largely influenced by this idea: to deal with all the boys as if they were or were meant to be gentlemen. . . ."

> If it is almost a true definition of a gentleman that he is one who never inflicts pain, then we shall have our hands full in the endeavor to instill into our thoughtless, self-indulgent charge a delicate consideration for the feelings of others, the grace of invariable courtesy to women, the habits of self-forgetfulness, respect for age, regard for another's rights, and tender care for the feeble and helpless and for the brute creation. This is in our ideal. . . .[28]

For Coit the basic, central quality of the gentleman was that of honor—or of what we might call today integrity. In 1860 he published anonymously in *The Horae Scholasticae,* the school magazine, a brief sketch which gives some idea of the kind of school he was trying to create and of the ideal character type that school was meant to produce. The piece begins with heavy sarcasm at the expense of "Sneakum," a student who was "ventilating the peculiar sentiments which he had picked up at the Apollonian High School and Young America Finishing Seminary, from which seat of enlarged views and expeditious progress he had been transferred by some unhappy accident to the quiet, obscure and oldtime B . . . [St. Paul's?] School, with its master [Coit?] who believed in human-kind and boy-kind altogether too much to be an experienced teacher of the present generation." To this unfortunate scholar, steeped in a disdain for "honor" and a disrespect for authority, Coit juxtaposed his ideal schoolmaster—and his own hopes:

> [The master] had worked many hours of many days to prove in act as well as by word to those who were interested in the subject, that there might be a school, where mutual honor and the law of kindness should prevail, where a feeling of traditional loyalty towards the school itself, as time went on, might be formed, and live, and grow, to the permanent well-being of every one who should ever come to be a scholar there; where, on the one side, there should be no spying, no mean taking advantage of age or position, but perfect truth, and a hearty, ready sympathy in all the interests of the boys; and on the other side no slying, no time serving, no vulgar spirit of contempt and opposition to a rule so just and kind, but frank, straight-forward dealing, a common scorn for the

current tricks of school rooms, and a healthy and good tempered interest in all the concerns of the school.

What was the quality which the master hoped most to instill into his students at his ideal school?

> Honour, boys, . . . [Coit wrote,] honour boys, is not a Chameleon, with one phase for gentlemen in society, and another for men pursuing their ordinary business, and another for boys at school. The honour which you ought to show to one another here is just the same which you ought to show when you are full grown to your fellow men. Honour will be honour in the dealings with me here. Honour is real manliness, which is able to look every one full in the face; not from the possession of vulgar brass, but from a free conscience that has nothing to fear because there is nothing to hide. Honour is real manliness which scorns to do or say anything in a corner, or behind the bush, which it dare not come out with boldly before friends and parents. Honour is real manliness, for it has the courage to speak and to do as its better knowledge dictates, and the steadiness, when it has started on the right track, not to fall back because of a sneering tongue, nor to turn aside to listen and be trapped by a lying one. Honour, boys, I say again is real manliness, and that is the tone I want to establish here. It would soon banish [schoolboy] . . . tricks . . . , for it loves the light that its deeds may be made manifest and approved.[29]

Coit did not work in a vacuum; the means he used to educate the honorable man were drawn from tradition, his own experience, and George Shattuck's wishes. The ideal course for the development of the school in the future had been laid out by Shattuck in his deed of gift. "We are desirous," he had said, "of endowing a school of the highest class for boys, in which they may obtain an education which shall fit them either for college or business, including thorough intellectual training in the various branches of learning, gymnastic and manly exercises adapted to preserve health and strengthen the physical constitution, such aesthetic culture and accomplishments as shall tend to refine the manners and elevate the taste, together with careful moral and religious instruction." Thus, the general lines Coit was to work within were broadly sketched; once he had obtained the confidence of the founder and trustees, he was free to fill them in according to his own ideas. The statement itself would appear in the school's promotional literature for over forty years. It sums up well the ideal educational pattern for the American gentleman of the Victorian age—a thorough training of the faculties of the intellect, the body, and the spirit.[30]

With only one significant exception, the basic organization of St. Paul's was decidedly unoriginal. Coit simply reproduced in Concord what he had seen at Muhlenberg's Flushing Institute and Kerfoot's College of St. James. St. Paul's daily schedule, for instance, was the same variant of the Fellenbergian schedules used by Cogswell and Bancroft, Muhlenberg, and Kerfoot. In the summer months the students rose to a bell at five A.M., had prayers at 5:45 and breakfast at six. They studied from seven until 1:30 P.M. with a fifteen-minute recess at nine and a half-hour at eleven. Dinner was served at two, after which the afternoon was free for recreation. The boys had tea at 6:30 P.M., followed by a study hour from eight to nine. The hour of the various activities changed a bit over the years, but the proportion of time devoted to each remained much the same.[31] The boy at St. Paul's led a far more supervised and regulated existence than a student at almost any contemporary academy, where, aside from attendance at chapel and classes, he was left much to his own devices.

St. Paul's training of the student's intellect was traditional, rigorous, and unadventuresome. A schoolmaster of the early eighteenth century would not have found the curriculum much changed if he had visited St. Paul's in the 1870s. In subject matter and outline it was the old "classical" course of the Latin Grammar school and the academy; it still centered on Latin, Greek, and mathematics, though by the 1870s English, French, and history had been added to St. Paul's six-year course.[32] The program of instruction was narrow but thorough. Coit himself was a severe but excellent teacher, with the rare gift of awakening interest in even the dull student. "You have mastered that very well; how beautiful!" he would remark to one of his own students; or, "My dear, that is a poor showing; I am afraid Homer would not recognize his own thoughts. Are you not well to-day?"; or, "Sam, that is not like you; I am afraid that you have neglected this. Is not that so?"[33] Perhaps as a result of Coit's own fastidious use of language St. Paul's graduates were noted for their command of English.[34]

One of Shattuck's aims in establishing St. Paul's was to provide "an education which shall fit . . . [boys] either for college *or business.*"[35] It was business, *not* college, that most graduates entered on leaving St. Paul's until well into the 1870s. From 1856 to 1864 the annual *Statement* reads: "The full course of instruction is designed to . . . prepare for admission to an advanced class in our best colleges, or for entrance upon a business life." Although after 1864 the "business life" phrase was dropped from the *Statement,*[36] as late as 1868, when the school had almost eighty students, only five went on to college. Of these four went to Trinity and only one to Harvard, despite the strong Harvard connections of the founder and trustees. The Trinity bias was due to Coit; Trinity was the only Episcopalian, the only "safe" college in New England. Coit—not unlike his contemporaries at the Phillips Andover Academy—was deeply suspicious of that sink of "soul-destroying" Unitarianism, Harvard. His suspicions came gradually to be reciprocated in Boston, which goes far to explain the surprisingly small number of students from Boston and Massachusetts at St. Paul's over the years.[37] Shattuck was a physician; his concern for the students' health and physical development equalled, and sometimes exceeded, his interest in their intellectual growth. Coit, on the other hand, had an almost obsessive dislike of being reminded that human beings were made of anything so vulgar as flesh. Visiting the swimming hole with a faculty member, he remarked, "The human form is not beautiful, is it?"[38] He had little or no knowledge of sports. Happening on a vigorous football game one day, he looked at the tumbling players, strode out on the field with his cane held high and exclaimed, "Tut, tut! No more of this!" It was carefully explained to him that football involved a certain amount of roughness; Coit mounted his carriage and rode away in silence.[39]

Despite Coit's almost complete lack of personal interest in sports, he encouraged them and they flourished at St. Paul's. For the first fifteen or so years, however, they were of a rather sporadic, informal nature. There were skating and sledding in the winter, hound and hares and tennis and an early, informal version of football—rugby (modern football had not been invented)

—in milder weather. A typical winter day might find the "younger portion of the family vigorously engaged in kicking football. It requires a good deal of skill to perform that operation well now, for a badly aimed kick is likely to send the player on his face on the ice."[40] In the absence of organized sports, informal types of exercise, like the very popular dancing lessons or the many excursions to the few points of interest in the surrounding countryside, were organized. As at Round Hill, a certain happy air of innocence hangs over the students' extracurricular activities in these early years, as in this 1858 account of a typical outing:

> Today we had a grand sleighride to the Shaker Village at Canterbury [about fourteen miles from the school]. Started at 8½ A.M. arrived at 11¼. Were very kindly received and entertained. In the afternoon, though it was Saturday, their usual holiday, the Shaker school for boys was called together for us to visit. Their school for boys occupies only three months in the winter, that for girls the same period in summer. The boys showed quite a good deal of proficiency in the ordinary branches of study. At the close of their exercises they sang us two songs, and wished us a happy New Year, which compliment we returned. There were three "Families" at C[anterbury], containing in all about 300. We stopped with the first of which Dav'd Parker is Chief Trustee. This numbers about 150. Our dinner was very nice. Sister Mary treated us in the very best and most lady-like manner. Her prim yet courteous bearing, her venerable grey head, and benignant face will long be remembered. Before leaving the boys made a few purchases of little articles of Shaker manufacture, as curiosities. When the boys were seated in the sleighs before the door, they returned the compliments they had received by singing the Carol "Good King Wenceslas." Then, giving them three cheers, we departed exceedingly pleased with our visit. Arrived at Millville [St. Paul's] safely at 6 P.M. The boys sang nearly all the way home. It was a beautiful day.[41]

In St. Paul's early years the students spent a great deal of time gathering or observing natural objects—flowers, minerals, and so forth. Prizes were offered for the best collections, and hours were spent on excursions to the surrounding woods or on trips like the one to Canterbury. These activities were possibly a result of the application of romantic educators' insistence on the direct observation of nature as the key to learning, or of the Transcendentalist belief (shared by George Shattuck) that the study of nature would reveal the ultimate oneness and divinity of all things. However, by the 1870s organized exercise had replaced romantic, Transcendentalist nature study at St. Paul's. Cricket and rowing had become the major outdoor activities. The area around the school was dotted with goodsized ponds, and as early as 1857 the boys themselves ordered a boat and began rowing races. Coit, perhaps with memories of the popular boating activities at the Flushing Institute, encouraged the sport. Until the coming of a professional rowing coach in 1878 this activity was managed by the students.[42]

In 1859 the students organized themselves into two cricket clubs (baseball was as yet in its infancy), and this, with rowing, remained the major sport until the 1880s. After that it endured at St. Paul's not because of any particular Anglophilia, but because of Henry Coit's idiosyncratic notions of what constituted a "gentlemanly" sport. Cricket had been introduced to America in the eighteenth century by, among others, Benjamin Franklin. With the influx of workers from the English Midlands in the early nineteenth century it became particularly popular in Philadelphia, source of so many of St. Paul's faculty and students. "Some games . . . ," Coit wrote, "have better associations than others. In the writer's judgment and experience, cricket is the best game to encourage. . . . The educational results are better than of most other games in promoting those moral qualities which belong to a right notion of manliness." "Moral qualities" or not, after the 1880s cricket at St. Paul's survived the temptations of baseball only with the studied encouragement of Coit and the faculty.[43]

In the late 1880s and 1890s football and ice hockey (particularly well suited to St. Paul's frigid climate) became major sports, and by the early twentieth century, with the introduction of trained coaches, they had reached (as at other schools) an almost professional level of competence. Recalling Coit's excursions on the football field, his attitude towards highly competitive athletics can well be imagined. "Whatever the example set by some of our young collegians," Coit wrote in 1891, "the ideal school will hold in check this monopoly of youthful energy. There will be great caution in allowing contests with athletic clubs from other schools."[44] Coit's ambivalent attitude towards organized athletics appears to be related to an old educational concern—the use of emulation, or competition for excellence among students.

Between about 1820 and 1850 at Round Hill and the Flushing Institute, the use of emulation as an educational device had been strongly condemned. Cogswell and Bancroft felt that competition stultified the development of the *individual* student by leading him to study simply to satisfy others rather than for the sake of the subject itself. Muhlenberg had gone even further; there was a significant difference between his aims in condemning emulation and those of Bancroft and Cogswell. Competition, Muhlenberg thought, discouraged the *average* (rather than the "individual") student who happened not to be academically talented. Moreover, it seemed disruptive to the organic, familial tone he was trying to create at his school. In a way his condemnation of emulation was a negative response to the strenuous competition and social disintegration which characterized Jacksonian America. In the deferential, status-secure society of Federalist America individual excellence threatened no one. In the egalitarian society of Victorian America, the excellence of a particular individual threatened everyone.

"Emulation," significantly, was hardly mentioned in St. Paul's early literature. From the very beginning prizes were offered for many activities—in other words, competition was encouraged. Its acceptance, however, was a qualified one—and nowhere more clearly than in the case of organized athletics. Unlike unorganized athletics, team sports allowed educators and other Americans to mitigate the deleterious effects of individualistic competition. They offered their participants all the pleasures of competition—*plus* the pleasures and possible benefits of cooperation. They allowed schoolmen to contain at least partially the possibly disintegrating effects of liberal individualism.[45]

George Shattuck's claim that St. Paul's was a nonsectarian school should be heavily discounted. Before everything else Henry Coit was an Episcopal priest, and St. Paul's was an Episcopalian institution: we can trace his influence most clearly in the cultivation, formal and informal, of his students' moral and spiritual faculties. In the early decades of the school the religious tone—as at the Flushing Institute—was that of "a moderate and reasoned high-churchmanship."[46] Many of the masters in these years were studying for the ministry, and Coit himself directed the studies of several. Muhlenberg's spirit and example pervaded the whole school (his picture hung on the wall of the main schoolroom until well into the twentieth century).[47] The formal religious activities of the school were carried on with a somewhat elaborate ritual along the lines which Muhlenberg had developed at the Flushing Institute. From dawn to dusk the school was suffused with the Episcopalian variant of evangelical Victorian pietism. A typical Sunday at St. Paul's would perhaps give any boy more of a dose of formal religion than he might wish. At 7:30 Holy Communion was celebrated; at nine, Morning Prayers, lasting about an hour. From ten to 11:30 they returned to the Chapel for an hour's service at which Coit preached a sermon. After this service they had an hour during which they were permitted to relax by reading books on religious subjects from a special "Sunday Library." At 3:15 they again went to Chapel where one of the clergyman masters preached another sermon. At 4:15 classes in Sacred Studies began, with those for Fifth and Sixth Formers conducted by Coit himself. Sundays closed with the singing by the whole school of Muhlenberg's hymn, "Now the day is past and gone"—a sentiment, one might think, gratefully shared by most of the students.[48] Aside from the massive infusion of formal religion on Sundays, there were also daily Chapel services and a special "Thursday Night Talk" on religious subjects given by Coit.

Besides the formal program of religious services to bring about the religious conversion and commitment of his students, Coit, much as Muhlenberg had done at Flushing, employed an intense personal moral suasion of the individual student. "Nothing," a memorialist has written, "claimed more imperiously his energetic interest than each boy's attitude toward what he considered the greatest thing in the world."[49] Other Protestants might depend upon the revival's instant conversion; Episcopalians looked instead to ritual, organization, and private Christian nurture to bring about the same ends. "It may not be amiss to notice here," the keeper of St. Paul's "Rural Record" wrote in 1858, "the great *revival movement* that is going on through the country, especially in the cities. In the larger cities and in many of the smaller, 'Businessmen's Prayer Meetings' are held daily, and very fully attended. A great interest and excitement is awakened. Conversions are numerous. I cannot help thinking that the Church's way, the regular and regularly directed observance of Lent, is the best kind of a Revival, the most lasting and effective, where it is carried out as it should be."[50] At St. Paul's Coit "carried it out" as Episcopalians thought it should be; the yearly confirmation class lay closest to his heart. "Thorough in his training, penetrating in his intuitions, he prepared each boy [for conversion and commitment/confirmation], as if he were the only boy, and made him feel that the choice he was making was the most momentous step in his life."[51]

With a sensitive or unstable child such intense Victorian pietism and continuing emotional pressure to "convert" might well lead to unfortunate results—as it did with one student of the 1870s, John Jay Chapman. In his third year at St. Paul's Chapman's biographer describes him thus:

> Traveling to and from the school on sleeping-cars, the presence of other boys did not keep him from kneeling openly beside his berth to say his prayers as if he were at home. There were legends at Concord of a woodland shrine of his own to which he would repair for religious rites. A schoolmate recalls a habit, when they sat next to each other in a schoolroom for Latin study, of passing his hands over the textbook as if warming them at a fire on the theory that the language would enter his system through the pores.

On the eve of Chapman's admission to the confirmation class Coit finally had to write to Mrs. Chapman that her son had become "very morbidly conscientious," and that he should leave St. Paul's to "have his mind somewhat diverted from the incessant strain of study and duty which seems to exercise it here." The actual crisis came, his son recalled, when Chapman, "without any warning to the rest of the team, . . . knelt and prayed in front of the wicket on the cricket field." Perhaps, everything considered, a natural confusion at St. Paul's. The school, however, was designed to mold not simply Christians, but Christian *gentlemen;* such enthusiasm was carrying things too far, even for Henry Coit. Chapman completed the rest of his secondary education at home with private tutors.[52]

In spirit Coit was closer in many ways to the fulfillment of Puritan educational goals than Bancroft and Cogswell had ever been. Jonathan Edwards's hope that schools which would lead to children's "conviction and conversion, and being trained up in vital piety" might be founded in New England was being carried out not by his direct intellectual descendants, Unitarians and Congregationalists, but by those he would probably have abhorred in his lifetime, Episcopalians.[53] It was understandable. At lunch one day at Oxford in the common room of Oriel College, John Henry Newman had remarked to Muhlenberg " 'that as so many of our [American Episcopal] clergymen came over from the Dissenters he thought they might be likely to go further, *i.e.*, to Rome.' "[54] While not too many Americans followed Newman to Rome, his observation on the origin of American Episcopal clergymen was perceptive. As Jonathan Edwards's (very often lineal) descendants turned from Geneva to Canterbury, they brought much of the spirit of the Dissenting sects into the Protestant Episcopal church in America.

For all the pervasiveness of Christian nurture as carried on at St. Paul's, surprisingly few students turned to the ministry for their life's work. Of the 3,250 alumni living in 1915, for instance, only 60—or 1.9 percent—had become clergymen; not a low figure by any means, but considering the environment fewer than one might reasonably expect.[55] Like Muhlenberg,, Henry Coit discovered that the children of the rich did not make a fertile field for nurturing clergymen.

Muhlenberg, his biographer noted, "grudged giving himself so largely to the sons of the rich." At the Flushing Institute he tried to have at least one-tenth of the students on scholarships, "always youths supposed to show some fitness for the sacred ministry, or for teaching."[56] Henry Coit too regretted that the high tuition necessitated by a "family school" limited St. Paul's to the sons of the rich.[57] Like the Flushing Institute, St. Paul's offered scholarships to poor but worthy boys. Of the 1,872 boys who attended St. Paul's in its first thirty-four years, about 150—or roughly 7 percent—were on full or partial scholarships, representing a cost to the school of over $50,000.[58]

As at Fellenberg's Hofwyl, the children of the poor never could be far out of mind for the student at St. Paul's. In 1866 Coit established, on a hill overlooking the school, a home for orphans of those who had died in the Civil War, though other homeless children were admitted as well. It provided an excellent opportunity to instruct the pupils in the proper exercise of Christian charity. The home, one alumnus recalled, "was ever an object lesson, while the little tramp and shuffle into chapel on Sunday of the mixed company in all kinds of clothes never ceased to be more than interesting." Henry Coit supplied the orphans with spiritual food, and his students very often brought them a basket of groceries. Every Sunday evening students would pass through St. Paul's with a charity box calling out, "A penny for the orphans!" Coit's memorialist noted that "these pennies in a few years built a substantial fence about the whole nine-acre lot assigned to the home."[59] Society would be organic only up to a certain point.

Educating "the sons of wealthy inhabitants of large cities," boys "from families of excellent social position"—as George Shattuck and Joseph Coit described St. Paul's students—was a unique responsibility. Henry Coit himself was a man of severe simplicity in his style of life, and the school reflected this. His students were schooled rigorously in inconspicuous consumption. Like the students at Flushing, St. Paul's boys lived in cramped dormitories, each in a somewhat barren little curtained cubicle, under the close, continual supervision of a resident master.[60] Many alumni felt that the simplicity of their early years was a sustaining influence throughout their lives. An early graduate, the novelist F. Marion Crawford, once returned from his palace in Sorrento to say that "he had felt all through his life the benefit of his early training at St. Paul's in simple living."[61]

Coit would brook no interference in his school from the parents of his students. Far removed from the great urban centers and from the world of Victorian nouveau riche ostentation, Coit and St. Paul's upheld older, sterner values. "Some fashionable women have turned away from the study door with such feelings of wounded pride and disappointment as perhaps they have never known before," a faculty member wrote. "I remember once [Coit] reading aloud at masters' meeting a letter from some vulgar woman laying down the law, and signing herself 'Your patron.' There was no comment, but such a gleeful laugh at the end!"[62]

Coit's students, of course, did not spend all their time at the school; vacations were long, and Coit expected them to maintain St. Paul's standards while on holiday. Before recesses (Coit and his family summered in a simple cottage in Newport) he would address his students thus:

> Now you are all going for a period of rest; some will be traveling; and some will be running loose, I fear, in various summer resorts. I pray that every St. Paul's boy will remember that he is a gentleman; that he will not forget what we have tried to set before you here; that he will spend his holidays in healthy outdoor sport and helpful reading, in recreation of mind and body that will fit him for the renewal work in September. . . . this school does not stand for the hotel manners popular at the seaside; this school does not stand for turning night into day, nor for morning hours lolling in bed, nor for the desecration of the Lord's Day now becoming so common.

He advised the students to use their vacations to study for prize essays on "The Life and Character of Oliver Cromwell" and on "The Merchant of Venice."[63]

More than admonition, however, Coit relied on the Christian faith ingrained into his students in their early years to keep them on the straight path when they came into their majorities. Imagine, he suggested to his students in an 1889 sermon, one of your number fifty years from now, in 1939:

> He has had his share of what is called pleasure, social enjoyments and distinctions, gayeties and sights, and keen physical excitement, and gratification of the senses, ease and travel, books and pictures and art, the love and appreciation of which is in so many cases a mere sham and pretense. What comfort or relief comes from these delights, when the real storms break and the spirit is thrown back upon itself for peace and inward satisfaction? The richest of men comes to a moment when all that wealth can purchase is worthless to him . . . surely as men sow, they reap, and none can think that pleasures or riches or honors or any other earthly props will stand the sweep and pressure of Eternity.

Conventional, perhaps—but one can imagine few other congregations of schoolboys where Coit's words would be so appropriate. The riches of the world, even the comforts of Joseph Duveen, were but snares; the only sure rock was conversion and commitment to Christ. Like the poor, the children of the rich were but sinners in the hands of God, suspended briefly over the pit of Eternity.

Many Victorians held the sentimental, romantic notion that young people were somehow "innocent." At its most vulgar level, this belief was expressed well in a late-Victorian bestseller by Frances Hodgson Burnett, *Little Lord Fauntleroy* (1884), in which the unsullied, innocent, natural goodness of a little American boy (with the inestimable help of his mother, "Dearest") reforms the cold heart of his grandfather, a corrupt English nobleman. At St. Paul's one of Henry Coit's major objectives was to preserve such childhood innocence in his students. "It was the strength of innocence for which he strove in himself and in his boys," a graduate remembered, "the strength of God's Spirit, unmixed with the knowledge of evil." To the Victorians, such innocence was best preserved like one of their arrangements of dried flowers—under glass, in isolation. An ideal figure to the Victorians was the child who, like Little Eva, died young, saved from worldly corruption, innocence preserved. One of Henry Coit's favorite sermons, occasioned by the death of a student at the school, similarly described "the boy, newborn at baptism, brought up a child of God in the Christian home, always faithful to his parents, never knowing any other life but the growth in loving obedience." But most St. Paul's boys lived and eventually went out into the world. Then, as one alumnus remembered, "there was a great 'let down' when we came into the college world and stood alongside boys of eighteen or twenty who had been through most of the temptations of the world, the flesh, and the devil. We did not *know* as much as they; we were not so *strong?"*[64] To which, Henry Coit might have answered:

> My strength is as the strength of ten
> Because my heart is pure.

St. Paul's location and rigid scheduling and supervision assured the safe isolation of the students' innocence from the contaminations of the world and of experience. However, a system which worked well for a school of fifty or even eighty students exhibited certain drawbacks by the time of Henry Coit's death in the 1890s, when the student body numbered between three hundred and four hundred. On visiting St. Paul's in 1902 George Edwards, an admittedly hostile critic, found that "there is such an elaborate system of control that friendly sympathy between the boys and the men is nearly impossible. The evil that results is that they feel they are in the hands of a system."[65] The breakdown in the Victorian familial spirit of St. Paul's had become apparent as early as 1893, when a new master recorded in his diary that the school "is pleasant eno' but for one great drawback the constant vigilance one must exercise and feeling that the boys may not be treated as equals in one sense. 'Tis so nasty to catch a boy doing what he ought not. And so many little things are done which one wishes to correct and does not feel that he can because constant nagging is the result."[66] With the growth in the school's size, the Victorian educational ideal of gentle, familial Christian nurture had become difficult to maintain; its more repressive aspects had come to the fore. By the time of Henry Coit's death innocence was not being preserved at St. Paul's: it was being enforced.

Perhaps the most obvious early testimony to Shattuck's vision and Coit's success came in 1865 with the founding of St. Mark's School in Southborough, Massachusetts. "I think it not far from the truth," one of Shattuck's sons commented, "that the success of St. Paul's suggested to Mr. [Joseph] Burnett the foundation of St. Mark's. . . ."[67] The younger Shattuck was not far off; it was not simply St. Paul's success, but Henry Coit himself who suggested to Joseph Burnett that he begin a church school in Massachusetts.[68]

Joseph Burnett was a Southborough boy who left the small village in 1835 at the age of fifteen; eventually, in the tradition Horatio Alger, Jr. is supposed to represent, he made a fortune for himself as a manufacturer of chemicals in Boston. He married into an old Boston family, had twelve children, and in his home town constructed "Deerfoot," an elaborate country seat where he played the local squire. Like George Shattuck, he was a fervent convert to Episcopalianism and was responsible for establishing an Episcopal parish in Southborough in 1862. He sent his eldest son, Edward, to St. Paul's early in the 1860s. By the middle of that decade St. Paul's was becoming increasingly crowded; when Burnett entered another son, Harry—with two more still to come—Coit suggested that he start his own school.

Burnett proceeded quickly. He bought an old estate in Southborough and persuaded one of St. Paul's trustees, Judge Isaac Redfield, to serve as a trustee also for St. Mark's, along with Josiah Gardner Abbot, a prominent Boston lawyer and politician. The Massachusetts legislature swiftly incorporated the new school and the trustees met for the first time in Boston in April 1865. At this point a full board was elected, consisting mostly of Episcopal clergymen. Among the most important was Muhlenberg's old pupil and Coit's mentor, the Reverend John Barrett Kerfoot, then president of Trinity College. They lost little time in finding a man to run the proposed school; on September 4 Kerfoot's nephew, the Reverend John Kerfoot Lewis, who had been educated at the College and Grammar School of St. James, was elected as St. Mark's first headmaster.

In only one important respect did St. Mark's basic organization differ from that of St. Paul's. At the Flushing Institute Muhlenberg had integrated the old role of the college tutor with that of the Lancasterian monitor: an older "post-graduate" student, still very close in age to the formal students, lived with the students and supervised all their activities. While Kerfoot too apparently used this system at St. James, Henry Coit replaced the monitors with regular adult faculty members. At St. Mark's, however, Lewis and later headmasters retained the monitors. A school guide described them as "six or seven boys chosen from the sixth form who 'are the representatives of the school, have certain duties and a general oversight of the life of the boys. They are supposed to stand for the school ideals and to exert their influence and leadership in all school matters.' "[69] This system, adopted in many later American boarding schools, had both faults and advantages. The role of the monitor was identical to that of the prefect in the English public schools; the prefect system was the source of some of the worst abuses of the English schools. On the other hand, the monitors provided an invaluable bridge between the faculty and students, lessened some of the schools' authoritarian aspects, and contributed to their familial spirit. Considering Coit's general policies, his avoidance of the system was understandable; however, St. Paul's probably lost as much as it gained.

Lewis was but the first of a number of headmasters St. Mark's would have over its first three decades—Henry Coits were hard to come by. Although the school prospered and grew, its administration did not become stabilized until the Reverend William Greenough Thayer became headmaster in the 1890s. There was almost an apostolic succession in the founding of the schools: Muhlenberg, following Cogswell and Bancroft's Fellenbergian example, had founded the Flushing Institute; Kerfoot, educated by Muhlenberg, founded St. James; St. Paul's was founded by an alumnus of Round Hill and successfully established by an alumnus of Flushing; St. Mark's would have as its first rector an alumnus of St. James, as its second an alumnus of Round Hill. By 1871 the second rector, Robert T. S. Lowell, could use the appellation "family school," confident that it would be recognized immediately by his readers.[70] The family boarding school had become a familiar American institution. Judge Huntington's early hope that St. Paul's would become an inspiration for other similar schools was being fulfilled.

Beneath the conventional surface of the family boarding school of the 1890s, some unnoticed but surprising developments had occurred, closely related to contemporary changes in American colleges and universities. Two-thirds of Yale's freshman class in 1826 had been sixteen years of age and *under*, while by 1851 two-thirds of the freshman class were seventeen and *over*.[71] Insofar as Yale was representative (and it was the most influential college in the United States before the Civil War), over the course of the nineteenth century the age of the American collegian had been raised by about four years. It had not been unusual for Joseph Buckminster or George Bancroft to enter Harvard at thirteen; by the 1890s such an event would be worthy of special notice. Cogswell and Bancroft had expected their students to enter Round Hill at about the age of nine. However, when Henry Coit was asked, "At what age do you think a boy ought to go away to school?" he replied, "Oh, do not let him leave his mother till he is thirteen."[72] By the 1880s and 1890s the age of the boy at St. Paul's—a secondary school—was almost the same as the age of the average college student of sixty or seventy years earlier. The young person who—like George Bancroft—might very well have graduated from college at sixteen was now graduating at twenty-one or twenty-two. Over the course of the nineteenth century the period of dependency for young people had been lengthened by about four years. And the nineteenth century invented a special concept to describe this four- or five-year period—"adolescence," a period of life until then barely known to the human race. On the surface, at St. Paul's and schools like it the studies of this period appeared to be filled with the traditional academic curriculum. Actually by the 1880s St. Paul's curriculum was remarkably similar in content and level of difficulty to the *college* curriculum of the 1820s.[73] George Ticknor's hope of 1821 had been realized. Harvard had not been turned into a "well-disciplined high school"; by the 1880s it was a university, supplied with freshmen prepared by curricula at least as demanding as St. Paul's. Similar in curriculum, in the age of students, and in organization, by the end of the nineteenth century St. Paul's and similar schools were, in effect, perfected versions of the American college of the 1820s.*

St. Paul's and other family boarding schools fulfilled the hopes of antebellum educational reformers in yet another way. From the Anthologists on, American intellectuals had almost unanimously called for the liberal education of the American businessman. "We want intelligent merchants and manufacturers as well as lawyers and doctors," Muhlenberg had written in 1828. "Merchants, manufacturers, and farmers," the Yale Report of 1828 had declared, "take their places in our public councils. A thorough education ought therefore to be extended to all these classes."[74] This is precisely what St. Paul's, other schools like it, and some American colleges began to accomplish in the late

*Needless to say, the Victorian infantilization of young people did not stop in 1900. From the best of motives child labor laws were extended to cover more and more occupations and the permissible age of school-leaving was pushed higher and higher. By the middle of the twentieth century it would not be unusual to find graduate students well into their thirties—a prospect which doubtless would have appalled George Ticknor and other antebellum educational reformers. In the 1960s, when the revolt of young people against nineteenth-century dependency, regulation, and enforced isolation from meaningful roles in their societies finally came, it would be excruciatingly painful and confusing for everyone concerned. But that is another story; the material to describe it is as yet almost completely unexplored.

Victorian era. In the early nineteenth century most Americans who attended college intended to become, and did become, professionals. But by the end of the century the colleges were educating more and more businessmen.[75] Much the same change in occupational distribution took place among prep school alumni. In St. Paul's early years, for instance, about half its graduates entered the professions, while only a third became businessmen. However, by the early twentieth century, less than a fifth of St. Paul's alumni were entering the professions, while almost two-thirds were becoming businessmen. The following table gives a precise indication of this shift.

Occupational Distribution of St. Paul's Graduates, 1858–1905[76]

Total	Number	Percent Professions	Percent Business
1858–60	6	50.0	33.3
1861–65	15	46.7	33.4
1866–70	49	42.8	40.8
1871–75	72	43.0	40.2
1876–80	167	40.1	46.6
1881–85	273	36.2	53.1
1886–90	349	33.2	52.7
1891–95	388	34.0	56.4
1896–00	449	23.6	63.6
1901–05	432	23.4	63.4

The decline in the proportion of alumni entering the professions was gradual until the years 1896–1900, when it suddenly dropped from over one-third to less than one-quarter. These were also the years of most abrupt growth for business occupations. This, however, was only an intesification of a long-term trend. The same trend was apparent in American higher education. Compare, for instance, the occupations of St. Paul's alumni with those of Harvard and Yale graduates:

Occupational Distribution of St. Paul's, Harvard and Yale Alumni at Twenty-Year Intervals, 1861–1905[77]

	St. Paul's		*Harvard*		*Yale*	
	Prof	Bus	Prof	Bus	Prof	Bus
1861–65	46.7	33.4	56.7	22.4	56.4	27.7
1881–85	36.2	53.1	54.1	31.1	63.9	29.1
1901–05	23.4	63.4	47.2	32.3	48.2	42.9

Like St. Paul's, Harvard and Yale moved from educating a preponderance of future professionals to educating a significant number of future businessmen. Despite constant popular exhortations to make education more "practical," more immediately utilitarian, over the course of the nineteenth century the family boarding school—and many American colleges—met with extraordinary success in extending traditional liberal education to the children of the leaders of the American industrial revolution and in graduating several generations of liberally, rather than vocationally, educated business leaders.

This was not precisely what either George Shattuck or Henry Coit had intended to do. "The majority of right-minded parents," Coit had written, "are more anxious that their boys should be gentlemen than scholars or successful businessmen."[78] Although scholarship as an ideal—at least in the sense that the Federalists would have understood it—seems to have slipped by the wayside at St. Paul's, during Coit's regime more and more of the alumni became businessmen. Insofar as Coit was turning the "sons of wealthy inhabitants of large cities" into gentlemen, they were bourgeois gentlemen. Coit apparently had no notion of the role his graduates would actually play in American society. They would be polite to women, respect their elders, and practice individualistic Christian charity. [79]

Coit was hardly alone in his inability to bridge the gap between his cultural ideals and contemporary social reality. "Went to see Morse's telegraph," Coit's mentor Muhlenberg jotted down in his diary about 1843, "—wonderful invention. With

Democracy and the advancement of physical science, man will be Lord, instead of God. I see another antichrist than that of Rome."[80] Coit's life in a way was one long variation on this theme —a *cri de coeur* against the spirit of the "other" Victorian America, the America of egalitarianism and materialism, of "Apollonian High Schools" and "Young America Finishing Seminaries," of the spirit of "enlarged views" and "expeditious progress" which he had protested in 1860. Somewhere in the bustle of America, he hoped, there might be a place for the old, the settled, the ordered. Appropriately enough, in his last years he turned more and more for friendship and spiritual consolation to the Cowley Fathers, an Episcopalian monastic order.[81]

If Coit's thought—or lack of it—was representative of his time, the bourgeois Christian gentleman was largely irrelevant to Victorian America. An isolated individual, Coit created an isolated institution, which in turn produced gentlemen who were to play isolated—though honorable and Christian—roles in American society. Coit could not imagine a significant place for the gentlemen he had created in the greater world beyond the walls of his institution. By the 1870s Joseph Buckminster's 1809 expectation—in fact, demand—that the Christian gentleman and scholar play an active and vital part on the broad stage of American affairs must have seemed to many something of an historical curiosity. That "pernicious notion of equality" which Buckminster denounced had permeated all of American society; since the time of Andrew Jackson there had seemed (Boston possibly excepted) little place in American public life for the gentleman, natural or artificial. Henry Coit's Victorian insistence on isolated innocence, familial Christian nurture, and individualistic perfection might well produce an honorable man; but there was too the possibility that he might be educating successful and vigorous businessmen who, outside the sphere of their immediate private worlds, were simply indifferent to the wider concerns of American society. While the Victorians' conception of the gentleman and the way in which he might be created was still vital and attractive enough to create St. Paul's and similar schools, it was left to the Progressives to define a new role in American society for the gentleman, and to devise new means by which to educate him.

Part III Progressives

Chapter VII

The Emergence of the Prep School

"The grand educational want of America at this present time," President James McCosh of Princeton told the National Educational Association in 1873, "is a judiciously scattered body of secondary schools, to bring on our brighter youth from what has been so well commenced in the primary schools, and may be so well completed in the better colleges."[1] It was in some respects the same question which had concerned the Anthologists and the Harvard reformers fifty years before: the problem of assuring a steady supply of well-prepared students in order to maintain or raise an institution's standards. It would be a major preoccupation of leaders in higher education through the last three decades of the nineteenth century.

If often on an uncertain course, over the three decades after McCosh spoke the American university would develop into much its present form. Despite their pretensions, before the Civil War American universities had been at best little more than good academies with a professional school or so attached. But by the First World War they rivaled and sometimes surpassed the institutions they were modeled on, the German universities of the nineteenth century. The great universities were built under the direction of a new breed of American, the academic entrepreneur. The Carnegies, Rockefellers, and Morgans had their counterparts in the academic world in university presidents like Charles W. Eliot of Harvard, William Rainey Harper of Chicago, Daniel Coit Gilman of Johns Hopkins, Andrew D. White of Cornell, and many others. Their roles bore about as much relation to those of the antebellum college presidents as did the role of the great corporation builder to that of the antebellum mill owner. From collegiate beginnings—or in some cases, from nothing—they created institutions that resembled, in influence, personnel, variety of services, and sometimes wealth, the contemporary industrial corporation.[2] And, like the corporation president, the university president found it necessary to seek out new sources of supply for his operation.

McCosh, a Scottish philosopher who had assumed Princeton's presidency in 1868, scoured all Europe for educational models which might prove useful for the United States. Although the German system of secondary education was excellent, he thought it inappropriate to the United States. The "endowed schools of England"—or public schools—were also excellent."A first-class English School," McCosh said, "if it does not impart much general knowledge, contrives, by its open-air exercise and the manliness of its school-life, to prepare youths for acting their parts in this world, and the high studies have sharpened the intellects of many, and produced a refinement among a select few such as you will scarcely find in another country." The difficulty with the English system was that it was only for the "select few." In "the utter want of provisions made for giving a higher-class education to the children of the poor, there is no advanced country in the world so deficient as England." If the English system was inappropriate to the United States, so were the schools of Ireland and Scotland.[3] But the situation in the United States seemed almost desperate: "Wide regions, even in some of the most advanced states, are without not only a high school to give higher instruction to the middle and lower classes, but even without an academy." The country's "natural" gentlemen were going undiscovered; the Jeffersonian dream of "raking twenty geniuses from the rubble annually" was not being fulfilled:

> there is a vast amount of talent lost to the country, in bright boys, fitted to do good in the higher walks of life,—in literature, in science, in statesmanship or the church,—being obliged to devote their life to manual occupations. I hold that in the secondary school is the main means of calling forth talent in every country. It seizes the most promising boys of

the primary schools and sends them up to college, or into the higher walks of life, where they have the means of distinguishing themselves and benefiting their country.[4]

What was the solution? McCosh suggested first, as Jonathan Edwards had done over a hundred years before, that wealthy individuals endow academies. "It would be far more to his credit for a man to have his name associated with academies such as Exeter and Andover, than to be handed down to posterity as the founder of some weakling college, ever ready to die, called Smith's College, or Jones's Scientific Institute, or Robinson University." Such schools might help fill the gap, but they would be of necessity scattered and sporadic. Drawing upon the recent example of the Freedman's Bureau, McCosh recommended another method, what he called "state and city endowments." Schools could be set up all over the country, as in Germany, open to rich and poor alike, well organized and well supervised. What McCosh was proposing, essentially, was a thorough and broadened public high school system, the path the United States would take in succeeding decades.[5]

Others had dealt with the problem before, and others would afterwards, but McCosh's 1873 speech occasioned a long and somewhat heated debate in his audience.[6] The essential themes that emerged would occupy American educators for the next three decades: Should secondary education be publicly or privately supported? Should public high schools prepare students for college or be terminal institutions, or both? It would be better, said James Wickersham, superintendent of the Pennsylvania common schools, to "increase the number of high schools than of academies or seminaries—every town build up a high school . . . , so providing classical, mathematical and scientific instruction. This we have in hand now in Pennsylvania. If other states do the same, we do away with the old academies." An academy principal, the Reverend Charles Hammond of Monson, Massachusetts, objected. High schools belonged to the system of "popular education," and could not prepare boys for college as academies especially organized for the purpose could. "Not one boy in fifteen hundred ought to see the inside of college," he stated flatly. "What would a community be if everybody went to college? (Cheers.) Men are born into the world to get a living, and do their work, and act their destiny. That destiny is, not to go to college, except for a certain number." Joseph White, another Massachusetts man, challenged Hammond. Local high schools, he said, provided many boys with a college preparation who could never have received it at a distant and expensive academy.

President Charles William Eliot of Harvard made the lengthiest reply to McCosh's speech. The mass of the population, he declared, would not support tax-financed college preparatory schools. The work of the public high schools was to "train their pupils in English, in mathematics, in classics a little, up to their seventeenth year. A small per cent go to college. From academies almost all go to college." Towards McCosh's scheme for large-scale government aid to the public schools, Eliot had nothing but horrified scorn. One drop of aid would be:

> a drop of poison. It demoralizes us, and weakens the foundation of our liberty. It interferes with the carrying-out of our destiny—the breeding of a race of independent and self-reliant freemen. I hope no words will go out from this Association which can be held to sanction, in any way or shape, a request from the government for education. I know of no more mischievous, insidious enemy to a free republic than this habit of asking help in good works which we ought to attend to ourselves.

Eliot was both an American and a nineteenth-century liberal; McCosh, being neither, had no such fears of governmental aid. Eliot, McCosh replied, "said tradesmen object to paying money to educate the minister's son and the lawyer's son. But what *we* say is: You pay money to open schools to which your own son may go. We want schools such that there shall be no poor boy in the country who shall not have within a few miles of him such a school as will enable him to go on to the highest place."[7]

McCosh's view would in the long run prevail. Over the next five decades American secondary education was drastically reorganized to meet the needs of a new industrial society. In 1870, for instance, there were only about 80,000 students in the secondary schools of the United States, schools which were still mainly academies. The 16,000 secondary school graduates of

1870 made up only about 2 percent of all the seventeen year olds in the country. Most of these students went on to college. By 1910, however, there were over 1,100,000 secondary school students in the United States, around 15 percent of the fourteen to seventeen age group.[8] In the space of just forty years American secondary education had undergone a drastic reorganization, from the predominantly classical, elitist, semi-private academy to the mass clientele of the job-oriented, egalitarian public high school.

Historians of education have usually described the growth of American secondary education as a unilinear institutional development: from Latin Grammar school to academy to public high school.[9] It was in the years from about 1870 to 1920, they would say, that the public high school became the predominant institution for a secondary education in the United States. If one were thinking in terms of centuries, this picture would be adequate; but on closer examination American secondary education in these years presents no such simple picture: a careful survey of these years reveals a splintering and proliferation of various institutional forms rather than any simple unilinear development. As the structure of American society grew more complex, so did the structure of American secondary education.

In 1870 there were only about 500 public high schools in the United States.[10] In Massachusetts alone in 1876 there were still at least 57 secondary schools which the state board of education could classify as academies.[11] Despite the large number of academies, however, an astute observer might have forecast the future: in the same year at least 190 public high schools were in existence in Massachusetts, at least two-thirds of them offering the same type of "English" education as the academies, and, more important, about one-third a college preparatory course.[12] By 1895, 41 percent of students admitted to American colleges and universities (especially those of the Middle West) were prepared in public high schools.[13] By 1910 there were at least 10,000 public high schools in the country; only a little over 11 percent of secondary school students were being educated in private schools.[14] However, while clear in retrospect, for contemporaries the road to the comprehensive public high school was a long and complex one. It was in just these years—the years of the decline of the academy, the growth of the public high school, and the emergence of the modern university—that the private family boarding school showed its most rapid increase. Aside from Exeter, Andover, St. Paul's, and St. Mark's, most of the more prominent boarding schools were founded in this period. The Lawrenceville School was refounded in 1883, Groton in 1884, the Taft School in 1890, Hotchkiss in 1891, the Choate School and St. George's school in 1896, the Middlesex School in 1901; Deerfield was reorganized in 1903; and the Kent school was founded in 1906. There was, obviously, some connection between the successful founding of these schools, the decline of the academy, the rise of the public high school, and the emergence of the university.

The connection might be outlined briefly as follows. Until the Civil War American secondary education was largely oriented towards the colleges; academies offered terminal "English" courses, but their main interest was, as often as not, a college preparatory course. The colleges drew their students either from the academies, private proprietary schools, or their own college preparatory departments. The system was adequate to meet the requirements of the nation's relatively small groups of professionals and wealthy, to train them in the same way, to impart to them much the same body of knowledge that had formed the curriculum for gentlemanly education in the West since the Renaissance. However, with industrialization and the reorganization of society that it entailed, this system no longer proved adequate. An industrial society needed a large number of trained workers with technical skills for mechanical, clerical, sales, and other occupations. While the colleges responded by grafting the specialized training of the university to their traditional liberal arts course, or by doing away with the latter entirely, the academies were slowly strangled by the growth of the comprehensive public high school, whose goals diverged more and more in these years from producing a liberally educated man to producing a narrowly, technically trained citizen. The last stand of the traditional liberal educators was made by the National Educational Association's college-oriented Committee of Ten. Their 1893 Report on Secondary School Studies, as a recent critic has claimed, "would [have held] the child to a prolonged exposure and thorough mastering of the few subjects that a remote college decreed that he had to study"[15]; in other words, to the traditional ideal of the liberally educated man. A major setback to traditional liberal education in the public schools was signaled by the 1918 publication of the *Cardinal Principles of Secondary Education* by the National Educational Association's Commission on the Reorganization of Secondary Education. These principles were, in the above writer's words, "student-oriented, life-centered, and socially directed"[16]—an appropriate preparation for the anonymous worker in a mass society, devised by men who would soon be calling themselves "progressive."[17]

The decline of the academy in the last decades of the nineteenth century meant that there was no longer an institution specifically geared to prepare students for college. The public high school was as yet unproven; in fact, according to some contemporary critics, the whole public school system was an utter disaster. Most of its pupils were "unable to read intelligently, to spell correctly, to write legibly, to describe understandingly the geography of their own country, or to do anything that reasonably well-educated children should do with ease." Doubtless an extreme view, but it expresses well the attitude of many towards the public high school. The well off and well educated were often distressed by the heterogeneous nature of its student body and its increasingly egalitarian social goals. Above all, they appear to have been distressed by the public high school's low academic standards and sheer educational ineffectiveness. Part of this was due to the emergence of teaching as a profession and the subsequent bureaucratization of public education systems. The experience of Boston may serve as a model for other American cities. As Michael Katz has described the situation there, the withdrawal of lay reformers from concern with the public schools in the 1850s "had left school systems open to capture by the professionals, who, quickly seeing the advantages of bureaucracy, had acted with dispatch to build large, hierarchical, differentiated, uniform and rigid organizations, which, in the 1870s, a new generation of lay reformers suddenly discovered with horror." An acrimonious and debilitating conflict between lay reformers and the new professionals ensued. The reformers lost, and the day of the impersonal urban educational bureaucracy dawned.[18] By the 1880s many well-to-do college-educated Bostonians viewed the public high schools with disgust and sought alternative institutions for their sons. Many college and university leaders felt with President Eliot that public high schools were incapable of training many students to the level a first-rate university should require of its applicants. For a steady supply of well-prepared students they often turned instead to—in fact, actively encouraged the foundation of—family boarding schools.

Early in the 1890s, for instance, President Timothy Dwight and others concerned with securing well-prepared students for Yale managed—with a certain amount of what can only be called ruthlessness—to have the Hotchkiss School in Lakeville, Connecticut, established. In 1885 Benjamin Hotchkiss, a native of Salisbury, Connecticut, had died in Paris after accumulating a considerable fortune as a pioneer munitions manufacturer. Despite the fact that Hotchkiss had been in the process of divorcing her to marry his French mistress, his widow Maria searched about for a suitable memorial to her errant husband. Neighbors suggested a hospital; Maria herself wanted to macadamize every road in the township. Instead, even though she was said not to be "particularly fond of boys," she found herself endowing a school for them.

President Dwight and others concerned with Yale's welfare had heard of Maria's bumbling attempts at philanthropy, rushed to Lakeville, and by a bit of artful moral armtwisting persuaded her to endow a college preparatory school for boys. On reading the legal documents Maria was outraged. "I have no interest whatever in a school for the pampered sons of rich gentlemen," she reportedly declared. "If this is not to be a public school, with its facilities open to boys of all classes, I shall have nothing further to do with it!" However, she was mollified when perpetual free tuition for six boys from the area was assured.

With Maria's gifts of land and $200,000 in bonds—and a tuition of $600 a year—the Hotchkiss School (briefly called "Yale Junior") opened in October 1892. Its first headmaster, E. G. Coy, was brought from the Phillips Academy at Andover, where he had taught Greek for over twenty years. Andover had long been a Yale feeder-school, and Hotchkiss's traditions would be decisively shaped by the traditions of Andover and Yale.

Relations between the founder and the school were strained from the beginning. One of Maria's desires, the school's historians write, "was to make Hotchkiss a small high school serving the needs of the neighborhood. Mr. Coy, backed by the board members from New Haven and his faculty, was determined that

Hotchkiss should be a boarding school in the tradition of Andover, Exeter, and Groton, [actually quite dissimilar traditions], a school serving the nation." Maria's further support of the institution was grudging; she left it nothing in her will, and quite possibly on muddy spring days thought wistfully of macadamized roads. But President Dwight and Yale were well satisfied; of the thirty members of Hotchkiss's class of 1896, twenty-eight were preparing for New Haven.[19] Dwight had assured Yale for many years to come of at least one sure source of students prepared to its standards. If the $600 tuition meant that they were very often the sons of (comparatively) "rich gentlemen"—well, that was unfortunate, but at least they would have no difficulty paying the college tuition.

Some years earlier to the south, in New Jersey, another college president with much the same needs and ambitions as Dwight had followed a similar, though not quite so dramatic, course. Not long after assuming his post at Princeton, President McCosh found that one of the major problems facing him was in attracting a large enough number of properly prepared students to the college. When there was a slight decline in enrollments in 1872, he became seriously alarmed. What was the matter? It was the lack of "feeding schools" in the middle states. "In New England," he explained to his trustees, "the colleges draw the majority of their students from schools endowed by the States, or by the towns, or by private benevolence. We have no such schools in New Jersey, in Pennsylvania, in Maryland, in Delaware." A father in the middle states who wanted to prepare his son for Princeton would naturally be attracted to one of the famous New England schools, like Andover of Exeter. There were dangers for Princeton in this situation. "From the day the youth enters the school," McCosh said, "he hears of no other college but Harvard, of its professors, of its students, of its games and generally of its vast superiority over all other colleges. It would require more courage than can be expected of a boy to resist this influence, and in the nine cases out of ten the boy destined for Princeton goes to a New England college, where the religion of his father's household is entirely ignored."[20] Princeton's friends, McCosh advised, could do the college no higher service than to endow preparatory schools.[21]

Like Dwight, McCosh found a legacy. He was overjoyed when

the trustees of the estate of John C. Green, a long-time benefactor of Princeton, began plans in 1878 to purchase the old academy in nearby Lawrenceville and endow it as the Lawrenceville School. Though dead three years in 1878, Green would certainly have approved of what his legatees were doing with his immense fortune. He himself had given about $1,500,000 to Princeton (of which his great-great-great-grandfather, Jonathan Dickinson, had been first president, and his great-great-grand father, Caleb Smith, first instructor) in his lifetime, and would have taken particular satisfaction in the Lawrenceville plan.[22] Green was born near Lawrenceville, then the hamlet of Maidenhead, in 1800. In 1810 he went off to the new academy which had been chartered there only two years before. He left the academy at Maidenhead at sixteen for New York City, where he entered the firm of N. I. and G. Griswold, which was involved in the China trade. His career followed the usual Horatio Alger pattern—he married his employer's daughter and prospered. In 1833 he joined Russell and Company, the most influential American merchant house in the Far East, and increased his fortune by dealings in silks and opium. He returned to the United States in 1839 with what was an immense fortune for the time. He increased it through investments in banking and railroads; when he died in 1875, he was reported to be worth over $5,000,000. Green and his brother, Henry Woodhull Green, chief justice and later chancellor of New Jersey, were both trustees of Princeton College and the theological seminary there.[23]

Before his death Green had discussed the possibility of starting some sort of secondary school to assist Princeton. Knowing intimately Princeton's problems in securing adequately prepared students, his legatees decided to follow this course. In 1879 they bought the property of Green's old academy (now the Lawrenceville Classical and Commercial High School) for $25,000 from Samuel Hamill, the proprietor for almost forty years. Intending to transform it into a first-rate college preparatory school, they entirely obliterated the old academy. As an historian of Lawrenceville has written, "the change was complete and entire; it was a new school that came into existence on the John C. Green Foundation."[24] Not until after 1899, under its second headmaster, Simon J. McPherson, would the Lawrenceville School make any attempt to claim relationship to the older academy—and its possibly nostalgic and generous alumni.[25]

At first the legatees throught of doing little more than enlarging and strengthening the old academy. But, as time passed and their ideas matured, this plan faded entirely. The new Lawrenceville, in personnel, plant, government, and spirit, would owe nothing to the old. A group of trustees, all connected in some way with Princeton were brought together: the legatees, Dr. Hamill, Barker Gummere, a Trenton lawyer, the Reverend Charles A. Aiken of the Princeton Theological Seminary, and William M. Sloane, professor of history at Princeton. The trustees' first step, in the words of Professor Sloane, was "to seek the best headmaster where he could be found, with entire disregard of local prejudice."[26]

One of the trustees, Charles E. Green, went to President McCosh to inquire about a suitable man. McCosh recommended a fellow Scotsman, James Cameron Mackenzie, the thirty-year-old principal of the Harry Hillman Academy in Wilkes-Barre, Pennsylania, for the post.[27] Mackenzie was born in Aberdeen, Scotland, in 1852 and brought to Wilkes-Barre—an area where many Scots had settled—by his mother about 1858. Until he was twelve he had at most only one term of formal schooling. However, he became a clerk in the local bookstore and educated himself. Deciding to teach in the public schools, he entered the Bloomsbury State Normal School. This soon seemed inadequate; in 1870, at eighteen, he made his way to New Hampshire and entered the Phillips Exeter Academy, from which, with the help of scholarships and odd jobs, he managed to graduate in 1873. He then returned to Wilkes-Barre, took a job in a local private girls' school, and entered Lafayette College, from which he graduated, a member of Phi Beta Kappa and valedictorian, in 1878. He was asked to join the faculties of Grinnell and Columbia colleges, but instead stayed in Wilkes-Barre as head of the girls' academy. He received his Ph.D. from Lafayette in 1882 and in the same year was asked to come to Lawrenceville. The trustees felt that their headmaster, even if not an ordained minister, should have some theological training, so Mackenzie, besides making plans for the new school, spent the year 1882–83 taking courses at the theological seminary and teaching Latin and Greek.[28]

The Lawrenceville trustees appear to have been almost completely undecided about the exact type of school they were to found; they knew they wanted to establish a secondary school which would help Princeton, but that was all. "We have written to

Mr. McKenzie [*sic*]," one trustee informed another, "to come down and have a conference as to the best mode of conducting the school. Keeping school is out of my line."[29] Mackenzie himself was somewhat at a loss: "I am at considerable disadvantage in not knowing more of your purposes," he wrote the trustees as he attempted to make a comprehensive plan for the proposed school.[30] Nevertheless, in October 1882 he was able to report to the trustees that "after visiting, pursuant to your instructions, the leading and representative preparatory Schools of the United States, conferring with their faculties, after corresponding with prominent educators, and after mature reflection, I desire to submit for your consideration the following suggestions touching the plan of boarding boys and the number and style of buildings for the proposed School at Lawrenceville."[31] James Mackenzie's plan for Lawrenceville would be followed for over two decades in remarkable detail; more than anyone else he was responsible for the school that ultimately emerged from Princeton's needs and John C. Green's bequest.

Among the many schools Mackenzie visited before making his plans for Lawrenceville were St. Paul's, the Phillips Andover Academy, and his own secondary school, Phillips Exeter. He also discussed the proposed school with a number of college men. As far as academic work went, the picture Mackenzie pieced together from the various schools was gloomy:

> It is admitted by the heads of the "Great Schools" that none of them are doing what ought to be done in the preparatory work. Andover, Exeter, East Hampton, St. Paul's and Adams each deplore some marked inability by reason of defective appointment or deficient endowment. Each one had some *sub rosa* confession of shortcoming. In not one can a good preparation for a high standard Sc[ientific?] Sch[ool?] be had. In not one are the modern languages properly or ably taught tho' this fact is deeply deplored by the faculties. Natural Science fares no better. The same is true in England . . .[32]

The problem of academic standards, however, was relatively easy to solve: attract a good faculty by offering above-average salaries. More important to Mackenzie (most of his report is devoted to the subject) was the manner in which the students would live. State-supported juvenile reform schools excepted, his plan for this was, so far as I can discover, unique in the United States at the time. "I recommend," he told the trustees:

> the "separate home" plan of boarding. These homes should be built at convenient distances from a main school building; should be large enough to hold a teacher and his family and not more than 25 boys; and should be under the immediate care of the teacher and his wife to organize and maintain a marked home life and supervision. . . . There should be a dormitory for the more matured in character and those of limited means who could not pay the necessary charges of the homes.

Such a plan would have definite advantages; it would work best, Mackenzie advised (possibly thinking of his own impecunious youth):

> were it possible to appropriate a sum sufficiently large to aid those in need. Its adoption would contemplate, in our case, a uniformity in the price of board at the different homes and at the dormitory; and further, a distribution of the boys, not according to means to pay board, but according to class or residence in the place. This, if effected, would render the dormitory a place of honor, as only those who could be trusted would be permitted to live there. Every new boy would be put in a Home for the first year at least. During this time his teachers could reform him if he needed reforming, or dismiss him if he were incorrigible. Some parents would prefer residence in a Home during the entire school course; others would prefer the dormitory; while others still would prefer, and see advantage in, spending part of the time in one, and the rest of the time in the other, place. The dual plan of boarding would incorporate all that is excellent in any plan, and it has the immense advantage of adaptability to meet emergencies. A boy could be remanded to a Home, if he were found unworthy of the constructive confidence reposed him by placing him in the dormitory.[33]

Mackenzie went on to spell out exactly the details and problems of his plan: the difficulty to be anticipated in attracting a proper faculty, the precise rates of board, the buildings that should be constructed, and so forth. All the educators he had spoken to envied him the opportunity Lawrenceville presented, he said. "Excepting Dr. Coit," he reported, "I believe I am correct in saying all the prominent Schools of New England would adopt the above scheme were they where we are now. Each independently practically suggested what I herein proposed." Mackenzie had presented his plan; the future of the school now depended on what kind of an endowment the legatees would make. Mackenzie had not inquired on this subject earlier, he said,

> preferring rather that the matter should open upon us gradually and basing confidence upon gentlemen whose experience in the management of a great college has doubtless revealed the essential conditions of a school that shall do for the Middle States, and orthodox, education what Exeter and Andover have done and are doing for New England and "Go as You Please" education. We must be well endowed after the "plant" is paid for. Garfield was right in declaring that a great university for him would be a log cabin, a rude bench with Mark Hopkins on one end and himself on the other. But Mark Hopkins can be obtained and held only by liberal, "ample" endowments.[34]

The trustees eventually provided about $1,000,000 for the construction of the school (it was designed by Peabody and Stearns of Boston and its grounds were laid out by Frederick Law Olmsted) and $250,000 in endowment funds.[35] While Lawrenceville may have been the best-endowed school in the country at the time of its founding, the tuition was set at a very high level: $500, the same as St. Paul's at the time.[36] And, as at Round Hill or St. Paul's, a high tuition meant a preselected student body; only the well-to-do could afford to send their sons to Lawrenceville, though the trustees did make provisions for a certain number of scholarships.[37]

Mackenzie gathered together a distinguished faculty, probably the best of any secondary school of the time. Lawrenceville offered three four-year courses of study; a classical and a scientific, which would prepare boys for college or scientific school, and, in the style of the old academies, a terminal English course.[38] In 1893 the English course was dropped, and Lawrenceville became completely a college preparatory school. In 1904 another year was added to the course at the beginning, making Lawrenceville a five-year school.[39]

Members of the faculties of both Andover and Exeter had predicted to Mackenzie that there would be considerable pressure for admission once the school got under way.[40] They were correct: the new school opened in the fall of 1883 with 112 boys—only 12 of whom had been students at the old academy. The new buildings were completed in 1885; in that year 138 boys from eighteen states were enrolled. By 1894 there were over 300 students and a faculty of 16; by 1898, 362 students and a faculty of 22. By then the student-faculty ratio was down to about 13:1, which compared favorably with St. Paul's 8½:1 in the same year.[41]

A novel claim appeared in Lawrenceville's publicity releases and in contemporary newspaper reports on the school. "The Lawrenceville School is to be on the model of the English schools at Rugby and Eton," trustee Caleb Green told a New York *Tribune* reporter, "with such modifications as a careful study of the educational methods in vogue here may suggest." Lawrenceville would be "a combination that will include the best features of the American and English preparatory school systems," the New York *Sun* reported; it would incoprorate the best of "the famous schools of New England—Exeter, Andover, and St. Paul's—with the well known characteristics of England's best schools," said the New York *Evening Post.*[42] While George Shattuck had been impressed by the English schools twenty-five years earlier, Lawrenceville's conscious claim that it would be in part directly modeled after them introduced a new note to the history of the family boarding school—American Anglophilia.

A natural, and considerable, Anglophilia had always been present in the United States. To Joseph Buckminster Britain had been that "island of the blessed"; in the 1830s Francis Grund, a former teacher at Round Hill, noted that young Bostonians could still talk, as their grandfathers had done, of England as "home." A rising young American like Charles Sumner might feel on a visit to England in 1839 that "he was coming home—coming as it were, to his father's hearthstone."[43] Before the Civil War, however, American Anglophilia had been qualified by a defensive nationalism; during the war the attitude of the British government towards the Union weakened even the most fervent Anglophile's attraction to England. But by the 1870s—in fact, about the time of the Centennial Year of 1876—old antagonisms had been almost forgotten. The image of Imperial England and its culture began to pervade and shape the social and cultural aspirations of thousands of Americans. The reasons for late-Victorian and Progressive Anglophilia are complex and difficult to assess—among others, the resolution of important diplomatic conflicts, the growth of racist "Anglo-Saxon" thought, foreign immigration to the United States, and the search for a usable American past.[44] In any case, as we saw earlier, by the 1880s Lord Bryce detected a cult of what he called "Anglomania" in the United States.[45] Lawrenceville's claim to be modeled in part on the English public schools was in keeping with the spirit of the age. The difficulty lies in determining precisely which aspects of the English public schools Lawrenceville actually copied.

James Mackenzie's experience was limited to American schools; what he learned of English schools he learned through reading or conversation. The one element in his plan for Lawrenceville which no earlier American school appears to have used was his "separate home" plan of boarding—the planned grouping of twenty-five to thirty boys with a master and his family in a house owned by the institution. This was precisely the system which Edward Thring had introduced at English Uppingham some thirty years earlier.[46] Since no other variation from established American practice was introduced at Lawrenceville, one can only assume that this is what was meant by references to the "best features" of the English schools in Lawrenceville's early literature. However, Mackenzie's heavy emphasis on the school as a family or a home was in the direct tradition of nineteenth-century American educational thought. In some respects Lawrenceville was a revival of the spirit of Round Hill or the Flushing Institute, from which St. Paul's, with its large size, dormitory life, and over-routinization, had drifted away. Mackenzie's plan also restored in a formal, institutionalized manner the conditions of the earliest American academies, at which students—ideally—had boarded with and been regulated by selected families of the town. In a way, the Lawrenceville School was an artificially reconstituted late-eighteenth-century village, a little educational Utopia, carefully isolated from the great world, in which familial nurture could be carried on free from outside distractions and temptations.[47]

Recognition came to Mackenzie and the school he had created at Lawrenceville almost immediately. President Eliot of Harvard visited it in 1886 and (excepting bathing facilities) pronounced it good. By 1894 Nicholas Murray Butler of Columbia could recommend it to a foreign educator as "the best equipped of the endowed secondary schools of America."[48] President McCosh had more reason than anyone to be pleased. "The magnificent endowment at Lawrenceville," he told his trustees in 1884, "is the most important contribution that has been given to our college of late years." As early as 1886 he could report that twenty boys prepared at Lawrenceville had entered Princeton that year. As Dwight would do for Yale a few years later, McCosh had secured for Princeton a steady source of students prepared to its satisfaction.[49]

Although private northeastern universities actively encouraged the foundation of family boarding schools, they were by no means solely dependent upon these schools for students, nor did graduates of our original group of fourteen schools ever constitute a majority of their freshmen classes. For instance, in the 1870s Harvard—as it had done in the 1820s—drew the largest proportion of its students from private sources. However, *within* the private sector, over the succeeding decade the freshmen prepared at private *boarding* schools would show as a group the most rapid rate of increase, as the following table indicates (percentages have been rounded off):[50]

Preparation of Harvard Freshmen in Selected Years

	1826		*1874*		*1883*		*1884*	
	#	%	#	%	#	%	#	%
Public High & Latin Schools	11	*42*	60	*36*	77	*30*	76	*32*
Academies	11	*42*	33	*19*	72	*26*	57	*23*
Private Proprietary Day Schools	1	*4*	13	*6*	36	*13*	48	*15*
Private Boarding Schools	3	*11*	4	*2*	23	*8*	31	*12*
Individuals	1	*4*	52	*31*	46	*17*	31	*12*

Even though between 1874 and 1884 the number of students

prepared at private boarding schools increased by about 600 percent, they still amounted to only about 12 percent of the freshman class of 1884. (Note that academies are *not* counted as boarding schools.) Although comparable figures are lacking, at Yale the proportion of students drawn from private boarding schools seems to have grown at a more rapid pace than at Harvard over the years. By 1907, for example, almost 40 percent (85 of 219 students) of the Yale freshman class was drawn from nine of our fourteen schools, while only about 20 percent (45 of 219 students) came from public high schools. (The rest of the freshmen were drawn from at least 52 different, largely private day, schools in every part of the nation.)[51] Despite the rise of the public high school, in 1909 the better private universities of the Northeast were still drawing, as they always had, the majority of their students from private sources—78 percent at Princeton, 65 percent at Yale, and 47 percent at Harvard, as compared to 9 percent at the University of Michigan or 8 percent at the University of Wisconsin.[52] Within this private group, however, the *boarding* school contingent seems to have grown the most in proportion to those from other types of schools. And, with all due weight given to scholarships, because of the expensive tuitions most of the students from the private boarding schools would necessarily have to have been the sons of the rich.

Reliance on the family boarding schools for well-prepared students placed many northeastern universities in an awkward position and altered drastically the tone of a hitherto rather simple social milieu. At Harvard, her historian writes, "about 1890 the Episcopal Church schools, together with Milton Academy and one or two Boston private schools, secured the social leadership." Neither family, race, nor wealth counted as much as graduation from certain schools, he claims. What was important "for a Harvard student with social ambition [was] to enter from the 'right' sort of school and be popular there. . . ." Yale's historian has noted that at the turn of the century "a growing distinction between the well-to-do prep-school men and the rest" of the students began to be apparent in the college, as "the rich and socially ambitious all congregated in a private dormitory." Yale's western alumni began to complain that "the best preparatory schools were all in the East and only the rich could afford them." And at Princeton "around the turn of the century there came an increasing influx of boys of wealth from private preparatory schools, such as the Hill, Lawrenceville, Andover, Exeter, and St. Paul's. In less than a decade the proportion of Presbyterians among the undergraduates dropped from two-thirds to less than one half, the number of Episcopalians doubled, and President Patton was heard to boast that he was head of the finest country club in America."[53] Actually, it is unlikely that Patton called Princeton a *country* club. Few country clubs existed in his day; the country club was a suburban institution and would not begin to influence the colleges until the 1920s.[54] Patton is more likely to have called Princeton one of the finest *men's* clubs in America. In the 1880s and 1890s the future Ivy League colleges were beginning to reflect the social patterns of the "wealthy inhabitants of large cities," whose sons they were more and more attracting. And among these students' fathers the metropolitan gentleman's club was becoming a central institution.[55] That the sons should reproduce the fathers' social patterns when they reached college was hardly surprising.

As we saw earlier, an ever-increasing proportion of prep school and college graduates became businessmen in the decades after the Civil War.[56] Educational leaders of the period were as emphatic on the necessity of well-educated men in "banking, transportation, manufacturing, mining, large-scale farming, and engineering" as those of the preceding two generations had been. "A young man who is going into business had better take an academic course . . . if he has any mind to train," declared President Eliot of Harvard. "That is an indisputable proposition, and there is no use in discussing it."[57]

While eager and willing to provide for and to educate the natural aristocrat in any line of endeavor, American educators were decidedly ambivalent about the artificial aristocrat. But what of the heirs of the successful businessman? What role was left for the son? "Inherited wealth," said President Eliot, as befitted a nephew of Andrews Norton and George Ticknor, "is an unmitigated curse when divorced from culture."[58] The sons of the rich, then, must be educated. But no college should—or would—depend entirely upon such students. Harvard, President Eliot told a former Overseer, must "be open equally to men with much money, little money, or no money, provided they all have brains. I care no more than you for young men who have no capacity for an intellectual life. They are not fit subjects for a college, whether their parents have money or not. I am inclined to think that you [Charles Francis Adams, Jr.] would be more tolerant than I of the presence of stupid sons of the rich." Only the *intelligent* sons of the rich were to go to college, then. But where did this leave the family boarding schools, which Eliot and other college educators were assiduously encouraging, and which were sending more and more of their alumni to college? President Eliot, for one, was quite definite about their intellectual quality: "It seems to me to be a great disadvantage to St. Paul's School at Concord, or to the Groton School," he told Adams, "that it is, as a matter of fact, a school for none but rich men's sons. It is a disadvantage because a school so composed is sure to be a poorer school than one which is resorted to by a better class of boys. It is simply impossible for St. Paul's or Groton to maintain a high intellectual standard. It would be just so with Harvard College if it became exclusively the resort of rich men's sons."

Since he lent his support to Groton and was quite happy to accept at Harvard thirty-two of its first forty-one graduates, there seems at first something disingenuous about such remarks on Eliot's part.[59] Particularly since he went on to add that "at this moment graduates of the public schools do better in college than the graduates of the private and endowed schools; and they are well-nigh sure to do better in after life, simply because they have won more personal power of work."[60] But Eliot was not being hypocritical; it was just that his liberalism, acquired in the mid-nineteenth century, was inadequate to encompass the changes that occurred in American society in the four or five decades before 1904. To Eliot the best society was the open society, in which all careers were open to the youth of talent and industry. Harvard existed in large measure to transform these natural aristocrats into gentlemen. But this did not mean that Harvard should ignore the artificial aristocrats. Since they started with several strikes against them, they, perhaps even more than the natural aristocrats, needed to be educated. In large part Eliot's uneasiness and inconsistency was inspired by the fact that there were simply so many *more* "rich men's sons" than there had been in his youth, and that so many of them seemed to want to go to Harvard.

Like all revolutions, the industrial revolution in America

brought power and wealth to new men. While there were not twenty millionaires in the United States in the 1840s, by 1892 there were over 4,000.[61] This was not an overnight development, but had begun with industrialization itself; a new artificial aristocracy of wealth had been apparent in cities like New York since the 1830s.[62] As early as 1853 in his *Potiphar Papers* the editor George William Curtis had satirized the ostentatious and awkward attempts of the Fifth Avenue *nouveaux riches* to create a viable style of life for themselves. The young gentleman who had lived at Brook Farm, sat at Emerson's feet, and helped Thoreau build his shelter at Walden, was to feel all his life that "to scale society is only to climb a golden stair. The more gold, the more distinction."[63] The Civil War accelerated the accumulation of larger and larger fortunes in the hands of more and more families. "There was a great increase in ostentation of life in the city," the publisher George Haven Putnam wrote of New York just after the war, "and there came into existence a division of society that could be called plutocratic." Putnam expressed well the feelings of men of established, modest wealth towards the newly rich of the 1860s. Inflation, he thought, had given people with fixed incomes a

> much smaller return in purchasing power or in securing the necessities of life, that for all practical purposes [their] income was seriously curtailed. Through the change in currency values, thousands of retired merchants, women, and others, no longer able to take advantage of business opportunities, were reduced to comparative poverty. These were the people who had constituted a large portion of the book-buying community. The *nouveaux riches,* who had made money out of shady contracts or through speculations in pork could not easily be reached by the publishers of standard literature.[64]

Though hardly illiterate, in the scale of their fortunes and scope of their operations men like Jay Gould, John D. Rockefeller, Cornelius Vanderbilt, or Leland Stanford did constitute a new element on the American scene. The style of life of the newly rich of late-Victorian America particularly grated on the sensibilities of men of established position. "When Americans who have become rich by trade or speculation," said one alumnus of the Flushing Institute in the 1880s, "assume the position, and effect, to the best of their blundering ability, the customs of an aristocratic class, it must be with utter lack of both memory and common sense."[65] Historians have agreed with such judgments. Why, one has asked, "did the business leaders from San Francisco to Bar Harbor have to live in their houses with libraries, billiard rooms, art galleries, several rooms in which to eat, at least one of which had to be two stories high and paneled to the ceiling, buildings sometimes equipped with small theatres and perhaps even a chapel capable of holding a considerable congregation?"[66] The answers are varied and complex (it was certainly more satisfying than sitting in a cottage and playing with one's money), but at least one was the wish to prove oneself a true gentleman. After all, it had been an American tradition, from Westover and Mt. Vernon on, to assert one's status in a great house. And, English nobles had great houses; should not their American counterparts have them too? The newly rich of late-Victorian and Progressive America showed a lack of neither memory nor of common sense.

One thing at least seemed clear to contemporaries: natural or artificial, America now possessed an aristocracy. "However democratic a nation may be in spirit and character," the popular English author Thomas Hughes told Americans in 1879, "and in its political and social constitution and organization, the time must come when it will breed a gentry, leisure class, aristocracy, call it by what name you will. . . ."[67] The United States, Hughes thought, had now reached that stage. For many educated Americans of established position the question was whether or not American aristocrats also constituted a class of Christian gentlemen and scholars. One contemporary, Frederick Law Olmsted—journalist, landscape architect, and executive secretary of the influential United States Sanitary Commission during the Civil War—thought that they might. Like Joseph Buckminster fifty years before, he had a scheme for uniting wealth, virtue, and intelligence. In Olmsted's case it was the Union League Club of New York, which he hoped to see become "a club of true American aristocracy, the legitimate descendents and armsbearers of the old dukes of our land; of our law-givers, [Union] loyalists. . . . We wish also to establish the fact that there is an 'aristocratic class' in New York, which in this respect is not European."

Olmsted suggested three distinct types of members to achieve the club's immediate aims during wartime and to continue its existence during peacetime. The first group, or hard core of the organization, should be the men described above, New Yorkers of colonial stock, "who had by character and ability risen to social, professional, and commercial eminence." The second group was to be composed of intellectuals, mainly artists and scientists, while for its third segment the club was to scour the city for promising younger men, "especially those rich young men of whom I see so many now who don't know what their place is in American society."[68] To others, however, it seemed important to catch all "those rich young men" even younger in order to transform them into a true American aristocracy. Thomas Hughes had a suggestion: why not introduce a system of boarding schools like the great public schools of England? After all, Hughes continued, "in the case of nations of the same race, and so nearly identical in character and habits as the people of the United States and the English, it may reasonably be assumed that a system which has borne such fruits in the one is at least worth the careful examination of the other."[69]

Immediate and vigorous exception was taken to Hughes's suggestion. The English public schools, one educational journal replied, "were good schools for the sons of the wealthy alone." It could not "assent to Mr. Hughes's belief either in the 'inevitable growth' in America of an exclusive aristocratic order, nor in the impossibility of so improving our common-school system as to render it 'thoroughly satisfactory' to all reasonable and patriotic persons, citizens of a republic, not of a monarchy."[70] Although neither Hughes nor his critics seemed to be aware of them, in St. Paul's and St. Mark's such schools already existed; through Round Hill, the Flushing Institute, and St. James's, thousands of well-to-do and well-educated Americans were already familiar with them. While hardly opposed to the improvement of the common-school system, such families were not willing to trust their sons to them. Who were these families?

St.. Paul's founder, George Shattuck, had married Anne Henrietta Brune of Baltimore, the sister of two of his schoolmates at Round Hill. The marriage linked Shattuck and his descendants with the Brunes of Baltimore, the newly rich Morisons of New England, and with a branch of the Eliot family. But the intermarriages of the Boston Brahmins are perhaps too familiar.[71] Consider the family connections of another Round Hill alumnus, Samuel Ward III of New York. On his banker-father's side Sam Ward was descended from various governors of Rhode Island; on his mother's side—Julia Rush Cutler—from Francis Marion, the South Carolina "Swamp Fox" of revolutionary fame, and from Benjamin Rush of Philadelphia, a signer of the Declaration of Independence. One of Sam's sisters married the American sculptor Thomas Crawford; another (Julia Ward) married the famous humanitarian Samuel Gridley Howe. Intellectually brilliant, socially charming, and financially unstable, Sam himself married Emily Astor, daughter of William Astor, a son of John Jacob I. Through Emily's mother the marriage tied Sam to the Livingstons and other old Knickerbocker families of New York. Various other connections linked Ward to scores of families from Georgia to Maine, from New York to San Francisco; he could travel from city to city and stay only with cousins. Sam Ward's situation was not unique.[72] By the 1870s ties of blood united scores of wealthy American families, particularly in the older urban centers of the East. A touch in Savannah on one strand of this web of kinship could cause vibrations in Philadelphia, New York, Baltimore, Boston, and other cities. Although the great industrial and financial fortunes of the late nineteenth century dwarfed those of Federalist and early-Victorian America, when newly wealthy Americans of the postbellum years looked for models for an appropriate style of life, they naturally referred first to the longer-established families—and only later to foreign models.[73] Thus, it was only natural that Sam Ward's Savannah cousin Ward McAllister should assist Sam's (comparatively) newly rich in-law, Mrs. William Astor, in her social wars. On a frivolous level, this was precisely the sort of union Frederick Law Olmsted urged for the membership of the Union League Club. And it was only natural that Round Hill's Sam Ward should see two of his nephews, John Jacob Astor II and F. Marion Crawford, attend St. Paul's School. The family boarding school was well established among the rich of antebellum America. Its expansion in the postwar years was due in some measure to the adoption by the newly rich of long-established styles of life and social and cultural goals. Such social adaptation also accounts to some degree for the increase in the number of rich students at northeastern universities in the same period. Higher education was valued not only for its own sake but as a status indicator for those who often cared little for its content. It is no wonder that educational leaders such as Eliot felt ambivalent about the family boarding schools and the students they were drawing from them.

There was more to the proliferation of family boarding schools after 1880 than the needs of the universities, traditional respect for education, status striving, or the adoption of older styles of life by the newly rich. In the two decades after the Civil War urbanization for the first time became a controlling factor in American life.[74] Americans had always felt ambivalent about their cities. Across the continent they founded and promoted city after city. At Harvard the moral philosopher Francis Bowen taught his students that "cities and towns are the great agents and tokens of the increase of national opulence and the progress of civilization."[75] But from the founding of Yale in 1701 to avoid the temptations of wicked Boston, to Thomas Jefferson's animadversions on urban corruptions, to Nathaniel Hawthorne's recommendation that cities be purified by periodically burning them to the ground, suspicion of and abhorrence towards the city had been an equally familiar theme.[76] In the 1870s and 1880s the negative aspects of the city seemed dominant to many Americans. The industrial city attracted not only native American workers from rural areas but millions of immigrants from southern and eastern Europe. The rural American blended fairly easily into the population; the most conspicuous city-dweller of late-Victorian and Progressive America was the foreigner. In some cities, he actually outnumbered the native Americans; for instance, in Chicago in 1890 the foreign-born population alone almost outnumbered the *entire* population of 1880. A native American such as Henry Adams was hardly alone in his feelings when he wrote that: "Not a Polish Jew fresh from Warsaw or Cracow, not a furtive Yacoob or Ysaac still reeking of the Ghetto, snarling a weird Yiddish to the officers of the customs—but had a keener instinct, an intenser energy, and a freer hand than he —American of Americans, with heaven knew how many Puritans and Patriots behind him, and an education that had cost a civil war."[77] By 1880 scores of native-born Americans would have heartily agreed with the New Yorker who wrote that whole areas of his city had become "so degraded that hardly a Republican will reside there."[78] In the light of such attitudes it would hardly be surprising that a 1903 survey of family boarding schools would state quite bluntly that they were being founded in part because of parents' feelings that "in certain localities the companions of the boy in all but the higher grades of day school are, from their nationality, objectionable personal habits, or what not, undesirable."[79]

It was the day too of the scandals of the Grant administration, of the corruption of innumerable city governments such as New York's under Boss Tweed. The new political machines were based in large measure on the immigrant vote, which was secured by providing special favors in a time before organized social welfare agencies had developed. Boss Tweed himself distributed $50,000 to the poor of his own ward on Christmas day of 1870, and gave $1,000 to each of his aldermen to buy coal for the needy. He could well afford it: in 1870 alone the Tweed Ring pulled in a million dollars a month from graft on New York's public works program.[80]

The effects of such corruption on public education were widespread and so strong that in 1874 a committee of the National Educational Association reported that a major drawback of the public schools was "one which afflicts our whole system of state schools. It is the interference of gutter politicians with these matters, about which they know nothing at all. Pandering to the prejudices of the rabble, for the sake of votes, they perpetually criticize and quarrel with every effort to elevate our schools, and so annoy able and sensitive teachers that they are driven out of the field and it is then confined to such incompetent hands that its course of study must be lowered or they cannot teach it."[81] It was little wonder that many parents refused to entrust their sons to the public schools.

By the end of the 1880s deteriorating urban conditions and rising tax rates, partially the result of political corruption based on the immigrant vote, had become so widespread that an acute British visitor, James Bryce, noted that "there is a strong tendency for rich men to migrate from the city to its suburbs in order to escape the city collector."[82] This movement of the well-to-do to the suburbs was particularly strong between 1870 and 1900, the years in which the majority of our fourteen schools were founded. What was happening to the Boston area was probably typical of many other contemporary American cities. As Boston expanded, Sam Warner has discovered, "the settlement line of the wealthy was always the farthest out from the center of the city, the largest in area, and the smallest in number of people." Before he was imprisoned, even Boss Tweed of New York established himself on a huge country estate in Greenwich, Connecticut. In these protosuburban areas "farming still went on and old villages remained, but sizable quantities of land were taken up by the wealthy either for estates or as streets of large suburban homes."[83] And, of course, the new suburbanite or estate-dweller had the same need to educate his children as the earlier farmer had had. Theodore Sizer has observed that with the growth of the city in the 1880s "the academy failed because it was fundamentally a rural institution, a school uniquely appropriate for a population thinly spread."[84] But a region of estates or of scattered suburban streets could not support a high school, public *or* private. Thomas Hughes offered suburban parents a solution. "However good your common-school system may be," he wrote, "you cannot have a thoroughly satisfactory school, so far as instruction is concerned, except in great centers of population; . . . [and] a large portion of the class in question [the rich] live too far from the great centers to make use of the best common schools, without sending their boys for long periods from under their own roofs. Some system of boarding schools, therefore, must be established. . . ."[85]

It was. Family boarding schools multiplied, their ranks joined by old academies which survived by transforming themselves into boarding schools. The same impulse which had sent so many urban children to Round Hill in the 1820s intensified tenfold in the 1880s. In 1884 the founders of the Groton School would state frankly that one of their motives was the "rapid growth of large cities."[86] In the 1880s many well-established urban private day schools found, like Boston's Noble's Classical School, that parents "were beginning to send their sons away to such boarding schools as St. Paul's, St. Mark's, and Groton."[87] The successful private day school would be careful to point out that it was situated, like one Philadelphia school, in "a central position in one of the best sections of the city, and . . . at the same time, removed from the undesirable surroundings and associations of the business centres."[88] But the family boarding schools flourished, meeting the needs of the new suburbanites as well as those of their well-to-do cousins who remained in a "silk-stocking" district of the politically corrupt city. They were country schools which were as much, paradoxically, the product of the growth of the industrial city and immigration as were the bureaucratic and rigid urban public high schools.

By the time of America's entry into World War I the fourteen schools listed in our introduction as the core group of prep schools were well-established and familiar American institutions, representative of a far larger group of schools. They were very expensive schools. In 1916 seven of them charged an average tuition of about $950 a year. Altogether, in the same year thirteen of them had a combined enrollment of 3,540 students and a total faculty of 320, for a student-faculty ratio of about 11:1. In 1915 eight of the schools had sent 449 students on to college. The largest was the Phillips Academy at Andover, with 562 students; the smallest was the Middlesex School, with 123 students.[89] On the basis of their history and traditions, they could be roughly divided into three groups. In the first were the direct descendants of the eighteenth-century academies—Andover, Exeter, and Deerfield. These schools were comparatively inexpensive, drew their students from a broader social spectrum, and imposed a less Victorian regimen than did the others. In the second group were the Episcopalian church schools—St. Paul's, St. Mark's, Groton, St. George's, and Kent. Generally, they drew their students from a rather restricted clientele of rich urban families, imposed an almost obsessively minute regulation on the life of their students, and had in common, naturally, a heavily religious orientation. In the last group were the nondenominational boarding schools—Lawrenceville, Hill, Choate, Taft, Hotchkiss, and Middlesex. They drew their students from much the same group as the Episcopalian schools and consciously attempted to strike a balance between the freedom of the academies and the heavily paternalistic discipline of the church schools. In 1916 all the schools had two objectives of equal, though often conflicting, importance: to prepare their students for entrance to college and to build character. To a greater or lesser degree they all believed that the best institution through which to fulfill these aims was the family boarding school.

By 1916 their image, for better or worse, would be fixed for the greater part of the twentieth century: the son of a St. Paul's rector of 1916 summed up the commonly held picture well. He described the schools as "self-sufficient and insular communit[ies], providing for [their] rather narrow clintele just what was expected—a conservative, gentlemanly preparation of body and mind for the Ivy League Colleges and for support of the economic, political and religious status quo."[90] So far as this picture goes, it is accurate. But it does not go far enough.

The family boarding schools of the 1880s and 1890s were founded in response to many motives, and would be shaped by a complex of often conflicting ideological and social traditions and pressures: among others, by a reaction against the rigidity of the emerging urban school bureaucracies, by the admission standards of the new universities, by the needs and aspirations of the urban and suburban rich, by much the same Victorian notions of childhood innocence and isolation as had molded St. Paul's and St. Mark's, and, not the least, by many parents' undefined hope that they provided the "best" education available for their sons.

The emergence of the private boarding school in significant number at the end of the nineteenth century was only one indication of an increasingly complex society. As the American public school system developed, it would be tied to the seemingly egalitarian neighborhood school concept, a concept which has often masked the reality of American education. Lawrence Cremin, however, has suggested that "the common school in its classic form was essentially a northern and western phenomenon and that it reached its apotheosis in rural and small-town America west of the Alleghenies. It thrived best where there was already a reasonable homogeneity of race, class, and religion, and where communities were not so large as to permit the development of substantially dissimilar ghettos. Wherever social or physical instances did become great, as in the South or in the larger cities, the public school tended to be less 'common.' "[91] In other words, almost from the beginning there has been a built-in social and economic segregation in urban American public schools. The private preparatory school was but one manifestation of an America that was becoming more socially and culturally pluralistic.[92]

❧ Chapter VIII

From Academy to Boarding School: The Case of Phillips Exeter

❧ On 20 and 21 June 1883, at almost the same time that Lawrenceville was being refounded, the Phillips Exeter Academy in New Hampshire was celebrating its one-hundredth anniversary. The guests and the speakers were distinguished. Among them were President Eliot of Harvard (who had gracefully declined the office of trustee a few years before[1]); the Governor of New Hampshire, Benjamin F. Prescott, class of 1850; the Governor of Massachusetts, Benjamin F. Butler, class of 1829; and a man who must have seemed a relic of another age—George Bancroft, class of 1811. The only thing that marred the proceedings was a certain tension between Butler and Eliot. Harvard was about to break tradition and for the first time in its history *not* award an honorary degree to the incumbent Governor of Massachusetts.[2] (The Overseers found Butler's character shady and his politics distasteful.) Otherwise, all looked well: the Academy, nationally famous, its investment funds totaling $237,448, had an enrollment of 206 and was just completing its tenth year under the principalship of Albert C. Perkins, the organizer of the festivities. Beneath the anniversary celebrations, however, Exeter presented a much unhappier picture. Few of the distinguished guests knew that only five weeks before Principal Perkins had submitted his resignation, or that it would be almost two decades before anyone would wholeheartedly praise the Academy as they did in that June of 1883.[3]

The problem Exeter faced in these years was typical of other academies as well: how to survive in the face of the growth of the public high school and the changing nature of higher education. Exeter's fate might have been that of academies in Gloucester, Marblehead, or Nantucket, Massachusetts, all of which became public high schools. It might have been that of the academies at Farmington and Gorham, Massachusetts, both of which became state normal schools. It might have been bought up and completely refounded like Lawrenceville, or the Milton Academy, which the Boston merchant, financier, and philanthropist John Murray Forbes endowed in 1884, hoping to transform it into the Round Hill he had attended as a youth.[4] But Exeter survived, not so much because of its impressive endowment as because of a group of concerned trustees and two strong principals, the unfortunate Charles Everett Fish and the luckier Harlan Page Amen. The story of its survival, of its transformation into a school which resembled George Bancroft's Round Hill, Mackenzie's Lawrenceville, or Coit's St. Paul's more than the Exeter of 1883 is representative of the situation of many other nineteenth-century academies.

When Exeter was founded in the late eighteenth century, academies, since they promoted education and thus the general welfare in an area the state was not willing to enter wholeheartedly, had been considered "public" schools, in much the sense in which the word was applied to the "public" schools of England. Throughout the nineteenth century, however, the legal and social definition of what could be considered "public" and what could be considered "private" had become more and more narrowly precise. Corporations, in particular, had generally grown to be defined as strictly "private" entities. With the growth and general popular acceptance of the common elementary school system the term "public," as it applied to educational institutions, had come to mean both state support and state control. After the Civil War this definition was extended to institutions of secondary education as well. The high school, by the 1880s, was thought of as the sole "public" secondary school. Many academies became normal schools, public high schools, or colleges. No longer could an academy be a "mixed" corporation; it must make a choice, become either public or private.

Like so many other academies, Exeter faced the problem of redefining its role. For a hundred years it had offered excellent, relatively cheap instruction to almost all applicants. It had never offered "education," in the sense that Woodrow Wilson used the word at Lawrenceville's centennial or in the sense that Fellenberg or Henry Coit understood it. It was one of the best-endowed corporations in New England. Would it disband? Become a public high school? A college? Exeter chose instead, hesitantly, almost despite itself, to become a boarding school. The choice was not so much consciously made by Exeter as it was made by Exeter's old, partial role as a college preparatory school.

In the 1880s Exeter's nature and aims were ill defined: it was partly a college preparatory school, partly a high school, and, as the centennial historian observed, had recently "taken on many of the features of a College."[5] Of the 1,047 boys who entered the Academy in the ten years Perkins was principal, for instance, only 427 went on to receive college degrees.[6] Most stayed at the Academy for less than two years.

Exeter's faculty was quite small. In 1884–85 it consisted of only seven men, including the principal, for a student-faculty ratio of 39:1.[7] By 1892–93 there were eleven faculty members, including the principal and a gymnasium director. The principal received $4,000 a year, while the salaries ranged from $1,000 for the gym director to $2,500 for the professor of ancient languages. The average salary, not including the principal's, was $1,700 a year, the median salary, $1,750.[8]

Exeter's student body was a miscellaneous lot, widely varying in age and social background: rich and poor, white and black, rural and urban: "ill-assorted and transient material," LeBaron Russell Briggs, dean of Harvard College, called it.[9] The average age of the eighty-eight members of the class of 1891, for instance, resembled that of a college more than a secondary school like St. Paul's, Hotchkiss, or Lawrenceville: it was twenty years and eight and a half months. The ages of the students ranged from sixteen and a half to almost twenty-six. Only thirty-nine members of this class had been in the Academy more than two years; only twenty-four had been at Exeter for the complete four-year course. Their religious backgrounds varied as widely as their ages: there were twenty-four Episcopalians and the same number of Congregationalists; eight listed no religion and another eight were Unitarians; seven were members respectively of the Presbyterian and Baptist churches; three were Methodists, two Lutherans, and five boys gave their denominations as Universalist, Orthodox, Liberal, Atheist, and Christian. Their politics varied as much as their religion: one sturdy soul supported the Farmers Alliance, but most—fifty-seven—were Republicans; six listed no party, while seventeen were Democrats, four were "Mugwumps," and three, "Independents."[10]

While students were drawn to Exeter from every part of the United States, the majority came, not unexpectedly, from New England. Of the 255 students at the Academy in 1884–85, 115 were from New England, 75 from the Middle Atlantic states, 32 from the Middle West, and 19 from the South. The states with the largest representations were New York (49), Massachusetts (46), and New Hampshire (45).[11] Unlike the students at St. Paul's, Exeter's students were drawn not mainly from large cities but from every type of place that existed in the United States—from rural areas, villages, small towns, big towns, and metropolises. In the session of 1884–85, for instance, 34 percent of the students came from places of under 4,000 population, 33 percent from places of 4,000–25,000, and 31 percent from places of over 25,-000.[12] Dean Briggs's observation was correct: the Academy's student body was varied indeed.

In the years after Principal Perkins's resignation, Exeter steadily declined. Although enrollment figures rose—255 in 1884, 281 in 1886, 325 in 1888, 355 in 1891—outward appearances were deceptive. After the session of 1890–91 Exeter's inner difficulties were reflected in a precipitous decline in enrollment —from the 355 of 1890–91 to 299 in 1891–92 to a disastrous 123 in 1895–96. Exeter's decline was due to several interrelated factors: a shift in the character of its student body, acute faculty problems, and the changing nature of American secondary and higher education in general.

The following table gives some suggestion of what was happening at Exeter in the late 1880s (the percentages have been rounded off):

Exeter Students at Colleges, 1873–1895[13]

	1873–83		1884–89		1890–94	
(1) Students Entering Exeter:	1,047		777		743	
(2) Attending College:	437	40%	138	18%	273	36%
(3) Harvard	210	49%	79	57%	118	43%
(4) Yale	152	35%	28	20%	60	21%
(5) Dartmouth	17	4%	2	1%	9	3%
(6) Princeton	24	3%	10	8%	5	1%
(7) Other Colleges	34	8%	19	14%	81	30%

Lines two and seven are of particular interest. In the years 1884–89 Exeter almost ceased being a college preparatory school; even in the years 1890–94, recovery to preparatory school status was by no means complete. The disastrous years 1884–89 led to an almost complete breakdown of Exeter's role as a "feeding school" for Harvard and Yale. After 1890, when Exeter was again sending more boys to college, its position was by no means restored: even in the bleak years 1884–89 Exeter graduates had gone to only thirteen colleges; in 1890–94 they went to forty-one different colleges. What had happened at Exeter in the late 1880s and early 1890s?

Many of Exeter's troubles sprang from two faculty members, George A. Wentworth, professor of mathematics, and his close friend, Bradbury Longfellow Cilley, professor of classics. Wentworth, the son of a poor New Hampshire farmer, graduated from Exeter in 1852 and with his roommate, Cilley, from Harvard in 1858. The same year Wentworth returned to Exeter as a teacher; Cilley followed him in 1859. Gruff, autocratic, undisciplined but warmhearted, Wentworth was a great bull of a man. His explosions were famous, but so were his kindnesses. For thirty-three years he was the strongest personality at Exeter. His friend, Cilley, was cut of much the same pattern. Wentworth was almost a small textbook factory in himself; over the years he churned out over thirty mathematics texts (usually during classes). He accumulated a considerable fortune and an international reputation. Parents sent their sons to Exeter because they had studied under Wentworth, or knew of him through his books.

With the retirement of Gideon Lane Soule after thirty-five years as Exeter's principal in 1873 it was generally expected that Wentworth, or perhaps Cilley, would be made the new principal. Neither, however, was chosen: the Academy's constitution required the principal to be a member of the "Church of Christ," and while both men were churchgoers, neither was a church member. The trustees chose instead Albert C. Perkins, a country boy who had graduated from Phillips Andover and Dartmouth and was in 1873 principal of a high school in Lawrence, Massachusetts.

Wentworth and Cilley made Perkins's years as principal, and those of his successors, Walter Q. Scott (1884–89) and Charles E. Fish (1890–95), miserable. Wentworth came into his classes when they were half over, permitted boys who had been expelled to attend his classes, and became the confidant of every troublemaker in the school. It was largely because of Wentworth that Perkins resigned in 1883 to become principal of Adelphi Academy in Brooklyn. For the year 1883–84 Wentworth and Cilley were in charge of the Academy, which they ran as a sort of benevolent despotism. Disciplinary standards declined drastically.[14]

When Walter Q. Scott arrived as principal in 1884, he faced a difficult task. Scott had been preparing to resign from the presidency of the Ohio State University because of a religious controversy when Exeter's trustees asked him to become principal. A Civil War veteran, a vigorous and breezy westerner, an ordained minister, he seemed the ideal man to restore order to the Academy. He was not. He had little knowledge of eastern schools and outraged tradition and sensibilities wherever he stepped. Moreover, he faced a positive lack of cooperation from Wentworth and Cilley, who quietly undermined him whenever they could. Order crumbled: one student riot followed another (all carefully reported in the New England press), until Scott asked for police protection for himself—a sure way to breed more trouble.[15] Scott attempted to bring about self-discipline among the pupils by establishing a student-council type of government. The effort failed completely.[16] On 20 June 1889, he gave up entirely and resigned the principalship—apparently to the surprise of the trustees, but certainly to the satisfaction of Wentworth and Cilley, who again were appointed to run the school until a new principal could be found.[17]

Many of Scott's troubles can be attributed to Wentworth and Cilley. But as much to blame for the Academy's difficulties were the changing demands of the colleges, particularly Harvard, the changing nature of Exeter's student body, and more elusive changes in the nature of the society of the town of Exeter and the larger American society.

St. Paul's School, even today, is a complete community unto itself. In the 1880s its grim red brick buildings (most, happily, either pulled down or burned in the last two decades) formed an isolated village. The same was true of the Lawrenceville School. On the other hand Phillips Exeter, in the 1880s merged almost imperceptibly into the surrounding town. And, by the 1880s, the town of Exeter was no longer the isolated village it had been in the late eighteenth or early nineteenth centuries. By 1890 its population was 4,284, and growing. In the 1880s, with machine works, cotton mills, brass works, pottery and drain-tile factories, and a carriage manufactory, it was already more than semi-industrial.[18] Moreover, the town was tightly woven into the New England transportation network. In 1883 the Boston and Maine Railroad ran six trains a day from Boston to Exeter, and vice-versa. (In fact, travel to Exeter was easier in the 1880s than it would be in the 1960s. In 1965 it took over two hours of driving on superhighways to reach Exeter from Boston; in 1883 one could leave Boston by train at 9:00 A.M. and be in Exeter at 10:38 A.M.[19]) The trains were as accessible to the students at the Academy as to the other residents of the town.

However, Exeter, like other academies, was only incidentally a boarding school. Until 1855, when a dormitory accommodating 42 boys was built, all the students lived with families in the town. Another dormitory was not constructed until 1893; it had room for only 52 students.[20] Of the 255 boys in the session of 1884–85, for example, only 82 lived in the school's dormitories.[21] Exeter was far less expensive than schools like St. Paul's or Lawrenceville. In 1885 the tuition was only $20 a term, or $60 a year.[22] It was not raised until 1890–91, when it went to $75 a year.[23] Added to the tuition, of course, students had to pay for their room and board; in 1884 in Academy-owned buildings it was $10 a year for room rent and about $3 a week for board. In private families it was $4.50 a week and up.[24] Figuring a school year of thirty-four weeks at $4.50 board a week, the total expenses would come to only $190 a year in the 1880s. The Academy always offered a certain number of scholarships—in 1888–89, twenty-four.[25] The rooms in the Academy-owned dormitory were reserved for the Charity Scholars.[26] It was such aid that enabled poor youths like James Mackenzie to attend Exeter.

"No distinctions have ever been made in the Academy by reason of pecuniary condition," the town of Exeter's historian claimed. "The poorest lad is as free to carry away the honors, and he is as much respected if he is deserving of respect, as the *millionaire.*"[27] One wonders. There was more to life at Exeter—or any other school—than academic "respect." The general tone of student life at the Academy under Principal Scott is somewhat coyly suggested by one of the school's historians:

> Nothing can be gained by repeating reports of the more lurid escapades and adventures of some of the more seasoned undergraduates of the day. Some of these, no doubt, are founded in fact, but, at all events, they would seem to fit more harmoniously in the pages of Fielding and Smollett than in the history of a boys' school.[28]

And that is precisely the point. In almost every respect the Phillips Exeter Academy of the 1880s was identical to the *unreformed* English public schools of the late eighteenth or early nineteenth centuries.[29] At both Exeter and the English schools the faculty was tiny and the classes were large. At both types of school Charity Scholars boarded in the institutions' buildings, while the majority of the students lived in private lodgings in the town and were left much to their own devices, which, considering the nature of the town of Exeter by the 1880s, offered considerable in the way of possibilities for experimentation. Exeter's students had not yet been—to use Philippe Ariès's word—"claustrated." With respect to Exeter's development after the 1880s, Ariès's description of the development of the English public schools is suggestive:

> Originally there was no distinction between the public schools and the other grammar schools or endowed schools. The

> latter were day-schools with only a few places for boarders who were scholarship boys; they drew their pupils from the town and neighborhood and from an extensive social field, as was the case in France. Towards the end of the eighteenth century, the gentry showed a certain reluctance to send its sons to the nearest grammar school, which was also attended by children from poorer homes. It was then that some of these grammar schools decided to specialize in the education of young gentlemen and became boarding-schools whose recruitment ceased to be regional in character and extended to the whole country; . . . The phenomenon remained basically the same [in both France and England]: a change from day-schools with a regional recruitment, from a varied social make-up to a limited aristocratic or middle-class recruitment. The result was that what had been a virtually unrestricted secondary education became a class monopoly, the symbol of a social stratum and means of its selection.[30]

This was precisely the pattern secondary education almost followed in the United States. By the 1880s those 6,000 academies of 1850 were fading away; like the English public schools, if an American academy wanted to survive, it had to become an expensive boarding school. But, compared to French or English developments, there was one crucial distinction on the American scene. Not only were many of the old academies becoming *public* high schools, but a vast network of *new* public secondary schools was being established. In the United States only to a limited and amorphous degree would secondary education become "a class monopoly, the symbol of a social stratum and the means of its selection." For the late nineteenth and early twentieth centuries at least, relative equality of educational opportunity—and thus of greater possibilities for social mobility—would distinguish the United States from other Western nations.

Contributing to Principal Scott's difficulties was a disruption in the Academy's long-standing relation with Harvard. Traditionally, Exeter had been a feeder-school for Harvard. Early in the ninteenth century the Congregational church in Massachusetts had split into two grups, the Orthodox Calvinists and the Unitarians. The latter maintained control of Harvard, which had been the cause of many of the university's difficulties in the

1820s.[31] The Andover branch of the Phillips family remained loyal to Orthodoxy, and assisted in establishing the conservative Andover Theological Seminary in 1808 as a counterweight to "infidel" Harvard. The Phillips Academy at Andover became more or less an appendage of the seminary; both institutions were governed by the same board of trustees until 1908.[32] For decades the Academy at Andover sent hardly a student to Harvard. Andover graduates were more likely to attend theologically orthodox institutions like Yale or Princeton. The Phillips Exeter Academy, on the other hand, while not formally Unitarian, became so latitudinarian as to be almost nonsectarian. It continued to be one of Harvard's main sources of students until the 1870s. By then, however, the old doctrinal differences had lost much of their importance. More important, in 1869 Charles W. Eliot was appointed president of Harvard.

President Eliot's total impact on all American education was immense but has yet to be properly assessed.[34] So far as Harvard was concerned, suffice to say that the place was revolutionized. Reform followed reform so swiftly that by the mid-1870s there was a strong, if unsuccessful, movement to remove Eliot. Among the first of Eliot's changes at Harvard was a broadening and raising of the college's entrance requirements. In 1870 Harvard required of its matriculants much of what it had required in the seventeenth century: Latin, Greek, and mathematics, along with a little history, geography, and English. By 1910 Harvard was accepting twenty-two subjects for admission.[35] The secondary schools would either prepare students in these subjects or not send them to Harvard or the many other colleges and universities that swiftly or slowly followed its example.

Exeter responded fairly quickly to changes in the colleges. Eliot changed Harvard's admission requirements first in 1872; by 1873–74 Exeter offered courses to meet the new demands in the sciences, French, and English.[36] The trustees had responded by asking Principal Perkins to teach physics and botany and Professor Cilley to teach French. The idea was so distasteful to Cilley that Oscar Faulhaber, a German, was hired to teach French and German.[37] Eventually, every time a college changed its entrance requirements, Exeter, and other secondary schools like it, had to add burdens to the existing faculty or hire new teachers qualified to teach the subject. As a consequence, the cost of secondary education rose while faculties became overworked and the teaching often perfunctory.

Exeter's curricular problems were complicated in these years by a revival of the "English" course, which had been dropped in 1848.[38] In 1871 Woodbridge Odlin, a resident of Exeter who had graduated from the Academy in 1817, offered the trustees a gift of $5,000 on the condition that an English department and professorship be established, particularly for the benefit of indigent town boys. The trustees were at first hesitant, but when the gift was widened to include a principal of $20,000 they decided to accept.[39] The English course was reintroduced in 1874 and grew gradually until it included, besides the regular studies in English, modern languages, mathematics and so forth, astronomy, logic, political economy, botany, and the history of Christianity. Exeter was becoming, by the 1880s, a junior college. In 1848 the trustees had done away with the English course because it "was liable to be filled with the idle and stupid.[40] By the 1880s the fears of 1848 seemed to have been fulfilled. Walter Scott increased the number of students at the Academy from 206 in 1882–83 to 325 in 1888–89 by filling up the comparatively undemanding English course. However, only 18 percent of the students who entered Exeter in his regime went on to college. And it was the English students who provided most of the rioters. Exeter, by 1888, was achieving a national reputation for rowdiness rather than scholarship.

While the trustees searched for a new principal, a search growing ever more difficult, Wentworth was again put in charge of the school.[41] Standards did not improve. The new principal was selected almost by accident. An 1878 alumnus of Exeter, Sherman Hoar (a well-known political reformer, later an Exeter trustee and United States Congressman from Massachusetts) volunteered to help in the search. On his way to interview a candidate Hoar stopped to visit his uncle, Senator George Frisbie Hoar of Massachusetts. The senator suggested one Charles E. Fish, then the head of a day school in Worcester, Massachusetts, for the post. The trustees were becoming desperate; after meeting five times in June 1890, they finally elected Fish Exeter's new principal on the twenty-fourth.[42]

The problems that faced Charles Everett Fish when he came to Exeter in 1890 seemed almost insurmountable: declining and ill-defined academic standards, riotous students, and a hostile faculty. Fish lasted only five years as principal; yet, when he left in 1895, the foundation for Exeter's full recovery under the next principal had been laid. Fish, a poor Massachusetts boy, was a graduate of Andover; he entered Harvard in 1874, then left to be principal of a Maine high school in order to earn enough money to send a sister through college. By great effort he managed to re-enter Harvard and complete his course in 1880. He then became principal of the Chicopee, Massachusetts, high school for five years, after which he opened the private school in Worcester from which he was called to Exeter's principalship.

Fish's task was difficult, but his personality made it doubly so. One historian of Exeter has aptly described him as "earnest, conscientious, and thoroughly well-intentioned," but also "fearful, irresolute, and devious."[43] Fish saw immediately upon arriving that the students must be brought under control. One way to do this was to extend the dormitory system and bring it more under the principal's direct supervision. This he did; his management of the dormitories, however, irritated Wentworth, who had heretofore had charge of them. Fish complained of lack of support, and the trustees, finally supporting a principal, sent Wentworth on a year's leave of absence. He never returned to Exeter's faculty again, although he later became a trustee.[44] Wentworth's absence removed one of Fish's largest obstacles—faculty noncooperation, if not downright opposition. However, it seriously hurt the Academy's public position. Wentworth had an immense reputation among the alumni and the public at large: if Wentworth was leaving, they asked—on top of the troubles of the past few years—what was becoming of the Academy? The number of applications to Exeter began to drop precipitously.

Added to the decline in applications was a significant shift in the decade between 1884–95 and 1894–95 in the type of place Exeter students came from. In 1894–95 Exeter, like St. Paul's, drew a very large percentage of its students from the twenty-five largest cities in the United States: 22.3 percent of the students at Exeter, 47.6 percent of the students at St. Paul's.[45] There were, however, important—and enlightening—differences in the composition of the student bodies at the two schools, as the following table indicates:

Origins of Exeter Students, 1884–85 and 1894–95, and of St. Paul's Students, 1894–95[46]

	1884–85 Exeter		1894–95 Exeter		1894–95 St. Paul's	
Size of Place	#	%	#	%	#	%
(1) Under 2,500	72	*29*	65	*33*	28	*9*
(2) 2,500–4,000	13	*5*	11	*6*	8	*3*
(3) 4,000–8,000	39	*16*	16	*8*	18	*6*
(4) 8,000–25,000	43	*17*	23	*12*	33	*10*
(5) 25,000–100,000	15	*6*	34	*17*	64	*20*
(6) 100,000–500,000	32	*13*	20	*10*	64	*20*
(7) Over 500,000	36	*14*	28	*14*	100	*31*
Total Sample	250	100.0	197	100.0	315	100.0

All we have learned of St. Paul's would lead us to expect precisely the data that appears above: 71 percent of its students came from cities of 25,000 and over. Most of the students from places of under 4,000 came from areas of estates or suburbs, such as Arden, New York, the Main Line of Philadelphia, or Babylon, Long Island. But while in 1894–95 St. Paul's drew over half of its students from cities of 100,000 and over, Phillips Exeter, much as it had done a decade earlier, drew only about a quarter of its students from such cities. What is most interesting is the area from which Phillips Exeter *lost* students in the same decade. In 1884–85 the Academy drew 33 percent of its students from cities in the 4,000–25,000 range; in 1894–95 it drew only 20 percent of its students from such places. This decrease was made up by a slight proportional increase in students from places of under 4,000, and by an increase of almost 300 percent in students from cities in the 25,000–100,000 range. The reasons for the attendance of the former group of students are fairly clear. Most of the places of under 4,000 from which the Academy's students came were not, as at St. Paul's, areas of estates or suburbs, but small hamlets or villages, which also probably had no facilities for secondary education. The boy who wanted to continue his education beyond the elementary subjects would have to leave home.

More puzzling are the reasons for the sharp increase in the proportion of students drawn from cities of 25,000–100,000 and sharp decrease in the proportion of students from cities in the 4,000–25,000 range. At the time both types of place were seeing a rapid growth in public educational facilities; why the Academy should show such a loss in representation from one group, and gain from the other, is obscure. What is clear, however, is that over the decade 1884–94 the Academy's student body was becoming polarized into two groups, one drawn from essentially rural areas, the other from highly urbanized places. One would expect that the differing experience and values the two groups brought with them would almost inevitably clash—amongst the students themselves, with the Academy's authorities, and with the town of Exeter itself.

That St. Paul's was located near Concord, Hotchkiss in Lakeville, or Lawrenceville in Lawrenceville was basically irrelevant to the life of those schools; self-isolated communities, little worlds unto themselves, they might just as well have been in Hartford, Northampton, or Greenwich. This, as we have seen, was not the case at Exeter, where the town merged almost imperceptibly into the Academy, and the Academy into the town: the students were not going merely to a boarding school but to the town of Exeter itself. And, in the 1880s it became apparent that the social fabric of the town had become too loose to hold the Academy's students. The controlled environment it had provided students for over a century seemed to be dissolving. To bring some order into the students' lives the trustees were forced to pass resolutions such as the following:

> Voted—That the Trustees of the Academy feel it their duty to adopt and enforce stringent action for the protection of their pupils from exposures to temptations and require the earnest cooperation of the householders in this strict compliance as to the rules of supervision of and reports of inmates and that the Trustees without necessarily impugning the character of the householder deem it to be the duty of the Board to instruct the Principal to withhold licenses from householders occupying houses in dangerous proximity to places, where there is reason to believe that illegal sales of liquor, gambling or other violations of law and decency occur.[47]

Virtual warfare between the young and the old, and between the Academy's authorities and town, ensued. Principal Fish was granted power to grant or to refuse licenses to householders. He exercised his power arbitrarily, not giving the townspeople reasons for his decisions to accept one house, or to refuse another. He constantly changed his mind, not only with the townspeople but with the students. He would dismiss students, then permit them to return. He hired private detectives to search out "evildoers" among the students, then denied that he had done so. He abolished Exeter's secret fraternities, causing widespread dissatisfaction. Finally, he felt himself so threatened from all sides that he asked for police protection and took to wearing brass knuckles. By October 1891 the trustees could discouragingly say that "being informed that the selectmen [of Exeter] are considering the subject of making further provision for the police of the town, [we] express the conviction that such provision is very desirable."[48] The reciprocal relation of school and society, of Academy and town, the old "familial" discipline of the Academy's first century, could no longer be maintained. Order could not be fully restored until the Academy, in effect, divorced itself from the town by building more dormitories. This was begun during Fish's principalship, but did not bear results until the next administration.

Fish's other most pressing problem was the restoration of Exeter's academic standards; this, in turn, was intimately associated with the type of student the Academy attracted and thus with disciplinary problems. Fish introduced a new marking system, and in October 1891 the trustees gave him the power to expell all students "who fail[ed] to attain an average rank of C or in the judgment of the Faculty . . . did not offer decided promise of rapid improvement. . . ."[49] Mass expulsions were the rule for the next few years. The main difficulty was still with the English course and the type and numbers of students it attracted. The trustees were unhappy about dropping the course; they realized that the only way to improve quality was:

> by discontinuing the English course of instruction, which would involve the giving up of the Odlin fund to the town of Exeter. This would occasion a serious loss of income. The interest of the Odlin legacy is about $1,000 a year, and the

> tuition from pupils taking the English course amount to more than $4,000 a year. And the expenses of the school would be in no respect lessened by the loss of those pupils, for the teaching force would have to be the same as now. This sum of $5,000 and upwards which the English department brings in, could not be dispensed with under present circumstances, without the most serious embarrassment to the operations of the school.[50]

The trustees, in other words, wanted to have their cake and eat it too; knowing that the English course lowered the Academy's standards and accentuated disciplinary problems, they were still unwilling to forego the revenue it brought in. They finally, however, decided to abridge the English course "so that it shall include only those studies required for admission to the best scientific schools and that all other English branches be struck out from the curriculum. . . ." The English course, in other words, was turned into a scientific course to prepare boys for Harvard's Lawrence Scientific School or Yale's Sheffield.[51] Since the conditions of Odlin's bequest were no longer being followed, the $20,000 fund was reluctantly turned over to the town of Exeter.[52] The school would divorce itself from its immediate environment. Exeter had finally decided on its future; it would be a college preparatory school. The old double function of so many academies—college preparation *and* a terminal education—was finally given up in favor of the former, single function. From now on the emphasis at Exeter would be on scholarship. The Academy, an alumnus of this period recalled years later, "was a new adventure, a new and very shocking world. There was no real discipline, no attempt to influence the boys; it was root-hog-or-die system. Do your work or get out, and the only measure of a boy's quality was his scholarship."[53] If at St. Paul's the gentlemanly and Christian aspects of the Christian gentleman and scholar type came to overshadow its scholarly qualities, at Exeter Christianity seemed irrelevant and gentlemanliness nonexistent.

By October 1892 Fish felt secure enough in the results of his massive housecleaning and reorganization to call the trustees' attention to a new service offered by Harvard, the Schools Examination Board. Established by President Eliot in 1892 to encourage closer cooperation between secondary schools and the university, the board offered the services of regular Harvard faculty members to examine thoroughly, for a small fee, "the regular work of instruction in any school—public, endowed, or private—of a grade to prepare boys for Harvard College or the Lawrence Scientific School."[54] The trustees responded by requesting a "thorough examination of the work of the Academy," and the board began its work in April 1893.[55] The Harvard faculty members made a distinguished group: in English, the dean of Harvard College, LeBaron Russell Briggs; in mathematics, the brilliant Maxime Bôcher; able and energetic Morris Hickey Morgan, professor of classical philology, in classics; Henry B. Hill, a pioneer in organic chemistry, in physics and chemistry; and Albert Bushnell Hart, a pioneer Americanist and former student of Henry Adams, in history.[56]

In general, the board found Exeter, somewhat to its surprise, good. There was, however, a certain coolness of tone to the final report:

> The object of the school as stated in the catalogue is to furnish "the elements of a solid education." This object the school accomplished well in the main; but there is manifest tendency to lower its standards, and to regard "the elements of a solid education" as equivalent to the requirements for admission to college. . . . [Exeter] undoubtedly exerts a considerable influence upon other schools of its class, and it ought therefore not merely for itself, but as an inspiration elsewhere, to maintain a high level of attainment and efficiency.[57]

Fish had succeeded in restoring Exeter's academic standards, but not to their former excellence. The examiners' major academic criticisms concerned the teaching of English, history, and modern languages. Not enough time was given to the first, the instruction in the second (being given by the gym director) was mechanical and insufficient, and the instructor in modern languages was simply incompetent.[58] Paul Hanus (professor of education at Harvard and secretary of the board), like almost everyone else concerned with secondary education at the time, recommended taking time from classics to expand the teaching of English.[59] The board also recommended the use of an entrance examination ("at least a knowledge of arithmetic might . . . be demanded," they said[60]), the purchase of a certain amount of minor equipment, a full-time history instructor, and another English instructor. The trustees followed the board's advice quickly and completely. The ineffectual instructor in modern languages was unceremoniously sacked, an entrance examination was introduced, books and maps purchased, and an instructor in history was hired.[61]

Perhaps as important to Principal Fish and the trustees as scholastic matters, however, were the Schools Examination Board's comments on the tone and discipline of the Academy. The final report said simply that "the relations between the teachers and the boys seem in general to be excellent"; the individual reports were far more revealing.[62] Albert Bushnell Hart found the general tone of the Academy "agreeable." The boys, he said, doubtless having expected the worst, "were, with perhaps one exception, uniformly well behaved and apparently accustomed to discipline." Dean Briggs found "the discipline of the class-room . . . decidedly better than it was two years ago." Most gratifying was the report of Morris Hickey Morgan, who had known the Academy well over the preceding few years:

> I went to Exeter with the strongest possible prejudice against the school, and returned in a very different frame of mind. I am glad to bear testimony to the effect that earnest hard work seems to be the leading characteristic of most of the pupils in the place. The boys in general seemed eager to learn. I saw but few indifferent, lazy faces, and these drew my attention chiefly from the strong contrast which they presented to most of the faces before me. The active measures which have lately been taken by the head of the school are doubtless known to your board, and to them I attribute the welcome change in the school from what it was when I first saw it some years ago.[63]

Opposition to Principal Fish, however, continued. Though he had the backing of the trustees—and Harvard—he was unable to gain the confidence of faculty, students, or townspeople. Standards might be improving, but registration was dropping precipitously—from 355 in 1890–91 to 123 in 1895–96. The trustees and the principal agreed that he was not the man to complete the job of rebuilding Exeter; on 30 March 1895, with good wishes on both sides, he resigned.[64]

The rebuilding of Exeter was completed under Harlan Page Amen, Principal from 1895 to 1913. It was he who firmly set Exeter on the path of becoming a true boarding school; a school which, while maintaining its traditions of a diverse student body and student independence, would gradually resemble more Round Hill, St. Paul's, or Lawrenceville than the Exeter of the 1880s or early 1890s.

Back in 1889–90, when the search for another principal had been under way, George S. Morison, an 1859 alumnus of the Academy, then a trustee and a nationally known civil engineer in New York, had urged the selection of Amen as principal.[65] He urged it again in 1895; two of the newer trustees, Sherman Hoar and S. Sydney Smith, traveled to Poughkeepsie, New York, to interview Amen. Amen, an 1879 alumnus of Exeter and graduate of Harvard, had been joint principal of the Riverview Academy in Poughkeepsie since 1882. Hoar and Smith must have been most persuasive, for Amen agreed to come to Exeter at a salary of $5,000 a year—$5,000 less than he was making from his school at Poughkeepsie.

Amen would accept the by now nationally unenviable post—but only on certain conditions. He demanded (1) that Exeter's tuition be raised from $75 to $100 a year in 1896; (2) that the principal's house be put in order and his salary raised to $6,000 in 1898; (3) that construction of new dormitories start immediately; (4) that he have complete power to hire and fire instructors; and (5) that their salaries be raised as soon as possible.[66]

Amen set about rebuilding the Academy in three ways. First, by removing undesirable boys and by bringing more and more of the students under the direct control of the Academy by building dormitories and buying houses; second, by building up a strong and well-paid faculty. The third requisite, the restoration of Exeter's reputation, would follow if the first two aims could be achieved. Construction and purchase of living quarters proceeded apace throughout Amen's regime; by 1903 he could happily write that "the school is gradually changing into a dormitory school, though about one third of the boys continue to room in private houses."[67] (Not until 1942 would all students live in the Academy's buildings.[68])

Amen's first appointment to the faculty showed how quickly he had penetrated to the core of Exeter's difficulty: he hired an athletic director to channel the boys' energies into activities less destructive than rioting. Order was restored quickly by the rather Draconian method, as he explained to the president of Dartmouth College, of "prompt dismissal of boys who prove vicious or weak."[69] He was (like any headmaster who hoped to run a moderately orderly school) ruthless in expelling boys who did not measure up to his standards. A letter he wrote one parent is typical:

> Ever since Karl's entrance to the school, you have failed, Mr. ———, to show confidence in the school and our intentions to treat Karl justly. On this account, we have been in a very hard position to treat Karl satisfactorily. We regret extremely that both you and Karl feel that we have been unfair to him and unduly harsh in his case. Considering the provocation we have had both from the character of his work and his indifference to begin his work promptly after his return to the school, we are conscious that we have not been unjust to him in our treatment of him. We must treat all boys alike. . . .
>
> We are not disposed to prolong an unpleasant correspondence or controversy. We must have the right to punish boys for their failure to attend to their regular studies here. We do not understand how you can expect a school to settle when a boy should be punished, and when not. We ask for nothing more than justice in this case, and are entirely willing to have you withdraw Karl from the school on the terms named in the catalogue.[70]

Poor Karl was but one of many: in 1903 Amen told an interested alumnus that he had "asked four hundred boys to withdraw from the school in the last eight years."[71] Unlike Scott or Fish, Amen won the confidence of the students almost immediately. Only two years after he took up his post, the class of 1897 could write that:

> Principal Amen's success here is well known. In two years the school has advanced wonderfully. The right man is in the right place. Two years ago Exeter occupied a position of apology before the public; today she has stepped aside from this position and stands frankly before the world in her old position of a school where they make MEN.[72]

MEN, but not *gentle*men. Exeter's gradual transformation from an academy into a boarding school was *not* accompanied by the introduction of the goal of molding students to a particular character or social type, as Philippe Ariès has suggested was the case with English and French schools.[73] "We do not understand how you can expect a school to settle when a boy should be punished, and when not," Amen had written a parent. The romantic and Victorian notions of childhood and of Christian nurture which had shaped American boarding schools from Round Hill on appear to have flowed around Phillips Exeter. The boy at Exeter was expected to be an autonomous individual on arrival, not a malleable object to be molded into a gentleman. At Exeter the training of the student's intellect, not his character (though the latter was not ignored), would remain the primary goal. The scholarly and gentlemanly aspects of the ideal type appear to be drifting apart. A listing of some prominent writers who were educated at Exeter and some who were educated at St. Paul's conveys something of the difference in spirit between the two types of school: from St. Paul's, Owen Wister, F. Marion Crawford, and Samuel Eliot Morison; from Exeter, Dwight Macdonald, Arthur Schlesinger, Jr., and Paul Sweezy.[74] Gentlemen and scholars, all, doubtlessly—but the emphasis is somewhat different.

If Exeter was not becoming a *family* boarding school, it was very definitely becoming a boarding school. Amen introduced organized athletics, reintroduced the student fraternities (now, however, closely supervised by faculty members), and made a point of bringing about closer contact between the students and the faculty. Amen himself knew every boy in the school. Each student was assigned a faculty member who was to stand *in loco parentis* to him.[75] Exeter, in other words, with no conscious intention of doing so, found itself in many important respects converging more and more towards the family boarding school type. With the tendency towards becoming a boarding school went higher expenses. In 1934-35 the Academy instituted a "flat rate" charge to the students of $1,050 a year, which covered board and tuition. While still considerably below the $1,400 charged by St. Paul's in the same year, proportionately the sum was far larger than the relatively modest charges of the late 1880s.[76]

In spite of drastic amputations, Exeter's enrollment rose from 191 in 1895 to 390 in 1903, and 572 in 1913. Amen also raised the quality, salaries, and numbers of the faculty. When he came to Exeter the faculty numbered 12 men who averaged $1,850 a year; when he died in 1913 it numbered 33, who received an average salary of $2,175.[77] By 1906 the student-faculty ratio was down to 15:1, which compared favorably to St. Paul's 7½:1 in the same year.

Part of Exeter's expansion was financed by a rise in tuition to $150 in 1899, but more came from a startling rise in gifts to the Academy, largely inspired by Amen. The resources of the school rose from $475,000 to $1,371,450 during his years as principal. Some of the increase was due to improved financial management, but more was due to Amen's constant involvement, with the trustees' support, of the alumni in the affairs of the school.[78]

Amen literally worked himself to death; only part of his correspondence survives, but it alone numbers almost 30,000 pages of letters. The trustees had to pass resolutions to force him to take vacations. He dropped dead on 7 November 1913. At his funeral one of the trustees could say, without exaggeration, that now, "at the end of eighteen years the Phillips Exeter Academy stands with its leadership not only restored but enhanced, and is as typical of the best in secondary education in democratic America as ever Rugby was in aristocratic England."[79]

The reference to Rugby would hardly have been made at Exeter's centenary thirty years before. But Exeter—and several other old academies—had changed and through change managed to survive the reorganization of American society and American education of the later nineteenth century. In 1883 it had been an eighteenth-century academy; in 1913 it was well on the way to its transformation into a boarding school much like St. Paul's or Lawrenceville. It became a boarding school not because of any new ideas about the child or education, but because the surrounding society of the town of Exeter no longer provided the communal control over the Academy's students which it had afforded for over a century. The reasons for this failure are complex, but one of the most important appears to have been the absorption of the town into a regional industrial complex.[80] Why this failure should have come to a head in the 1880s is unclear: Exeter had had rail service for decades, and mills had been present there for some time before. In no sense did the town become an industrial slum; on the surface it looked as bucolic as ever. But that the town failed the Academy is undeniable. In the transition from community to society, from *Gemeinschaft* to *Gesellschaft,* the institution was forced to take on many of the functions that the wider community had once performed. If George Bancroft, dead only twenty-two years in 1913, could have looked in on his alma mater he might have been very well pleased; starting from very different premises, every day it was coming to resemble more and more the Round Hill he and Cogswell had founded ninety years before.

❧ Chapter IX

The Resurgence of the Gentleman: Groton and the Progressive Educational Ideal

(*To the tune of "Jingle Bells"*):

Let us now explain
What we mean to be.
That boy there will be a judge
And that one a M.D.
That one's a Diplomat,
To London he'll be sent,
And the one who's manliest of all,
We'll make him President.

—"The Coming Men of Choate," 1900[1]

❧ In the spring of 1901 the newly elected Vice President of the United States was despondent about his political future. As often happened, Theodore Roosevelt received encouragement from his old friend, cousin of his beloved first wife Alice Lee, the Reverend Endicott Peabody, rector of the Groton School in Massachusetts. "It is very unlikely that I shall be able to go on in politics after my term as Vice President is over," Roosevelt told Peabody, "and when I have gone out of public life I shall be able to do very much less in trying to steer straight young fellows of the right type, who ought to take an interest in politics. Therefore

I am peculiarly anxious to use the next two or three years to good purpose so far as I am able, and you are giving me a chance to do this."

Peabody had suggested to Roosevelt an elaborate plan to attract young college men to government service. Throughout the summer of 1901 Peabody and Roosevelt busily enlisted the participation of others in their scheme.[2] However, in September an assassin's bullet intervened; though Roosevelt found a wider scope for his ambitions, both he and Peabody continued to attempt to educate the sons of the rich towards a career of public service. In doing so, Peabody and Roosevelt—the former through precept, the latter through example and exhortation—were creating a new role for the gentleman in American society. In the Progressive era the Victorian image of the isolated and socially aloof gentleman was transformed into a picture of the gentleman as the perfected social democrat—the disinterested public servant. While each of the three presidents of the Progressive era—Theodore Roosevelt, William Howard Taft, and Woodrow Wilson—was demonstrably a Christian gentleman and scholar, and while each president had strong ties with the family boarding school, it is at Endicott Peabody's Groton School that the transformation of the role of the gentleman can best be seen.[3]

As early as Groton's twentieth anniversary in 1904, Peabody could look about and be content. Starting with 24 boys in 1884, by 1904 the school numbered 158 and had received $700,000 in gifts. The high point of the anniversary celebrations in 1904 came when President Theodore Roosevelt, who had two sons at Groton, drew up in a coach-and-four and delivered the main oration.[4] "There are," Peabody had written Roosevelt in extending his invitation to Groton, "great possibilities latent in our body so that you might legitimately look upon it as not entirely apart from your great work of the development of the Nation."[5] There were possibilities indeed; a few months later Peabody broke a long-standing rule in order to let a student, Kermit Roosevelt, leave school in term in order to go to Washington when his father was installed in his own right as President of the United States. "We are not likely to have requests for boys to attend their father's inaugurations after this," he wrote to the President. "I only wish we were!"[6] Peabody was wrong. On the fiftieth anniversary of his school, in 1934, not only had it grown in numbers, wealth, and reputation, but again there was a President of the United States with two sons at Groton present to deliver an address. This President, however—Franklin D. Roosevelt—was a graduate of Groton, not simply a concerned friend.[7]

The attendance of Presidents or sons of Presidents at a particular school is not necessarily, of course, a sign of either social or educational success. Nevertheless, few men have seen their work come to such complete fruition within their own lifetime as did Endicott Peabody. When he retired in 1940, after fifty-six years as rector of Groton, it was to public praise and a justified sense of private satisfaction. For those Americans who were even aware of the institution, he *was* the private preparatory school; perhaps more than any other man in the twentieth century he fixed in the American consciousness the public image of the private preparatory school and its headmaster: vigorous, moralistic, and Anglophile—but withal, curiously attractive. The picture was, of course, only part of the truth: Franklin Roosevelt's administration was the fruition of forty years' effort on Peabody's part, the ultimate justification of the school he had founded in 1884.

Endicott Peabody was a product of the Massachusetts Brahmins, that group which, uniquely in nineteenth-century America, united wealth with culture. His great-grandfather, Joseph Peabody of Salem, founded the family fortune in the confused years after the Revolution, when new families from Boston's outports were rapidly replacing the merchants who had dominated New England's maritime trade in the colonial years. Joseph Peabody accumulated, for those days, an immense fortune from his worldwide shipping ventures—part of it, like that of Lawrenceville's John C. Green, from the opium trade between China and India. When he died at the age of eighty-seven in 1844 his credit was said to be as good as the government's. His wealth enabled his son, Francis, to spend his life as a gentleman dilettante in Salem, dabbling in artistic and scientific matters. Francis's son, Samuel Endicott Peabody, returned more to his grandfather's traditions. He spent only one year at Harvard, then went around the world as a supercargo in one of his grandfather's ships. On his return he married Marianne Cabot Lee, daughter of John C. Lee of Salem, founder of the influential financial firm, Lee, Higginson and Company. It was into this affluent, if simple and provincial society, that Endicott Peabody was born in 1857, the third of five children.

Peabody's childhood was spent conventionally and pleasantly at the family's main residence in Salem and at various summer homes. However, in 1871, when Peabody was thirteen, a great change took place in the life of his family which would influence all his future career. The first American banking house in London, the center of the nineteenth-century financial world, had been founded by George Peabody of Baltimore, a very distant relative of the Salem Peabodys, who had in turn brought over Junius S. Morgan of Hartford as his partner. The firm was extremely profitable and Peabody immensely popular in England. Maintaining the family connection after Peabody's death, Morgan asked Samuel Peabody and his brother-in-law to join him as partners in the London nucleus of what would become the great House of Morgan. So it was in 1871 that the Peabodys of Salem sailed for what would become a seven-year stay in England.

Endicott and his older brother, Francis, had to be educated. The question was where. From a visiting Scotsman in America the Peabodys had heard of the first new major English public school of the Victorian era, Cheltenham. There Endicott would spend his next five years. His childhood in Salem apparently was the perfect preparation for Cheltenham. "I think that at first," a schoolmate recalled years later, "to most of the School the brothers Peabody, as foreigners, were a distinct disappointment, for they were so adaptable, and fitted into our narrow and rather exclusive life, as though they had always been English."[8] He developed there a life-long love of athletics and exercise, of cricket, of fives and racquets, and rowing.

In 1876 he finished Cheltenham and went home to Salem for the summer; he returned to England that year to attend Trinity College, Cambridge. "Cambridge," Peabody's biographer writes, "he found perfectly delightful for the three and a half years he was there. He had a short-tailed collie, he rowed and played cricket."[9] He also grew to like Dickens, Thackeray, Tennyson, and Arnold. He studied hard and received a first-class degree in the lower law tripos. In 1880 he followed his family back to the United States and entered Lee, Higginson and Company, his grandfather's investment firm—seemingly a thoroughly conventional young mid-Atlantic gentleman.

Tall, strong, graceful, and handsome, young Peabody was a striking figure—his contemporaries called him the "Sun God."[10] He impressed with his sincerity and inspired confidence in everyone he met. But however bright his prospects, there seemed to be something lacking on State Street at Lee, Higginson and Company. An anonymous poem—"The Arctic Expedition, 1875"—which appeared in Peabody's school magazine while he was a student at Cheltenham expresses that something well:

It pulseth still within our veins—
The gen'rous strain of Norseman's blood;
The restless spirit still remains,
And goads us o'er th' encircling flood,
When one had thought all motives cold,
Save love of self, and lust of gold.

Oh joy! Amid a jaded world
With slumb'rous luxury o'ercast,
When faith seems dead, and lips are curled
To sneer at each enthusiast,
To find true hearts are beating still,
And leap to work their country's will![11]

Although Peabody later said that about all he learned from Cheltenham "were things to be avoided and not to do,"[12] and while his biographer discounts any direct influence upon Peabody of his years at Cambridge, his informal education up to this point had been saturated in the spirit expressed by this poem. Beginning in the late 1850s the English public schools had undergone a process of gradual laicization. "The accent on the chapel remained," their most recent historian writes, "but the official combination of vigour and the Christian spirit, with both geared to educational ends, became popular as muscular Christianity."[13] By the time Peabody reached Cheltenham this trend was quite distinct. "The doctrine of the stiff-upper-lip was no part of the public-school code of the Arnoldian period," David Newsome has observed. "This gradually came in with the manliness cult of the 1870's and 80's. For it would never have done for Empire builders and games players to exhibit their emotions."[14] Cheltenham, where Peabody spent five years, was a nexus of this spirit—it sent a majority of its graduates into the armed forces, and a particularly high proportion into the Indian Army.[15] At Cambridge too Peabody came under influences more significant than the formal curriculum. At college he read and was deeply influenced by the biography of the pioneer English Christian Socialist Charles Kingsley.[16] Earlier in the century Kingsley and F. D. Maurice had begun an idealistic movement to broaden the social base of the Church of England and to attack the evils of industrial capitalism. The spirit, if not the precise program, of the movement was expressed particularly well in Thomas Hughes's *Tom Brown's Schooldays,* which is steeped in nostalgia for an organic, Christian commonwealth and in the ethos of muscular Christianity. Although the immediate ends of the Christian Socialist movement were unfulfilled, it made a deep and lasting mark on the Church of England, English radical thought—and on Endicott Peabody, who spent a good deal of his time while at Trinity teaching in a Sunday School staffed by Cambridge undergraduates in a poor section of the town.[17]

It was this complex of inchoate ideals and notions—of the Anglo-Saxon mission, of a lurking distrust for industrial capitalism, of a hope for an organic Christian community—that Peabody brought with him to State Street. "His ambition," an historian of Groton writes, "was frankly to stay in business until he could make enough money to retire and devote himself to good works and the service of his fellow men."[18] This was no spirit for a proper young broker; nor did Peabody find such a compromise with his ideals comfortable. In his uncertainty he turned for counsel to Phillips Brooks, then rector of Trinity Church in Boston, and inquired about the ministry.

"If," Brooks said, "it appeals to you as the most interesting thing in the world to tell people about Christ, you had better come in. Does it appeal to you?"

"Well," Peabody remembered thinking, "that was pretty satisfactory. It was perfectly simple and true, so much better than arousing your feelings. My whole heart leapt up."[19]

Overcoming strong opposition from his staunchly Unitarian family, Peabody entered the Episcopal Theological School in Cambridge to train for the ministry. "One can find no evidence," his biographer states, "that his studies at this period produced a very strong effect on his mind. He was by nature a believer rather than an enquirer."[20] Although Peabody—like most boarding school headmasters—was a moralist rather than an intellectual, this judgment gives too little weight to the theological school and to the social and intellectual milieu in which he found himself.

At that time Boston was feeling the full impact of immigration, industrialization, and urbanization. Slums abounded, conflict between capital and labor and between various ethnic groups was endemic. Whole areas of the city seemed wasteland; one writer called Boston's dreary South End a "social wilderness," another, "the city wilderness."[21] Boston's situation was not unique among American cities of the time. In every part of the nation, groups of Protestant clergymen began to attempt a realistic analysis of the nature of industrial society and to search for ways in which the ills that society was so evidently creating might be ameliorated. By the turn of the century the efforts of these moderately progressive clergymen would be known as the Social Gospel movement.[22] Conservative clergymen of the time, Henry May has observed, "were *chiefly* concerned to prove the rightness of existing institutions and to head off change." Social Gospel spokesmen, on the other hand, "were *primarily* concerned with the search for a better society. Instead of insisting on the all-sufficiency of individual regeneration as a solution for social problems, they sought, however unsuccessfully, for concrete measures of improvement and listened, however critically, to contemporary proposals for change."[23] Episcopalians were not immune to this trend—indeed, they were among its leaders and were responsible for some of its most radical aspects. Some Protestants found it odd, as the *Christian Union* wrote in 1891, that "the Episcopal Church—the Church of wealth, culture, and aristocratic lineage—is leading the way."[24] Actually, it was not so odd. Since the 1840s, when William Augustus Muhlenberg had left the Flushing Institute to begin his work in New York City, Episcopalians had built up a rich tradition of concern with urban social problems.[25] Moreover, Episcopalians were early and deeply influenced by Charles Kingsley and the English Chrisian Socialists, whose work would eventually come to serve as important precedents for the broader American Social Gospel movement.[26] Endicott Peabody's English education had familiarized him with these trends at their point of origin.

When Peabody entered the Episcopal Theological School in Cambridge in 1880 it had been in existence only thirteen years. Its founder, Benjamin Tyler Reed, had declared that the school's "professors . . . should be selected from the Evangelical class, who believe in the doctrines of the Church as declared at the Reformation. . . . I would by all means avoid the appointment of men who would magnify the forms of the Church above its teachings, or who would imitate any of the ceremonies of the Papal Church." Reed's strictures reflected the relatively simple, Low Church nature of early Boston Episcopalianism. Cassocks, colored stoles, candles and crosses, elaborate ritual—all seemed strange and foreign to most Boston Episcopalians. Not, however, to *all* Boston Episcopalians. A High Church element, deeply influenced by the Oxford Movement, centered about Boston's Church of the Advent, which gradually introduced practices that made Roman Catholic services seem rather simple by contrast and proved extremely distressing to a whole series of Massachusetts bishops.[27] The Episcopal Theological School, however, reflected more of a Broad Church attitude, which early came to be Peabody's position as well. "With High Churchmen or Ritualists," he wrote to a friend in 1882, "I can have little sympathy in thought, altho' I may like them well as men—but I do not see things as they see them and never shall."[28]

While the Theological School was not suspected of High Church tendencies, its proximity to Harvard subjected it to unfounded intimations of heresy, and its liberal teaching methods made it anathema to the High Church element in Boston. In fact, the School sometimes seemed to outsiders to be simply a Harvard department. In the 1870s Harvard feared that it was not attracting students because of its reputation for Unitarianism; in an effort to change this image, President Eliot attempted to attract institutions of other denominations to Cambridge. Harvard therefore was extremely cordial to the Theological School; its students were given full access to the Harvard Library, and—until the School's authorities finally intervened—it was listed in the university's catalogue with no indication that it was in fact a wholly independent institution.[29]

Although this atmosphere was stimulating to Peabody, he was impatient to do good. In January 1882 he answered a call to serve as a temporary minister at the mining town of Tombstone, in the

Arizona Territory. ("Well," the *Tombstone Epitaph* remarked editorially, "we've got a parson who doesn't flirt with the girls, who doesn't drink beer behind the door and when it comes to baseball, he's a daisy."[30]) While Peabody always discounted the significance of this episode, in later years the aura of the frontier West at its most romantic—of the Earps, of Cochise and of Geronimo—stood him in good stead with his students. After seven months in Arizona Peabody returned home and threw himself into the life of the theological school and of the Boston area with renewed vigor. He studied hard, courted his cousin, Fanny Peabody, taught Sunday School, and, in true Kingsleyian fashion (his letters of the period are studded with references to Kingsley[31]) worked in the Boston missions. But his restlessness continued. While still at the Theological School the idea of starting an Episcopal boarding school for boys occurred to him.

In the winter of 1882–83 the headmaster of St. Mark's School, the Reverend James Coolidge, resigned, and William E. Peck was given a temporary assignment to the post. Since Peck was not a clergyman, someone was needed to conduct the school's religious services. Peabody was asked to fill in, spent a few weeks at St. Mark's and fell in love with the whole idea of the church school. There seemed to be a possibility that St. Mark's trustees would elect him as the next headmaster. While he was waiting to hear from St. Mark's a close friend, the Reverend Leighton Parks, rector of Emmanuel Church in Boston, suggested that if he were not elected he might well consider starting a school himself. In the meantime, Henry Coit asked Peabody to come to St. Paul's as a junior master. Phillips Brooks counseled him to spend a year at St. Paul's in order to gain experience, but the idea of his own school grew more and more persuasive. Peabody made his final decision when St. Mark's trustees, as he wrote an old friend, chose "Peck permanent headmaster of Southboro' having set aside the byelaw which required a Presbyter [clergyman]. Thereby they have made it a lay school and if it seems right for me to do so, I hope to start a church school."[32]

Early in 1883 Peabody made a visit to the home of some relatives by marriage, Mr. and Mrs. James Lawrence, at Groton Massachusetts. Mrs. Lawrence, a devout Episcopalian, suggested that since the nearest Episcopal church was fourteen miles away, Peabody might start one in Groton. Peabody demurred, but then

Mrs. Lawrence suggested that if he were to start a school in Groton, her husband and his brother, Prescott Lawrence, would be happy to buy a site for it. The Lawrences and Peabody looked over a nearby farm of ninety acres and called in Frederick Law Olmsted, the landscape architect, to examine it. The Lawrences then donated it to the as yet unfounded school. The gift was made by the Lawrence brothers in memory of their sister, Gertrude Lawrence, the wife of Peabody's brother, John.

Peabody had astonishingly little difficulty raising funds and gaining support for his school. He went to see a friend in Cambridge, Arthur Carey, who gave him $5,000; he then went to a friend of Carey's, William Wells, who gave him another $5,000. He was so pleased he told his father, who gave him yet another $5,000. Within a few weeks he had raised $34,000, with the promise of an additional $5,000 if a guarantee fund could be raised. He asked two friends to serve with him as the faculty, both classmates from the Episcopal Theological School—the Reverend Sherrard Billings, and Peabody's cousin, the wealthy and eccentric William Amory Gardner (who had been raised by his equally wealthy and eccentric aunt, the art patroness Isabella Stewart Gardner).[33]

The next step was a board of trustees. Peabody met no problems at all here. Phillips Brooks agreed to serve as president; William Lawrence, a relative by marriage of Peabody and soon-to-be dean of the Episcopal Theological School, as secretary; and his father, Samuel Endicott Peabody, as treasurer. Besides Peabody himself, the other members were William C. Endicott, a cousin who would be elected a member of the Harvard Corporation in 1884; his father's old business associate, J. Pierpont Morgan, Sr.; another relative by marriage, James Lawrence; and his old friend the Reverend Leighton Parks.

Why was the completely inexperienced Peabody able to gather such support in so short a time at so comparatively tender an age? With no suggestion of facetiousness, one has the impression that it was in no small measure a matter of "setting Cotty up." It was almost a family affair; practically anyone involved in the matter was closely related in one way or another to someone else. (The Peabodys were not much given to exogamy; in 1885 Endicott married his first cousin, the beautiful Fanny Peabody, while his two older brothers and younger sister all married members of the Lawrence family.) This cousinage was naturally concerned to see that so promising a young member of the family was properly established in life. And Peabody seemed promising indeed: handsome, intensely earnest, and modest, he inspired confidence then, as always, in everybody who came in contact with him. He was a simple man, but of a massive simplicity. The qualities which so attracted people to him while young and enabled him to exert influence over others as he became older are not apparent in anything he ever wrote. His personal impact, however, is suggested by an old Grotonian's anecdote. Peabody was a very large man, but moved with extraordinary lightness. One day at Groton two boys were standing at one end of the library, a very large room. Shortly, they began to feel peculiar; they looked about, and there, at the far end of the room, was Peabody. No one had heard him enter the room, but his presence was *felt.* The twentieth century has no name for this quality; only in memory does it survive the passage of time.

Peabody was also almost certainly the beneficiary of the bruising battle between lay reformers and professional educators over the nature and control of the Boston public schools which had rocked the city for years and culminated in 1884 with the victory of the professional educators.[34] It was hardly coincidence that one of the lay leaders of the battle, Charles Francis Adams, Jr., would be among Peabody's early supporters and would send his sons to Groton. As public educators locked themselves within rigid bureaucracies, the well-to-do often turned to private schools where they might feel some direct relation to the teachers who were educating their children. The poor were not so fortunate.

Peabody's decision to found a boarding school was the logical outcome of his own experience. Most of his life had been spent in tight, organic communities—the small world of his family in Salem, Cheltenham, Trinity, and then the Episcopal Theological School. A school of his own would be another such environment, another intimate, organic community in which everyone knew everyone else and shared common values and goals. And, in a way Peabody's choice of a career and his decision to found a school returned him closer to the traditions of his forebears than would have been the case if he had remained on State Street at Lee, Higginson and Company. His forebears' energy, ingenuity, and imagination had gone into establishing novel enterprises which outlasted their own lifetimes. For Peabody routinely to have maintained what his ancestors had established would have been a negation and rejection of their example. All his life Peabody had probably been exposed to talk of trade, of stocks, bonds, and debentures. To spend years as a functionary in the familiar worlds of finance or business would have presented him with no novel challenge, nor would it have offered him much opportunity to be his own man. However, in establishing a school —which was in one sense another family firm—Peabody duplicated in a novel sphere the entrepreneurial roles of his forebears, expressed uniquely his own personality, and relived the experience of the patriarchal organization-founder.

Peabody's decision to found an institution, moreover, placed him squarely within one of the main cultural movements of his age. Since the time of the Anthologists early in the nineteenth century there had been a steady campaign in America to embody and perpetuate cultural values and practices in instituions. Muhlenberg's work, some of the implications of Horace Bushnell's thought, the founding of St. Paul's and other schools—all were representative of this impulse. In the form of colleges and universities, in institutions such as New York's Cooper Union, Baltimore's Peabody Institute, the New York or Boston public libraries, this campaign had met with considerable success in the decades before the Civil War. There had been a brief flurry of anti-institutionalism among Abolitionists and Transcendentalists, but these groups exerted a limited impact on the main currents of American thought and social development.[35]

What had been a steady stream of institution and organization founding in the decades before the Civil War became a positive flood in the years between 1865 and 1920. Besides hundreds of other organizations, by the end of the century the United States even had, in the manner of the French Academy's self-appointed "immortals," a National Institute of Arts and Letters. By World War I the institutional thinness of which the Anthologists had complained had been completely repaired. These years saw the birth of the great American symphony orchestras, museums, philanthropic foundations, the reorganization of American publishing, the development of serious national magazines and a cultivated audience to read them, and, in astonishing variety, the organization of the professions. American medicine underwent a tightening of standards beginning in the 1870s; the American Bar Association was founded in 1878. Most striking was the proliferation of learned societies: in the 1870s at least 79 were established, and in the 1880s, 121.[36] By the First World War the dreams of the Anthologists had been more than fulfilled: the United States had developed a vigorous and truly American structure of high culture. It was no coincidence that while Endicott Peabody was establishing Groton, his cousin Henry Lee Higginson was founding the Boston Symphony Orchestra: both men were the heirs of an old American tradition of trust in the efficacy of institutions to shape American life for the better.[37]

Peabody and his trustees had in mind an exact picture of the type of institution they wished to establish, and of their reasons for doing so. The trustees stated this clearly in the "Preface to Records" which they drew up for the school. Peabody, they wrote:

> . . . wished to make an attempt to found a boy's school in this country somewhat after the manner of the Public Schools of England.
>
> As these schools, under the influence of the Church of England, have developed a type of manly Christian character, he believed that a School, under the influence of the Protestant Episcopal Church, would do a similar work in this country.
>
> He was assured by men experienced in such matters that, owing to changes in methods of education and the rapid growth of large cities, there was a demand for such an institution. . . .
>
> After bringing the plans to a certain point, a meeting of several gentlemen who had consented to assist him was called and the whole matter was placed in their hands as Trustees.[38]

The broader reasons for Groton's founding came, then, from several sources. We have already discussed at some length the impetus given to the establishment of boarding schools because of "changes in methods of education and the rapid growth of large cities."[39] With the exception of the reference to the English public schools much the same thing might have been written about the founding of St. Paul's in 1855 or of St. Mark's in 1865.

And, in 1883–84 the notion of founding boarding schools was in the air: certainly the refounding of the Lawrenceville School must have had some influence on Peabody's decision to start Groton and on those who supported him. Several newspapers had carried stories on Lawrenceville at exactly the same time that Peabody and the Lawrences were thinking of a school at Groton. It can hardly be complete coincidence that Peabody called on the same firm of architects, Peabody and Stearns of Boston, and on the same landscape architect, Frederick Law Olmsted, who were at the very moment designing Lawrenceville, to design the Groton School.[40]

More important is the reference to the English public schools. The 1880s were a period of intense Anglophilia in America; the reference to the English public schools was standard rhetoric. Peabody himself declared that Cheltenham had only a negative influence on Groton's organization. Actually, in formal organization, Lawrenceville with its house system resembled an English public school more than would Groton. Groton's organization seems to have owed more to St. Mark's—and thus to the College of St. James, Muhlenberg's Flushing Institute, and indirectly, to Round Hill, Fellenberg's Hofwyl, and the early nineteenth-century American college—than to English example. And it was, after all, St. Mark's example which had initially inspired Peabody to start a school of his own. However, to outsiders—and often even to insiders—Groton would seem English, as would St. Mark's or St. Paul's. Few would realize that both American and English schools long had been developing along parallel, but independent, lines. So far as the organization of the American boarding school was concerned, Peabody made no significant innovations; his influence would come in the new spirit he introduced to the schools and in the new emphasis he would place on already familiar elements of the organization.[41]

The trustees' initial "Announcement" to parents of the goals of the proposed institution was as clear as their image of the school:

> . . . Especial attention will be paid to preparing boys for college, but the object of the school will not be the less to provide a thorough education for those who are to enter upon the active work of life.

> Every endeavor will be made to cultivate manly, Christian character, having regard to moral and physical as well as intellectual development.[42]

Peabody himself insisted again and again that Groton was to be first of all a church school, primarily designed to build character, only secondarily meant to be a "mere" preparatory school.[43] Peabody believed, in best nineteenth-century fashion, that the ideal environment in which to build character was the family; therefore Groton would be a family. The persistence and intensity of the use of the familial image to describe institutions is astonishing. "To understand Groton one must understand the importance of the family idea," Peabody's biographer insists:

> Peabody never, in his own mind, was able to nor wished to dissociate the two concepts of family and religion. A good family *was* religious to his mind. Further, the importance of the family in the whole human scheme of things is paramount. Where family life was wholesome and happy he believed that all would be well with the church and state; where family life was false or untrue or cheap all human institutions failed. Therefore it was the most natural thing in the world for him to think of his school as being simply a large family. To him the words *in loco parentis* meant just that. At the center of the big school family his own family grew and the beautiful home and family life was presided over by Mrs. Peabody, the most gracious and beautiful of wives and mothers. He and she said good night to every boy in the school every night when they were there. If they were away the senior master did it. In addition to formal chapel services, every night there were family prayers in each house. The Peabodys knew all about every boy at school, his other family, his relations, and their doings. There was an intimacy at the heart of things that was peculiar to the genius of the place.[44]

Although by the 1880s such familial imagery—the heritage of the American moral philosophers, of Muhlenberg and of Horace Bushnell—was already somewhat shopworn, it proved to be remarkably persistent, as the quotation above, first published in 1944, attests. While the idealization of the family in popular thought probably reached its zenith with the "togetherness" notions of the 1950s, well into the 1960s—almost a century after the intellectual world from which the familial image first emerged had expired—American boarding schools would still be conceiving of themselves as idealized families.[45]

The image of the school as a family did not exist in an intellectual vacuum; one reason for its persistence was contemporary developments in the public schools. In the 1820s Joseph Green Cogswell had charged that the new factories were making their child laborers "just as completely machines as the spindles they manage."[46] By the 1870s and 1880s, though many children who might earlier have been laborers were now in schools, their situation was in some respects still the same. Again and again in their drive for autonomy, efficiency, and bureaucratization, public school administrators, Michael Katz has observed, "described their school systems as factories and used metaphors based on the corporation and the machine."[47] And the metaphors slipped over into practice: by the time of the First World War many public schools were actually being operated as "efficient" factories.[48] "The fatal weakness which is fastening on our schools," one critic of the public schools wrote as early as 1880, "is succinctly suggested in this figure [of the school as factory]."[49] Charles Francis Adams, Jr., claimed that public school systems were "huge, mechanical, educational machines, or mills," which combined "the principal characteristics of the cotton-mill and the railroad with those of the model state's prison."[50] Significantly, Adams sent his sons to Groton. It was difficult to build character in a factory. To private schoolmasters the family symbolized everything the factory was not: it was idiosyncratic, intimate, and moral. Faced with a choice between sending their children to public schools modeled on factories or to private schools modeled on families, many well-to-do parents made the obvious decision.

Peabody's success with his school seems to have been almost foreordained. Within a few months of Groton's founding, Phillips Brooks was being besieged for information; within a few years Groton was known throughout the Northeast. "I doubt if you know how keenly I have watched and sympathized with your success," Theodore Roosevelt wrote Peabody less than four years after the school had been established. "I think you are doing a most genuine service to America—and by the way, I am delighted especially because you are doing it in a thoroughly American way, from baseball down and up. It has been a great comfort to me to think of small Ted [then two years old] at your school. . . ."[51] Peabody's own reputation grew with that of the school. In 1889 he was asked if he wished to be considered for the presidency of Columbia University—an offer which he sensibly declined. ("It is a place . . ." he told William Endicott, with a characteristic recognition of his own limitations, "which I could not fill to the satisfaction of the Trustees or yourself.")[52]

Groton opened in October 1884 with 27 boys. "I beg you," Phillips Brooks wrote, "not to let the school get too large in its second year. I wish that there need be no more than thirty boys."[53] But the next year there were 46 boys and by 1896, 110. Above all, Peabody wanted to maintain a close, personal atmosphere at Groton. A church school, he once remarked, must remain "comparatively small if it is to retain the family aspect, where all the members, old and young, may know each other intimately. . . ."[54] In this he was not completely successful. When the school reached 180, remembered Ellery Sedgwick, who had been a student, faculty member, and trustee at Groton, "everything grew more institutionalized, a little more metallic, a little less human."[55] Their small size is the most striking difference between American prep schools and the English public schools. While English schools ranged in numbers up to a thousand students, American schools remained comparatively small: in 1916 St. Paul's had only 363 students, Groton 166, St. Mark's 140, and Middlesex 123. American schools were small schools. Their size appears to be directly attributable to the persistence of the image of the school as an idealized family.[56]

Peabody had constant difficulty gracefully—and not so gracefully—refusing parents who wanted to place their sons at Groton. In this, as in many other things, he looked first to the example of older American schools. However, one of his most trusted advisers, William Lawrence, advised him that "St. Paul's and St. Mark's seem to be so varied in their application methods that Groton will have to create its own rules."[57] Since Peabody, at least in the school's early years, kept his administrative records in messy little memoranda books or in his head, there would often be slip-ups.[58] In 1890 John Hay wrote asking for the admission, whenever there was space, of his sons Adelbert and Clarence. In case Peabody was not sure of his credentials, Hay offered Phillips Brooks, Thomas Jefferson Coolidge, Francis Amasa Walker, Henry Adams, William C. Endicott, and Oliver Wendell Holmes as references. But neither Adelbert nor Clarence made it; Peabody became confused with his waiting lists and they ended up in other schools. The safest thing to do, as always, was to follow Emily Post's example: she entered one son at birth and the other at the age of two.[59]

That same doting, almost obsessive, concern about their sons which characterizes so many of the parents we have discussed from Joseph Buckminster's on was apparent among the fathers of Peabody's pupils. Charles Francis Adams, Jr., for instance, offered Peabody endless advice on how to educate his twin sons, John and Henry. J. Pierpont Morgan, Jr., took infinite pains over the treatment of his rather unpromising son, Junius.[60] Peabody usually responded by writing the parent a reassuring letter and proceeding on his own way. In general, parents were well pleased with what Peabody was accomplishing with their sons at Groton. Admiral Alfred Thayer Mahan's attitude was representative: "I will not allow this occasion to pass," he wrote Peabody, "without expressing to you my entire satisfaction with the growth and development of Lyle's [Lyle Evans Mahan] character and moral tone, as apparent to us, during his stay at the school. His standards of action and habits of thought, as I see and hear them, and by which I judge, are the guarantee of the wholesome influence exerted by yourself and your associates. That he at times may fall short of best ideals is an infirmity common to man, and in no way imputable to others."[61]

Although many rich men sent their sons to Groton, it was by no means solely a school for rich men's sons, as President Eliot thought. While a few students, such as Averell Harriman, Junius Morgan, or Payne Whitney, might be the sons of immensely rich men, more typical of the Groton father were men like Theodore Roosevelt, or James Roosevelt, his distant cousin of Hyde Park—the middling sort of rich. And not all of the students were even the sons of the middling rich. "In this 'rich boys' school'," Ellery Sedgwick remembered of Groton in its early years, "I found many boys as poor as I, and at the time my father was very poor. . . . I am mistaken if term bills were not of major concern to at least half the parents."[62] "Poor," of course, like "rich," is a relative term. Sedgwick was hardly the son of a poor clerk or factory worker. Parents who sent their sons to Groton seem, in fact, to have been much the same type as those the unsuccessful second Round Hill School had appealed to almost twenty years earlier—"men who unite with a competence, intelligence and a love of culture."[63] They were men of the "Mugwump" type—of established families with traditions of public service, financially secure though not necessarily very rich, and, perhaps most important, well educated. They were, in a word, gentlemen.[64]

At the time Peabody founded Groton the place of the gentleman in American society in general and in American education in particular was ill defined. Once it had seemed clear that the goal of American education, of American schools, colleges, and universities, was to produce Christian gentlemen and scholars. Most American educators would have agreed with President Noah Porter of Yale when he wrote in 1870 that "it is a legitimate and important function of the college, to form the character to moral and religious excellence. Education should not and cannot be limited to the culture of the intellect and the tastes."[65] But by the 1880s and 1890s this no longer seemed a self-evident proposition. As American colleges gradually transformed themselves into universities, as the map of knowledge was swiftly subdivided into increasingly narrower specialties, the role of the educator and the goals of higher education changed as well. No longer would it seem one of the primary aims of the academic man to build character amongst his charges. From being intellectual jacks-of-all-trades, from situations in which one man might find himself teaching political economy, evidences of Christianity, mathematics, and Latin, college professors were transformed in these years into masters of one well-defined intellectual discipline, disciplines with standards and demands of their own which might very often conflict with collegiate ideals. The image of the academic man changed in these years from that of the gentleman and scholar to that of the expert.

The last thing that Endicott Peabody wanted to do at Groton was to educate experts; his primary goal was to build character. However, every day the universities seemed to demand the inculcation of higher and higher levels of expertise amongst their applicants; such demands often seemed directly at odds with what Peabody and other boarding school leaders were trying to accomplish. At Groton the confrontation between the university and the secondary school, between the expert and the gentleman, between intellect and character, came in 1893 when Harvard's Schools Examination Board was asked to investigate and evaluate Peabody's eight-year-old school.

Between 1892 and 1894 the Harvard Board examined eleven schools.[66] Early in 1893, a month or so before it began a similar examination of the Phillips Exeter Academy, the board set to work at Groton. With one exception, all the examiners were members of the Harvard faculty.[67] They were instructed to make a full report on every aspect of the institution—the curriculum, pedagogical methods, faculty, equipment—and particularly on "the general atmosphere of the school—whether kindly, inspiring, and refining or otherwise."[68] The reports of the individual examiners were consolidated by the secretary of the board, Paul H. Hanus, professor of education at Harvard and the man largely responsible for the founding of the Harvard Graduate School of Education, and then sent to the school examined.[69] The final report on the academic aspects of Groton must have caused Peabody no little consternation: if he had seen the original individual reports of the Harvard faculty members he might well have despaired altogether. Like those on most of the other schools examined, the papers on Groton read like the tales of a nineteenth-century British traveler in darkest Africa: conditions were primitive, and the attitude of the natives uncertain.

As at other academic secondary schools of the period, Groton's main scholastic emphasis was on the classics—Greek and Latin. John H. Wright, professor of Greek at Harvard and later dean of the graduate school, spent March 29 and 30 observing the teaching of these subjects. He saw many things that pleased him:

> the use of Latin as a living speech in the First Form [seventh grade], taught by Mr. Peabody, where little boys quoted Latin sentences and idioms with the greatest freedom, and in the Second Form . . . where boys of fourteen read aloud from Caesar with appreciation and understanding. The use of intelligible and clear English in all translations: The demand that the students should understand the subject matter and course

of thought: subordination of grammatical lore to practical uses:The frank relation between teachers and pupils as between members of the same family.[70]

All in all, however, Wright was not favorably impressed with the final result: "The fact," he wrote, "that so long a time is spent on Greek and Latin and so little familiarity with their literature is gained has its depressing effect on the observer, as the teachers say it has on themselves." What was wrong? The major problem seemed to be the college entrance requirements, especially those of Harvard. Teachers had to prepare students for specific examinations for each college, which led to disjointedness and discontinuity in the study of Greek and Latin.[71] Wright's rather lukewarm report was the brightest of all the examiners': the others painted a decidedly unflattering portrait of Groton's academic competence.

The investigation into the teaching of mathematics at Groton was made on March 16 and 17. The instruction in mathematics was, at best, mediocre. "The masters," the examiner wrote, but then crossed out, "do not know how to handle their classes." They seemed unprepared, and needed "to study the work of good teachers. They should take time to visit other schools where they could see plans of class management and methods of teaching in operation." The examiner was taken aback at the masters' schedules: "I do not know what time they have for study," he said. "It seemed to me that they were on duty either in or out of school continuously. They ought certainly to have some time for daily preparation for coming work."[72]

The examiner in science, Theodore W. Richards, probably the foremost experimental chemist of his time, was somewhat more satisfied—with what there was of science. Groton taught only one scientific course, physics, which met but once a week. It was taught well, however. "The plan," Richards conceded, "pursued at Groton of not attempting more than is possible satisfactorily to fulfill, is a very excellent one. It is much to be desired that the way may soon be cleared for a course in Chemistry similar to the one already started in physics."[73]

Modern languages fared worse. "The class-room work consists, as a rule," wrote Hugo K. Schilling, a young instructor in German, "solely in the monotonous routine of reciting the prepared lesson . . . [it] lacks life and 'snap' throughout. A great deal of valuable time is lost in the recitations through the teachers' slowness and indecision in asking questions."[74] If the teaching of modern languages was poor, the instruction of history was almost nonexistent. "So little History is taught that during several of the recitation periods," reported Ephraim Emerton, Harvard expert on the Renaissance and Reformation, "I found myself reduced to visiting recitations in classics with a view to discovering if any instruction in History was conveyed to the pupils by indirection." The principal history instructor was William Greenough Thayer. "His methods are good," Emerton thought, "but I found that he pitched his teaching too high for the comprehension of his boys. Much of his very intelligent and rapid talk went over their heads and must rather have confused than instructed them."[75] Instruction in English was somewhat more satisfactory. "On the whole," wrote LeBaron Russell Briggs, dean of Harvard College, later president of Radcliffe and a confidant of Peabody, "I believe that the Groton School sends to us boys well-equipped in English: . . . it must be a rough boy indeed who can come away from Groton without some knowledge of English."[76] And some knowledge, after all, was better than none.

Academically, then, the examiners found Groton at best mediocre, at worst incompetent. Aside from their lengthy, specific, and detailed criticisms of the curriculum and suggestions for its improvement, their strongest negative comments were on the academic quality of the teachers. As Paul Hanus wrote to Peabody in the final report:

> The most difficult problem presented to you is unquestionably the selection of teachers who shall combine with the personal qualities you desire the other qualities as scholars and teachers which are needed to place your school on the high level you seek to attain. The Board are impressed with the frequent conflict noticeable between these two sets of requirements. They find that the personal and social demands are on the whole thoroughly well met by your assistants,—but they perceive also that the scholarly and pedagogic side of their work suffers very much by comparison.[77]

Dean Briggs specified just what was wrong with the faculty: "The underteachers are drawn to the school by the picturesqueness of the Groton idea," he wrote:

> The word "picturesque" is Mr. Peabody's own: . . . These young men love him and the boys and the school and the beautiful open spot among the hills; but the teaching instinct in them, and the idea of consecration to teaching seem at times rather limp and feeble. In the classroom some of them are . . . "amateurish"—cultivated men with little notion of discipline—perhaps even of thoroughness. Moreover, the British character of the school in language and dress, though natural to the Master much of whose boyhood and early manhood was spent in England, seems in the other teachers imitative, and not quite true. One or two of these teachers show pretty clearly . . . "Britannia Plate". . . . the truly English urbanity of the Master becomes in the submasters . . . a kind of artificial language, a suburbanity, if I may say so, for which even their kindness to the boys does not wholly atone.[78]

To this point in the confrontation, the score would seem to be "Experts 10, Gentlemen 0." But despite this damning picture of the academic side of Groton, it may be surprising to discover that, in general, the reports of the various examiners were favorable—indeed, at times rapturous—about the school as an educational environment. And, of the eleven schools the board examined, Groton can be placed academically at about the middle: if it nowhere approaches the excellence of the Roxbury Latin School, neither does it suggest the academic nadir of the Peekskill, New York, Military Academy.

The examiners had been instructed to comment on the aim and general tone of the school. Peabody's aim was primarily to create an atmosphere in which "manly, Christian character" would be nurtured, only secondarily to prepare boys for college. In his chief aim, if the examiners are to be trusted, Peabody had become, only a little over eight years after founding Groton, completely successful.

"No description," the examiner in mathematics declared, "of the classwork taken by itself would convey an adequate idea of what the school is doing for the boys."[79] The examiner in modern languages, Hugo Schilling, summed up best the impression the nonacademic aspects of Groton made on the Harvard experts. Peabody, Schilling wrote, in words startlingly reminiscent of descriptions of Muhlenberg's Flushing Institute made over sixty years earlier:

> takes a personal interest in every one of his pupils and treats them with the greatest kindness and consideration; and it is not exaggeration to say that they all love and admire him. Teachers and pupils live together like members of one large family and their relations to each other are characterized by mutual respect and confidence, and at the same time by a total absence of stiffness and constraint. The boys seem to enjoy the company of their instructors (who are mostly young men) as much as that of their fellows, and they seek it at home, on their walks and even in their sports which by the active participation of most of the teachers, including the principal himself, acquire a high tone not frequently met with elsewhere. There is a delightful air of refinement about the whole school; indeed, all the influences which are brought to bear upon the minds of the boys are elevating and inspiring. It is the aim of the principal to educate, not merely to instruct his pupils; and there can be no doubt that he is eminently successful.[80]

The final score in the confrontation between the university and the boarding school was "Experts 10, Gentlemen 10": Groton afforded mediocre instruction, but excellent education. The Harvard faculty members were caught in a dilemma which they hardly recognized and made little attempt to resolve. As the decades passed and the image of man grew increasingly fragmented, academic experts would be even less sure of the proper goals and methods of education than the Harvard examiners of 1893 had been. By the middle of the twentieth century the goal of undergraduate education, so far as most university professors were concerned, would be to produce promising graduate students.

Boarding school leaders came to feel a constant fear that all their work might be undone in the new universities. They felt that something had been lost in the transformation of the antebellum, paternalistic, "character-building" college into the laissez-faire university, which left the student much to his own devices. Here Harvard seemed the greatest offender; to many it appeared that Charles W. Eliot had realized the 1820s plans of his uncle, George Ticknor, only too thoroughly. "Is it all nonsense to fool yourself into thinking," Peabody told President Roosevelt, "as President Eliot seems to think, that you are treating men in a peculiarly manly way when you give them full scope and no advice —stand off and watch things go wrong and still say nothing and finally when you consider that things have become too bad stop them or try to stop them altogether. That is not what the authorities are paid for!"[81] Bishop Lawrence had tried to reassure Peabody earlier: "Harvard," he said, "may be taking more maturity and steadiness of purpose for granted than the students have. If a boy is immature and unsteady in purpose, he had better pass a year or two in a college under the old system and then come to Harvard. She has ceased to be a College and is now a University, tho' her Governors know very well that there is much yet to be done, especially in the line of personal relations of Professors and students: and in that line, great strides are being taken."[82]

As distressing to Peabody as the laissez-faire attitude of university authorities was the "undemocratic" social system which began to become apparent among undergraduates in the 1890s. Yale, with its secret societies, was an offender here, but even more invidious was Harvard and its clubs. Worst was the Porcellian Club, which drew many Groton alumni as members. "It seems to me," Peabody said as early as 1895, "to separate the men from the life of the University and to produce a sort of self-conscious and exclusive spirit which are most injurious to reality and enthusiasm and the American spirit. I think that along with this comes an indifference to religious ideals, and indeed to high moral aims." Peabody called for reform of the clubs in 1895; eleven years later he was still complaining that the influence of Harvard's clubs might be "permanently harmful" to the student. "A man must be sane and well established morally," he told Porcellian member Theodore Roosevelt, "in order to withstand the luxury and the indifference that he will find perhaps especially in . . . [the Porcellian] Club. . . ."[83]

Peabody's criticisms would not begin to be answered until 1909, when A. Lawrence Lowell, as president of Harvard, reversed some of Eliot's policies. In the 1920s Peabody's hopes would see a certain fulfillment with the introduction of the communal "House System"—which brought about closer contact between the undergraduates and faculty, and broke the power of the club system—at Harvard and eventually at some other colleges. In the meantime, boarding school leaders would redouble their efforts at character building. They would hope to make innocence and responsibility a habit, so that, as Dean Briggs wrote of Peabody, "even when innocence is lost in college, something in the Groton idea will never quite leave the Groton boy, so that the Groton boy who falls, will, in time, be lifted up again."[84]

While Peabody continued to improve the school, the Schools Examination Board Reports seems to have been passed over in silence, with the acquiescence of at least one of the trustees.[85] Some of the faults indicated in the report were corrected as the school grew: in 1893 it was a school of only one-hundred boys and could not afford to diverse a program. Nevertheless, it *was* a college preparatory school. Of the forty-one students who graduated from Groton between 1889 and 1893, inclusive, only one went directly to work; the other forty went on to college—thirty-two to Harvard and eight to Yale.[86] As a college preparatory school, it had to improve its academic standards as it grew. "We have got," one of the trustees was pointing out to Peabody as late as 1902, "to satisfy not only the parents that want their sons taken care of but parents of intellectual ambition who want their boys taught in the best way."[87] The years between 1884 and 1904, however, were ones of building. Not until after 1904, when the school was well established socially, physically, and financially, did Groton's rise to relative academic excellence begin.[88]

At least in its early years, then, Groton's appeal to parents was not due to its intellectual eminence. Parents were attracted to Groton for other reasons. By the end of the nineteenth century there was an already ancient tradition among many rich American families of sending their sons away to a family boarding school. Among the students at Round Hill in the 1820s had been John Lothrop Motley, F. Tudor Gardiner, William Lawrence, John Murray Forbes, and Theodore Sedgwick. Among the students at Groton would be J. Lothrop Motley ('97), W. Tudor Gardiner ('10), William R. Lawrence ('97), R. Murray Forbes ('92), and, of course, Ellery Sedgwick ('90).[89] Similar matchings could be extended almost indefinitely. For three or four generations such families had sent their sons away to school; Peabody was the beneficiary of a long-established tradition.

The nature of Peabody's Episcopalianism also was probably an important factor in attracting parents. Many of Groton's students came from the Boston area. While the dominant tradition of Boston Episcopalianism was of the Low—or Broad—Church variety, St. Paul's maintained a tradition of High Church Episcopalianism. George Shattuck ended his life as a member of Boston's Church of the Advent, which outdid the Roman Catholics in its ritualism.[90] St. Paul's drew largely on the Middle Atlantic states, where the High Church tradition was very strong. New England Episcopalians would hesitate to send their sons to Concord—there were, for instance, only six students from Boston at St. Paul's in the session of 1894–95.[91] Groton offered Boston and other Broad Church Episcopalians a "safe" church school for their sons, and also was more attractive to non-Episcopalians than was St. Paul's. Significant too in attracting students, and in explaining Groton's great reputation, was a fortuitous element—Peabody's strategic social position. It was the age of the investment banker; through his family Peabody was connected to two of the most powerful investment banking firms of the day—Lee, Higginson and Company, and the House of Morgan. The Higginsons and Morgans sent their sons to Groton, and others followed their example. This seems to be the only reasonable explanation why the rich and devout Jewish investment banker, Jacob Schiff, would have made inquiries about sending his son Mortimer to Groton, an almost oppressively Christian school.[92] Through his close friendship with Theodore Roosevelt, Peabody was obviously well connected in the worlds of politics and public affairs. It was fortuitous too that among his supporters should be his cousin William C. Endicott, or his acquaintance, Thomas Jefferson Coolidge—men whom a recent study of American imperialism has singled out as two of the most influential figures of the late nineteenth-century American "establishment."[93] Peabody was literally situated at the crossroads of the most significant avenues of power of his day. In part, parents surely sent their sons to Groton because Peabody was a Peabody, not because Peabody was a schoolmaster. No other boarding school leader of the day—not even Horace Dutton Taft—could match Peabody's unique social position.

The reasons parents sent their sons to Groton, then, are many; in the case of such a large group they are also elusive. However, the rationale of Charles Francis Adams, Jr., for sending his twin sons to Groton perhaps expresses the thoughts of many other fathers. "I have been so much occupied of late years that I have been wholly unable to give that time and attention to my two boys which every boy ought to receive from his father," Adams told Peabody. "This is one of my leading reasons for sending them to boarding school. They have been almost wholly under female control; and they have done pretty much as they pleased. I have been quite dissatisfied with the progress they have made at school, but have not seen my way to bettering it. There was a lack of discipline and correct method in their teaching which seemed to me to auger ill for the future. I hope this will be corrected at Groton." But Adams—a brilliant man himself—did not place much stock in high academic grades, nor did he expect them from his sons. Neither of the boys do I regard as brilliant," he continued. "This I am glad to say; for I take but little stock in youthful brilliancy of scholarship. Looking back over my own experience, I can say that not a single one of the boys who used to be my envy and admiration at school have in subsequent life made any mark. They have all fallen by the way from one cause or another; generally because premature growth is deceptive." Adams felt instead that "the three qualities of energy, persistency and courage, which show themselves more or less in school life, have, as I have gone on, seemed to me the telling factors later." These above all else were the qualities which Adams hoped Peabody could instill in his sons. If Peabody could do this, Adams said, "I should have small doubt as to the final result."[94]

Adams was suggesting that Peabody do with his sons just what Peabody had set out to do—to build "manly, Christian character" into his charges. As Edmund Morgan suggested of the seventeenth century Puritan father, Adams's intense and overscrupulous concern with his children led him to send them away to be educated.

Charles Francis Adams, Jr., was a very rich man, a grandson of Peter Charndon Brooks, the wealthiest Boston merchant of his day. His concern with his sons' moral character suggests a continuing theme in American popular thought and among wealthy parents as well. It was a simple theme: the rich child is apt to be the spoiled child. In popular Victorian thought wealth led to luxury, luxury led to immorality, immorality led to vice, and vice led to the destruction of the republic. The Pilgrim Fathers, one American moralist said in 1838, had laid the foundations of America upon their own "severe virtues":

> The first was *Industry,* without which it was impossible to render their conditions tolerable; in its train followed *Frugality,* the exercise of which, at all times desirable, was rendered imperious by circumstances; *Perseverance,* essential to the success of all human efforts. . . .[95]

A mad rush for riches, however, was undermining these virtues. At best, only moderate wealth—a "competence"—was socially acceptable; even this must come as the reward for personal morality, or virtue. And, unfortunately, virtue was not inheritable. In children's fiction and in the self-help literature of the Victorian age, Richard Weiss has noted, "the portrayal of the wealthy man's son as a weak, wicked, and generally unpleasant character" was common and consistent.[96]

To a surprising degree, wealthy Americans seem to have agreed with such sentiments. George Shattuck worried that St. Paul's students would be "lacking in the wholesome stimulus of prospective want." Charles W. Eliot felt poor boys were more likely to do better in college and in life than were rich boys, since the former had "won more personal power of work."[97] Coming from two paragons of industry and accomplishment who themselves had been raised in extremely affluent circumstances, such sentiments may appear curious. But the notion that inherited wealth had a deleterious effect on children was widely shared and persistent. As late as 1909 a rector of St. Paul's was making much the same observation: "It is hard," Henry Ferguson told his trustees, "to impress the necessity of hard work upon boys who feel none of the incentive for labor that is provided by poverty. The life of too many children . . . is made up of an almost unbroken series of pleasures and indulgences. Such a life cannot be expected to develop habits of wholesome exertion of mind or body. . . . Such children are apt to pass through a very difficult period while they are learning how to study, and have to yield their wills to discipline."[98] In a society in which status was based mainly on achievement rather than ascription, many seem to have agreed that the socialization of the children of the rich presented peculiar problems.

In the 1880s and 1890s parents and boarding school leaders found their efforts at building character undermined from a source other than simple wealth—the prevailing cultural temper of the age. In these years the children of the rich were presented simultaneously with an alternative model to "manly, Christian character"—effeminate, pagan *anomie.* The *fin de siècle* was the age of the *Yellow Book,* of Mallarmé, of Oscar Wilde, of art-for-art's sake. Imminent destruction, revolution, or cataclysm threatened the Western world, many feared.[99] The Anglo-Saxon race, some thought, was declining; Puritan virtues lingered like insubstantial ghosts in a depopulated New England countryside. The tendency of the age was, in Max Nordau's famous concept, towards *degeneration.*[100] To many parents and boarding school leaders the children of the wealthy seemed particularly susceptible to such temptations. There were too many object lessons in practical degeneration among prep school alumni themselves—like Edgar Saltus, St. Paul's '72. Saltus wrote perverse, dilettanish novels with gaudy titles like *The Pomps of Satan* (1906). As Eric McKitrick describes them, their setting was "most often that of New York Society, whose vulgarity was transformed in . . . [Saltus's] frenetic imagination, into a kind of fastidious and aristocratic immorality which it never really possessed." Saltus's private life was marked by confusion, scandal, and divorce, which Henry Coit must have shuddered to contemplate.[101]

Besides the deleterious effects of wealth and temptations towards degeneration, boarding school leaders faced still another potential obstacle in their efforts to build character among their students—the simple complacency, or tendency to rest upon their assumed status, of the wealthy. "I know the people behind St. Paul's and Groton and St. Mark's," the social critic John Jay Chapman once wrote the rector of St. Mark's. "They are the stupidest, the nicest and about the most protected and safely rich people in the land. The Gardners, the Burnets, the Delanos . . . uninformed, timid and comfortable people."[102] As with the parents, so with the sons. In an analysis made in the early 1950s Charles McArthur discovered that among Harvard undergraduates the academic achievement of public school graduates consistently outranked private school alumni. Private school graduates were more often than not content with the "gentleman's C"; public school alumni strove towards the highest grades available. McArthur characterized the basic outlook of the private school alumni as one of *being,* that of the public school students as one of *becoming.*[103]

McArthur's categories are too loose to be useful as analytical tools, but they are suggestive. Most of the private school alumni probably came from well-to-do families. Such families had already achieved "success" in conventional American terms; their sons might very well have felt that the grade ladder was not worth the climbing, that the pleasures of ascribed status were far more rewarding than the "greasy-grind" challenge of achieving high academic status for its own sake.[104] This attitude of *being,* rather than *becoming,* among the well-to-do was expressed clearly in "An Ideal Boy" a little essay written by a boarding school student in 1906:

> An ideal boy I think would be a boy fifteen years of age; tall, of average weight for his size, blonde, strong, well up in sports, plucky and "fair and square". At the same time he could do well in his studies and be well liked among his classmates. He ought to be jolly, slightly mischievous so as not to be called a "goodie-goodie" or a "sissie." He should be reverent, obedient and honest, truthful, manly and clean in both body and soul. He should not swear (slang is allowed), nor should he be "dead gone" on the female sex. He might live in the city in the vacations, go to Choate in the fall, winter and spring, and either to the mountains or to the seashore in the "good old summer time." His father should have enough money so as not to worry about his financial affairs. The boy should have two brothers and a sister. He should not get all he wants; which, if he did, would make him selfish and really unsatisfied.
>
> If a boy should have all these characteristics he would indeed be "An Ideal Boy."[105]

Such a static attitude was basically aristocratic, the antithesis of the classically bourgeois "severe virtues" of "Industry, Frugality and Perseverance," which Victorian and later moralists celebrated. It was also just the attitude which Charles Francis Adams, Jr., hoped Peabody could prevent his sons from adopting. Above all, it was subversive of that elusive "character" which Peabody and other boarding school leaders considered it their main aim to instill in their students.

The concept of character is an ancient one; it had always been thought to be one of the essential attributes of the gentleman. In the nineteenth and early twentieth centuries it became one of the central concepts in educational thought. It is also one of the most difficult to define. Henry Coit came close to it when he spoke of the quality of "honour"; Robert T. S. Lowell spent the whole of his novel *Antony Brade* trying to demonstrate how it worked in action.[106] The idea of character was part of a complex of nineteenth-century notions about the ideal man which included the concepts of "honor," "manliness," and the "whole man" (father to the twentieth-century's ubiquitous "whole child").[107] In a way, the use of the notion of character was an attempt to democratize the older image of the gentleman, to free it from association with a particular social class.

In the nineteenth century "character" had at least two, not necessarily mutually exclusive, meanings. The first derived from an often mechanical application of nineteenth-century faculty psychology, in which an individual's "character" was simply the sum of his inborn faculties. In the thought of some boarding school leaders, one developed manly, Christian character, or the whole man, by the discipline, or training, of the intellectual, moral, and physical faculties. The proper discipline of these faculties would lead to the development of the faculty of the will, the power to make right choices—or, in other words, to character. In a speech to the students on the tenth anniversary of his school, William Choate expressed this meaning of character perfectly: "It is a school for training your minds in knowledge and the habit of study. It is a school for training your bodies for strength and perfect health. It is a school for developing your characters."[108]

Character, however, meant more to the nineteenth century than the sum of a man's faculties; the notion conveyed also a certain quality of an individual's personality. William James once expressed that quality clearly:

> A man's character is discernible in the mental or moral attitude in which, when it came upon him, he felt himself most deeply and intensely active and alive. At such moments there is a voice inside which speaks and says: "*This* is the real me!"

At such a moment, James continued, one always felt:

> . . . an element of active tension, of holding my own, as it were, and trusting outward things to perform their part so as to make it a full harmony, but without any *guaranty* that they will. Make it a guaranty . . . and the attitude immediately becomes to my consciousness stagnant and stingless. Take away the guaranty, and I feel (provided I am *ueberhaupt* in vigorous condition) a sort of deep enthusiastic bliss, a bitter willingness to do and suffer anything . . . and which, although it is a mere mood or emotion to which I can give no form in words, authenticates itself to me as the deepest principle of all active and theoretic determination which I possess . . .[109]

The psychologist Erik Erikson has observed of this definition that although "James uses the word 'character' " he is describing what Erikson considers "a sense of identity, and that he does so in a way which can in principle be experienced by any man." "Character," or "a sense of identity," as Erikson describes it, is "a *subjective sense* of an *invigorating sameness* and continuity."[110] How, then, did Peabody and other boarding school leaders go about nurturing a sense of identity in their students?

One thing seemed certain: the present must be linked to the past, a sense of permanence and institutional tradition which would support the growth of a sense of identity must be swiftly established in a family boarding school. Instant tradition, however, was rather hard to come by; but perhaps it could be invoked immediately—through architecture and through ritual. The same problem had faced English schoolmasters earlier in the century. Before the Victorian age, most English public schools were small and mean. "I envy Winchester its antiquity," Thomas Arnold had said upon becoming headmaster of Rugby, "and am therefore anxious to do all that can be done to give us something of a venerable outside, if we have not the nobleness of old associations to help us."[111] American schoolmasters felt much the same need as Arnold. So, with the chapel at St. Paul's School Henry Coit helped create what is one of the most beautiful Gothic Revival structure in the United States. When Groton built a chapel in high Perpendicular Gothic style in the late 1890s Bishop Lawrence was quite conscious of its purpose. "This Chapel, then," he said at its opening, "with its pointed arches and carved finials, will suggest to the worshipping boys all that is finest and most chivalrous in the history of the Anglo-Saxon people. . . ."[112] Such searching for traditions could at times be ludicrous. In 1897, for instance, William Choate opened the school bearing his name with elaborate rituals. His sardonic brother Joseph was not impressed; "have you heard," he asked his wife, "of the supremely silly proceedings at the opening of the 'Choate School' [?] I should think that even William would have revolted at the 'open barge' . . . and the 'banquet', and the 'procession' and the earth from 'Ex Judge Choate's Birthplace.[']"[113] Ludicrous perhaps, but not silly; such actions demonstrated a fine sense of what it took to create lasting institutional traditions.

Architecture and ritual gave a school a larger sense of historical and cultural continuity—an institutional identity. Within the school itself invariable, day-by-day routine provided the students with a sense of extreme stability and personal continuity. Groton's schedule followed the Fellenbergian one used by most American boarding schools since the 1820s. On a typical day in about 1904 or 1905 Groton students rose early, had breakfast, and went immediately to chapel, where Peabody, dressed in priest's robes, led them in prayers, hymn, and a psalm. Immediately after chapel the boys and masters assembled in the main room of the "Schoolhouse," or classroom building. Each student sat at his desk until a bell rang. Then, silence, until Peabody—invariably dressed in a dark blue suit, starched white collar and white bow tie—appeared and mounted a dais. He then took the day's schedules and announced, "First Form—History. . . . Second Form—Latin. . . ." and the boys filed out for the first class of the day. Four hours later the school assembled in the same room. From the dais Peabody took the mail, read detentions, and made announcements. Then it was to the dining hall for midday dinner, where the school stood as Peabody invoked an impersonal, unvarying blessing. The afternoons were devoted to athletics, in which the masters (including Peabody himself until

1894) often played on the teams. At supper Peabody appeared again in his familiar blue suit and white bow tie and asked the blessing. After the supper the boys returned to the schoolroom, where Peabody read from the New Testament, then knelt and led the school in prayers. After this, the boys filed out, each one shaking Peabody's hand and saying "Goodnight, sir," while he replied, "Goodnight, my boy."[114]

There was hardly a moment of the day during which the school authorities did not know what an individual student was doing. Such close supervision was understandable among those who were responsible for other people's children, but at times it could seem oppressive. However, beneath the routine, there was often a warm, personal note at Groton. Lonely and unhappy when he arrived at Groton, Ellery Sedgwick remembered that Peabody took him into the life of his own family and "rescued me from complete unbelief in myself and gave me a degree of self-confidence which through all changes and chances I have never quite lost." But no more than had Muhlenberg's Flushing Institute did Peabody's Groton resemble a family. As the school grew, it became a somewhat rigid institution at which the boy who did not "fit in" was apt to be miserable. "The organization of boarding school," Dean Acheson remembered of his years at Groton, ". . . devoured my early freedom. School life was organized from the wakening bell to the policed silence which followed lights-out. All was organized—eating, studying, games, so-called free time, the whole thing. One could understand and accept rendering unto Caesar the things which were Caesar's, the control of one's external life. The mind and spirit were not Caesar's; yet these were demanded too. And I, for one, found it necessary to erect defenses for the last citadel of spiritual freedom." Acheson, however, was unusual. Most students seem to have liked Groton—or at least thought it had been good for them: of the thirty-four members of the class of 1934, twenty-five were the sons of graduates.[115]

Life at Groton was by no means all routine. Peabody read to the boys from Kipling and other authors, his family held open house, and there was the usual amount of schoolboy horseplay. And, at times intimate glimpses of the great world penetrated even Groton's isolation. For instance, one Sunday morning in the 1880s little Ellery Sedgwick hid himself away between the wrestling mats in the gymnasium to indulge in the forbidden pleasures of *Ben Hur*. He heard a noise and covered himself more carefully. Peering out, he saw a woman with a girlish figure being playfully pursued by a black-bearded man in white flannels. The woman was Isabella Stewart Gardner, who was visiting her faculty-member nephew, William Amory Gardner. The man was John Singer Sargent, then painting a portrait of "Mrs. Jack" which would become notorious. But at Groton such visions of nymphs and satyrs were rare.[116]

American parents, Peabody thought, had "a tendency to overindulge their children, to wish to make life easy for them, a natural result of which is that the children sometimes lack intellectual and moral and physical fibre."[117] At Groton and other schools the students were provided with a considerable amount of corrective salutary deprivation. At St. Paul's and Groton the boys roomed in barren little cubicles, and if they were ever indulged in anything as sybaritic as a *warm* shower the fact has gone unrecorded. ("If you think that the cold showers were the only Spartan element," a Groton alumnus recalled, "you should have seen the long soapstone wash basins with only cold water, you should have lived in the long dormitories with only open partitions and curtains and with all windows required to be open every night.")[118]

Although some of the students' mothers and fathers might appear in the society pages of the metropolitan newspapers, the social and economic distinctions of the outside world were rigidly excluded from the school. The boys all wore almost identical dark blue suits and white collars. They were given a quarter for a week's allowance—with five cents of that going to the collection plate on Sunday.[119] Despite such thoroughgoing egalitarian immersion in the ethos of muscular Christianity, Theodore Roosevelt still felt it necessary to urge Groton students *truly* to pursue the strenuous life by not taking along champagne and butlers when they went on camping trips to the Adirondacks.[120] Endicott Peabody could hardly be blamed if some of his charges escaped inculcation with the "severe virtues" of bourgeois Victorian Puritanism. A few Groton alumni might wallow in luxury after graduation, but they surely did so with guilty consciences.

Erik Erikson has observed that an important element of a secure sense of identity is "trust in oneself and others." The adolescent, he writes, "looks most fervently for men and ideas to have *faith* in, which also means men and ideas in whose service it would seem worth while to prove oneself trustworthy."[121] At Groton part of this need was met by Peabody and his faculty. Peabody, an alumnus remembered, "was the *pater familias,* and the boys instinctively trusted him even when they criticized him." Always just, but not particularly sympathetic, Peabody "was determined to be liberal—if it killed him." Above all, Peabody "made it quite plain to boys that each must live his own life—that no one else could do this for him." Ellery Sedgwick made what is perhaps the most succinct characterization of the impact of this perfect father-figure: "Born in the days when hopes of a perfected world seemed possible, never ill, with a wife lovely as she was beloved, knowing nothing but happiness, he looked on trouble as transitory and held it firmly underfoot."[122]

At Groton and other family boarding schools the need for trust was met not only by the headmasters but by the faculty members. Unlike boys at American public schools, who in these years were being taught more and more by women (by 1900 over 70 percent of American teachers were women; by 1925 83 percent), students at Groton and other family boarding schools were taught exclusively by men.[123] To them, "culture" and schooling were not made to seem almost exclusively feminine pursuits. More than most American youths of the time, they were exposed early, intimately, and constantly to a wide range of mature masculine figures whom they might accept or reject as models.

While schools such as Lawrenceville or Choate divided their students between dormitories and houses where married couples acted as surrogate parents for the boys, at Groton and St. Paul's there was no "house system." (Peabody thought that the system led to the formation of undesirable student cliques.) Although the Peabody family's own living quarters were attached to the main dormitory, at Groton and St. Paul's no married men acted as dormitory masters. For the young bachelors who lived in the dormitories the master's lot could be a trying one.

Peabody and other boarding school leaders placed enormous emphasis on the quality of their faculties. "The teachers make the school," Peabody stated flatly. But what kind of a teacher? That he should be a good scholar went without saying. "You must have an intelligent man, you want an intellectual man; and yet there are things distinctly more important." Above all, a teacher "must be a man of lively manner, he must be a man of fine character, and he must be a man who loves boys. That is the essence of the whole thing—a man who takes up the work at school because he cares for boys, and they know it; they know it within an hour or two of the time the man arrives at the school."[124]

At Groton, an alumnus recalled, Peabody himself "hired the masters. He sat in their classes. He listened to their suggestions. When they returned from a trip to Boston he sat up and cross-examined them." He knew all their strong and weak points. "Those who did not measure up to the requirements he eliminated."[125] Most family boarding schools tried to bring back such outstanding alumni as showed an interest in teaching. At Groton, for instance, Ellery Sedgwick served on the faculty before turning to magazine editing. At St. Paul's by 1915 exactly a quarter of the forty-eight members of the faculty were alumni of the school. Needless to say, private school leaders did not ask of their teachers the formal requirements which public school systems were more and more demanding. However, such posts were not open, as a St. Paul's rector stated bluntly, "to alumni who, after passing listless years at college, think that perhaps they would like to take up a congenial country life."[126]

If the Harvard examiners are to be trusted, Peabody had succeeded very early in bringing an outstanding group of young men to Groton. As the Harvard examiners also noted, the demands on the faculty were continuous and intense. Day in and day out, morning and night, in the dormitories, in the classrooms, and on the athletic fields, they spent hardly a moment away from their students. In 1916 an independent observer at St. Paul's concluded that "the masters, generally speaking, have too heavy a program." It was not that their duties in themselves were particularly taxing; it was the fact that "a master can rarely let down completely and be away from his charges [that] entails a nervous strain. If any program could be worked out so that a master would have some time, either each day or each month, completely to himself, it would assist in relaxing his tensions." The observer's general remarks on the character of St. Paul's faculty were strikingly similar to the 1893 observations of the Harvard examiners about the Groton faculty. "The masters are distinctly above the average of secondary-school teachers in personal qualities," he reported. "They have the characteristics of leaders of boys. It may not be inappropriate to say that, taken as a whole, they have native qualities better suited for leadership than the average college or university instructor."[127] This would seem to fulfill Erik Erikson's prescription for adolescence to the letter. At a time when American public school systems were becoming rigid and impersonal bureaucracies, Groton, St. Paul's, and other family boarding schools maintained in practice the ancient ideal of education as an intimate association between the young and the mature.

In the Victorian period the ideal of preserving childhood innocence had often ended—as at St. Paul's under Henry Coit—in placing youths in positions of extreme dependence. The Progressive era, however, saw a certain mitigation of this trend. In colleges and secondary schools throughout the country academic authorities introduced plans for student government. If the young were to be trained in habits of responsibility, they could not be left completely dependent—a certain amount of autonomy had to be restored to them. "You may ask what the reason for this self-government is," a faculty member at one family boarding school wrote in 1905:

> It is simply to impress the idea of responsibility on the individual members of the School, a responsibility for the welfare and good of the School; so that when we get out into the world we may be good citizens and have some responsibility for the welfare of our country. That I think, is the main reason. A less important reason is to give us some understanding of Parliamentary proceedings.[128]

At Groton, however, the student government movement was ignored. Peabody hoped to achieve similar ends through what he called "the monitor system, or the prefect system." This "scientific system" was meant to "use the boys as fellow workers with the masters to prevent evil arising." The prefects were outstanding Sixth Form (senior) boys, responsible for a great deal of minor disciplinary and administrative work. "The prefect," Peabody said, "takes the position of the older brother in the family."[129] To some of the younger boys it sometimes seemed that the prefects, in concert with the Sixth Form, actually ran "the family."[130] The prefects were supposed to serve as models of character and responsibility to the younger students. The post was highly prized. Franklin Roosevelt's keenest disappointment at Groton was that he was not made a prefect.[131] (He was extremely gratified when Franklin, Jr., was made Senior Prefect in 1933). At Groton, then, while the students' rights and duties were clearly defined, only to a limited degree was autonomy granted to a small and carefully selected number of youths.

Peabody's heavy reliance on the prefect system was his most significant innovation in the formal organization of the boarding school. Even here, it was the emphasis he placed on the system rather than the system itself which was novel. Peabody was familiar with the prefect system in the English public schools. There, housemasters delegated so much authority to the prefects that they in effect ran the schools. (In the 1880s, for instance, when a Marlborough head prefect reported that the place was on fire, his housemaster is said to have roared: "That part of the house is your department, not mine."[132]) Peabody also had seen the monitor-prefect system in operation at St. Mark's, where he had been first inspired to found a school of his own. The system at St. Mark's had originated in Muhlenberg's adaptation of the Lancasterian monitorial system at the Flushing Institute.[133] One has the impression that the authorities at St. Mark's placed not nearly so much emphasis on the system as Peabody would at Groton. Nor did Peabody's use of prefects resemble, in several important respects, the English system. American prefects were never granted as much power as were the English. And "fagging," the single most conspicuous element of the English prefect system, was not used in the United States. Fagging—the use of the younger boys by the older as servants—was the source of most of the abuses of the English system. It was consciously avoided at Groton.[134] Even so, American educational leaders were suspicious of the system. "It is absolutely inapplicable in our country," said President Eliot, "except, indeed, in a school like Groton, where a quite extraordinary control can be exercised by the masters."[135]

Little room for innovation in the curriculum existed at Groton or at any other preparatory school. "The studies of a school which sends practically all its pupils to college," Peabody wrote, "are generally determined by the university authorities."[136]

Within the curriculum, the only area of experimentation left open to preparatory schools was that of pedagogical method. Here, Peabody and his peers tended to be most conservative. In an address to a group of New England educators Peabody once recounted the following anecdote:

> [I visited] one of the great schools of England, a school which wins more scholarships at the universities than almost any other school, and I was talking to one of the leading men in the school. I said: "What do you think of Froebel's methods, and of the theories of the German educationalists?" He replied: "Oh, they are all rot" (laughter). "They do very well for German boys, but they won't do for English boys," he said; "What we do is to give a boy a Latin grammar and make him learn it, that is the only way to teach" (applause). That theory obtains throughout the schools of England to a great extent, and yet I say that the influence of the schools upon character is greater than the influence of our schools today.[137]

Peabody relied on the close familial relationship of the masters and the boys to supply motivation. And, if the laughter and applause from his audience are any indication, many other American educators of the time would have agreed with his views. Although boarding school leaders eagerly took advantage of outside educational experts, progressive pedagogy made almost no widespread impact on them.[138] In a limited sense, boarding schools were already progressive—perfect unions of the school and the community. Boarding school men, however, were not rigidly opposed to progressive educational methods. At Groton, for instance, in a pure example of the progressive project method, little Joseph Alsop wrote a history of China which was then printed by the students on their own press. For the most part, though, Peabody and others simply felt that most progressive methods were weak, undemanding—and thus a cheat to the student. Their attitude was summed up well in remarks made by Horace Dutton Taft to Peabody concerning the Lincoln School in New York City, one of the best progressive schools of its time:

> The Lincoln school is whaling away with an exceptional set of highly paid experts. I am unable to judge what the results

> are. I hear violent opinions both ways, but I feel certain that methods that might produce good results with such exceptional teachers would be calamitous when used by ordinary teachers. On the other hand, I am sure that a good many boys are subjected to the training of our orthodox schools who ought to have something different. The trouble is that the only other schools, as a rule, are schools with patent methods, often fraudulent.[139]

Besides pedagogy, another area of possible innovation open to the boarding school was that of the cultivation of the physical faculties—which usually meant organized athletics. Here prep school leaders felt a far deeper involvement than with pedagogy. Students in the Federalist era had exercised for the most part in a natural, casual way—they played spontaneous, traditional games, they fished, rode, ran, and swam. The Jahn system of gymnastics introduced to the United States at Round Hill had been short-lived. In the Victorian period highly organized and highly competitive team sports had slipped into the extracurriculum largely at the instigation of the students themselves. They had aroused considerable misgivings in educators such as Henry Coit. In the Progressive era, however, a new generation of schoolmen embraced athleticism as a primary instrument of moral education and student control. In American colleges and secondary schools by the turn of the century organized athletics—particularly football—almost buried all other aspects of school life.[140] At Phillips Exeter athletics assumed such proportion that overambitious students had to be dismissed when it was discovered that they had hired professionals to play on the Academy football team. By 1907 Lord Bryce, in declining an invitation to speak at Groton, said that it was perhaps just as well, for he "should have felt bound to take up my parable against the present excessive devotion to athletics," which the boys would have received "with indignation."[141]

At Groton athletics became one of the most pervasive of the school's activities. Peabody considered it a superior instrument for building character. "Football," his biographer wrote, "he privately admired because it is a game that is rough and hard, requiring courage, endurance, and discipline. Instinctively he trusted a football player more than a non-football-player, just as the boys did."[142] The same, of course, could be said for scores of other activities, athletic or not. One may speculate that football was a particularly appropriate educational device for the age: what better preparation for the wars of the trusts and the corporations than the battles between highly organized athletic teams? Peabody was amazed, as he told Theodore Roosevelt, when President Eliot "attacked me for holding that there was something beneficial in American football that was beneficial for the growing youth of the country."[143]

Peabody's athleticism should be seen in the context of his age. Never did Groton approach the hysterical devotion to football—or the corruption that went with it—which characterized many American colleges of the time. Peabody always wanted to win—but according to the rules of the game and the code of the gentleman. Since the masters played with the boys, sports at Groton could never get too far out of hand. Peabody himself was responsible for a national reformation of football. On 16 September 1905, when collegiate football seemed to be reaching a new peak of brutality and corruption, he suggested to President Theodore Roosevelt that "a complete revolution could be worked if we could get the coaches of Harvard and Yale and Princeton together, and persuade them to undertake to teach men to play football honestly. You are the one man, so far as I know, who could accomplish this without much effort."[144] The President followed Peabody's suggestion. A White House conference on football was called for 9 October 1905. The conference led to a nationwide reorganization of the game.[145] Peabody could well be content; the gentleman's code had been upheld.[146]

American Progressives were obsessed with purity and cleanliness: they wanted to purify politics, to clean up the cities, to conserve our precious natural resources, to avoid waste, to be efficient. So, at Groton Peabody used athletics not only as a means of moral education but to insure "pure and clean and righteous living in the school."[147] His rationale for this was typical of the time, and is worth quoting at length:

> It seems to me of the utmost importance that there should be nothing of the nature of loafing in a school. The curse of American college life and of school life is loafing (applause). Boys and men get together in a sociable way and sit round a

> room and talk and gossip, and a little scandal comes in, and then evil. The tone of loafers is always low. You can avoid that easily in a school, because you have the great advantage of athletics. One has not the slightest hesitation in saying that to run a school on a high standard of morality without athletics would be a practical impossibility. Athletics are of the most importance in establishing righteousness in the school. What do the boys do? What do they talk about? For moral evil you have got to consider the care of the body, and the best thing for a boy is to work hard and then, after a short interval, to play hard, and then to work hard again and then to play hard again and then, when the end of the day has come, to be so tired that he wants to go to bed and go to sleep. That is the healthy and good way for a boy to live.[148]

The logic of this passage seems inescapable: athletics were a substitute for sex, the playing field was a surrogate for the bed. The Victorian obsession with the preservation of childhood innocence led almost inexorably to the Progressive notion that the pure youth was the exhausted youth.

Throughout the nineteenth century Americans held an ambivalent view of nature. On the one hand it was seen as beneficent—a paridigm of God's message to man, from which the child could learn the proper relation of the individual to the cosmos. But the nineteenth century also conceived of nature as irrational chaos—an unfathomable abyss from which almost any horror might unexpectedly erupt. The notion that somehow the young were closer to the forces of nature, that at any moment they might erupt with unnameable excesses, became widespread in the Progressive era. "Pubescent boys and even girls," the psychologist G. Stanley Hall, father of the child-study movement, wrote in 1911, "often feel like animals in captivity. They long intensely for the utter abandon of a wilder life, and very characteristic is the frequent discarding of foot and head dress and even garments in the blind instinct to realize the conditions of primitive man."[149] Some of these tensions were released in the Spanish-American War; similar ones would be played out on the athletic fields of the nation.

Such intense and devoted effort, such stern but loving care, such thorough immersion in the ethos of muscular Christianity

—but even still some contemporaries had doubts about the very idea of the family boarding school. "Whether the 'cloister' theory, even in the modernized and charming form in which it appears at Groton," observed Dean Briggs of Harvard in 1893:

> —is the right theory, whether the isolation of one hundred sons of rich men—a separation from fathers and mothers, from poor men's sons and from a city life into which they must afterwards plunge and in which they must be exposed to all manner of temptations (temptation from which, except in vacation, they are watchfully shielded from at the school)—whether this isolation is not a mistake; whether the boys should not meet city life by day, and meet every night the counteracting influence of their own homes,—all this may well be doubted.[150]

Briggs was questioning here the whole tradition of romantic Christian nurture, the ideal of preserving the innocence of childhood into a pure and responsible maturity, free from the corruptions of the world. This ideal Peabody, like Muhlenberg and Coit, subscribed to without question. "Keep innocency," Peabody told his students, "for that will give a man peace at the last." In the Progressive era as in the Victorian, the gentleman must still be educated in isolation. But in the Progressive era the image of the gentleman and, more important, the role of the gentleman in American society, underwent a significant metamorphosis. In an altercation with a parent, Peabody once indicated his notion of the gentleman and his role thus:

> The difficulty [with the father] was that he believed being a gentleman is something which happens, whereas, of course, it must be accomplished. There is a most awful amount of rot talked about it today. A lot of people seem to think that because poverty is dreadful and laboring men are badly treated, it is wrong to have good manners and be decent and live up to standards. The idea of apologizing for being a gentleman! It is almost as bad as talking forever about one's possessions or family. The worst thing of all is to be a drone, to do nothing, and boast of it. Being a gentleman is a responsibility, that's what it is.[151]

At Victorian St. Paul's, the gentleman had been conceived of as a decent, virtuous Christian—well educated, considerate of the poor, women, and the old—but with no special role to play in American society. The Progressive gentleman, however, was to occupy somewhat the same position as his Federalist forebear: above all he was to be *responsible*—responsible not simply to himself but to his society. "The self-reliant, simplified public-servant," a successor of Henry Coit could declare by 1917, "caring only for whatsoever things are honorable and of good report, should be the normal product of St. Paul's School."[152] Better than anyone else, Theodore Roosevelt summed up the role of the Progressive gentleman. "I feel most strongly with you," he wrote to Endicott Peabody in 1894, "about drilling into the minds of such boys as are many of yours that they must use aright the gifts given them and that they must render service to the State of a non-remunerative kind. Of course by service to the State I not only mean politics, but I mean work to raise the condition of the people in our great cities; work for cleanliness of mind and body generally."[153]

The notion that a major aim of education should be training towards public service was not unique to Theodore Roosevelt, St. Paul's, or Groton. It was one of the primary aims of the Progressive movement, and, more particularly, of the Social Gospel movement within American Protestantism. In an effort to apply Christian ethics to the problems created by industrial capitalism, Protestant clergymen turned more and more from an emphasis on individual salvation to a drive towards social redemption through social reform. Episcopalians were in the forefront of this movement. Peabody himself had been exposed to the earliest stirrings of the movement at both the English and American Cambridges. While he was firmly establishing Groton in the 1890s, back at his alma mater Dean George Hodges was making the Episcopal Theological School a center of Social Gospel thought.

Bostonian Social Gospelers, Arthur Mann has suggested, can be divided into two groups: "the moderates, who wished to Christianize capitalism; and the radicals, who wished to socialize Christianity." Peabody, of course, belonged to the former group, although he had no articulated social philosophy. "He was not profound," one of his alumni said in an observation that could be extended to his social views, "but he was alert and intelligent and completely devoid of any shame about changing his mind when he thought he was wrong. This was disconcerting."[154] (It was a trait equally disconcerting in some Groton alumni.) But however loosely, Peabody would probably have subscribed to what Arthur Mann has described as the four basic themes of the moderate Social Gospelers: "a fear of Marxism and Nationalism as well as Spencerian sociology and Summerian economics; a marked desire for instruction in the facts of American economic life; a readiness to adopt meliorative reforms rather than drastic changes; and a willingness to back honest reformers with Christian brotherliness. The basic assumption was that capitalism was not organically evil or unworkable, but rather a good economic system suffering from exploding yet easily removable unchristian practices."[155] Directly and indirectly, these were the attitudes with which Groton inculcated its students. That they should bear a striking resemblance to Franklin Roosevelt's New Deal is hardly surprising.

The message of the Social Gospel was spread to a generation of young Americans in colleges and universities in every part of the nation. Young people were constantly urged to devote their lives to the public service.[156] Theodore Roosevelt waged a one-man campaign amongst college youth to abjure Victorian Mugwumpery with its disdain for practical politics and to enter enthusiastically upon a public career. "The man with a university education," he exhorted college students in a speech which reads almost like a paraphrase of Joseph Buckminster's 1809 Phi Beta Kappa address, "is honor bound to take an active part in our political life, and to do his full duty as a citizen by helping his fellow-citizens to the extent of his power in the exercise of the rights of self-government."[157] In Boston at seminaries and colleges students were urged, in much these neo-Federalist terms, to face the problems of the day. Beginning in the 1880s at Harvard Endicott Peabody's distant relation Francis Greenwood Peabody taught a course on the "Ethics of the Social Question" (fondly known as "Peabo's drainage, drunkenness and divorce"), which attempted to unite Christian ethics and the emerging social sciences.[158] Francis Peabody and others urged a generation of collegians to take up what Arthur Mann has aptly called "the gentleman's burden." The Social Gospel educators "endowed the Boston seminarian and collegian with the idea that he stood between the plutocrat and the proletarian, that he was neither grasping nor degraded, but altruistic and refined, and with social science know-how. The burden was clear: to safeguard society against subversion from extreme and antithetical elements."[159] It was the message of the Anthologists, couched now in social rather than cultural terms, all over again. Such teachings bore fruit in the conversion and commitment of thousands of collegians to lives of social service. One immediate result, for instance, was the social settlement movement, sparked largely by young college graduates.[160]

Earlier in the century, the tradition of Christian nurture had arisen in reaction to too heavy a reliance on revivalistic conversions. "Never is it too early for good to be communicated," Horace Bushnell had written in 1847. "Infancy and childhood are the age most pliant to good. And who can think it necessary that the plastic nature of childhood must first be hardened into stone and stiffened into enmity towards God and all duty, before it can become a candidate for Christian character!"[161] Do not depend upon revivals, Bushnell had recommended; concentrate instead upon the gradual Christian nurture of the child within the Christian family and home. This was the technique which Muhlenberg and Coit had followed within an institution, the family boarding school. As with Christian nurture, so with Progressive nurture: it was the method which Endicott Peabody would use at Groton to insure the gradual inculcation of the child with the ethos of the Social Gospel.

Progressivism provided "those ideas to have *faith* in," which Erik Erikson considers so necessary for a firm sense of identity. Progressive nurture involved the saturation of the youth in the concept of public service and his awakening to a deep interest in public affairs. Victorian Christian nurture had been summed up in Muhlenberg's dictum that "the pupil must be made to perceive that the law of God is the Law of the School."[162] Progressive nurture was summed up in Peabody's dictum that "in a Christian country the aim of the school-master is nothing less . . . than to help his pupils to become citizens of the commonwealth of Christ."[163] To do this, the boarding school had to be more than a family: "The church boarding school," a rector of St. Paul's would be writing by 1923, "should be a sort of social settlement among the prosperous."[164] This Groton had been since its founding.

To begin with, Peabody, as a Groton alumnus recalled, constantly and incessantly "urged the boys to go into the professions and keep away from Wall Street."[165] As early as March 1888, "thinking that it would be a good thing for the fellows to be a little better posted on things in general," Peabody had begun presenting nightly a fifteen-minute digest of foreign and domestic news.[166] By the 1890s the Groton student had available to him many of the leading periodicals of the day which dealt with important public issues: *Harper's Monthly,* the New York *Evening Post,* the Boston *Evening Transcript,* the *Outlook, Scribners,* and the *Century.*[167] When the students opened the pages of their school magazine they would almost invariably find a piece which attempted to "prepare in a more palatable form for the young a food of real value—a knowledge of the politics of the country."[168] Formal student debates, long a popular activity in American colleges and secondary schools, were another means of inculcating the students with an interest in public service. In 1898, for example, Groton students debated on subjects such as the Turkish indemnity question, the protection of Alaskan seals, and the annexation of Hawaii.[169] Progressive nurture was by no means limited to Groton. For instance, in 1884 at St. Paul's under Henry Coit a typical subject set for the English Composition Prize had been a perfect expression of Victorian Mugwumpery: "The Elective Franchise: Should It Be Restricted, and How?" By the turn of the century, however, St. Paul's students were writing on subjects such as these:

1898—The Search for the North Pole as a Training for Heroism
1899—The Causes of the Decline of the Spanish Empire
1900—Abraham Lincoln's Place in History
1902—The Future of the American Negro
1903—Rome's Conquest of Carthage; or, Results of Marconi's System of Wireless Telegraphy
1905—The Americans As Rulers of Alien Races
1906—The Japanese Character; or, The Automobile: Its Influence on the Habits and Character of the American People

1908—The Powers and Prerogative of the President of the United States
1910—The Responsibility of the United States in the Philippine Islands
1912—The Effect of Luxury on National Development
1913—The Panama Canal[170]

By 1920 St. Paul's Sixth Form class in Sacred Studies would even be using the Christian Socialist Walter Rauschenbusch's *The Social Principles of Jesus* as its text.[171]

The transition from Victorian isolation to Progressive social commitment at St. Paul's did not take place without objections. Early in the twentieth century the *Horae Scholasticae,* the student journal, was transformed into a sort of junior muckraking magazine. In 1910, on the *Horae's* fiftieth anniversary, the editors asked for comments from alumni on their new policy. James C. Knox, who had been a student and master at St Paul's under Henry Coit, took a dim view of the journal's progressive tone. His views were probably representative of many of the earlier generation. "I do not think a boy's journal need concern itself very much with the spirit of the age," he wrote. "It should reflect the natural life of childhood, which I have more than a suspicion will not change materially in the future any more than it has in the past. A boy is a conservative being—content to ignore the world." Knox, of course, was mistaken. The idea—and the very experience—of childhood is always in flux. As a society changes, its ideal types change. With such shifts the aims and methods of education also change. Politically, the ideal product of Christian nurture was the nineteenth-century liberal; the ideal product of Progressive nurture would be the twentieth-century social democrat.[172]

One of the aims of Progressive nurture was to create a new relationship between the rich and the poor. Fellenberg's Hofwyl had included schools for both the children of the rich and the children of the poor. They did not mix, however. From a safe distance the children of the rich were taught "that their first duty is to use the means which Providence has placed at their disposal in a way likely to prove beneficial to the less fortunate members of the community."[173] The poor, in turn, would learn self-respect and a belief that their superiors had only their best interests at heart.[174] In this way, social discord would be prevented and the organic nature of society maintained. At Victorian St. Paul's Henry Coit's orphan asylum overlooking the school had served much the same purpose—whatever it did for the orphans, it provided St. Paul's students with object lessons in the exercise of Christian charity. There would be no such separation of the rich and the poor at the Progressive family boarding school. Dean Briggs's observation that Groton students were separated "from poor men's sons, and from a city life into which they must afterwards plunge," was true only to a limited degree. Groton students probably learned more about and saw more of the urban poor at the school than they would have if they had lived in a silk-stocking city district or in a suburb.

Among the most popular and ubiquitous of the secular preachers of the Social Gospel was Jacob Riis, who began touring boarding schools at least as early as 1893 with his magic lantern and his vivid slides depicting how the "other half" lived in the slums of the great cities. Yearly, Riis visited one school after another: Groton, St. Paul's, Hill, St. Mark's, Lawrenceville, Choate, and others. He brought his graphic images of the city and its problems, from which so many of their parents were fleeing, to the children of the well-to-do. "I trust that I shall be able to sow seed that will open up and bear a hundredfold," he told Peabody (with whom he became quite friendly) after his first visit to Groton. He did. He not only raised money for his activities, but persuaded many children of the wealthy to take an active part in social reform movements.[175]

College students could go to work in a city slum settlement; Groton brought the children of the poor to the country. In 1893 Peabody established the Groton School Camp on Squam Lake "to provide two weeks' camping for poor boys from Boston and near-by parishes, several contingents coming each summer." Groton students served in relays throughout the summer as counselors at the camp.[176] Groton's example was followed by many other family boarding schools. Nor were Groton's students completely isolated from the town of Groton. The schools' student Missionary Society took part in many of the town's activities.[177]

Grotonians were exposed to a constant parade of some of the most prominent public figures of the day exhorting them to do something about the nation's social needs. Booker T. Washington came and talked about the Negro problem. (Peabody considered "B. Washington and T. Roosevelt as the 2 great Americans for young men to back up."[178]) There was always cousin Theodore Roosevelt, preaching secular sermons such as the following one of 1904 to the students:

> You are not entitled, either in college or in life, to an ounce of privilege because you have been to Groton—not an ounce, but we are entitled to hold you to exceptionable accountability because you have been to Groton. Much has been given you, therefore we have a right to expect much of you. . . . I was glad to hear the rector when he asked you to be careful not to turn out snobs. Now there are in our civic and social life very much worse creatures than snobs, but none is more contemptible. . . . The interest you take in him is, can a man accomplish anything? If he cannot, then let him give place to one who can.[179]

Roosevelt would often travel up to Groton in the 1890s to enchant the boys with fireside tales of his bully adventures as Police Commissioner of New York City. But moral exhortation was never missing from this parade of Progressives. The conservationist Gifford Pinchot would look menacingly at the students and declare: "Fortunate is the man so rich he does not have to work; but twice fortunate is the rich man who works hard though he does not have to."[180]

Progressive nurture was not limited to a saturation in pressing domestic questions. Students at family boarding schools were also urged to turn their attention to the role of the United States among the other great nations of the world. As early as 1895, Alfred Thayer Mahan—then still Captain Mahan—was speaking to Grotonians on the role of sea power in history.[181] It was timely, for America's export version of Progressivism would be imperialism.[182] The outbreak of the Spanish-American War in 1898 and the subsequent acquisition of an American empire aroused tremendous interest among boarding school students. Peabody himself was exhilarated; this was much more exciting than football. Many of his classmates at Cheltenham had entered the Indian Civil Service; since his days in Tombstone his own missionary impulse had been kept dampened only with considerable effort. The Groton library was shortly stocked with Woolsey's *American Foreign Policy,* Lord Roberts's *Forty-One Years in India* and Pasha's *Fire and Sword in the Soudan.*[183] In the midst of the war, Peabody suggested to Henry Cabot Lodge, a powerful member of the Senate Foreign Relations Committee, that Grotonians might even be of some use in the new American empire. Lodge was modestly encouraging:

> I have read your letter . . . with a great deal of interest, and I agree with all you say, not only as to the opportunities which will come with our new acquisitions for our young men of education and standing, but also as to the immense importance of having good administration and the highest class of officials in those islands which we take from Spain. We cannot however put them on just the same plane as the English colonies, but either districts . . . or territories. . . . I do not think we shall send out many men from this country to govern in those islands as England sends men to India. If we take the Philippines or any part of them . . . we shall need there for the district government . . . a class of men precisely like those employed by England in India. . . . Of course everything at present is unsettled and will so continue until after the peace. . . . You may rest assured that I appreciate the importance of this matter and shall keep it steadily in mind.[184]

Anti-imperialistic sentiments were never absent among boarding school leaders or students. However, the possibility of spreading the virtues of American Progressivism to the lesser breeds without the law and of emulating mother England was intensely appealing to schoolboys. The inquiry of a student at the Choate School, addressed to a visiting Englishman, John Hobson—the father of modern theories of imperalism—was typical of the enthusiasm American expansion aroused in some of the young:

> I have learned that you are the author of several books on sociological subjects and as you have a son [Harold Hobson] here at school, I thought I should like to read some of your works. I selected your study of "Imperialism" as that is a subject as interesting to Americans as to Englishmen. At first

I found it rather hard reading, but as I progressed I became more interested, especially in that part which refers to "Imperalism and the Lower Races."

I think that imperialism is a help to the lower races, not a detriment. The supremacy of the English race above all others is acknowledged, and their coming into an uncivilized country and their settlement there would, I think, help to raise the people to a higher and better state.

If imperialism should be stopped by the nations of the world, would not everything be at a standstill? Would not the races now becoming civilized under the influence of English and American occupation, be reclaimed to savagery? Would the valuable products of the colonies be exported as heretofore? Each nation would draw back, as it were, into its own shell, never raising its head to look around, but entirely absorbed in its own affairs.

Perhaps I have been a little presuming in speaking thus freely, but I am sure you would like my real opinion. I hope you will be so kind as to reply, for a letter from you in THE BRIEF would be greatly appreciated by us boys.[185]

Hobson, in one of his most succinct statements of the anti-imperialist position, did reply.[186] The letter, however, probably did little to deter schoolboy dreams of Gordon and Khartoum or of Roosevelt and San Juan Hill.

Peabody's strong interest in America's role abroad influenced his students. Many Grotonians—such as Joseph C. Grew and Sumner Welles—would enter the American Foreign Service. For the next forty years Peabody was indefatigable in his efforts to promote their ambitions for domestic or foreign positions in the American imperium. Groton alumni would be playing significant roles in shaping American foreign policy well into the second half of the twentieth century. Peabody, however, was in no sense a howling imperialist; he simply believed that if America was to have an empire, it should be a Progressive empire—honestly administered by well-educated gentlemen, pure, clean, and Christian.

Progressive nurture would lead to the creation of the compleat social democrat—the gentleman as perfected public servant. That public *service* also meant public *power* was an idea not lingered upon long by Peabody or others. Like Thomas Jefferson and John Adams (great-grandsons of both, incidentally, sent their sons to Groton), Peabody and Theodore Roosevelt believed in government by the true *aristoi;* insofar as Groton was creating such gentlemen, neither man would have questioned their fitness to rule.

Groton's alumni were ambivalent about the effects of their four-to six-year saturation in Progressive nurture. George Martin, for instance, felt that Peabody might just as well have saved his breath. When Peabody "urged the boys to be true to themselves and drop out of their parents' income class," Martin wrote, "they did not hear him. They were going to make enough money to be able to send their sons to Groton." Ellery Sedgwick too had mixed feelings about Progressive nurture. "In season and out," he remembered, "public service was held up to every boy as a shining goal. It is God's mercy that all of us didn't go into it!"[187]

An extraordinary number of Groton alumni, however, did enter public service. Most became businessmen; but being a businessman hardly precluded public service. In 1933, shortly before its fiftieth anniversary, this tiny school with fewer than a thousand alumni out of college could number among its graduates one man serving as President of the United States; two men who had served as Secretary of State; three senators; a congressman; ministers or ambassadors to Japan, Turkey, Canada, Denmark, Greece, Switzerland, the Dominican Republic, El Salvador, and Cuba; a governor-general; two state governors; two assistant secretaries of the Navy; one of the Treasury; one of the Army; two lieutenant-governors; a police commissioner of New York City; a civil service commissioner of New York, and a governor of the Federal Reserve Bank.[188] It was a staggering record; in later years it would remain equally impressive.

The crown of Endicott Peabody's career came with the election of Franklin D. Roosevelt to the presidency in 1932. Peabody himself voted for Hoover, as he told an alumnus, "thinking that he was the best man to deal with the economic questions and counting it wise for him to have a chance to carry out the policies which he had inaugurated." Franklin had been "a quiet, satisfactory boy of more than ordinary intelligence, taking a good position in his form but not brilliant. Athletically, he was rather too slight for success. We all liked him . . . I have always been fond of him, following his career with much interest and keeping in close touch with him in connection with his boys."[189] As the New Deal progressed, Peabody's somewhat detached view turned to one of outright enthusiasm. Friends might tell him that Franklin was slippery, and not to be trusted.[190] But then Peabody too had that rather disconcerting habit of being "completely devoid of any shame about changing his mind when he thought he was wrong." Friends might accuse Franklin of being too much of a "politician" in tinkering with the civil service and consorting with the likes of Jim Farley. But Peabody had learned his lessons from Theodore Roosevelt well. "The right course in political life must be very difficult to discover and pursue," he wrote. Theodore had had to deal with Boss Platt of New York, "counted one of the worse Republican highwaymen of his time." Franklin might have to consult with Farley in order to put through his programs.[191] So far as Peabody was concerned, there would be no mugwumpery at Groton.

By 1936 Peabody was completely won over to the New Deal. "I am in hearty agreement with you," he wrote Roosevelt shortly after that year's presidential election, "in what seems to me the two great purposes of your life: first, making it possible for all the people of the nation who are willing to work being given an opportunity to do so and to carry on work under worthy conditions; secondly, to join with others who are like-minded in endeavoring to bring peace to the nations."[192] While Franklin might be pragmatic as to means, Peabody always knew that deep within they both shared the Progressive gentleman's vision of the Christian commonwealth.

Progressive nurture, though obviously effective at Groton, was not limited to that school alone. It pervaded the family boarding schools in the two to three decades before the First World War, and for a considerable period thereafter. For instance, the alumni of the Phillips Exeter Academy, which had been transformed into a boarding school only around the turn of the century, compiled a record of public service almost as impressive as Groton's. Of the 2,517 students who graduated from the Academy between 1920 and 1929 fully 25.3 percent held elective or appointive offices in federal, state, county, or local governments.[193]

"In the usual course of national aggrandizement," Joseph Buckminster had prophesied in 1809, "it is almost certain that those of you, who shall attain to old age, will find yourselves the citizens of an empire unparalled in extent." Within the lifetimes of many in his audience Buckminster's vision would be fulfilled beyond his most fantastic dreams. "Truth, truth," Buckminster had added, "is indeed the ultimate object of human study." But the educated gentleman must always remember "that we all owe something to society." Elitist but not exclusive, neo-Federalist Progressive nurture did not end with the larger Progressive movement. Students at family boarding schools would be exhorted to pursue careers of public service—and of public power —well into the twentieth century.

"I think the success of any School can be measured by the contribution the Alumni make to our national life," a young aspirant to Congress named John Kennedy told his fellow alumni at the fiftieth anniversary of the Choate School in 1946. There was one field, Kennedy went on, "in which Choate and the other private schools of this country have not made a contribution, and this is in the field of politics. It's perhaps natural that this should be so. In America, politics are regarded with great contempt; and politicians themselves are looked down upon because of their free and easy compromises. . . . [but] we must recognize that if we do not take an interest in our political life we can easily lose at home what so many young men have so bloodily won abroad. I don't think this will happen. But it is the great challenge of our times."[194] The careers of scores of Groton and Phillips Exeter alumni—not to mention his own later life—decisively disproved Kennedy's observation that private school alumni had made no "contribution" to American political life. To a degree—even though some of its members were unaware of it—the Federalist dream of a nation inspired and led by a gentlemanly elite had been fulfilled by the middle of the twentieth century. But while the ideal had been achieved in some measure, the exhortatory rhetoric lingered on, frozen in its nineteenth-century mold: Kennedy's words could be inserted into a speech of Theodore Roosevelt or Endicott Peabody with no sense of incongruity. Whether the rhetoric and world-view of Theodore Rooosevelt and Endicott Peabody was appropriate to the middle of the twentieth century was another matter—and perhaps not one for which the family boarding schools should be held responsible.

Notes

Introduction

1. *Charles Francis Adams, 1835–1915: An Autobiography* (Boston, 1916), pp. 21,20.

2. Frank D. Ashburn, *Fifty Years On: Groton School, 1884–1934* (New York, 1934), p. 185.

3. MS Minutes of the Board of Trustees, January 17, 1941, Office of the Administrative Vice-Rector, St. Paul's School, Concord, New Hampshire.

4. "Private School Graduates in *Who's Who in America,*" *Bulletin of Educational Philanthropy,* IX (Chicago, 1956), 3. Unfortunately, the schools were not specified.

5. George E. Mowry, *The Era of Theodore Roosevelt, 1900–1912* (New York, 1958), p. 106.

6. Roosevelt was educated by private tutors before entering Harvard in 1876. Carleton Putnam, *Theodore Roosevelt: The Formative Years 1858–1886* (New York, 1958), pp. 116–28.

7. Robert Gutwillig, "The Select Seventeen: A Guide to Upper-Class Education," *Esquire,* LIV (November 1960), 162–63.

8. See Stephen Birmingham, "The New England Prep School," *Holiday,* XXXV (February 1964), 38 ff. Birmingham, with as many qualifications as Gutwillig, listed 14 New England schools as his core group: Groton, St. Paul's, St. Mark's, St. George's, Kent, Taft, Hotchkiss, Choate, Middlesex, Deerfield, Phillips Exeter, Phillips Andover, Canterbury, and Portsmouth Priory. One observer even managed to run her core list of schools up to 130: see Lucy Kavaler, *The Private World of High Society* (New York, 1960).

9. For the first suggestion of the use of that sturdily American word "independent," see Frank S. Hackett, "Independent School," *Outlook,* 26 May 1926. The lengthy debate over the adoption of the adjective can be followed in the *Private School News,* II (15 June 1926), *et seq.*

10. R. Freeman Butts and Lawrence A. Cremin, *A History of Education in American Culture* (New York, 1955), pp. 417, 421.

11. Elmer Ellsworth Brown, *The Making of Our Middle Schools: An Account of the Development of Secondary Education in the United States* (New York, 1903), pp. 393–97.

12. Arthur Mann, *Yankee Reformers in the Urban Age: Social Reform in Boston, 1880–1900* (New York: Harper Torchbooks, 1966), p. 7.

13. See below, p. 334.

14. Dixon Wecter, *The Saga of American Society: A Record of Social Aspiration, 1607–1937* (New York, 1937), p. 241.

15. E. Digby Baltzell, *Philadelphia Gentlemen: The Making of A National Upper Class* (Glencoe, Ill., 1958), p. 313.

16. *Ibid.,* pp. 293, 305. A line must be drawn somewhere; quite arbitrarily, we will consider the schools on Baltzell's list (excepting the two southern schools, Episcopal High and Woodbury Forest), as *our* core group of schools.

17. C. Wright Mills, *The Power Elite* (New York, 1956), pp. 63–66.

18. G. William Domhoff, *Who Rules America?* (Englewood Cliffs, N.J., 1967), pp. 16–17, 22–23.

19. Baltzell may well be correct in his assertions concerning the upper-class nature of these schools. If he is, the American upper class has been a singularly powerless one. In any case, Baltzell, Mills, and Domhoff all rely on listing in a *Social Register* as the basic determinant for membership in the upper class. However, criteria for such listings are and were so eccentric that they strike me as being of extremely limited usefulness. I would suggest that the existence or nonexistence of an American upper class in the nineteenth century must begin with an empirical analysis of tax lists, wills, and so forth, along the lines followed by Jackson Turner Main in his *Social Structure of Revolutionary America* (Princeton, 1965). My suspicion is that one would eventually find not a single "upper class," but several different "sub-cultures of the rich," often in conflict with one another, or even ignorant of each other's existence.

The following pages, obviously, concern only those rich parents who sent their sons to boarding schools. It is perfectly possible (though I think it highly unlikely) that in 1895 the majority of rich New Yorkers, for instance, sent their sons to public high schools. It is possible that a majority sent their sons to private day schools. Or perhaps a majority had their sons tutored at home. My point is that until we know exactly *who* the "rich" were at any one time or place, sweeping generalizations about the class nature of private boarding schools are premature.

20. Harold U. Faulkner, *The Quest for Social Justice, 1898–1914* (New York, 1931), p. 22; see below, pp. 0).

21. Kenneth Keniston, "You Have to Grow Up In Scarsdale to

Know How Bad Things Really Are," *New York Times Magazine,* 27 April 1969, pp. 27 ff.

22. For a more complete development of some of these themes, see James McLachlan, "The City, the School, and the Suburb: An Historian's View," in *The City in American History: A Report of the Twelfth Yale Conference on the Teaching of Social Studies. . . .* (New Haven, 1967), pp. 57–67.

23. James MacGregor Burns, *Roosevelt: The Lion and the Fox* (New York, 1956), pp. 236–37.

Chapter I

1. Edward Everett, in Eliza Buckminster Lee, *Memoirs of Rev. Joseph Buckminster, D.D., and of his Son, Rev. Joseph Stevens Buckminster* (Boston, 1849), p. 391.

2. "On the Dangers and Duties of Men of Letters; An Address, Pronounced before the Society of OBK, on Thursday, August 31st, 1809," *Monthly Anthology,* VII (September, 1809), 145–60.

3. John Gorham Palfrey, *A Discourse on the Life of John Thornton Kirkland, D.D., LL.D., Late President of Harvard College. . . .* (2nd ed.; Cambridge, 1840), p. 35. Italics mine.

4. Adams quotation from John R. Howe, Jr., *The Changing Political Thought of John Adams* (Princeton, 1966), p. 142; Edwin Harrison Cady, *The Gentleman in America: A Literary Study in American Culture* (Syracuse, N.Y., 1949), pp. 5, 3, and chs. I-V *passim.*

5. John Adams to Thomas Jefferson, 15 November 1813, in Lester J. Cappon, ed., *The Adams-Jefferson Letters* (2 vols.; Chapel Hill, N.C., 1959), I, 397–402.

6. Thomas Jefferson to Peter Carr, 7 September 1814, reprinted in Roy J. Honeywell, *The Educational Work of Thomas Jefferson* (Cambridge, 1931), p. 223.

7. *Ibid.,* p. 11. In this case Jefferson was writing specifically of his 1779 *Bill for the More General Diffusion of Knowledge.*

8. Lee, *Memoirs of Buckminsters,* chs. VII–XI and *passim.*

9. Palfrey, *Kirkland, passim;* Samuel Eliot Morison, *Three Centuries of Harvard* (Cambridge, 1936), pp. 195–96.

10. For the Anthology Society, see Lewis P. Simpson's excellent "Introduction" to his *Federalist Literary Mind: Selections from the Monthly Anthology and Boston Review, 1803–1811, Including Documents Relating to the Boston Atheneum* (Baton Rouge, 1962), pp. 3–41, and Mark A. DeWolfe Howe, ed., *Journal of the Proceedings of the Society Which Conducts The Monthly Anthology and Boston Review . . .* (Boston, 1910), pp. 3–25.

11. The eleven other original members were: Arthur Maynard Wal-

ter, a Boston lawyer; Buckminster; Joseph Tuckerman, Unitarian minister and pioneer urban humanitarian; William Tudor, Jr., the first editor of the *North American Review;* Peter Oxenbridge Thacher, brother of Samuel and later judge of the Boston Municipal Court; Thomas Gray, a Unitarian minister; William Wells, an English-born schoolmaster and bookseller; Edmund T. Dana, brother of Richard Henry and a lawyer; and John Collins Warren and James Jackson, both physicians and members of the Harvard Medical School faculty. Howe, *Journal,* pp. 298–99.

12. *Federalist Literary Mind,* p. 40.

13. Quoted in Henry Adams, *History of the United States of America during the First Administration of Thomas Jefferson* (9 vols; New York, 1889), I, 83–84.

14. "Preface," *Monthly Anthology,* I (1805), i–iii, reprinted in Howe, *Journal,* pp. 5–8.

15. Simpson, *Federalist Literary Mind,* pp. 28–31. Buckminster's comments on Liverpool were obviously intended to apply to the cultural situation in Boston: "The city of Liverpool has now reached that point of wealth, at which societies, which have been hitherto merely mercenary and commercial, begin to turn their attention to learning and the fine arts, that is, when they perceive that something more than great riches is necessary to make a place worthy of being visited, and interesting enough to be admired." Buckminster, "Literary Institution in Liverpool," *Monthly Anthology,* IV (1807), 597–601. Articles in the *Anthology* were not signed; a fairly complete list of attributions can be found in Howe, *Journal,* pp. 317–28.

16. Robert Hallowell Gardiner, "An Essay Upon the Multiplicity of Our Literary Institutions," *Monthly Anthology,* IV (1807), 113–16, 184–186.

17. For full accounts of this group, see Orie W. Long, *Literary Pioneers: Early American Explorers of European Culture* (Cambridge, 1935), and Van Wyck Brooks, *The Flowering of New England* (New York, 1936), pp. 73–134.

18. [John T. Kirkland,] "Literary Institutions—University," *North American Review,* VII (1818), 270. Kirkland's article was based on notes by Edward Everett. See David Tyack, *George Ticknor and the Boston Brahmins* (Cambridge, 1967), p. 271, n. 1.

19. Edward Everett to George Bancroft, 23 August 1819, George Bancroft MSS, Massachusetts Historical Society, Boston. The Society is cited hereafter as MHS; for an excellent discussion of the Anthologists' ideas in general, and Buckminster's in particular, see Daniel Howe, "The Unitarian Conscience: Harvard Moral Philosophy and the Second Great Awakening, 1805–1861" (Ph.D. dissertation, University of California, Berkeley, 1967), ch. VII.

20. On the attitude of the Scotch reviews towards America, see John Clive, *Scotch Reviewers: The Edinburgh Review, 1802–1815* (Cambridge, 1957), pp. 168–69, 175.

21. Cogswell reviewed a new edition of Nathaniel Ward's seventeenth-century *The Simple Cobbler of Aggawam in America* in *The Monthly Anthology,* VI (1809), 34–47.

22. [Anna Eliot Ticknor, ed.,] *Life of Joseph Green Cogswell as Sketched in His Letters* (Cambridge, 1874), *passim.*

23. "On the Means of Learning, and the State of Learning, in the United States of America," *Blackwood's Edinburgh Magazine,* IV (1818–1819), 546–53, and "On the State of Learning in the United States of America," *ibid.,* 641–49. The quotations are from p. 547.

24. Joseph Green Cogswell to George Bancroft, 3 July 1819, Bancroft MSS, MHS.

25. [Sidney Willard,] "State of Learning in the United States," *North American Review,* IX (1819), 240, 243.

26. For an example of this usage, see "Account of Westminster-School . . . ," *Monthly Anthology,* III (1806), 636.

27. On college entrance requirements throughout the nineteenth century, see Edwin C. Broome, *A Historical and Critical Discussion of College Entrance Requirements* (New York, 1903).

Discovering how, by whom, and where students entering an American college before the late nineteenth century were prepared is extraordinarily difficult. Intensive research has produced very little solid information. Consider, for example, Harvard's class of 1755; information on their precollegiate education is available for only seven of the twenty-seven members of the class. Of these, three were prepared by their ministers, two at the Cambridge Latin Grammar school, and two by local tutors. This is hardly enough information on which to base a firm generalization; that available for later classes is not much better. (Clifford K. Shipton, *Biographical Sketches of Those Who Attended Harvard in the Classes 1751–1755. . . .* [*Sibley's Harvard Graduates,* vol. XIII] [Boston, 1965], 512–686.)

For Yale, somewhat more information is available. For example, almost all members of Yale's class of 1815 were prepared, publicly or privately, by Yale graduates. Information—at times difficult to interpret—is available for forty-eight members of this class of seventy-one. Ministers prepared twenty-three students, or almost half of the sample. They were largely local pastors, though it appears that a few clergymen were in the habit of taking two or three boys at a time to live with them and fit them for college. Laymen apparently tutored eleven boys in or near the students' homes, while three seem to have gone to local private schools. Only eleven boys prepared in formal institutions: seven at academies, and four at Latin Grammar schools (in this case all at New Haven's Hopkins Grammar School). The only generalization I would venture on this subject is that, at least before 1820 or so, college preparation seems to have been largely a private, noninstitutional, affair. Franklin B. Dexter, *Biographical Sketches of the Graduates of Yale College. . . .* (New Haven, 1912), VI, 729 ff.

28. For a charming account of one northern tutor's stay with a southern planting family, see Philip Vickers Fithian, *Journal and Letters,* H. D. Farish, ed., (Williamsburg, 1943).

29. Butts and Cremin, *History of Education,* pp. 124–26; Robert Middlekauff, *Ancients and Axioms: Secondary Education in Eighteenth-Century New England* (New Haven, 1963), p. 151; Carl Bridenbaugh, *The Colonial Craftsman* (New York, 1950), pp. 167–68.

30. Edmund S. Morgan, *Virginians at Home: Family Life in the Eighteenth Century* (Williamsburg, 1952), pp. 11–12.

31. Emit D. Grizzell, *Origin and Development of the High School in New England Before 1865* (Philadelphia, 1923), p. 29; Middlekauff, *Ancients and Axioms,* pp. 128–37.

32. Frederick Rudolph, *The American College and University, A History* (New York, 1962), p. 281; Thomas Jefferson Wertenbaker, *Princeton, 1746–1896* (Princeton, 1946), pp. 89–91.

33. Middlekauff, *Ancients and Axioms,* p. 151; Butts and Cremin, *History of Education,* p. 260.

34. The Nonconformist academies had their origin in the Act of Uniformity of 1662. This statute required the English clergy to subscribe unquestioningly to the Anglican prayer book. Admission to Oxford and Cambridge, the only universities in England, was made dependent upon acceptance of the Thirty-Nine Articles of faith of the Anglican church. Within a few months of the passage of the act over two thousand rectors and vicars—almost one-fifth of the whole English clergy—resigned from the Church of England. Some of these "dissenting" clergymen established schools, which they called academies, to ensure that their successors would receive a thorough traditional education. At least seventy such institutions were founded in the eighteenth century. Their curricula embraced not only the classical subjects taught at the old universities, but also gradually introduced, throughout the eighteenth century, more modern subjects. The course offered by these academies resembled a combination of today's secondary and higher education. (For the English academies, see: H. McLachlan, *English Education Under the Test Acts: Being the History of the Non-Conformist Academies, 1662–1800* [Manchester, 1931], pp. 1–2, 143–52; J. W. Ashley Smith, *The Birth of Modern Education: The Contribution of the Dissenting Academies, 1660–1800* [London, 1954]; Brian Simon, *Studies in the History of Education, 1780–1870* [London, 1960], pp. 26–38, 56–62.)

The excellence of the academies attracted not only Dissenters and ministerial students but also Anglicans and laymen from all social backgrounds who wanted an education other than that offered in the universities, which appear to have gone into a decline after about 1760. [See Nicholas Hans, *New Trends in Education in the Eighteenth Century* (London, 1951), p. 51.] "Outside of the colleges and universities of Scotland," one observer has written, "the academies run by Dissenters gave the best instruction obtainable for youth in Britain." [Michael Kraus, *The Atlantic Civilization: Eighteenth Century Origins* (Ithaca, N.Y., 1949), p. 291.]

Americans were familiar with the English Dissenting academies and with the men who operated them. English and American Dissenters shared a common intellectual milieu; the works of Dissenting intellectuals and schoolmasters such as Richard Price, Isaac Watts, or Phillip Doddridge were as eagerly read and as influential in the colonies as in the mother country. Benjamin Franklin, in his widely circulated *Proposals Relating to the Education of Youth in Pennsylvania* (1749), outlined a plan of education remarkably similar to that of many English academies. However, at our present state of knowledge, it seems premature to draw any conclusions more final than these on the origins of the American academy. [For Franklin's academy, see *The Papers of Benjamin Franklin,* Leonard W. Labaree, ed., (New Haven, 1961), III, 395–421, esp. n. 6, 397–98. For an account of the academy, the nucleus of the future University of Pennsylvania, see Edward P. Cheyney, *History of the University of Pennsylvania, 1740–1940* (Philadelphia, 1940), pp. 71–81.]

The name "academy" itself has no particular significance. In seventeenth-century Europe the word was used indiscriminately to describe several different kinds of institutions, and in the following century it fit well with the Enlightenment's general reverence for the classical past. Most Dissenters were probably familiar with it from the type of school proposed by John Milton in his 1644 essay, "Of Education." [*The Works of John Milton,* Frank M. Patterson, ed., (18 vols.; New York, 1931–35), III, 275–91. See also Brown, *Making of Our Middle Schools,* pp. 155–61.]

35. Robert H. Bremner, *American Philanthropy* (Chicago, 1960), p. 21.

36. "Thoughts on the Revival of Religion in New England," *The Works of President Edwards* (4 vols.; New York, 1857), III, 413–16.

37. John Phillips to Samuel Phillips, 24 May 1762, in Charles H. Bell, *Phillips Exeter Academy in New Hamsphire, A Historical Sketch* (Exeter, 1883), p. 90; Myron R. Williams, *The Story of Phillips Exeter* (Exeter, 1957), p. 12.

38. Nehemiah Cleaveland, *The First Century of Dummer Academy . . .* (Boston, 1865), pp. 17–23 and *passim.*

39. Claude M. Fuess, *An Old New England School: A History of Phillips*

Academy, Andover (Boston, 1917), pp. 13–53; Williams, *Story of Phillips Exeter,* pp. 7–27.

40. Bernard Bailyn, "The Origins of American Politics," *Perspectives in American History,* I (1967), 15 and *passim;* Bailyn, *The Ideological Origins of the American Revolution* (Cambridge, Mass., 1967), esp. pp. 94–159.

41. Quoted in Fuess, *An Old New England School,* p. 23.

42. *Ibid.,* pp. 55–57. Phillips's emphases throughout.

43. For a brilliant account of the background of the experience, see William Haller, *The Rise of Puritanism* (New York: Harper Torchbooks, 1957).

44. Edmund S. Morgan, *The Puritan Family: Religion and Domestic Relations in Seventeenth-Century New England* (New York: Harper Torchbooks, 1966), pp. 90–92.

45. Fuess, *An Old New England School,* pp. 58, 67; Williams, *Story of Phillips Exeter,* p. 14.

46. Fuess, *An Old New England School,* p. 59. The interpretation of Phillips's intentions is mine, not Fuess's.

47. *Ibid.,* pp. 59–60.

48. Williams, *Story of Phillips Exeter,* p. 23.

49. Fuess, *An Old New England School,* pp. 76–79.

50. Williams, *Story of Phillips Exeter,* pp. 13–14, 19–20; Fuess, *An Old New England School,* pp. 47–48.

51. *Ibid.,* pp. 72–74.

52. *Academic Freedom in the Age of the College* (New York: Columbia Paperbacks, 1961), p. 123.

53. Oscar Handlin and Mary Flugg Handlin, *Commonwealth: A Study of the Role of Government in the American Economy: Massachusetts, 1774–1861* (New York, 1947), pp. 98, 99, and esp. pp. 93–112. Also enlightening on this point in relation to the academies are: Bernard Bailyn, "Education as a Discipline: Some Historical Notes," in John Walton and James L. Kuethe, eds. *The Discipline of Education* (Madison, Wis., 1963), pp. 125–39, and Theodore R. Sizer, "The Academies: An Interpretation," in *The Age of the Academies* (New York, 1964), pp. 2–5.

54. Fuess, *An Old New England School,* pp. 83–85, 80; Williams, *Story of Phillips Exeter,* pp. 46–47, 49.

55. Harriet Webster Marr, *The Old New England Academies Founded before 1826* (New York, 1959), p. 109.

56. *Ancients and Axioms,* p. 152.

57. The following brief account is based on: Butts and Cremin, *History of Education,* pp. 125–27, 196–98, 206–209; Brown, *Making of Our Middle Schools,* pp. 228–57; Marr, *Old New England Academies, passim;* Middlekauff, *Ancients and Axioms,* pp. 138-53; Grizzell, *Origin and Development of the High School,* pp. 29–37; George F. Miller, *The Academy System of the*

State of New York (Albany, 1922), pp. 19–131; James Mulhern, *A History of Secondary Education in Pennsylvania* (Philadelphia, 1933), *passim*; Edgar W. Knight, *The Academy Movement in the South* (n.p., n.d.), *passim;* and Sizer, *Age of the Academies,* pp. 46–48.

58. From the Minutes of the Trustees, 24 December 1819, in Edgar W. Knight, ed., *A Documentary History of Education in the South before 1860* (5 vols.; Chapel Hill, N.C., 1949–53), IV, 27.

59. Grizzell, *Origin and Development of the High School,* "Table IV," p. 31. The figures on incorporation in New England are as follows: to 1800, 42 academies; 1801–20, 81; 1821–40, 190; 1841–60, 107.

60. Butts and Cremin, *History of Education,* p. 127.

61. Marr, *Old New England Academies,* p. 127.

62. The connection between the residential idea and the American college is clear in the following extract from the Diary of William Woodbridge, Exeter's first Preceptor: " 'Exeter Academy was opened in April, 1783. During the war few young men could be educated. A crowd of such were ready to fill up the Academy. By charter, no boarders in a family where morning and evening prayers were not maintained should be admitted to the privileges of the Academy. Such a prohibition would break up the Academy at once. One expedient only remained: I must make them my family, as in college. In order to do this, the students were called to the Academy at one half after five in summer, and before sunrise in winter.' " Exeter *News-Letter,* 5 July 1895, as reprinted in Lawrence M. Crosbie, *The Phillips Exeter Academy, A History* (Norwood, Mass., 1923), p. 49.

63. Fuess, *An Old New England School,* p. 76.

64. Crosbie, *Phillips Exeter,* pp. 128, 192.

65. Clifton Johnson, *Old-Time Schools and School-Books* [1904] (New York: Dover Publications, 1963), p. 148.

66. *Ibid.,* pp. 148–49.

67. Knight, ed., *Documentary History,* IV, 27. See too the 1812 plea of the Raleigh (North Carolina) Academy in the Raleigh *Register,* 2 October 1812, *ibid.,* IV, 24–26; Johnson, *Old-Time Schools,* pp. 149–50; Marr, *Old New England Academies,* pp. 120–27.

68. William Gilman Perry, "In the Thirties," *Bulletin of The Phillips Exeter Academy,* III (March 1907), 29.

69. Cogswell, "Means of Learning," 547, 548.

Chapter II

1. "School Education," *North American Review,* IX (1819), 188–89.
2. Honeywell, *Educational Work of Jefferson,* pp. 58–61.

3. For a survey of this movement, see Ellwood P. Cubberley, *Public Education in the United States: A Study and Interpretation of American Educational History* (rev. ed.; Cambridge, 1934), pp. 340–66.

4. Quoted in Tyack, *George Ticknor,* p. 43.

5. George Bancroft to Edward Everett, 12 October 1819, in Mark A. DeWolfe Howe, *The Life and Letters of George Bancroft* (2 vols.; New York, 1908), I, 67.

6. Cogswell to George Ticknor, 18 February 1816, in Anna Ticknor, *Cogswell,* p. 44.

7. Cogswell to Mrs. Prescott, 28 October 1819, *ibid.*, pp. 114–15.

8. Although there is no systematic study of romantic educational thought in English, Hugh M. Pollard, *Pioneers of Popular Education* (Cambridge, 1957), is in many respects rewarding on this group.

9. For a clear exposition of the ideas of Rousseau, Pestalozzi, and their followers, see S. J. Curtis and M. E. Boultwood, *A Short History of Educational Ideas* (2nd. ed.; London, 1956), chs. XI, XIII, and XIV.

10. Johann Heinrich Pestalozzi, *How Gertrude Teaches Her Children . . . and an Account of the Method,* trans. Lucy E. Holland and Francis C. Turner, ed. Ebenezer Cooke (Syracuse, N.Y., 1894), p. 195.

11. *Ibid.*, pp. 87, 145–46.

12. H. Courthope Bowen, *Froebel and Education through Self-Activity* (New York, 1897), *passim;* see too Charles de Garmo, *Herbart and the Herbartians* (New York, 1896), pp. 3–11 for Herbart's debt to Pestalozzi.

13. Butts and Cremin, *History of Education,* p. 219.

14. "Character of Rousseau," *Monthly Anthology,* III (1806), 190–91.

15. Joseph Neef, *Sketch of A Plan and Method of Education, Founded on An Analysis of the Human Faculties and Natural Reason, Suitable for the Offspring of A Free People, and for All Rational Beings* (Philadelphia, 1808). In 1804 and 1805 William Maclure, a wealthy and philanthropic Scots industrialist who was planning to emigrate to the United States, visited Pestalozzi and tried to persuade him to go to Philadelphia and establish a school there. Though Pestalozzi refused, Maclure succeeded in bringing one of his disciples, Neef, to the new republic. In 1809 Neef opened a school run on the purest Pestalozzian principles in Philadelphia. The school was successful, but Neef wanted it located in the countryside; in 1812 he moved it to Village Green, Pennsylvania. There the neighbors were suspicious of the possibly atheistic Alsatian and his odd practices. In 1816 Neef moved the school again, this time to Louisville, Kentucky. The move proved unwise; students would not follow him to the remote village in the wilderness. The enterprise collapsed; Neef became a farmer until called by Maclure in 1825 to establish Pestalozzian schools at New Harmony, Indiana, the Utopian colony sponsored by Maclure's friend, the philanthropic Scots industrialist, Robert Owen the elder,

who had also been deeply influenced by Pestalozzi. Will S. Monroe, *History of the Pestalozzian Movement in the United States* (Syracuse, N.Y., 1907), pp. 9–108.

16. Robert Hallowell Gardiner, "Neef's Method of Education," *Monthly Anthology,* VII (1809), 264–71.

17. Cogswell to Elisha Ticknor, 8 December 1817, in Anna Ticknor, *Cogswell,* pp. 70–71.

18. Kate Silber, *Pestalozzi, The Man and His Work* (London, 1960), *passim.*

19. Anna Ticknor, *Cogswell,* p. 81 n.

20. Cogswell to Mrs. Prescott, October 28, 1819, *ibid.,* p. 115.

21. *Ibid.,* p. 81 n.

22. Silber, *Pestalozzi,* p. 285.

23. See Fellenberg's autobiographical sketch in *Letters From Hofwyl by A Parent, on The Educational Institutions of De Fellenberg* (London, 1842), pp. 48–61; and Pollard, *Pioneers of Popular Education,* pp. 42–45.

24. Quoted in *ibid.,* p. 44.

25. Quoted in Charles A. Bennett, *History of Manual and Industrial Education Up to 1870* (Peoria, Ill., 1926), p. 128.

26. Lewis Flint Anderson, *History of Manual and Industrial School Education* (New York, 1926), p. 91.

27. John Griscom, *A Year in Europe. Comprising A Journal of Observations in England, Scotland, Ireland, France, Switzerland, the North of Italy, and Holland. In 1818 and 1819* (2 vols.; New York, 1823), I, 382–83.

28. In 1814 a contemporary described all the elements thus: "The 1st is, a farm intended as a model; 2nd, an experimental farm; 3rd, a manufactory of agricultural implements; 4th, a workshop employed in the improvement of agricultural mechanism; 5th, a school of industry for the poor; 6th, a seminary for children of the higher class; 7th, an academy of theoretical and practical agriculture; and lastly, a school for the instruction of [school] masters;—and there is not one of these separate departments that does not derive some advantage from its connexion with the others." John Attersoll, *Translation of the Reports of M. le Comte de Capo-d'Istria and M. Rengger, upon the Principles and Progress of the Establishment of M. de Fellenberg, at Hofwyl, Switzerland* (London, 1820), p. 9.

29. *Ibid.,* p. 38.

30. *Ibid.,* p. 15 n.

31. Cogswell to Elisha Ticknor, 6 June 1818, Anna Ticknor, *Cogswell,* p. 81.

32. Attersoll, *Translation,* p. 13; Griscom, *A Year in Europe,* I, 393.

33. *Threading My Way: Twenty-seven Years of Autobiography* (New York, 1874), p. 161.

34. William C. Woodbridge, "Sketches of Hofwyl, and The Institutions of M. de Fellenberg. . . .," printed as an appendix to *Letters from Hofwyl.* Woodbridge's thirty-six letters from Hofwyl were first published in his magazine, the *American Annals of Education and Instruction,* beginning in 1831. Fellenberg himself considered them "the most complete view which has yet appeared of my plans, and of the means which I employ for their accomplishment." Since *Letters from Hofwyl* conveniently brings together all of Woodbridge's scattered reports, further references will be to it rather than to the *American Annals.*

35. Woodbridge, "Sketches of Hofwyl," p. 236. Woodbridge's italics.

36. Walter B. Kolesnick, *Mental Discipline in Modern Education* (Madison, Wis., 1958), pp. 10–29, 89–112.

37. Woodbridge, "Sketches of Hofwyl," pp. 244–45.

38. Quoted in *ibid.,* p. 328.

39. *Ibid.,* p. 246. For several of the student schedules used at Hofwyl, see *Letters from Hofwyl,* pp. 124–25.

40. Owen, *Threading My Way,* p. 166.

41. [Henry Brougham,] "Mr. Fellenberg's Establishments at Hofwyl," *Edinburgh Review,* XXXI (December 1818), 152.

42. Gabriel Compayré, *Herbart and Education by Instruction* (London, 1908), p. 81. In later years Fellenberg apparently discontinued this practice. See *Letters from Hofwyl,* pp. 126–27.

43. Woodbridge, "Sketches of Hofwyl," p. 288 ff.

44. Attersoll, *Translation,* pp. 13, 14.

45. *Ibid.,* p. 15.

46. Woodbridge, "Sketches of Hofwyl," pp. 271–72.

47. *Ibid.,* p. 279.

48. Cogswell to Elisha Ticknor, 1 September 1818, in Anna Ticknor, *Cogswell,* pp. 87–88.

49. Morgan, *Puritan Family,* p. 104.

50. For an excellent analysis of common sense—or "moral"—philosophy, the intellectual base from which the Anthologists operated, see Daniel Howe's "The Unitarian Conscience." Donald Harvey Meyer's "The American Moralists: Academic Moral Philosophy in the United States, 1835–1880" (Ph.D. dissertation, University of California, Berkeley, 1967) is the best broad consideration of the subject.

51. M. Howe, *Life and Letters of Bancroft,* I, 20.

52. Russell B. Nye, *George Bancroft, Brahmin Rebel* (New York, 1944), pp. 21–22, 29–30.

53. *Ibid.,* p. 36; Bancroft to Norton, 9 April 1820 and 1 August 1820; Bancroft to Kirkland, 17 September 1820, Bancroft MSS, MHS.

54. Bancroft to Everett, 3 December 1820; Bancroft to "Dear Sir,"

5 November 1820; Bancroft to ———, 13 November 1820, Bancroft MSS, MHS; Bancroft to Aaron and Lucretia Bancroft, 30 December 1820, George Bancroft MSS, American Antiquarian Society, Worcester, Mass. The Society is cited hereafter as AAS. It is difficult to determine precisely what Bancroft learned from Schleiermacher, since the latter's ideas on education were not fully developed until 1826. He had written a considerable amount on education before 1820, but very little had been published. Schleiermacher's lectures in the winter semester of 1820–21 were extremely theoretical and were concerned largely with discipline. Bancroft was probably influenced by the two main general concepts Schleiermacher put forward in these lectures: (1) the necessity of relating school and home training to one another, and above all (2) the use of external punishment only as an aid to development of self-discipline in the child. Schleiermacher, "Vorlesungen über Gegenwirkung, Strafe und Zucht (1820/21)," *Pädagogische Abhandlungen und Zeugnisse,* vol. II of Erich Weniger, ed., *Friedrich Schleiermacher: Pädagogische Schriften* (Düsseldorf and Munich, 1957), pp. 171–202.

55. Kirkland to Bancroft, 26 May 1819; Bancroft to Kirkland, 6 July 1819, Bancroft MSS, MHS. Italics mine.

56. Bancroft to "Dear Sir," 5 November 1820, Bancroft MSS, MHS. I have been unable to determine which of several contemporary Berlin schools Bancroft was referring to in this letter. For the reformation of Prussian education and Pestalozzi's influence on it, see Pollard, *Pioneers of Popular Education,* pp. 87–90.

57. Matthew Arnold, *Higher Schools and Universities in Germany* (2nd. ed.; London, 1882), pp. 120-25; Bancroft to Levi Hedge, 6 March 1821, Bancroft MSS, MHS.

58. Nye, *George Bancroft, Brahmin Rebel,* pp. 49–57; Howe, *Life and Letters of Bancroft,* I, 121–53.

59. MS Journal, 27 October 1821, Bancroft MSS, MHS. Reprinted in M. Howe, *Life and Letters of Bancroft,* I, 128–29.

60. Since Bancroft certainly knew of the work of Pestalozzi and Fellenberg through Schleiermacher and Cogswell (he had met and corresponded with Cogswell while in Germany), it seems odd that he did not make the relatively short trips to Yverdun or Hofwyl when he stopped in Berne in October 1821. Although I have found no indication in the Bancroft MSS at the Massachusetts Historical Society, American Antiquarian Society, or New York Public Library that Bancroft visited Hofwyl, the usually accurate author of two excellent biographies of Bancroft, Russel Nye, states that he "visited Hofwyl, where he discussed education with Fellenberg and his staff." Nye, *George Bancroft* (New York, 1964), p. 27.

61. Bancroft spent only three weeks in August 1821 in England, and all of that in London, where he saw little more than the usual tourist sights and a few Unitarian chapels. M. Howe, *Life and Letters of Bancroft,* I, 114–21.

62. Philippe Ariès, *Centuries of Childhood: A Social History of Family Life* (New York: Vintage Books, 1965), pp. 283, 284, 285. Italics mine.

63. Cogswell to Elisha Ticknor, 8 December 1817, in Anna Ticknor, *Cogswell,* pp. 70–71.

64. George C. Shattuck, Sr., to George C. Shattuck, Jr., 24 August 1825, Shattuck Family MSS, MHS.

65. Constance McLaughlin Green, *The Rise of Urban America* (New York, 1965), *passim.*

66. Charles N. Glaab and A. Theodore Brown, *A History of Urban America* (New York, 1967), p. 84.

Chapter III

1. Bancroft to Aaron Bancroft, 6 June 1821, Bancroft MSS, AAS.

2. Cogswell to Bancroft, 3 August 181[9?], Bancroft MSS, MHS.

3. Norton to Bancroft, 29 December 1821, Bancroft MSS, MHS; Howe, *Life and Letters of Bancroft,* I, 156.

4. Bancroft to Norton, 18 September 1822, Bancroft MSS, MHS. This letter appears never to have been sent.

5. Bancroft to Samuel A. Eliot, 3 December 1822, Bancroft MSS, MHS.

6. Nye, *George Bancroft, Brahmin Rebel,* pp. 63–64.

7. Bancroft to Samuel A. Eliot, 2 April 1823, Bancroft MSS, MHS.

8. Samuel Eliot Morison, "The Great Rebellion in Harvard College, and The Resignation of President Kirkland," Colonial Society of Massachusetts *Transactions,* XXVII (1927–30), 91–93, 88, 65.

9. Jeremiah Day, MS "Report of the Course of Instruction in the College, during the year ending Sep 9th, 1818," Miscellaneous [Yale] Corporation Papers, Beinecke Library, Yale University, New Haven, Conn.

10. Morison, "Great Rebellion," p. 66; the Yale figure is based on a comparison of the date of birth and date of entrance to college of all freshman listed in*Memorial of the Class of 1830, Yale College* (Hartford, 1871).

11. George Wilson Pierson, *Yale College: An Educational History, 1871–1921* (New Haven, 1952), p. 142; Morison, *Three Centuries of Harvard,* pp. 90, 179.

12. See above, p. 29

13. George P. Schmidt, *The Old Time College President* (New York, 1930), p. 78; the Yale figure is based on a comparison of the date of birth and date of entrance to college of all freshmen listed in William Wheeler, *Statistics of the Class of 1855, of Yale College* (New Haven, 1859).

14. James Freeman Clarke, *Autobiography, Diary, and Correspondence,* ed. Edward Everett Hale (Boston, 1899), pp. 34–42. For similar remarks on Yale in the 1820s, see Julian M. Sturtevant, ed., *Julian M. Sturtevant, An Autobiography* (New York, 1896), pp. 84–85, 90–91.

15. George Ticknor, *Remarks on Changes Lately Proposed or Adopted in Harvard University* (Boston, 1825), p. 7.

16. Tyack, *George Ticknor,* p. 96. My description of Harvard relies heavily on Tyack's excellent account, esp. pp. 90–128.

17. Ticknor to Prescott, 31 July 1821, reprinted in *ibid.,* p. 97.

18. Bancroft to Eliot, 3 December 1822, Bancroft MSS, MHS.

19. Bancroft to Samuel A. Eliot, 2 April 1823, Bancroft MSS, MHS.

20. Joseph G. Cogswell to John T. Kirkland, 21 October 1822, MS Harvard College Papers, Harvard University Archives, Widener Library, Cambridge. The Harvard Archives are cited hereafter as HUA.

21. Ticknor, *Cogswell,* p. 135; M. Howe, *Life and Letters of Bancroft,* I, 66.

22. Joseph Green Cogswell and George Bancroft, *Prospectus of a School to be Established at Round Hill, Northampton, Massachusetts* (Cambridge, 1823), p. 4.

23. *Ibid.,* pp. 20, 3, 5.

24. *Ibid.,* pp. 6–7. Italics mine.

25. *Ibid.,* p. 9.

26. *Ibid.,* pp. 9–16, 19.

27. *Ibid.,* pp. 16–17.

28. Bernard Wishy, *The Child and the Republic: The Dawn of Modern American Child Nurture* (Philadelphia, 1968), pp. 12–13, 17–18.

29. Quoted in John Spencer Bassett, "The Round Hill School," American Antiquarian Society *Proceedings,* XXVII (1917), 33.

30. *Ibid.,* 32, 48; Nye, *George Bancroft, Brahmin Rebel,* pp. 72, 69.

31. "Great Rebellion," 102.

32. Eliot to Bancroft, 25 August 1823, Bancroft MSS, MHS.

33. A search of the Harvard College Papers for this period reveals no other instance of a similar action by the Harvard Corporation. The agreement between Cogswell and Bancroft and the Corporation was apparently made in January 1824. The mortgage was dischargeable on three months notice; Cogswell made the first quarterly payment of interest ($120) in July 1824. Bancroft to John Davis, 4 February 1824; Cogswell to John Davis, 12 July 1824, Harvard College Papers.

34. The figure of 50 students was arrived at by comparing the

names of 291 Round Hill alumni listed in Joseph Green Cogswell, *Outline of the System of Education at the Round Hill School With a List of the Present Instructers and of the Pupils From Its Commencement Until This Time* (Boston, 1831), pp. 19–24, with lists of Harvard alumni for this period in *Quinquennial Catalogue of the Officers and Graduates, 1636–1930. Harvard University.* (Cambridge, 1930).

35. The quotation is from Morison, *Three Centuries of Harvard,* p. 220.

36. Tyack, *George Ticknor,* pp. 99, 100–107.

37. Reprinted in Howe, *Life and Letters of Bancroft,* I, 175–76. Cf. with the schedule used at Hofwyl, *Letters from Hofwyl,* pp. 124-25; with the schedule at Pestalozzi's Yverdun, in Mehdi Nakosteen, *The History and Philosophy of Education* (New York, 1965), p. 340; and at Schulpforta, in Bancroft to Levi Hedge, 6 March 1821, Bancroft MSS, MHS.

38. Bancroft to Jane Bancroft, 5 November 1823, Bancroft MSS, AAS.

39. "Round Hill School," 36.

40. Cogswell and Bancroft to Jeremiah Day, 19 March 1828, Jeremiah Day MSS, Beinecke Library, Yale University (though signed by both Cogswell and Bancroft, the body of this letter is in Bancroft's hand); Nye, *George Bancroft, Brahmin Rebel,* pp. 72–73; Bassett, "Round Hill School," pp. 56–57.

41. George C. Shattuck, Jr., to George C. Shattuck, Sr., 10 January 1828, Shattuck Family MSS.

42. Cogswell and Bancroft to Jeremiah Day, 19 March 1828, Day MSS.

43. *Prospectus,* pp. 11, 9.

44. Samuel Ward III to Samuel Ward II, 17 December 1826, Ward Family MSS, Manuscript Division, New York Public Library. The library is cited hereafter as NYPL.

45. George C. Shattuck, Jr., to George C. Shattuck, Sr., 4 February 1827; Shattuck, Sr., to Shattuck, Jr., 1 March 1827, Shattuck Family MSS.

46. While there were twenty-six professors at Hofwyl, only eight lived with the students and were responsible for their conduct. Discipline was left largely to the "masters," very often graduates of Hofwyl themselves, who "reside[d] constantly with the pupils." Fellenberg felt that a good classical or French scholar did not necessarily make a good educator. *Letters from Hofwyl,* pp. 88-89.

47. Bancroft to Jane Bancroft, 5 November 1823, Bancroft MSS, AAS; George C. Shattuck, Jr., to George C. Shattuck, Sr., March ——, 1825, Shattuck Family MSS.

48. M. Howe, *Life and Letters of Bancroft,* I, 176.

49. For the practices at Hofwyl, cf. above pp. 60–62..

50. For a listing of these books and articles, see Monroe, *Pestalozzian Movement,* pp. 215–33. Beginning in January 1819, *The Academician,* the first American journal devoted solely to educational matters, ran a long —and somewhat misleading—series of articles on Pestalozzi. See "Pestalozzi's Method of Teaching Religious and Moral Principles, &c. to Children," *The Academician,* I (9 January 1819), 215–16, *et. seq.*

51. While Cogswell had been interested both in Fellenberg's academy for upper-class children and in his programs for the education of the poor and for agricultural instruction, most other Americans who visited Hofwyl concentrated on the latter. Americans, in fact, passed through about twenty years' infatuation with Fellenberg's ideas on these subjects. In 1824—the year after Cogswell and Bancroft opened Round Hill—a Fellenberg School, heavily emphasizing agricultural instruction, was established in Winsor, Connecticut. Several manual training or agricultural schools were begun in the United States in the 1820s and 1830s. The main attraction of Fellenberg's plan for Americans was that it not only promised to improve students' morals and health, but also to make a school self-supporting. At one American Fellenberg school (the Fellenberg Academy, established in Greenfield, Massachusetts, in 1831), students worked on the school farm for three hours a day; it was claimed that such work actually turned a profit for the school. In the 1830s dozens of American colleges introduced work-study plans inspired by Pestalozzi and Fellenberg—with results which were usually futile, comic, or both. (See: the notices in the *Connecticut Courant,* 28 May 1824 and 14 June 1824, as reprinted in Vera M. Butler, *Education As Revealed by New England Newspapers Prior to 1850* [Philadelphia, 1935], pp. 196–97; *ibid.,* p. 198; Bennett, *Manual and Industrial Education,* pp. 182–206; Anderson, *History of Industrial Education,* pp. 95–96; *First and Second Annual Reports of the Fellenberg Academy* [Greenfield, Mass., 1834], p. 5; Rudolph, *American College and University,* pp. 217–18.)

Pestalozzian pedagogical practices did not have a widespread impact on American education until the late 1850s, when they were taught to prospective teachers from every part of the nation at the Oswego (New York) Normal School. Monroe, *Pestalozzian Movement,* pp. 159–93.

52. See above, p. 60.

53. See above, pp. 23–24; Honeywell, *Educational Work of Jefferson,* pp. 165–66.

54. In New England and a few other parts of the United States, Cogswell wrote, "it is rare that a child destined to live by the labour of his hands, cannot find the means of acquiring quite as much book learning, as will be useful to him in his business, and often a great deal too much to allow him to remain contented with his lot and place in

life." Cogswell, "On the Means of Learning," p. 547.

55. Bancroft to Lucretia Bancroft, 1 January 1832, Bancroft MSS, AAS.

56. George Ticknor to Samuel A. Eliot, 13 September 1823, in Anna Ticknor, *Cogswell,* p. 137.

57. Computed from Cogswell, *Outline of the System of Education,* pp. 19–24. The state-by-state distribution was as follows: Massachusetts, 99; New York, 46; South Carolina, 34; Maryland, 32; Georgia, 18; Rhode Island, 12; Pennsylvania, 7; West Indies, 5; Mississippi, 4; Mexico, 4; 3 from each of Maine, Virginia, North Carolina, Louisiana, and Lower Canada; 2 from each of Connecticut, New Hampshire, Delaware, Ohio, Brazil, and "Transatlantic"; and 1 from each of Tennessee and Michigan.

58. "T.G.A." [Thomas Gold Appleton], "Some Souveniers of Round-Hill School," *A Sheaf of Papers* (Boston, 1875), p. 10.

59. M. Howe, *Life and Letters of Bancroft,* I, 169.

60. *A Relation of the Island of England,* Camden Society, 1897, p. XIV, quoted in F. J. Furnivall, ed., *The Babees Book* (1868), and reprinted in Ariès, *Centuries of Childhood,* p. 365.

61. Lawrence Stone, *The Crisis of the Aristocracy,* 1558–1641 (Oxford, 1965), p. 683. Stone does not connect this with his own observation on the preceding page that "by the early seventeenth century . . . peers and gentry began to congregate in a limited number of fashionable schools, which became more exclusively upper-class in composition."

62. Morgan, *Puritan Family,* pp. 76, 77, and *Virginians at Home,* pp. 22–23. Of the Congregationalist northerners, Morgan suggests "that Puritan parents did not trust themselves with their own children, that they were afraid of spoiling them by too great affection." Of the practice in the Anglican South, he writes: "One of the reasons seems to have been that parents were afraid of spoiling their own children; they did not trust themselves with the knotty problems of discipline although they had no hesitation in assuming responsibility for the children of others." This seems too plausible.

63. William L. Sachse, *The Colonial American in Britain* (Madison, Wis., 1956), ch. V.

64. *Centuries of Childhood,* pp. 365, 366.

65. See above, pp. 46–47.

66. See above, p. 42.

67. Stone, *Crisis of the Aristocracy,* p. 681.

68. See above, p. 68.

69. Wishy, *Child and the Republic,* pp. 13–17.

70. George C. Shattuck, Sr., to [R?] Shurtleff 7 August 1828, Shattuck Family MSS. The senior Shattuck's handwriting is almost illegible; the bracketed "evil" in the last phrase of the quotation might also be

read as "coil." In this particular case Shattuck was discussing not his son but his daughter.

71. The eleven cities, in descending size and with number of Round Hill students from each, were New York City (13); Philadelphia (4); Baltimore (21); Boston (8); New Orleans (1); Charleston (18); Washington (0); Salem (3); Albany (1), Richmond (1); and Providence (2). There were 9 students from Savannah, 4 from Natchez, and 1 from Wilmington. For the cities, see J.D.B. De Bow, *Statistical View of the United States: A Compendium of the Seventh Census* (Washington, 1854), p. 192. For the student list, see the Round Hill student journal, *Literary Recreations,* I (9 May 1829). This is the only list which provides both the state *and* locality of origin of Round Hill's students.

72. Endicott Peabody, "Academic Influence," in Alfred E. Stearns et al., *The Education of the Modern Boy* (Boston, 1925), p. 108.

73. *Centuries of Childhood,* p. 368.

74. Samuel Ward III to Samuel Ward II, 1 August 1826, Ward Family MSS. My italics.

75. George C. Shattuck, M.D., "The Founding," in *Memorials of St. Paul's School* (New York, 1891), p. 21.

76. See note 74 above.

77. See above, p. 30.

78. "Original Papers in Relation to a Course of Liberal Education," *American Journal of Science and Arts,* XV (January 1829), 297–351.

79. Tyack, *George Ticknor,* pp. 204–12; Harry Miller Lydenberg, *History of The New York Public Library, Astor, Lenox and Tilden Foundations* (New York, 1923), pp. 1–50.

80. G. H. Bode to George C. Shattuck, Sr., 12 August 1827, Shattuck Family MSS.

81. George C. Shattuck, Jr., to George C. Shattuck, Sr., 24 November 1827, Shattuck Family MSS.

82. Joseph G. Cogswell to Benjamin Silliman, 23 July 1827, Silliman MSS, Beinecke Library, Yale University; Cogswell and Bancroft to Jeremiah Day, 19 March 1828, Day MSS. A penciled note on the former letter reads: "If they have 4 evangelists & Greek reader it will be accepted."

83. Cogswell and Bancroft to Jeremiah Day, 19 March 1828; Cogswell and Bancroft to Day, 2 April 1828, Day MSS.

84. G. H. Bode to George C. Shattuck, Sr., 12 August 1827; Cogswell to Shattuck, 28 August 1827, Shattuck Family MSS.

85. George Bancroft, unfinished MS essay, "Of the Liberal Education of Boys," n.d., p. 7, Bancroft MSS, Manuscript Division, NYPL. In his *George Bancroft, Brahmin Rebel,* Russell Nye dates this essay to 1823; in his *George Bancroft* he dates it to 1828.

86. "Of the Liberal Education of Boys," p. 8.

87. See above, p. 65.

88. Cogswell to Bancroft, 3 March 1830, Bancroft MSS, MHS.

89. Harry N. Scheiber, "A Jacksonian as Banker and Lobbyist: New Light on George Bancroft," *New England Quarterly,* XXXVII (1964), 363–72; Howe, *Life and Letters of Bancroft,* I, 178–84; Nye, *George Bancroft, Brahmin Rebel,* pp. 82–84, 143–46.

90. Appleton, "Some Souveniers of Round-Hill School," p. 13.

91. Round Hill was incorporated in February 1829. It was capitalized at $20,000, and 200 shares of stock at $100 a share were offered. Most of the stockholders were either former Anthologists, Harvard reformers, or individuals who had sons or other relatives at Round Hill. Among them were: George Ticknor (10 shares); Israel Thorndike (10); G. W. Lyman (5); P. C. Brooks (5); Samuel A. Eliot (2); Andrews Norton (2); T. H. Perkins (Sr. and Jr., 2 each); N. Appleton (1); F. Walker (1); Daniel Webster (1); B. W. Crowinshield (1); F. W. Brune (1), and Tappan and Co. (5). The directors of the corporation then leased the school back to Cogswell and Bancroft. See printed broadside, *An Act to Incorporate the Proprietors of the Round Hill Institution,* dated 18 February 1829, in Shattuck Family MSS. The stockholders are listed in script on the bottom of this copy of the *Act.* A further notation reads: "cost exceeded $30,000."

92. Harvard was at no time, of course, solely dependent upon Round Hill for students; only five of the fifty-six members of the freshman class in 1829 were Round Hill graduates. Most of the freshman class were prepared in academies (information on only thirty-eight of the fifty-six students is available):

Preparation of Harvard Freshmen, 1829

	Percent	& Number
Academies	36	(14)
Private Proprietary Schools	26	(10)
Latin Grammar Schools	21	(8)
Clergymen	10	(4)
College Preparatory Departments	5	(2)

Based on data in Waldo Higginson, *Memorials of the Class of 1833 of Harvard College. . . .* (Cambridge, 1883).

93. Bassett, "Round Hill School," pp. 61–62; Anna Ticknor, *Cogswell,* pp. 163–85. Bassett suggests that an important cause of Round Hill's financial difficulties was the failure of many southern parents to pay their sons' fees.

94. On Webster, see above, n. 91. Round Hill's Robert Hayne was not the Senator's son, but probably one of his innumerable nephews.

95. "Means of Learning," p. 548.

96. Cogswell to Mrs. Prescott, 3 December 1834; 14 September

1834; 14 April 1836, in Anna Ticknor, *Cogswell,* pp. 193–94, 192–93, 202.

97. John Hope Franklin, *The Militant South, 1800–1861* (Cambridge, 1956), chs. VII and VIII.

Chapter IV

1. John Murray Forbes to T. T. Forbes, 6 June 1828, in Sarah Forbes Hughes, ed., *Letters and Recollections of John Murray Forbes* (Boston, 1899), p. 50.

2. Alvin W. Skardon, "William Augustus Muhlenberg: Pioneer Urban Church Leader," (Ph.D. dissertation, University of Chicago, 1960), pp. 135–36.

3. Thomas Kelah Wharton, MS Journal, entry for December 1832, pp. 221-22. Manuscript Division, NYPL.

4. Clifton H. Brewer, *A History of Religious Education in the Episcopal Church to 1835* (New Haven, 1924), p. 262.

5. Charles C. Tiffany, *A History of the Protestant Episcopal Church in the United States of America* (New York, 1895), p. 259.

6. Both characterizations are products of the historiography of the 1930s. On the latter see Dixon Ryan Fox, "The Protestant Counter-Reformation in America," *New York History,* XVI (1935), 19–35.

7. Possibly because his first biographer, Anne Ayres (a disciple of Muhlenberg), destroyed his papers after completing her work. (*The Life and Work of William Augustus Muhlenberg* [New York, 1880].) It must be supplemented by Skardon's exhaustively researched "Muhlenberg." See too Richard C. Becker, "The Social Thought of William Augustus Muhlenberg," *Historical Magazine of the Protestant Episcopal Church,* XXVII (1958), 307–23.

8. Skardon, "Muhlenberg," pp. 13–45; Ayres, *Muhlenberg, passim.*

9. Winthrop S. Hudson, *American Protestantism* (Chicago, 1961), p. 98.

10. Quoted in Skardon, "Muhlenberg," p. 45.

11. *Ibid.,* pp. 61–82.

12. *Ibid.,* pp. 83–91.

13. Muhlenberg to Jackson Kemper, 22 December 1824, in *ibid.,* pp. 96–97.

14. *Ibid.,* pp. 98–112.

15. William W. Manross, *A History of the American Episcopal Church* (3rd ed.; New York, 1959), pp. 202, 213, 238; Hudson, *American Protestantism,* pp. 55–57.

16. See William G. McLoughlin, *Modern Revivalism: Charles Grandison Finney to Billy Graham* (New York, 1959).

17. Timothy L. Smith, *Revivalism and Social Reform In Mid-Nineteenth-Century America* (New York, 1957), p. 46.

18. *Ibid.*, p. 30.

19. See Muhlenberg, *Evangelical Catholic Papers: A Collection of Essays, Letters, and Tractates. . . .*, comp. Anne Ayres (New York, 1875).

20. Quoted in William Warren Sweet, *Indiana Asbury-De Pauw University, 1837–1937: A Hundred Years of Higher Education in the Middle West* (New York, 1937), p. 26.

21. Donald G. Tewksbury, *The Founding of American Colleges and Universities before the Civil War; with Particular Reference to the Religious Influences Bearing Upon the College Movement* (New York, 1932), p. 28.

22. Hofstadter, *Academic Freedom*, pp. 209–19.

23. Brewer, *History of Religious Education*, pp. 228–32, 247–48.

24. *Ibid.*, pp. 94–101.

25. [William Augustus Muhlenberg], *The Application of Christianity to Education: Being the Principles and Plan of Education to be Adopted to the Institute at Flushing, L.I.* (Jamaica, L.I., 1828).

26. Muhlenberg wrote to a friend that his Institute would "be of the same grade as the famous one at Northampton"; he referred to Round Hill in his promotional literature; he wrote glowingly of Cogswell in later years, and appointed him to the Board of Visitors of the college he ultimately added to the Institute. See: Muhlenberg to Jackson Kemper, 11 February 1828, in Skardon, "Muhlenberg," p. 124, and cf. also pp. 135–36. For more similarities between Round Hill and the Flushing Institute, compare Cogswell and Bancroft's 1823 *Prospectus* with: [Muhlenberg], *The Studies and Discipline of the Institute at Flushing, L.I.* (n.p., 1830); Muhlenberg, *Christian Education: Being an Address delivered after a Public Examination of the Students at Flushing, L.I. July 28, 1831* (New York, 1831). For Muhlenberg's admiring remarks on Cogswell's "sound views of education, various learning, and experience in the instruction and government of boys," see his "The New Episcopal Schools," *Journal of the Institute at Flushing*, II (April 1834), 82–83. (Printed sources relating to the Institute are very difficult to locate; most of the materials the author has used were found in the William H. Handley Collection of Long Island Americana, Long Island Room, Smithtown Public Library, Smithtown, L.I., N.Y.)

27. Muhlenberg to Kemper, 25 July 1827, Skardon, "Muhlenberg," p. 116.

28. Muhlenberg to Bishop William R. Whittingham, 25 August 1841, in Hall Harrison, *Life of the Right Reverend John Barrett Kerfoot, D.D., LL.D., First Bishop of Pittsburgh, with Selections from His Diaries and Correspondence* (2 vols.; New York, 1886), I, 36.

29. *Application of Christianity*, p. 7n.

30. *Ibid.*, pp. 6–7.

31. *Ibid.*, pp. 6–9.

32. *Ibid.*, p. 6.

33. *Ibid.*, pp. 11–12. The full curriculum of the Institute, like contemporary academies, offered both "English" and "Classical" programs. The curriculum, Muhlenberg promised, "will comprise all the branches of a thorough English education, including Mathematics, Natural History, and Philosophy, as far as they can be advantageously pursued, Vocal Music, Instrumental Music and Drawing, when for either of them there is decided talent. The Latin and Greek, or Spanish and French languages, according as the pupil is destined for the counting room, or the college. The classical course may be continued until it is an equivalent for a collegiate one; as it will be in the case of the Tutors, with whom the pupils, after they are sufficiently advanced, may study. . . . No pains will be spared to make well grounded scholars in the dead languages." *Ibid.*, pp. 17–18.

34. *Ibid.*, pp. 14–18; Skardon, "Muhlenberg," p. 120 ff.

35. *Puritan Family*, pp. 133–35, 19, 3–12.

36. Gladys Bryson, *Man and Society: The Scottish Inquiry of the Eighteenth Century* (Princeton, 1945), pp. 171–72.

37. "The Unitarian Conscience," ch. V.

38. Barbara M. Cross, *Horace Bushnell: Minister to a Changing America* (Chicago, 1958), pp. 14, 58–60 and *passim;* see too William R. Taylor, *Cavalier and Yankee: The Old South and American National Character* (New York, 1961), pp. 146–48 and *passim.*

39. *Application of Christianity*, p. 6.

40. See above, p. 108.

41. Quoted in Ayres, *Muhlenberg*, p. 133.

42. Skardon, "Muhlenberg," pp. 113–15, 138.

43. *St. Paul's College* (n.p., 1835), pp. 19–20; Ayres, *Muhlenberg*, ch. VIII.

44. The geographical origin of the students at the Institute was as follows for the respective years:

	1832	1834	1839
New England:	2	1	1
Middle Atlantic:	54	56	43
South:	12	18	17
Northwest:	—	2	2
Foreign:	—	—	1
Total	68	77	64

Note that Round Hill's New England representation is almost completely absent, and that enrollment dropped after the Panic of 1837.

Compiled from : *Journal of the Institute at Flushing,* I (November 1832), 15–16; *ibid.,* II (January 1834), 18–20; and *Catalogue of the Professors, Instructers, and Students of St. Paul's College and Grammar School, for the Session of 1838–39; together with the Studies and Discipline of the Institution, and Observations addressed to Parents intending to place their Sons in the Same* (New York, 1839), pp. 1–8.

45. For a vivid description of urban health and sanitation measures in the 1830s, see Charles Rosenberg, *The Cholera Years: The United States in 1832, 1849, and 1866.* (Chicago, 1962), ch. I.

46. Edward E[verett] Hale, "The State's Care of its Children: Considered as A Check on Juvenile Delinquency," in Philadelphia House of Refuge, *Prize Essays on Juvenile Deliquency* (Philadelphia, 1855), p. 16.

47. Rev. T. V. Moore, "God's University; or, The Family Considered as A Government, a School, and a Church, the Divinely Appointed Institute for Training the Young for the Life That Now Is, and for That Which Is to Come," in *ibid.,* pp. 60–61.

48. Hale, "State's Care of its Children," p. 15.

49. In his Twelfth Annual Report to the Massachusetts Board of Education, reprinted in Mary Peabody Mann, *Life of Horace Mann* (4 vols.; Boston, 1891), IV, 245–68.

50. Rev. Caleb Stetson, in a speech before the Middlesex County Association for the Improvement of Common Schools, *The Common School Journal,* I (1839), 60.

51. Josiah Quincy, *A Municipal History of the Town and City of Boston* (Boston, 1852), pp. 21–22.

52. Brown, *Making of Our Middle Schools,* pp. 297–321; Butts and Cremin, *History of Education,* p. 263.

53. MS Records of the Board of Trustees of the Phillips Exeter Academy, 1 August 1848. Treasurer's Office, Jeremiah Smith Hall, the Phillips Exeter Academy, Exeter, N.H.

54. Butts and Cremin, *History of Education,* p. 239.

55. Marr, *Old New England Academies,* pp. 287–91.

56. Rush Welter, *Popular Education and Democratic Thought in America* (New York, 1962), p. 103.

57. *The Working Man's Advocate,* I (24 April 1830), 4, quoted in Lawrence A. Cremin, *The American Common School: An Historic Conception* (New York, 1951), p. 39.

58. Rev. Charles Hammond, "New England Academies and Classical Schools," *American Journal of Education,* XLIV (September 1866), 425.

59. David S. Snedden, *Administration and Educational Work of American Juvenile Reform Schools* (New York, 1907), pp. 10–20.

60. Richard L. Rapson, "The American Child as Seen by British

Travelers, 1845–1935," *American Quarterly,* XVII (1965), 520–34. This may, of course, indicate a good deal more about British than American children.

61. Harriet Martineau, *Society in America* [1834], ed. Seymour Martin Lipset (New York: Anchor Books, 1962), pp. 310–11. See especially Lipset's comments on the American family in his Introduction, pp. 28–30.

62. Frances Trollope, *Domestic Manners of the Americans* [1832], ed. Donald Smalley (New York: Vintage Books, 1960), p. 213.

63. Rev. John B. Kerfoot to Mrs. Kerfoot, 9 September 1843, in Harrison, *Life of Kerfoot,* I, 86.

64. *Centuries of Childhood.*

65. Wharton MS Journal, entry for December 1832, pp. 222–23.

66. *Ibid.*

67. *Application of Christianity,* pp. 10–11.

68. *Studies and Discipline,* pp. 9–10.

69. *Christian Education,* p. 3.

70. *Application of Christianity,* pp. 12–14.

71. Cf. the Yale Report of 1828: ". . . in this country, where offices are accessible to all who are qualified for them, superior intellectual attainments ought not to be confined to any description of persons. *Merchants, manufacturers,* and *farmers,* as well as professional gentlemen, take their places in our public councils. A thorough education ought therefore to be extended to all these classes."

72. E.g., *Journal of the Institute at Flushing,* I (February 1833), 13; II (January 1834), 16–18; *ibid.,* (May 1834), 130. In the 1830s and 1840s the condemnation of the use of emulation became almost a cliche among American educators. See Merle Curti, *The Social Ideas of American Educators* (rev. ed.; Paterson, N.J., 1961), pp. 59, 123.

73. Harrison, *Life of Kerfoot,* I, 22–24; Arthur Stanwood Pier, *St. Paul's School, 1855–1934* (New York, 1934), pp. 6–7.

74. *Journal,* pp. 238–39.

75. Muhlenberg to Rev. John B. Kerfoot, 9 May 1848, Harrison, *Life of Kerfoot,* I, 130–31. Muhlenberg's italics.

76. Muhlenberg to Rev. John B. Kerfoot, 28 January 1851, *ibid.,* I, 136.

77. Ayres, *Muhlenberg,* p. 100.

78. Walter Hougton, *The Victorian Frame of Mind, 1830–1870* (New Haven, 1957), p. 233.

79. Skardon, "Muhlenberg," pp. 140–51; John F. Woolverton, "William Augustus Muhlenberg and the Founding of St. Paul's College," *Historical Magazine of the Protestant Episcopal Church,* XXIX (1960), 192–218.

80. Skardon, "Muhlenberg," pp. 152–55; Brewer, *History of Religious Education,* pp. 262–63.

81. For a good brief account of St. James, see Hall Harrison, "The College of St. James (1843–1864)," in Bernard C. Steiner, *History of Education in Maryland* (Washington, 1894), 258–60.

82. Harrison, *Life of Kerfoot,* I, 21–43.

83. Edith Rossiter Bevan, "Fountain Rock, The Ringgold Home in Washington County," *Maryland Historical Magazine,* XLVII (1952), 19–28; Thomas J. C. Williams A History of Washington County, Maryland. . . . Including a History of Hagerstown (2 vols.; Hagerstown, 1906), I, 278.

84. "Bishop Whittingham's Address," *Opening Services. . . . Outline of the Discipline, Studies, Etc., St. James Hall, near Hagerstown, Washington County, Maryland* (Hagers-Town, 1842), p. 9. Aside from the bishop's address, this is almost a word-for-word copy of Muhlenberg's *An Account of the Grammar School, or Junior Department, of St. Paul's College* (New York, 1842).

85. MS Circular of St. James's Hall (Addressed, "J.B. Kerfoot to Rt. Rev. W. R. Whittingham," marked, "Rec. Nov. 15 [1841]"), Subject File, Maryland Diocesan [Episcopal] Manuscripts, Rare Book and Manuscript Room, Peabody Institute Library, Baltimore.

86. Of the 117 students at St. James in 1857–1858 only 18 were from north of the Mason-Dixon line. The largest number (42) were from Maryland. *Register of the College of St. James, and the Grammar School . . . 1857–58* (Baltimore, 1859), pp. 9–13; *Register of the College of St. James and the Grammar School . . . 1848–49* (Baltimore, 1849), pp. 5–8; Williams, *History of Washington County,* I, 341–42.

87. Harrison, *Life of Kerfoot,* I, 270–301. In 1869 Henry Onderdonk (1822–95), member of a prominent Episcopalian family, leased the deteriorating buildings of St. James's from the trustees, made extensive repairs, and reopened it as a secondary school for boys. The present (1968) St. James School is therefore (like Lawrenceville School in New Jersey or Deerfield Academy in Massachusetts) an essentially new and different institution built on a moribund foundation. For a fuller account of the College of St. James, its collapse and its influence, see James McLachlan, "The Civil War Diary of Joseph H. Coit," *Maryland Historical Magazine,* LX (1965), 245–60.

88. Bushnell, *Christian Nurture* (New Haven: Yale Paperbacks, 1967), *passim;* Cross, *Horace Bushnell,* pp. 64–72.

Chapter V

1. Alexander V. G. Allen, *Life and Letters of Phillips Brooks* (2 vols.; New York, 1900), II, 634.

2. Shattuck, "The Founding," p. 21.

3. Caleb Bradlee Davis, D.D., *A Brief Sketch of the Life of Prof. George Cheyne Shattuck, H. U. 1831* (Boston, 1894), p. 3.

4. Shattuck, "The Founding," p. 6.

5. Josiah Quincy to George C. Shattuck, Sr., 3 January 1831, Shattuck Family MSS.

6. Timothy Walker to 'George C. Shattuck, Sr., 8 January 1830, Cornelius C. Felton to George C. Shattuck, Sr., 25 October 1830, Shattuck Family MSS. Unless otherwise indicated, further citations refer to the junior Shattuck.

7. "I prefer seeing St. James going on," Shattuck wrote of the school's difficulties during the Civil War, "but if that may not be I want to see Church education prosper elsewhere." Though he had been an extremely generous contributor to the school throughout its history, he did not feel able to spend the $3,000–$4,000 a year necessary to keep the school going during the War. He was responsible for seeing that Kerfoot was offered the presidency of Trinity College when St. James was finally forced to close. George C. Shattuck to Rt. Rev. W. R. Whittingham, 20 June 1864, Vertical File, Maryland Diocesan MSS; Pier, *St. Paul's School,* p. 32; Harrison, *Life of Kerfoot,* I, 48, 279–80; Shattuck, "The Founding," p. 15; Davis, *Life of Shattuck,* p. 5.

8. Mills, *Power Elite,* p. 106.

9. Manross, *History of the American Episcopal Church,* p. 173.

10. John T. Morse, "Memoir of Henry Lee," Massachusetts Historical Society *Proceedings,* XIX (2nd series, 1905), 256.

11. Baltzell, *Philadelphia Gentlemen,* p. 246.

12. Manross, *History of the American Episcopal Church,* pp. 230–31.

13. "Unitarian and Episcopalian Affinities," *New Englander,* III (1845), 557–59.

14. Shattuck, MS essay beginning "I have been asked to put in writing how I became interested in schools for boys . . .," Shattuck Family MSS, vol. 21a. Although undated, from internal evidence this essay appears to have been written in 1889. Cited hereafter as "Schools for Boys MS."

15. One person's influence might extend much farther than one might first suppose: rich New Englanders seem to have formed one great extended family in the nineteenth century. Think, for example, of the possible combinations of these familiar New England family names: Oliver-Wendell-Phillips-Brooks-Adams.

16. From William Brooks's Journal for 18 October 1839, reprinted in Allen, *Life of Phillips Brooks,* I, 43.

17. Manross, *History of the American Episcopal Church,* p. 246.

18. *Horace Bushnell,* p. 56.

19. Shattuck, MS Diary, entry for 10 October 1854, Shattuck Family MSS.

20. From surviving receipts in the Shattuck Family MSS it appears that the elder Shattuck had invested widely and shrewdly in various New England textile manufacturing firms.

21. Shattuck, "The Founding," p. 14.

22. Shattuck, Schools for Boys MS.

23. Shattuck, "The Founding," pp. 15–16.

24. Shattuck, Schools for Boys MS.

25. Pier, *St. Paul's School,* p. 34.

26. Bishop' Carleton Chase to George Cheyne Shattuck, 30 September 1854, in bound volume, "Copies of Letters Concerning the Founding of St. Paul's School, the Selection of a Rector, Etc. 1854–1876. Taken from the Letter-File Albums of Dr. George C. Shattuck." Safe, Archives Room, Sheldon Library, St. Paul's School, Concord, N.H. Cited hereafter as "SPS Founding MSS." St. Paul's collections are referred to hereafter as "SPS Archives."

27. "J.H.C." [Joseph Howland Coit], "Subsequent History," in *Memorials of St. Paul's School,* p. 31; Pier, *St. Paul's School,* p. 13.

28. Shattuck, "The Founding," p. 21.

29. Shattuck, Schools for Boys MS.

30. Shattuck, "The Founding," p. 21.

31. Chase to Shattuck, 10 March 1855; Huntington to Shattuck, 12 February and 26 February 1855, SPS Founding MSS.

32. Huntington to Shattuck, 2 February 1855, SPS Founding MSS.

33. Huntington to Shattuck, 16 March 1855; see also Chase to Shattuck, 27 March 1855, SPS Founding MSS.

34. Huntington to Shattuck, 27 June 1855, SPS Founding MSS.

35. Chase to Shattuck, 7 August 1855, SPS Founding MSS.

36. Shattuck to Huntington, 9 August and 20 August 1855, Shattuck Autograph Folder, Safe, SPS Archives.

37. J. H. Coit, "Subsequent History," pp. 32–34.

38. Chase to Shattuck, 7 August 1855, SPS Founding MSS; Shattuck to Huntington, 9 August 1855, Shattuck Autograph Folder; Marble to Shattuck, 15 September 1855; Howard to Marble, 19 September 1855; Chase to Shattuck, 6 October 1855, SPS Founding MSS.

39. Chase to Shattuck, 6 October 1855, SPS Founding MSS.

40. Chase to Shattuck, 23 October 1855; Marble to Shattuck, 11 October 1855; Chase to Shattuck, 21 November 1855, SPS Founding MSS.

41. Marble to Shattuck, 22 November 1855; H. A. Coit to Shattuck,

5 December 1855, SPS Founding MSS; J. H. Coit, "Subsequent History," p. 34.

42. See above, p. 316; n. 62.

43. Shattuck to Huntington, 28 October 1856, Shattuck Autograph Folder. Unfortunately, Shattuck did not name the schools he had visited.

44. For a classic example of this view, see George C. Edwards, "The Private School in American Life," *Educational Review,* XXIII (1902), 264–80.

45. The members of the Anthology Society certainly were. See the long article by "T.L." (apparently an English correspondent), "Account of Westminster-School—Of Its Foundation, Masters, Ushers, Present Method of Instruction, Expenses of Education, &c. &c," *Monthly Anthology,* III (1806), 636–41.

46. The standard works on the English public schools have long been Edward C. Mack's *Public Schools and British Opinion, 1780 to 1860. . . .* (London, 1939) and his *Public Schools and British Opinion Since 1860: The Relationship between Contemporary Ideas and the Evolution of An English Institution* (New York, 1941). T. W. Bamford's *Rise of the Public Schools: A Study of Boys' Public Boarding Schools in England and Wales from 1837 to the Present Day* (London, 1967), in many respects supersedes Mack's studies, and throws a completely new light on the history of public schools.

Among the most illuminating pieces in the vast literature on the public schools are Denis W. Brogan, *The English People: Impressions and Observations* (New York, 1948), pp. 18–56; Harold Nicholson, *Good Behaviour: being a Study of Certain Types of Civility* (Boston: Beacon Paperbacks, 1960), pp. 247–67; and T. W. Bamford, "Public Schools and Social Class, 1801–1850," *British Journal of Sociology,* XII (September 1961), 224–35. Rupert Wilkinson's *Gentlemanly Power: British Leadership and the Public School Tradition* (London and New York, 1964) is an often-suggestive speculative essay.

47. Brogan, *The English People,* p. 20.

48. Bamford, *Rise of the Public Schools,* p. 11.

49. For reasons which will become clear, many parents were afraid to trust their sons to these schools. Many boys had tutors, or were educated in private schools at home or abroad. Bamford, "Public Schools and Social Class," p. 232–33.

50. Rev. John B. Kerfoot to Mrs. Kerfoot, 9 September 1843, Harrison, *Life of Kerfoot,* I, 86.

51. Bamford, *Rise of the Public Schools,* p. 47.

52. *Ibid.,* pp. 78–80. For Eton, see George R. Parkin, *Edward Thring, Headmaster of Uppingham School: Life Diary and Letters* (2nd ed.; London, 1900), pp. 25, 19, and esp. ch. II; for Harrow, Phyllis Grosskurth, *The*

Woeful Victorian: A Biography of John Addington Symonds (New York, 1965), pp. 22–41.

This raises the somewhat thorny problem of the sexual life of the boys at American boarding schools. The peculiar thing is that nowhere in the literally reams of manuscript materials I examined (and I was granted unrestricted access through about 1940 at most of the schools I visited) have I found *any* mention of such activities—no accounts of pregnant maids, no homosexual episodes, not even a slightly higher birthrate in Exeter, New Hampshire, than in nearby towns. My first thought was that this was not the type of conduct which would be written about or preserved in the nineteenth century. However, material considerably more damaging or intimate than accounts of youthful sexual escapades relating to many famous persons is still carefully preserved in school archives. Making all due allowances for Victorian sexual prudery, I can only conclude that American boys were not getting much heterosexual *or* homosexual physical contact. (The psychological relationships which must have developed among students are another matter, and one best left to novelists.)

While homosexual activity appears to have been rife in English public schools until well into the nineteenth century (and not uncommon thereafter), not even a careful reading between the lines seems to turn up similar conduct in the American schools. (Though some instances there surely must have been.) Bamford suggests that homosexual activity in the English public schools was considerably reduced by two means. First, in the tradition of Fellenberg or the American schools, by the minute regulation of the student's every activity, so that the authorities knew what the boy was doing at every minute of the day. Second, at mid-century, by the quite conscious introduction of and almost hysterical overemphasis on organized athletics. (He quotes one English headmaster thus: "One reason for the tremendous emphasis on 'healthy games'—compulsory cricket or football several times a week, and no slacking—has been the master's desire to leave no room for anything else. 'My prophylactic against certain unclean microbes was to send the boys to bed dead tired,' the headmaster of the United Services College admitted to his most distinguished Old Boy." [Bamford, *Rise of the Public Schools,* p. 82; cf. pp. 80–83.])

The difficulty with this interpretation for the United States is that some American headmasters *resisted* a heavy emphasis on organized athletics, which became very popular after the Civil War largely at the instigation of the students themselves. Perhaps the search for cultural analogies between the two nations can be carried too far. As a recent study (Steven Marcus, *The Other Victorians* [New York, 1965]) makes quite clear, nineteenth-century English sexual activity was inextricably intertwined, consciously and subconsciously, with the contemporary English class structure. (Perhaps the strong sado-masochistic element in English sexuality was in a way a reflection of the upper-former—fag, master—servant, extremely hierarchical, structure of English society. The English attributed to their lower classes much the same heightened sexuality that white Americans usually reserve for black Americans.) The standard of conduct of the upper reaches of American society was set not by an aristocracy (with all the tendencies, which aristocrats very often exhibit, to act out immediately their impulses), but by a much more amorphous, more fluid, and less self-assured *haute bourgeoisie.* With the possible exception of the South and certain southerners, American schoolmasters had no aristocratic traditions or actual aristocrats to contend against—only "the sons of wealthy inhabitants of large cities."

In the 1820s George Ticknor (see above, p. 76) had complained about the contraction of venereal diseases by Harvard undergraduates, whose age was then about the same as that of prep school students of the late nineteenth century. Over the course of the century, at least so far as students in boarding schools were concerned, the Victorian ideal of the preservation of childhood innocence in a secluded environment was obviously triumphant. Not only was the period of dependency for young people considerably extended, but sexually they were effectively neutralized. Whether it amounted to successful sexual repression or sexual sublimation is a moot point. For most, masturbation and fantasy were probably the main recourses. And, perhaps there *was* something to all those schoolboy tales of saltpeter in the *blanc mange.*

53. Arthur P. Stanley, *The Life and Correspondence of Thomas Arnold* (New York, 1877). For a twentieth-century version of the Arnold legend, see the biography by his American grandson: Arnold Whitridge, *Dr. Arnold of Rugby* (New York, 1928), *passim.* Arnold's immediate effect on the day-to-day workings of Rugby was quite limited; he spent most of his time writing (very perceptive) essays on social problems of the day. See T. W. Bamford, *Thomas Arnold* (London, 1960), *passim,* and Bamford, *Rise of the Public Shools,* pp. 51–54.

54. Arnold and Thring, particularly the latter, are constantly referred to in the correspondence, memoirs, and biographies of American private schoolmasters of the late nineteenth and early twentieth centuries. One has the impression that Arnold is invoked as a matter of form, while the real influence and example came from Thring. E.g., see Frank D. Ashburn, *Peabody of Groton, A Portrait* (New York, 1944), pp. 22–30 and *passim;* the memoirs of the man who built the Choate School, George St. John, *Forty Years at School* (New York, 1959), *passim;* and Claude M. Fuess, *Creed of A Schoolmaster* (Boston, 1939), pp. 164–65.

55. Parkin, *Edward Thring,* p. ix; on the building of Uppingham, see pp. 55–92.

56. *Ibid.*, p. 68.

57. See in particular, Edward Thring, *Education and School* (London and Cambridge, England, 1867), and Thring, *Theory and Practice of Teaching* (rev. ed.; Cambridge, England, 1885).

58. See John A. McPhee, *The Headmaster: Frank L. Boyden of Deerfield* (New York, 1966).

59. *Rise of the Public Schools,* p. 34.

60. Paul Ward, *Reminiscences of Cheltenham College* (London, 1868), pp. 1–2.

61. Henry A. Coit, D.D., "An American Boys' School—What It Should Be," in James P. Conover. *Memories of a Great Schoolmaster* (*Dr. Henry A. Coit*) (Boston and New York, 1906), p. 193. Coit's article originally appeared in the *Forum* magazine in September 1891.

62. Shattuck, "The Founding," p. 17; Scrapbook of Obituary Notices of Henry Augustus Coit, Safe, SPS Archives; James Carter Knox, *Henry Augustus Coit, First Rector of Saint Paul's School, Concord, New Hampshire* (New York, 1915), pp. 10–14.

Chapter VI

1. J. H. Coit, "Subsequent History," p. 34.

2. Chase to Shattuck, June [?] 1856, SPS Founding MSS.

3. Chase to Shattuck, 10 March 1856, SPS Founding MSS; Chase to Huntington, 21 May 1856, Shattuck Autograph Folder.

4. Chase to Shattuck, June [?] 1856, SPS Founding MSS. St. Paul's tuition was $300 from 1856 to 1863, $400 from 1864 to 1866, $500 from 1867 to 1890, and $600 from 1891 to 1900. This did not include extras —dancing lessons, equipment, etc. See the annual *Statement of St. Paul's School, Concord, N.H., with the List of the School. . . .* (Concord), for 1858–1900. Cited hereafter as *SPS Statement.* The attendance figures are from *Directory of the Alumni of St. Paul's School, List of the Deceased Alumni, List of Former Masters and Trustees, together with a List of the School* (Concord, 1915), p. 161.

5. *Directory of the Alumni of St. Paul's School . . .*, p. 161.

6. Figures calculated from the "List of the Students" in the annual *SPS Statement* for the respective years.

7. Owen Wister, "Dr. Coit of St. Paul's," *Atlantic Monthly,* CXLII (1928), 765.

8. St. Paul's School MS "Rural Record," entry for 12 September 1857, Safe, SPS Archives. A six-volume manuscript journal of events at St. Paul's, kept by various hands from 1857 to 1902, cited hereafter as SPS MS Rural Record.

9. J. H. Coit, "Subsequent History," pp. 38, 40, 78.

10. H. A. Coit to Shattuck, 28 February 1862, SPS Founding MSS.

11. J. H. Coit, "Subsequent History," pp. 78–80.

12. Chase to H. A. Coit, 4 July 1863, Letterbox, Safe, SPS Archives: J. H. Coit "Subsequent History," p. 129 n.; Daniel Coit Gilman to H. A. Coit, 8 April 1876; Curtis to H. A. Coit, 20 June 1870; Godkin to H. A. Coit, 30 [?] 1874, Letterbox, SPS Archives.

13. Wister, "Dr. Coit," pp. 766, 756.

14. Knox, *Henry Augustus Coit,* p. 40.

15. Biographical information from Conover, *Memories of a Great Schoolmaster,* pp. xiii-xxi; direct quotations from Pier, *St. Paul's School,* p. 5.

16. Wister, "Dr. Coit," 765.

17. Chase to Huntington, 21 May 1856; Chas to Shattuck, [?] June 1856, Shattuck Autograph Folder.

18. Conover, *Memories of a Great Schoolmaster,* p. 86.

19. Wister, "Dr. Coit," 765.

20. H. A. Coit to William White 16 November 1886, H. A. Coit Autograph Folder, Safe, SPS Archives.

21. Wister, "Dr. Coit," 761.

22. *Ibid.*

23. Conover, *Memories of a Great Schoolmaster,* p. 102.

24. Coit, "An American Boys' School," p. 209.

25. *Ibid.*, p. 206.

26. Robert Lowell, *Antony Brade* (Boston, 1874), pp. 24–26.

27. Quoted in Cady, *Gentleman in America,* p. 78.

28. Coit, "An American Boys' School," pp. 206–208.

29. Reprinted in Pier, *St. Paul's School,* pp. 38–40.

30. J. H. Coit, "Subsequent History," p. 35; cf. *SPS Statement 1858,* p. 3.

31. J. H. Coit, "Subsequent History," pp. 36–37.

32. In the 1870s St. Paul's curriculum was constructed as follows:

First Form: Geography, Latin, Mathematics, History, French, Sacred Studies
Second: English, Latin, Mathematics, History, French, Sacred Studies
Third: English, Latin, Greek, Mathematics, History, Sacred Studies
Fourth: English, Latin, Greek, Mathematics, History, French, Sacred Studies
Fifth: English, Latin, Greek, Mathematics, History, Sacred Studies
Sixth: English, Latin, Greek, Mathematics, Sacred Studies

Pier, *St. Paul's School,* pp. 94–96.

33. Conover, *Memories of a Great Schoolmaster,* p. 36.

34. Wister, "Dr. Coit," 759.

35. See above, p. 167. Italics mine.

36. Compare *SPS Statement 1864,* p. 4, with the *SPS Statement 1865,* p. 4, and later years.

37. Pier, *St. Paul's School,* pp. 19–20.

38. *Ibid.,* p. 277.

39. Knox, *Henry Augustus Coit,* pp. 19–20.

40. SPS MS Rural Record, 4 March 1857.

41. SPS MS Rural Record, 2 January 1858.

42. SPS MS Rural Record, 6 June 1857; Pier, *St. Paul's School,* p. 155. Boating became a popular sport at Harvard in the late 1840s and 1850s; the first Yale-Harvard race was held on Lake Winnepesaukee, not far from Concord, in 1852. The early popularity of crew at St. Paul's was probably due in large measure to a desire to emulate the colleges. Morison, *Three Centuries of Harvard,* pp. 314–15.

43. St. Paul's historian writes that Henry Coit—characteristically—encouraged cricket because of "the fact that besides being a healthy form of exercise it was clean and rather picturesque and brought out no vulgar shouting. . . ." Pier, *St. Paul's School,* pp. 81–82, 147; SPS MS Rural Record, 18 June 1859; Baltzell, *Philadelphia Gentlemen,* p. 358.

44. Pier, *St. Paul's School,* p. 267, "An American Boys' School," pp. 196–97.

45. It would be tempting to ascribe the rise of highly competitive organized athletics in the nineteenth century to Charles Darwin's ideas about the survival of the fittest, natural selection and so forth. However, nowhere in the materials examined for this study were the names of Darwin, or those of two of his most influential disciples, Herbert Spencer and William Graham Sumner, even mentioned. Considering its heavy emphasis on the virtues of social competition, Social Darwinism would probably have been repellent to most boarding school leaders, who hoped for a cooperative, organic society.

46. Knox, *Henry Augustus Coit,* pp. 94, 93.

47. Conover, *Memories of a Great Schoolmaster,* p. xix.

48. Pier, *St. Paul's School,* pp. 127–28.

49. Knox, *Henry Augustus Coit,* pp. 104, 105, 106.

50. SPS MS Rural Record, 23 March 1858. The keeper of the Rural Record until 1861 was the Reverend Francis Chase, a son of Bishop Chase of New Hampshire and Coit's chief assistant in these years. On the revivals of the years immediately before the Civil War, see Smith, *Revivalism and Social Reform, passim.*

51. Knox, *Henry Augustus Coit,* pp. 121, 122.

52. Mark A. DeWolfe Howe, *John Jay Chapman and His Letters* (Bos-

ton, 1937), p. 21; H. A. Coit to Eleanor Jay Chapman, 25 November 1876, in Richard B. Hovey, *John Jay Chapman, An American Mind* (New York, 1959), p. 10; Chanler A. Chapman, *The Wrong Attitude: A Bad Boy at a Good School* (New York, 1940), p. 40.

53. See above, p.35.

54. From Mulhelberg's Journal for 17 September 1843, reprinted in Ayres, *Muhlenberg,* pp. 166–67.

55. *Directory of the Alumni of St. Paul's School . . .*, p. 163.

56. Ayers, *Muhlenberg,* p. 154.

57. Conover, *Memories of a Great Schoolmaster,* p. 168.

58. J. H. Coit, "Subsequent History," p. 145.

59. Conover, *Memories of a Great Schoolmaster,* pp. 140–41; Pier, *St. Paul's School,* pp. 67–68.

60. Conover, *Memories of a Great Schoolmaster,* p. 145.

61. *Ibid.,* pp. 7–8.

62. *Ibid.,* pp. 25–26.

63. Knox, *Henry Augustus Coit,* pp. 104, 105, 106.

64. Conover, *Memories of a Great Schoolmaster,* pp. 103, 106.

65. Edwards, "Private School in American Life," p. 271. Although Edwards did not identify the schools he discussed by name, from internal evidence they are readily recognizable to anyone familiar with their history.

66. Willard Scudder, MS Diary, entry for 25 September 1893, SPS Archives.

67. George B. Shattuck, "The Centenary of Round Hill School," Massachusetts Historical Society *Proceedings,* LVII (1923), 209.

68. Albert E. Benson, *History of Saint Mark's School* ([Cambridge, Mass.], 1925), p. 11.

69. [Porter E. Sargent], *A Handbook of the Best Private Schools of the United States and Canada* (Boston, 1915), p. 32.

70. *Extracts from the Report of the Head-Master, Robert Lowell, D.D. St. Mark's School* (Boston, 1871), p. 6. The memory of Round Hill, incidentally, died hard; in 1865 yet another "Round Hill School" was founded in Northampton. The school was "designed to meet a supposed want of an increasing class in our American community—men who unite with a competence, intelligence and a love of culture, and who, therefore, fully appreciating the systematic training given in our best Academies, as Andover, Exeter, and Williston, covet for their sons a mental discipline no less thorough. They would be glad, however, to connect with it also a more direct personal and kindly influence from the teacher and the family than these public institutions can furnish, and at the same time to avoid the serious evils always incident to any large collection of youth, even under the best attainable supervision. . . . It is intended that

the discipline of the Round Hill School shall be modelled after that of a well-regulated family." *Anual Circular of the Round Hill School, Northampton, Mass. 1866–67* (Northampton, 1866), pp. 1, 3. I have not been able to discover the fate of this school.

Joseph Burnett remained treasurer of St. Mark's until his death in 1894 and apparently interfered more with his school than most of the short-term headmasters would tolerate. At least this is the inference of a letter from Bishop William Lawrence, a long-time trustee of St. Mark's, written to Endicott Peabody at the time of Burnett's death. See Lawrence to Peabody, 16 August 1894, Endicott Peabody MSS, Houghton Library, Harvard University, Cambridge, Mass.

71. See above, p. 75.

72. Conover, *Memories of a Great Schoolmaster,* p. 6.

73. Cf. Jeremiah Day's Report of 1818 (see above, p. 74) with St. Paul's curriculum as detailed in the annual *SPS Statement* during the 1880s.

74. See above, p. 128.

75. Bailey B. Burritt, *Professional Distribution of College and University Graduates,* "United States Bureau of Education Bulletin, 1912, No. 19" (Washington, 1912), *passim.*

76. Figures recalculated from *Directory of the Alumni of St. Paul's School* . . . , pp. 162–63. The original table is based on the occupations of the 3,250 alumni of St. Paul's *living* in 1915. Of the 3,250 the occupations of 3,140 are known.

77. *Ibid.,* figures for Harvard and Yale recalculated from Burritt, *Professional Distribution,* Tables 2 and 6, pp. 80, 83.

78. See above, p. 164.

79. See above, p. 166.

80. Reprinted in Ayres, *Muhlenberg,* p. 162.

81. Conover, *Memories of a Great Schoolmaster,* p. 180.

Chapter VII

1. James McCosh, "Upper Schools," *Addresses and Proceedings of the National Educational Association, Session of the Year 1873* . . . , p. 23. Title and place of publication vary; cited hereafter as *NEA Proceedings.*

2. Laurence R. Veysey's *The Emergence of the American University* (Chicago, 1965), is a comprehensive account of this movement.

3. *NEA Proceedings, 1873,* pp. 23–27.

4. *Ibid.,* p. 31.

5. *Ibid.,* pp. 31–35.

6. Of the many earlier discussions, see especially: W. F. Phelps, "The Duties of an American State in Respect to Higher Education,"

NEA Proceedings, 1866, pp. 83–94; W. P. Atkinson, "The Place of Classical Studies in an American System of Education," *ibid.,* pp. 59–70. For later discussions, see Noah Porter, "Preparatory Schools for College and University Life," *ibid., 1874,* pp. 42–58, and the NEA's report inspired by McCosh's speech, "Report on Intermediate (or Upper) Schools," *ibid.,* pp. 9–22.

7. *NEA Proceedings, 1873,* pp. 37–49.

8. Martin Trow, "The Second Transformation of American Secondary Education," *International Journal of Comparative Sociology,* II (September 1961), 146.

9. E.g., cubberley, *Public Education,* p. 255 and *passim;* Brown, *Making of Our Middle Schools, passim.*

10. Cubberley, *Public Education,* p. 627.

11. George A. Walton, "Appendix E: Report on Academies," *Fortieth Annual Report of the* [*Massachusetts*] *Board of Education: . . . 1875–76* (Boston, 1877), pp. 176–78.

12. Abner J. Phipps, "Appendix B: High Schools of Massachusetts . . . ," *ibid.,* pp. 47, 46.

13. Rudolph, *American College and University,* pp. 282–84.

14. Cubberley, *Public Education,* p. 267.

15. Edgar B. Wesley, *NEA: The First Hundred Years: The Building of the Teaching Profession* (New York, 1957), p. 74.

16. *Ibid.,* p. 76.

17. Lawrence A. Cremin's "The Revolution in American Secondary Education, 1893–1918," *Teachers College Record,* LVI (March 1955), 295–308, provides an excellent overview of these years. Cremin's *The Transfomration of the School: Progressivism in American Education, 1876–1957* (New York, 1961) is the best survey of American secondary education for this period. On the Committee of Ten, see Theodore R. Sizer, *Secondary Schools at the Turn of the Century* (New Haven, 1964). For a highly critical view of educational developments from the Committee of Ten to *Cardinal Principles,* see Richard Hofstadter, *Anti-Intellectualism in American Life* (New York, 1963), pp. 323–41.

18. Richard Grant White, "The Public-School Failure," *North American Review* (December 1880), pp. 537–50, as quoted in Edward A. Krug, *The Shaping of the American High School* (New York, 1964), p. 9; Michael B. Katz, "The Emergence of Bureaucracy in Urban Education: The Boston Case, 1850–1884," *History of Education Quarterly,* VIII (1968), 155–88, 319–57.

19. Lael Tucker Wertenbaker and Maude Basserman, *The Hotchkiss School: A Portrait* (Lakeville, Conn., 1966), pp. 35–41, 14, 16, 1.

20. James McCosh, MS *Reports to Board of Trustees,* 12 February 1880, quoted in T. J. Wertenbaker, *Princeton,* pp. 313–14.

21. *Ibid.*, June 1872, p. 314.

22. *Ibid.*, p. 294; Roland J. Mulford, *History of the Lawrenceville School, 1810–1935* (Princeton, 1935), pp. 6–7.

23. Mulford, *Lawrenceville,* pp. 50–51.

24. *Ibid.*, pp. 87–89. The history of the older academy is in itself interesting. It was one of the many academies that was deeply influenced by Cogswell and Bancroft's example at Round Hill. See the *Trenton Federalist,* 29 April 1829 (reprinted in Mulford, *Lawrenceville,* pp. 20–22); the advertisement for the academy is almost a paraphrase of Cogswell and Bancroft's *Prospectus.*

25. "Simon John McPherson," *Lawrenceville Bulletin,* CIX (April 1919), 7–17.

26. *Twenty-five Years of Lawrenceville. Address of Wm. M. Sloane, Founders' Day, June 16, 1908,* reprinted in Mulford, *Lawrenceville,* p. 90.

27. McCosh to Mackenzie, 5 June 1882, *ibid.*, p. 95.

28. *Ibid.*, pp. 81, 93–95.

29. Caleb S. Green to Samuel Hamil, 9 June 1882, *ibid.*, p. 91.

30. James Cameron Mckenzie, MS "Original draft plan for the organization of the Lawrenceville School. Submitted to the Residuary Legatees of the John C. Green Bequest, October, 1892," typescript copy, Archives Room, John Dixon Library, The Lawrenceville School, Lawrenceville, N.J. (The original is in the school's vault). Cited hereafter as Lawrenceville Founding MS. In quotations from the MS I have expanded Mackenzie's contractions.

31. *Ibid.*, p. 1.

32. *Ibid.*, p. 5.

33. *Ibid.*, pp. 1–3.

34. *Ibid.*, p. 9.

35. Mulford, *Lawrenceville,* pp. 87–88.

36. In the old Lawrenceville academy the tuition had been $350 a year; by 1894 at the new school it would range from $400 to $650, depending upon the location of the room. *Ibid.*, pp. 97, 107.

37. After the first few years the endowment of $250,000 proved inadequate. Lawrenceville ran into constant financial difficulties in its first few decades, difficulties not helped by its reputation for great wealth. Ibid., pp. 182–83.

38. The academic aims of the school were set forth in the Minutes of the Trustees thus: "1. Instruction in the Classical Course shall be of such a character as to fit students for the Freshman Class of any American college. 2. Instruction in the Scientific course shall be of such a character as to fit students for the first class of any American scientific or technical school. 3. The English course shall aim to provide instruction in such branches as shall at the same time secure a solid and

comprehensive discipline and provide a good foundation for general culture." *Lawrenceville School, John C. Green Foundation* (Princeton, 1883), p. 9.

39. Mulford, *Lawrenceville,* pp. 102, 128.

40. Lawrenceville Founding MS, pp. 3–4.

41. Mulford, *Lawrenceville,* pp. 97–98; *Directory of the Alumni of St. Paul's School . . . ,* p. 161.

42. New York *Tribune,* 1 April 1883; New York *Sun,* 29 June 1883; New York *Evening Post,* 9 June 1883; see too Philadelphia *Press,* 12 June 1883.

43. See above, p. 21; Francis Grund, *Aristocracy in America: From the Sketch Book of a German Nobleman* (New York: Harper Torchbooks, 1959), pp. 175–76; David Donald, *Charles Sumner and the Coming of the Civil War* (New York, 1960), p. 57.

44. See above, p. 155. A full-scale study of late nineteenth-century American Anglophilia and of actual English influences on American culture would be most useful. In only one area of American culture—architecture—has it been definitively traced: Vincent J. Scully, Jr., *The Shingle Style: Architectural Theory and Design from Richardson to Wright* (New Haven, 1955), esp. pp. 19–53. See too: Cushing Strout, *The American Image of the Old World* (New York, 1963), esp. Ch. VIII, "The Old Sweet Anglo-Saxon Spell"; Taylor, *Cavalier and Yankee, passim;* Richard Hofstadter, *Social Darwinism in American Thought* (rev. ed.; Boston, 1955), pp. 170–200.

45. See above, p. 155.

46. See above, p. 153. How Thring arrived at his system is still unknown. The "cottage-plan" of boarding children had been first introduced in the Belgian town of Geel early in the nineteenth century in connection with the mentally ill.

47. This atmosphere is very well conveyed in the "Lawrenceville Stories," a series of novels written by Owen Johnson at the turn of the century. See esp. Johnson, *The Eternal Boy, Being the Story of the Prodigious Hickey* (New York, 1909). By the 1920s the notion of the "school as a community" was quite conscious. At St. Paul's, for instance, there was talk of developing the school "on the line of the New England Village Community." SPS MS Trustees' Minutes, 15 October 1920.

48. Charles W. Eliot to Mackenzie, 15 February 1886; Nicholas Murray Butler to M. Gabriel Compayré, 29 May 1894, Mackenzie Committee of Ten Folder, Lawrenceville Archives.

49. McCosh, *Reports,* 18 February 1884, in T. J. Wertenbaker, *Princeton,* pp. 314–15; *ibid.,* p. 161.

50. The 1826 figures are from *H. U. Memoirs, 1830* (Boston, 1886). There were 48 members in this class; data on only 26 are available.

There were 167 freshmen in 1874 (preparation of 6 unknown); the 1883 figure (268, 12 unknown), includes not just freshmen but *all* entrants; there were 246 freshmen in 1884 (preparation of 2 unknown). The 1874, 1883, and 1884 figures are based on the MS Harvard College Admission Books, vol. IV, 1874/1888, in the HUA. They are at best approximate. (The 1874 figure for students prepared by individuals is probably grossly misleading.) An accurate analysis of the Admission Books would take an eidetic memory, a computer, and a team of researchers. See the bibliography for a full description and discussion of these MSS.

The public high schools contributing the largest numbers of freshmen in 1884 were those of Cambridge, Waltham, Newton, and Salem, Massachusetts. The following schools sent the largest single contingents: Phillips Exeter Academy—26; Boston Latin School—20; Hopkinson's (a private proprietary day school in Boston)—18; Roxbury Latin School—13; Noble's (another private Boston day school)—also 13. Of our other schools, St. Paul's sent 9, Phillips Andover 7 (it had sent 12 the previous year), and St. Mark's, 2.

51. Data from *The Freshman Blue Book* (n.p. [New Haven], n.d. [1907]). Note that these data and those for Harvard above are not comparable because of differences in the base of computation. There were 220 freshmen in 1907; data for only 1 are unavailable. The 9 schools, with the number of students from each, were as follows: Phillips Andover—30; St. Paul's—17; the Hill School—13; Lawrenceville—11; Hotchkiss—4; Taft—4; Phillips Exeter—3; St. George's—2; Groton—1.

52. Percentages from *Fourth Annual Report of the Carnegie Foundation for the Advancement of Teaching . . . October, 1909* (New York, 1910), p. 148.

53. Morison, *Three Centuries of Harvard,* pp. 421–22; Pierson, *Yale College,* pp. 235, 391; Henry Wilkinson Bragdon, *Woodrow Wilson: The Academic Years* (Princeton, 1967), p. 272.

54. Bragdon's source for Patton's remark was an interview conducted in 1940. Bragdon, *Woodrow Wilson,* n. 9, pp. 458–59.

55. See especially, Wecter, *Saga of American Society,* ch. VII, "The Gentleman and His Club," pp. 252–88.

56. See above, pp. 000.

57. Charles W. Eliot to R. T. Crane, 12 September 1901, Charles W. Eliot MSS, HUA.

58. Quoted in Morison, *Three Centuries of Harvard,* p. 330.

59. For the Groton-Harvard figures, see: Hugo K. Schilling, MS Report on Modern Languages at Groton [1893], Groton Folder, [Harvard University] Schools Examination Board Reports and

Papers, HUA. Cited hereafter as Harvard SEB MSS.

60. Eliot to Charles Francis Adams, Jr., 27 May 1904, and 9 June 1904, Eliot MSS. Never particularly consistent or rational on anything that touched Harvard's preeminence, Eliot concluded the correspondence by declaring that "even the stupid fellows are better off in Harvard than they would be anywhere else." On another occasion he wrote: "To lose altogether the presence of those who in early life have enjoyed the domestic and social advantages of wealth would be as great a blow to the college as to lose the sons of the poor." Quoted in Morison, *Three Centuries of Harvard,* p. 330.

61. Richard Hofstadter, *The Age of Reform: From Bryan to F.D.R.* (New York, 1955), p. 136.

62. Douglas T. Miller, *Jacksonian Aristocracy: Class and Democracy in New York, 1830–1860* (New York, 1967), ch. VII.

63. Gordon Milne, *George William Curtis and the Genteel Tradition* (Bloomington, Ind., 1956), pp. 72–73, 29, 235.

64. George Haven Putnam, *Memories of A Publisher, 1865–1915* (New York, 1916), pp. 21, 6.

65. Richard Grant White, "Class Distinctions in the United States," *North American Review,* CXXXVII (1883), 242.

6h6. Edward C. Kirkland, *Dream and Thought in the Business Community, 1860–1900* (Chicago, Quadrangle Books, 1964), p. 33 ff.

67. "The Public Schools of England," *North American Review,* "Part I," CXXVIII (1879), 352–71; "Part II," CXXIX (1879), 37–52. The quotation is from p. 371.

68. Frederick Law Olmsted to Wolcott Gibbs, 5 November 1862, in Henry W. Bellows, *Historical Sketch of the Union League Club of New York: Its Origins, Organization, and Work, 1863–1879* (New York, 1879), pp. 11–16.

69. "Public Schools of England," 371.

70. " 'The Public Schools of England,' " *New England Journal of Education,* IX (3 April 1879), 216–17.

71. See Cleveland Amory, *The Proper Bostonians* (New York, 1950), *passim.*

72. For the rather extraordinary Ward Family connection, see the genealogical chart at the end of Maud Howe Elliott, *Uncle Sam Ward and His Circle* (New York, 1938).

73. On reference group theory, see Robert K. Merton, *Social Theory and Social Structure* (rev. ed.; Glencoe, Ill., 1957). In the future, if significant and convincing work on an American "upper-class"—a concept which I have regretfully chosen not to use in this study—is to be done by historians, they would do well to begin with family and kinship systems. Much of the basic material is already available; to such studies

the historian should bring the skills of the genealogist, the statistician, the demographer, the anthropologist, and an indefinite amount of *sitz-fleisch.*

74. The best general social history of this period is still Arthur M. Schlesinger, *The Rise of the City, 1878–1898* (New York, 1933).

75. Daniel Boorstin, *The Americans: The National Experience* (New York, 1965), pp. 161–68; Francis Bowen, *The Principles of Political Economy Applied to the Condition, the Resources, and the Institutions of the American People* (Boston, 1856), p. 91.

76. Morton and Lucia White, *The Intellectual versus the City* (New York: Mentor Books, 1964), *passim.*

77. *The Education of Henry Adams* (New York: Modern Library, 1931), p. 238.

78. Dorman B. Eaton, *The Independent Movement in New York as an Element in the Next Elections and A problem in Party Government* (New York, 1880), p. 55.

79. Oscar Fay Adams, *Some Famous American Schools* (Boston, 1903), p. 337.

80. Seymour Mandelbaum, *Boss Tweed's New York* (New York, 1965), *passim.*

81. "Report on Intermediate (or Upper) Schools," *NEA Proceedings, 1874,* p. 15.

82. *The American Commonwealth* (2 vols.; New York, 1908), I, 681.

83. Sam B. Warner, Jr., *Streetcar Suburbs: The Process of Growth in Boston, 1870–1900* (Cambridge, 1962), p. 58.

84. Sizer, *Age of the Academies,* p. 40.

85. "Public Schools of England," 369, 370.

86. See p. 253.

87. Richard T. Flood, *The Story of Noble and Greenough School, 1866–1966* (Dedham, Mass., 1966), p. 23.

88. *Catalogue of Rugby Academy . . . 1873–1874* (Philadelphia, 1874).

89. Figures computed from [Porter E. Sargent], *A Handbook of American Private Schools* (Boston, 1916), p. 284 ff., and from various school catalogues and histories. The fourteen schools in our original group were: Andover, Exeter, Hill, St. Paul's, St. Mark's, Lawrenceville, Groton, Taft, Hotchkiss, Choate, St. George's, Middlesex, Deerfield, and Kent. The average tuition figure is based on the following schools: St. Paul's, St. Mark's, Groton, Taft, Hotchkiss, Choate, St. George's, and Middlesex. Deerfield is the school *not* included in the group of thirteen.

90. Roger W. Drury, *Drury and St. Paul's: The Scars of a Schoolmaster* (Boston, 1964), p. 60.

91. *The Genius of American Education* (Pittsburgh, 1965), p. 66.

92. For a more complete exploration of this theme through the 1960s, see McLachlan, "The City, the School, and the Suburb."

Chapter VIII

1. MS Minutes of the Board of Trustees, 17 June 1879. Treasurer's Office, Jeremiah Smith Hall, The Phillips Exeter Academy, Exeter, N.H. Cited hereafter as PEA Trustees' MSS.

2. *Phillips Exeter Academy. . . . Exercises at the Centennial Celebration. . . . 1883* . . . (Exeter, 1883), *passim;* Williams, *Story of Phillips Exeter,* pp. 60–62.

3. PEA Trustees' MSS, 8 May 1883. All figures on student enrollments, etc., are calculated from the annual *Catalogue of the Phillips Exeter Academy* for the appropriate year. Cited hereafter as *PEA Catalogue.*

4. Marr, *Old New England Academies,* pp. 289, 294–95; Richard Walden Hale, Jr., *Milton Academy, 1798–1948* (Milton, Mass., 1948), pp. 31–50.

5. Bell, *Phillips Exeter Academy,* p. 46.

6. Crosbie, *Phillips Exeter,* p. 128.

7. *PEA Catalogue, 1884–85.*

8. "Budget, 1892–93," PEA Trustees' MSS, 4 June 1892. At Lawrenceville in the 1880s an instructor in modern languages was offered a salary of $1,800 if living in the school's buildings, $2,200 if living outside. The average faculty salary there in 1892–99 was about $2,300, Mulford, *Lawrenceville,* pp. 90, 107.

9. LeBaron Russell Briggs, MS "Report on English at Groton," [1893], p. 4, Groton Folder, Harvard SEB MSS.

10. "Senior Class Statistics," *The Pean,* VIII (1891), 19.

11. *PEA Catalogue, 1884–85.*

12. See table, p. 231.

13. Figures and percentages calculated from the annual *PEA Catalogues* and from Crosbie, *Phillips Exeter,* pp. 128, 140–41, 151–52. The figures for the first two periods are for alumni *receiving degrees* from colleges; for the third period, for alumni *entering* colleges.

14. PEA Trustees' MSS, 18 July 1883. Perkins's position had not been made easier by a trustees' resolution of 1873 that placed most effective power in the hands of the faculty, i.e., Wentworth: "Whereas it is desirable, at the beginning of . . . the Administration of the Academy by a new Principal, that the respective powers and duties of the Principal and Faculty should be precisely defined, therefore, *Voted:* that all questions of discipline, determination of the merit or demerit of the students, and recommendation of candidates for situations on the Charity Foundation be settled by vote of the Faculty; but that the conduct and administration of the Academy in all other respects whatever be confided to the Principal alone, subject only to his responsibility

to the Board." PEA Trustees' MSS, 17 June 1873. Perkins, in other words, had all the responsibility and almost none of the power. While Henry Coit was Pope at St. Paul's, Perkins was just the Patriarch of Constantinople—*primus inter pares*—at Exeter.

15. See the scrapbooks of newspaper clippings for the period in the Thompson Library, PEA.

16. PEA Trustees' MSS, 18 June 1888; 20 April 1889.

17. PEA Trustees' MSS, 20 April 1889; 28 August 1889.

18. Charles H. Bell, *History of the Town of Exeter, New Hampshire* (Exeter, 1888), pp. 340–42.

19. For the train schedules, see *"News-Letter" Hand-Book of Exeter, 1883* (Exeter, 1883).

20. Crosbie, *Phillips Exeter,* p. 192.

21. *PEA Catalogue, 1884–85.*

22. *PEA Catalogue, 1885–86.*

23. *PEA Catalogue, 1891–92.*

24. *PEA Catalogue, 1884–85.*

25. PEA Trustees' MSS, 18 June 1888.

26. Bell, *History of Town of Exeter,* p. 298.

27. *Ibid.*

28. Williams, *Story of Phillips Exeter*, p. 68.

29. See above, pp. 150–53.

30. *Centuries of Childhood,* pp. 312–13.

31. See above, p. 82.

32. Fuess, *An Old New England School,* pp. 140–56.

33. In 1908 the seminary moved to Cambridge, and its buildings became the property of the academy.

34. For a short account of Eliot's administration, see Morison, *Three Centuries of Harvard,* pp. 329–99.

35. Broome, *College Admission Requirements,* pp. 48–52, 103; Rudolph, *American College and University,* p. 285.

36. *PEA Catalogue, 1873–74.*

37. Crosbie, *Phillips Exeter,* p. 295.

38. See above, p. 121.

39. PEA Trustees' MSS, 2 February 1871; *PEA Catalogue, 1873–74; PEA Catalogue, 1883–84.*

40. See above, p. 122.

41. PEA Trustees' MSS, 17 June 1889.

42. PEA Trustees' MSS, 24 June 1890.

43. Williams, *Story of Phillips Exeter,* p. 71.

44. PEA Trustees' MSS, 17 October 1891; 20 February 1892.

45. In 1900 there were 161 cities in the United States with a population of 25,000 and over. They are listed in *United States Twelfth Census:*

1900, Population, I, Table XXII, pp. lxix–lxx. The twenty-five largest cities, and the numbers of students at Phillips Exeter and St. Paul's in 1894–95 from each, was as follows (for the source of the student data see n. 46 below):

City	Exeter		St. Paul's	
1. New York City (Includes Brooklyn)	18		52	
2. Chicago	4		13	
3. Philadelphia	1		20	
4. St. Louis	3		8	
5. Boston	7		6	
6. Baltimore	2		1	
7. Cleveland	—		1	
8. Buffalo	—		—	
9. San Francisco	1		2	
10. Cincinnati	—		4	
11. Pittsburgh	—		8	
12. New Orleans	—		1	
13. Detroit	1		3	
14. Milwaukee	—		—	
15. Washington, D.C.	1		6	
16. Newark	—		1	
17. Jersey City	—		—	
18. Louisville	—		—	
19. Minneapolis	—		—	
20. Providence	—		2	
21. Indianapolis	3		—	
22. Kansas City, Mo.	—		2	
23. St. Paul	—		2	
24. Rochester	—		4	
25. Denver	—		4	
	41	22.3%	140	47.6%

46. Lists of the students and their places of origin are given in the *PEA Catalogues* for 1884–85 and 1894–95, and the *SPS Statement* for 1894–95. They were matched with "Table 91—Population of Places Having at Least 2,500 Inhabitants in 1900: 1900 and 1890," in *Abstract of The Twelfth Census of the United States, 1900* (Washington, D.C., 1904), p. 135 ff.

47. PEA Trustees' MSS, 26 September 1891.

48. PEA Trustees' MSS, 17 October 1891.

49. PEA Trustees' MSS, 3 January 1891; 21 February 1891; 18 October 1891.

50. "Report of the Committee on restricting the number of Students in the Academy," PEA Trustees' MSS, 20 May 1891.

51. PEA Trustees' MSS, 12 June 1891.

52. PEA Trustees' MSS, 16 April 1892.

53. Quoted in Williams, *Story of Phillips Exeter,* p. 71.

54. *Harvard University. Schools Examination Board. Announcement.* Printed broadside, dated 22 June 1892, Harvard SEB MSS. The Schools Examination Board is discussed fully in Chapter IX below.

55. PEA Trustees' MSS, 15 October 1892.

56. Julian Lowell Coolidge, "Mathematics, 1870–1928," in *The Development of Harvard University Since the Inauguration of President Eliot, 1869–1929,* ed. Samuel Eliot Morison (Cambridge, 1930), pp. 249, 251; Herbert W. Smyth, "The Classics, 1867–1929," *ibid.,* pp. 48–49; C. L. Jackson and G. P. Baxter, "Chemistry, 1865–1929," *ibid.,* pp. 263–64; Morison, *Three Centuries of Harvard,* pp. 349, 376.

57. [Paul H. Hanus], MS "[Final] Report on The Phillips Exeter Academy, June 9, 1892," Exeter Folder, Harvard SEB MSS. Unless otherwise noted, the other SEB reports cited in this chapter are all in the Exeter Folder.

58. LeBaron Russell Briggs, MS "Report on English at Exeter," *passim;* Albert Bushnell Hart, MS "Report on History at Exeter," *passim;* Hanus, "[Final] Report on Exeter," p. 19, Harvard SEB MSS.

59. *Ibid.,* p. 18.

60. *Ibid.*

61. The modern language instructor was Oscar Faulhaber, who had been hired in 1871. When the students tried to present the Academy with a portrait of him the trustees resolved "that no portrait could be placed in the Academy without their approval, and that no living person's portrait could be placed in the Academy chapel." PEA Trustees' MSS, 16 June 1893; 21 October 1893; 18 December 1893; 17 June 1895. Faulhaber was the one instructor whose classes had been criticized as undisciplined; the trustees were taking no more chances in this area. See too *PEA Catalogue, 1894–95,* p. 7.

62. Hanus, "[Final] Report on Exeter," p. 19, Harvard SEB MSS.

63. Hart, "History at Exeter," pp. 19–20; Briggs, "English at Exeter," p. 10; Morgan, MS "Report on Classics at Exeter," pp. 16–17, Harvard SEB MSS.

64. PEA Trustees' MSS, 17 June 1895.

65. PEA Trustees' MSS, 11 May 1895; Williams, *Story of Phillips Exeter,* p. 73.

66. PEA Trustees' MSS, 17 June 1895.

67. Amen to Clement C. Gaines, 13 February 1903. MS Principals'

Letter-press Books, Attic, Jeremiah Smith Hall, The Phillips Exeter Academy. Cited hereafter as PEA Principals' MSS.

68. Williams, *Story of Phillips Exeter,* pp. 114–35.

69. Amen to William J. Tucker, 28 January 1903, PEA Principals' MSS.

70. Amen to Alonzo ———, 2 February 1903, PEA Principals' MSS.

71. Amen to William A. Scott, 13 February 1903, PEA Principals' MSS.

72. "Harlan Page Amen," *The Pean,* XIII (1897), 161.

73. See above, p. 68.

74. This sort of thing probably shouldn't be carried too far. What would one make of the three most prominent writer-alumni of the Choate School, in Wallingford, Connecticut—John Dos Passos, Alan Jay Lerner, and Edward Albee?

75. Crosbie, *Phillips Exeter,* pp. 164, 172.

76. Williams, *Story of Phillips Exeter,* p. 132: *SPS Statement, 1934–35.*

77. Crosbie, *Phillips Exeter,* p. 158.

78. PEA Trustees' MSS, 19 December 1898; 18 February 1899.

79. William DeWitt Hyde, president of Bowdoin College, quoted in Williams, *Story of Phillips Exeter,* p. 84.

80. Although it extends beyond our immediate subject, in this respect the recent work of Robert Weibe is most suggestive. "America during the nineteenth century was a society of island communities," Wiebe writes. "Weak communication severely restricted the interaction among these islands and dispersed and power to form opinion and enact public policy. Education, both formal and informal, inhibited specialization and discouraged the accumulation of knowledge. The heart of American democracy was local autonomy. . . . Almost all of a community's affairs were still arranged informally.

"My purpose is to describe the breakdown of this society and the emergence of a new system. The health of the nineteenth-century community depended upon two closely related conditions: its ability to manage the lives of its members, and the belief among its members that the community had such powers. Already by the 1870's the autonomy of the community was badly eroded." *The Search for Order, 1877–1920* (New York, 1967), p. vii. Wiebe's general remarks appear to be an exact description of the situation of Exeter, New Hampshire.

Chapter IX

1. George E. Carmichael, "The Coming Men of Choate" (1900), *The Choate School Brief,* IV (April 1903), 52.

2. This interesting episode can be followed in: Theodore Roosevelt to Endicott Peabody, 7 May 1901; 10 April 1901; 12 July 1901; 18 July 1901; Malcolm Donald to TR, 16 July 1901; TR to Malcolm Donald (copy), 18 July 1901; A. Lawrence Lowell to Peabody, 24 July 1901, all in the Endicott Peabody MSS, Houghton Library, Harvard University. See also TR to Peabody, 22 April 1901; TR to George Hinckley Lyman, 22 April 1901; TR to Richard Derby, 29 May 1901, and TR to William Church Osborn, 10 July 1901, all in *The Letters of Theodore Roosevelt,* Elting E. Morison *et al.,* eds., (8 vols.; Cambridge, 1951), III, 62, 75–76, 80, 91.

3. Roosevelt's ties to Groton are discussed in this chapter; Wilson's appreciation of Lawrenceville is cited above, p. 13. Taft's connection with the family boarding school came through his brother, Horace Dutton Taft, who founded the Taft School in Watertown, Connecticut, in 1890. The presidents of the Progressive era sometimes found themselves in amusing situations with the boarding schools, as in 1914 when Horace Taft reported to his brother on a student debate. The theme, he explained, was " 'Resolved that the Progressive Party Deserves the Support of the American People.' Isn't that a pleasant subject for a debate with the Taft School?" To which, a few days later, his brother replied that he was very happy "that your school won the debate on the question of the usefulness of the Progressive party, and I am also glad that you held the negative." Horace Dutton Taft to William Howard Taft, 22 April 1914; W. H. Taft to H. D. Taft, 26 April 1914; William Howard Taft MSS, Manuscript Division, Library of Congress, Washington, D.C. The library is cited hereafter as LC. On the early years of the Taft School—which stood in somewhat the same relation to Yale as did Hotchkiss—see Horace Dutton Taft, *Memories and Opinions* (New York, 1942).

4. Frank D. Ashburn, *Fifty Years On: Groton School, 1884–1934* (New York, 1934), pp. 33–35.

5. Peabody to Roosevelt, 27 August 1903, Theodore Roosevelt MSS, Manuscript Division, LC.

6. Peabody to Roosevelt, 19 November 1904, Roosevelt MSS.

7. Ashburn, *Fifty Years On,* p. 193.

8. Sir Walter Lawrence to Mrs. Endicott Peabody, 19 August 1935, in Frank D. Ashburn, *Peabody of Groton, A Portrait* (New York, 1944), p. 19.

9. *Ibid.,* p. 31.

10. Ellery Sedgwick, "Three Men of Groton," *Atlantic Monthly,* CLXXVIII (1946), 68.

11. And so on for eleven stanzas more. *The Cheltonian,* (March 1876), p. 142.

12. Ashburn, *Peabody,* p. 16.

13. Bamford, *Rise of the Public Schools,* p. 58.

14. David Newsome, *Godliness and Good Learning: Four Studies on A Victorian Ideal* (London, 1961), p. 83.

15. Bamford, *Rise of the Public Schools,* pp. 219–20.

16. Ashburn, *Peabody.*

17. Ashburn, *Fifty Years On,* p. 10.

18. *Ibid.*

19. Ashburn, *Peabody,* p. 36.

20. *Ibid.,* p. 43.

21. Mann, *Yankee Reformers,* pp. 1–5.

22. Charles Howard Hopkins, *The Rise of the Social Gospel in American Protestantism, 1865–1915* (New Haven, 1940), pp. 196–97.

23. Henry F. May, *Protestant Churches and Industrial America* (New York, 1949), p. 148.

24. Quoted in *ibid.,* p. 185.

25. Clyde Griffen, "An Urban Church in Ferment: The Episcopal Church in New York City, 1880–1900," (Ph.D. dissertation, Columbia University, 1960), *passim.*

26. May, *Protestant Churches,* pp. 149, 182–85.

27. Quoted in James Arthur Muller, *The Episcopal Theological School, 1867–1943* (Cambridge, 1943), p. 17.

28. Peabody to Julius W. Atwood, [May/June 1882], in Peabody MSS, and also reprinted in Ashburn, *Peabody,* p. 57. (Whenever possible further reference to Peabody's letters are made to the printed rather than the MS version.)

29. Muller, *Episcopal Theological School,* pp. 50–53.

30. Quoted in Ashburn, *Fifty Years On,* p. 11.

31. Ashburn, *Peabody,* pp. 60,61.

32. Peabody to Julius A. Atwood, 10 May 1883, in *ibid.,* p. 63.

33. Peabody to Samuel A. Green, 17 January 1884; 24 January 1884, Samuel A. Green MSS, MHS.

34. Katz, "Emergence of Bureaucracy," *passim.*

35. Stanley Elkins's suggestive remarks about nineteenth-century American anti-institutionalism (*Slavery: A Problem in American Institutional and Intellectual Life* [Chicago, 1959], pp. 27–37, 140–206) have been perhaps overly persuasive. The neglect of the continuing *pro*-institutional tradition in American thought has led, I believe, to a certain distortion in two brilliant studies related to this theme, George M. Frederickson's *The Inner Civil War: Northern Intellectuals and the Crisis of the Union* (New York, 1965), and John L. Thomas, "Romantic Reform in America, 1815–1865," *American Quarterly,* XVII (Winter, 1965), 656–81. The tradition Ralph Waldo Emerson was reacting *against*—that of

his father, William Emerson, and of the Anthologists and the moral philosophers—deserves more serious and sympathetic attention than it has yet received.

36. Schlesinger, *Rise of the City,* pp. 220–22; John Higham, *History* (Englewood Cliffs, N.J., 1965), pp. 8–10.

37. Mark A. DeWolfe Howe, *The Boston Symphony Orchestra* (Boston, 1931), *passim*; Bliss Perry, *The Life and Letters of Henry Lee Higginson* (Boston, 1921), *passim.*

38. Reprinted in Ashburn, *Peabody,* p. 67.

39. See above, pp. 213–16.

40. See above, p. 202.

41. An extremely careful comparison has revealed only one completely unmistakeable direct borrowing from Cheltenham at Groton: in typography and layout the two school journals—*The Cheltonian* and *The Grotonian*—are identical.

42. Reprinted in Ashburn, *Peabody,* p. 68.

43. *Ibid.,* pp. 72–73.

44. *Ibid.,* p. 71.

45. On the origins of the familial image, see above, pp. 115–16; for its use in the 1960s see the article on the Choate School by Richard J. Margolin, "The Prep School World Adjusts to the Real World," *New York Times Magazine* (5 January 1969), p. 27 ff. Such familial imagery was by no means limited to secondary schools. In 1902, for instance, William Rainey Harper, president of the young University of Chicago, characterized the student social system there thus: "The theory of the system may be summed up in the statement that the University is one family, socially considered, of which the President is the head. . . ." Quoted in Richard J. Storr, *Harper's University, The Beginnings: A History of the University of Chicago* (Chicago, 1966), p. 166.

46. See above, p. 55.

47. Katz, "Emergence of Bureaucracy," p. 167.

48. Raymond E. Callahan, *Education and the Cult of Efficiency* (Chicago, 1962), *passim.*

49. Gail Hamilton, *Our Common-School System* (Boston, 1880), p. 91.

50. Charles Francis Adams, Jr., *The New Departure in the Common Schools of Quincy and Other Papers on Educational Topics* (Boston, 1881), pp. 60–63.

51. Brooks to Peabody, 21 March 1885; Roosevelt to Peabody, 20 March 1889, Peabody MSS.

52. Peabody to William C. Endicott, 14 March 1889, William C. Endicott MSS, MHS; Phillips Brooks to Peabody, 16 March 1889, Peabody MSS.

53. Brooks to Peabody, 21 March 1885, Peabody MSS.

54. In a speech to the Groton Historical Society, reprinted in full in Ashburn, *Peabody,* pp. 73–76.

55. Sedgwick, "Three Men of Groton," p. 70.

56. For the figures on the American schools, see above, p. 216. In 1962 Eton had 1,190 students, Rugby 715, Cheltenham 468, and Uppingham 589. Bamford, *Rise of the Public Schools,* p. 331.

57. Lawrence to Peabody, 12 September 1888; 24 August 1888, Peabody MSS.

58. The memoranda books are in the Peabody MSS.

59. John Hay to Peabody, 20 April 1890; 21 June 1892; 10 September 1892; and 3 October 1898; Mrs. Edwin Main Post to Peabody, 4 January 1902, Peabody MSS.

60. See Adams to Peabody, 28 September 1885; 26 October 1887; 19 September 1888; 19 January 1889; 28 January 1889; 12 February 1889; 21 October 1889; 19 March 1891; and 2 January 1892; Morgan to Peabody, 9 February 1905; 2 January 1906; 10 January 1906; 7 April 1906; 21 May 1906; 6 September 1907; 12 September 1907; 8 January 1908; 9 April 1909; 19 July 1909; 28 July 1909; 18 August 1909; and 8 September 1909, Peabody MSS.

61. Alfred Thayer Mahan to Peabody, 18 February 1898, Peabody MSS.

62. "Three Men of Groton," pp. 66–67.

63. See above p. 333, no. 70.

64. On the Mugwump type, see Hofstadter, *Anti-Intellectualism,* pp. 174–76; for a full discussion of the backgrounds of this group, see James McLachlan, "The Genteel Reformers, 1865–1884," (unpublished Master's Essay, Columbia University, 1958), pp. 12–26.

65. Noah Porter, *The American College and the American Public* (New York, 1870), p. 211.

66. The other ten schools examined were: 1892—St. Mark's School; 1893—Milton Academy, Peekskill Military Academy, Phillips Exeter Academy, Roxbury Latin School, Salem High School, Watertown (Mass.) High School; 1893–94—Mt. Hermon School; 1894—Clinton (N.H.) High School, and Newton (Mass.) High School.

67. The non-Harvard member of the board was William C. Collar, principal of the Roxbury Latin School.

68. *Schools Examination Board. Instructions to the Examiners. Harvard University.* Printed broadside in Harvard SEB MSS.

69. Henry W. Holmes, "The Graduate School of Education, 1891–1929," in Morison, ed., *Development of Harvard University,* pp. 518–24.

70. John H. Wright, MS "Report on Classics at Groton," p. 4, Groton Folder, Harvard SEB MSS. A short title is used in all following

references to the MS Reports on Groton, all of which are in the Groton Folder in the SEB MSS.

71. *Ibid.*, p. 5. This was a constant complaint among all the schools examined. Teachers continually felt their work hampered and fragmented by the widely differing requirements of the various colleges. The problem would not be resolved until the establishment in 1900 of the College Entrance Examination Board and the gradual adoption of uniform college entrance requirements. See Claude M. Fuess, *The College Board: Its First Fifty Years* (New York, 1950), pp. 34–46. Groton adopted the board's system when Harvard did, in 1906.

72. "Mathematics at Groton," pp. 8, 9–10. This report is not signed. Harvard SEB MSS.

73. Theodore W. Richards, "Science at Groton," pp. 1–2, Harvard SEB MSS.

74. Hugo K. Schilling, "Modern Languages at Groton," p. 10, Harvard SEB MSS.

75. Ephraim Emerton, "History at Groton," pp. 1, 2, Harvard SEB MSS. Thayer was Peabody's most trusted lieutenant. In 1894 he became headmaster of St. Mark's, which he built into a school rivaling Groton and St. Paul's.

76. LeBaron Russell Briggs, "English at Groton," p. 10, Harvard SEB MSS.

77. [Paul H. Hanus], "Final report on Groton," p. 2, Harvard SEB MSS.

78. Briggs, "English at Groton," p. 2 Harvard SEB MSS.

79. "Mathematics at Groton," p. 7, Harvard SEB MSS.

80. Schilling, "Modern Languages at Groton," p. 16, Harvard SEB MSS.

81. Peabody to Roosevelt, 30 January 1906, Roosevelt MSS.

82. Lawrence to Peabody, 21 August 1887, Peabody MSS.

83. Peabody to Dr. J. C. Warren, 26 June 1895, J. C. Warren MSS, MHS; Peabody to Roosevelt, 30 January 1906, Roosevelt MSS.

84. Briggs, "English at Groton," p. 2, Harvard SEB MSS.

85. William Lawrence to Peabody, 26 January 1894, Peabody MSS.

86. Schilling, "Modern Languages at Groton," p. 3, Harvard SEB MSS.

87. William Lawrence to Peabody, 9 September 1902, Peabody MSS.

88. Ashburn, *Peabody,* pp. 136–37.

89. For Groton's alumni rolls, see Ashburn, *Fifty Years On,* p. 185 ff.

90. See Henry A. Coit, *The Resurrection Life. A Sermon In Memory of the Late George C. Shattuck, M.D., Preached at the Church of the Advent, Boston, On Low Sunday, 1893* (Boston, 1893).

91. See p. 343, n. 45.

92. For various reasons, Schiff decided not to send Mortimer to Groton. For a lively, overly ingenious, and slightly inaccurate account of this episode, see Stephen Birmingham, *"Our Crowd": The Great Jewish Families of New York* (New York: Dell Paperbacks, 1968), pp. 218–19. Rich New York Jews at this period were apt to keep their sons at home and send them to Julius Sachs's excellent and highly respected Collegiate Institute.

Although anti-Semitic incidents at various schools have certainly occurred (see *ibid.*, p. 437), my own studies reveal no definite pattern of anti-Semitism on the part of boarding schools. In the masses of material I examined I found only three direct references to Jews, none of them overtly anti-Semitic in character. Based solely on my own experience, I would guess that until shortly after World War II Jewish students were accepted on a quota basis. In the late 1940s some schools unconsciously conveyed the vaguely anti-Semitic attitude common among well-to-do Christian Americans of the time—a genteel anti-Semitism of the T. S. Eliot sort, but none the less unpleasant for its gentility.

In fact, comparatively few Jews seem to have applied to these schools—understandably, considering their avowedly strong Christian orientation. For instance, after sampling Choate's admission applications for the 1920's and 1930's my impression is that the majority of applicants were Episcopalians, followed in number almost equal to each other by Presbyterians, Congregationalists, and Roman Catholics. (MS Admission Applications, Storeroom, Administration Building, The Choate School, Wallingford, Conn.)

If the references to Jews are scanty, those to Roman Catholics are almost nonexistent. Well-to-do Roman Catholics seem to have sent their sons to these boarding schools; perhaps on a quota basis, perhaps not. (One would surely think that the Episcopalian schools would have tried to reserve a large majority of places for members of their own denomination.) Comparable Roman Catholic boarding schools were founded early in the twentieth century—the Canterbury School in New Milford, Connecticut, in 1915, and Portsmouth Priory in Rhode Island in 1926. Canterbury was founded by Catholic laymen and had no direct ecclesiastical connections. Portsmouth Priory was founded by the Revernd J. Hugh Diman, who, as an Episcopal priest, founded and was headmaster of the Episcopalian St. George's School in Newport from 1896 to 1917. After conversion to Catholicism he was ordained a Roman Catholic priest and founded Portsmouth Priory; his memory is not highly honored among Episcopalians. Diman—in the one com pletely unambiguous example of direct English influence upon

American schools—imported English Benedictines to staff his new school.

93. Ernest R. May, *American Imperialism: A Speculative Essay* (New York, 1968), pp. 44–48.

94. Adams to Peabody, 19 September 1888, Peabody MSS.

95. James Watson Williams, *The Passion for Riches* (Utica, N.Y., 1838), pp. 16–17.

96. Richard Weiss, *The American Myth of Success: From Horatio Alger to Norman Vincent Peale* (New York, 1969), ch. I.

97. See above, pp. 145, 208.

98. *The Annual Report of the Rector to the Corporation of the School, October 28th, 1909* (Concord, N.H., 1909), pp. 4–5. Cited hereafter as *SPS Rector's Report.*

99. For explorations of various aspects of this mood, see Frederick C. Jaher, *Doubters and Dissenters: Cataclysmic Thought in America, 1885–1918* (New York, 1964), *passim;* and Barbara Miller Solomon, *Ancestors and Immigrants: A Changing New England Tradition* (Cambridge, 1956), *passim.*

100. Cf. Edmund Gosse, "The Decay of Literary Taste," *North American Review,* CLXI (1895), 109–17, and Theodore Roosevelt, "Social Evolution," *American Ideals and Other Essays Social and Political* (New York, 1904), pp. 303–28. The Roosevelt essay was first published in 1895.

101. Eric McKitrick, "Decadence and Bohemianism in the 1890s," (unpublished Master's Essay, Columbia University, 1951), pp. 14, 19–20.

102. John Jay Chapman to William Greenough Thayer, 30 September 1929, carbon copy in Peabody MSS. Chapman was on one of his perennial anti-Catholic crusades; in this case he was trying to whip up opposition to Al Smith among Episcopalians.

103. Charles McArthur, "Personalities of Public and Private School Boys," *Harvard Educational Review,* XXIV (Fall, 1954), 256–62.

104. McArthur's notions should be approached with caution; it is quite possible that private school alumni were "achieving" in areas and in ways which might well have escaped the recognition of the academic observer.

105. "An Ideal Boy," *The Choate School Brief,* VII (June 1906), 16.

106. See above, pp. 164–66.

107. For an excellent discussion of the notion of the "whole man," see George R. Peterson, *The New England College in the Age of the University* (Amherst, Mass., 1964), pp. 27–51; for an equally good discussion of the related concept of "manliness," see Veysey, *Emergence of the American University,* pp. 28–32.

108. "Judge Choate's Address," *The Choate School Brief,* VII (June 1906), 7.

109. William James to Mrs. James, [ca. 1878], in Henry James, ed., *The Letters of William James* (2 vols.; Boston, 1920), I, 199–200.

110. Erik H. Erikson, *Identity: Youth and Crisis* (New York, 1968), pp. 20, 19.

111. Quoted in Bamford, *Rise of the Public Schools,* pp. 11–12.

112. "The Sermon Preached at the Consecration of St. John's Chapel, Groton School, on Saturday, 13 October 1900, by the Right Reverend William Lawrence, D.D., Bishop of Massachusetts," *Consecration of St. John's Chapel . . .* (Boston, 1900), pp. 18–19.

113. Joseph H. Choate to Carrie Choate, 3 June 1897, Joseph H. Choate MSS, Manuscript Division, LC.

114. George W. Martin, "Preface to A Schoolmaster's Biography," *Harper's Magazine,* CLXXXVIII (January 1944), 157–58. Martin was a member of Groton's class of 1906.

115. Sedgwick, "Three Men of Groton," p. 68; Dean Acheson, *Morning and Noon* (Boston, 1965), p. 24; Ashburn, *Fifty Years On,* p. 193.

116. Sedgwick, "Three Men of Groton," p. 70.

117. Endicott Peabody. "The Aims, Duties, and Opportunities of the Headmaster of an Endowed Secondary School," *School Review,* XVII (1909), 527.

118. Private communication to the author.

119. Sedgwick, "Three Men of Groton," pp. 66–67.

120. Martin, "Schoolmaster's Biography," p. 161.

121. *Identity,* pp. 128–29.

122. Martin, "Schoolmaster's Biography," pp. 162, 157; Sedgwick, "Three Men of Groton," p. 68.

123. Willard S. Elsbree, *The American Teacher* (New York, 1939), pp. 194–208, 553–54.

124. Endicott Peabody, "The Continuous Moral Influence of the School Through College and Through Life," *School Review,* VII (1899), 622–23.

125. Martin, "Schoolmaster's Biography," p. 157.

126. [Samuel S. Drury], *SPS Rector's Report, 1915,* p. 16.

127. Dr. M. V. O'Shea, "Educational Conditions and Needs of St. Paul's School," *SPS Rector's Report, 1916,* pp. 43, 38.

128. Francis A. Shinn, "Self-Government," *The Choate School Brief,* (June 1905), 1–2; Rudolph, *American College and University,* p. 369 ff.

129. Peabody, "Continuous Moral Influence," pp. 621–22.

130. See, for example, George Biddle, "As I Remember Groton School: A Chapter of Autobiography, 1898–1904," *Harper's Magazine,* CLXXIX (1939), 293.

131. Burns, *Roosevelt,* p. 14.

132. Wilkinson, *Gentlemanly Power,* p. 30.

133. See above, p. 180.

134. Ashburn, *Peabody,* pp. 98–99. For Peabody's views on the English public schools, see "Appendix A: Endicott Peabody's Comparison of American and English Schools," in *ibid.,* pp. 421–26.

135. Eliot's remarks were made in direct response to Peabody's "Continuous Moral Influence," which was originally delivered as a speech before the New England Association of Colleges and Preparatory Schools. Eliot, "Discussion," *School Review,* VII (1899), 631–32.

136. Peabody, "Aims, Duties, and Opportunities," p. 523.

137. Peabody, "Continuous Moral Influence," p. 621.

138. Almost every conceivable aspect of St. Paul's—from the curriculum to the bacteria on the workmen in the school's dairy—was investigated by various experts between about 1910 and 1930. See the *SPS Rector's Reports* for the period. Sometime between 1904 and 1920 Groton was visited by Abraham Flexner, one of the most acute educational experts in the nation, "for the purposes of a general survey, which led to considerable changes." Ashburn, *Peabody,* pp. 136–37 n. I have not been able to locate Flexner's report, which should be of considerable interest.

139. Horce Dutton Taft to Peabody, 27 April 1927, Peabody MSS. For a good short account of the remarkable Lincoln School—founded by Abraham Flexner in 1917—see Cremin, *Transformation of the School,* pp. 280–91.

140. For a superb account of this development, see Frederick Rudolph's chapter on "The Rise of Football" in his *American College and University,* pp. 373–93.

141. James Bryce to Peabody, 17 April 1907, Peabody MSS.

142. Ashburn, *Peabody,* p. 100.

143. Peabody to Roosevelt, 25 January 1906, Roosevelt MSS.

144. Peabody to Roosevelt, 16 September 1905, Roosevelt MSS.

145. Rudolph, *American College and University,* pp. 375–77.

146. As the years went on, Peabody's uneasiness with collegiate football continued. See, for example, Peabody to LeBaron R. Briggs, 8 November 1916, reprinted in Ashburn, *Peabody,* pp. 229–30.

147. Peabody, "Continuous Moral Influence," 627–28.

148. *Ibid.*

149 G. Stanley Hall, *Youth: Its Education, Regimen, and Hygiene* (New York, 1911), p. 125.

150. Briggs, "English at Groton," p. 1, Harvard SEB MSS.

151. Sedgwick, "Three Men at Groton," p. 68; Ashburn, *Peabody,* p. 222.

152. [Samuel S. Drury], *SPS Rector's Report, 1917,* p. 10.

153. Roosevelt to Peabody, 10 October 1894, Peabody MSS.

154. Martin, "Schoolmaster's Biography," p. 156.

155. Mann, *Yankee Reformers,* pp. 106–114, 77–78.

156. Rudolph, *American College and University,* pp. 359–69.

157. Theodore Roosevelt, "The College Graduate and American Life," *American Ideals,* p. 61. This talk was published as a magazine article in 1894.

158. David B. Potts, "Social Ethics at Harvard, 1881–1931: A Study in Academic Activism," in Paul Buck, ed., *Social Sciences at Harvard, 1860–1920: From Inculcation to the Open Mind* (Cambridge, 1965), pp. 91–128.

159. Mann, *Yankee Reformers,* p. 124.

160. See esp. Allen F. Davis, *Spearheads for Reform: The Social Settlements and the Progressive Movement, 1890–1914* (New York, 1967), pp. 23–39 and *passim;* Peterson, *New England College,* pp. 172–95.

161. Bushnell, *Christian Nurture,* p. 14.

162. See above, p. 114.

163. Peabody, "Aims, Duties, and Opportunities," 528.

164. [Samuel S. Drury], *SPS Rector's Report, 1923,* p. 4.

165. Martin, "Schoolmaster's Biography," 161.

166. *The Grotonian,* VI (March 1888), 8.

167. *Ibid.,* XIII (February 1897), 121.

168. *Ibid.,* XII (February 1896), 77.

169. *Ibid.,* XIV (February 1898), 91.

170. All from the *SPS Statement* for the respective years.

171. *SPS Statement, 1920–1921,* p. 37.

172. *Horae Scholasticae* (9 June 1910), 198–99; for the equation of American Progressivism with the contemporary movement for social democracy in the Western world, see George E. Mowry, "Social Democracy, 1900–1918," in C. Vann Woodward, ed., *The Comparative Approach to American History* (New York, 1968), pp. 271–84.

173. *Letters from Hofwyl,* p. 164.

174. See above, p. 60.

175. Jacob A. Riis to Peabody, 10 April 1893; 29 March [1893]; 1 December 1905; 11 May 1906, Peabody MSS; see too Riis, *The Making of An American* (New York, 1901), p. 192 ff., and James C. Mackenzie to Riis, 18 January 1895, Jacob A. Riis MSS, Manuscript Division, LC.

176. Ashburn, *Peabody,* pp. 102, 231.

177. Peabody to Mr. Fiske, 24 July 1923, reprinted in *ibid.,* pp. 267–269.

178. Martin, "Schoolmaster's Biography," p. 159; Booker T. Washington to Peabody, 5 May 1898; 19 May 1898; 23 November 1900, Peabody MSS; Ashburn, *Peabody,* p. 210.

179. Reprinted in Ashburn, *Peabody,* pp. 176–77.

180. Martin, "Schoolmaster's Biography," p. 159.

181. *The Grotonian,* XII (December 1895), 39.

182. For a lucid and convincing discussion of imperialism as a manifestation of Progressivism, see William E. Leuchtenburg, "Progressivism and Imperialism: The Progressive Movement and American Foreign Policy, 1898–1916," *Mississippi Valley Historical Review,* XXIX (1952–53), 483–504.

183. *The Grotonian,* XV (November 1898), 37; (December 1898), 58; (January 1899), 76.

184. Henry Cabot Lodge to Peabody, 17 August 1898, Peabody MSS.

185. Clarence E. Hale to John A. Hobson, 8 March 1903, in "Letters to Authors," *The Choate School Brief,* IV (April 1903), 11.

186. Hobson was spending a year in the United States as a visiting professor at the University of Wisconsin. His reply is worth reprinting in full:

> I am proud that you should have read my book upon "Imperialism" but pained that it should have failed to convince your mind of the grave dangers which attend the national policy (or impolicy) thus designated. You think that the forcible seizure by England or the United States of a country occupied by a "lower race" and the forcible maintainance of government by the "higher race" may be an education and a civilizing process by which the lower race may gain.
>
> The radical assumptions contained in this view are that there is only one sort of civilization and that the Anglo-Saxon peoples have got so much more of it than the others, that they can impart it to the lower races. Now there is no reason to suppose that there is only one sort of, or one path to, civilization: there are so many types of civilization as there are races and natural environments.
>
> There is no reason to suppose that, with the best intentions and the best efforts, England can implant the political, religious and social institutions, and the valuations and methods of conduct which constitute her civilization, in India; or that the United States can do this in the Philippines. Each nation may claim that she is doing it, but the claim will not bear investigation. What an Anglo-Saxon nation can do is to fasten on the lower nations their "forms" of justice, their "forms" of government, but they will remain there unassimilated in the life of the people, a "foreign" body. Those who believe in the principles of "self-government" and "self-development" for which Washington and Lincoln stood, will not believe

that good government or any other art of civilization can be imposed autocratically by any nation upon any other nation. You cannot take the *flora* and *fauna* from a tropical country, plant them in the soil of a frigid country and expect them to grow; similarly with those delicate plants which we term the arts of civilization: you may, of course, raise them artificially as "exotics" in hothouses, you can not implant them in the hearts of the people. The claim that this is actually done is one which almost always rests upon the statement of the "civilizing power," and will not stand an impartial examination.

You can keep formal order in the Philippines, as we English can in India, but it is at the expense of progress; for true progress implies internal growth in an atmosphere of progress; for true progress implies internal growth in an atmosphere of liberty, and this condition is denied. As for the talk to the effect that these lower races enjoy more real liberty under our rule than under the rules, often tyrannical, which they might set up, this is sheer sophistry: the progress of a people towards liberal self-government always passes through various stages of despotism and oligarchy, and it may well be true that their natural development has at present reached a low stage of government. But let them alone and they retain at any rate some chance of natural progress: establish imperial control from outside, you check all progress.

One of your ablest statesmen, the late Mr. Reed, put the matter of imperialism with as much wisdom as wit when he said, "Many Americans seem to think that America has a mission to carry 'canned civilization' to the heathen." If civilization were a commodity that could be "canned" and preserved, and the same sorts suited the digestion of all races, the argument for imperialism, as beneficial to the lower races, would be plausible.

But you can't "can" civilization; and the sorts of civilization these lower races need must be grown by themselves, for themselves, in their own soil.

This is the sound doctrine of American democracy embodied in the famous saying of Abraham Lincoln, "No man is good enough to govern another, without the other's consent."

If no man, then no nation. The sentiment of Abraham Lincoln is good enough, true enough, and sufficiently comprehensive for me, an Englishman. I suggest that it remains good enough for Americans. (Hobson to Hale, 12 March 1903, *ibid.,* pp. 15–16).

187. Martin, "Schoolmaster's Biography," p. 161; Sedgwick, "Three Men of Groton." p. 70.

188. Ashburn, *Fifty Years On,* pp. 165–78; Ashburn, *Peabody,* pp. 317–23.

189. Peabody to Harrison Dibblee, Jr., 19 December 1932, Peabody MSS.

190. William C. Endicott to Peabody, 1 August 1933. Peabody MSS.

191. Peabody to unnamed correspondent, 1936, reprinted in Ashburn, *Peabody,* p. 345.

192. Peabody to Franklin D. Roosevelt, 12 November 1936, Peabody MSS.

193. *Report of the Principal to the Trustees, 1957–1958* (Exeter, N.H., 1959), p. 12.

194. *The Choate Alumni Bulletin,* VIII (November 1946), 74–75.

Notes on Sources

The history of education touches on almost all aspects of a particular society. Therefore, the contemporary historian of education—whether he wishes to or not—almost invariably finds himself writing in that vague genre called "cultural history." This book is no exception. It draws on such a wide variety of primary and secondary sources that a conventional bibliographical apparatus would be of little use to the scholar. Since the notes provide a running commentary on the sources, I have chosen to discuss only two matters below: first, general works relating to the history of American education, and second, the major manuscript and archival collections used in the preparation of this study.

Lawrence A. Cremin's *The Wonderful World of Ellwood Patterson Cubberley: An Essay on the Historiography of American Education* (New York, 1965), is a comprehensive and suggestive introduction to the historiography of American education. Though presently badly in need of revision, Bernard Bailyn's *Education in the Forming of American Society: Needs and Opportunities for Study* (Chapel Hill, 1960), has been of great conceptual suggestiveness for students of American social and educational history. Bailyn's book should be read along with one of the seminal works in contemporary social and educational history, Philippe Ariès *Centuries of Childhood: A Social History of Family Life* (New York, 1965). The best survey of the history of American education now available is R. Freeman Butts and Lawrence A. Cremin's *A History of Education in American Culture* (New York, 1955), written from a progressive viewpoint and now badly outdated. All students of the history of American education await Professor Cremin's massive history of American education, now in progress, with considerable interest.

Although the history of education is afflicted with a plethora of studies of individual institutions, ranging in quality from the dismal to the brilliant, it strangely lacks contemporary studies of particular types of institution of the quality of Frederick Rudolph's *The American College and University, A History* (New York, 1962). For example, there is no history of the American kindergarten or of American primary education; we lack histories of major institutions such as the American academy and the reform school. There is no history of college preparation in the United States, of the American college student, or of professional education. Not the least, no history of American secondary education has appeared since Elmer E. Brown's *Making of Our Middle Schools* in 1903. The present work does not pretend to be a comprehensive study of even private boarding schools for boys; it is hoped that it will suggest further studies in the history of American secondary education in general, and of boarding schools in particular.

An exhaustive bibliography of books and articles relating to the private preparatory school is Pauline Anderson's *A Selected Bibliography of Literature on the Independent School* (Milton, Mass., 1959), which deals not only with the type of school discussed here, but with schools for girls, military schools, and others. However, for this work general circulation materials proved to be of limited usefulness. Far more valuable to the historian are publications of the schools themselves—annual catalogues, student magazines and newspapers, alumni magazines, official reports, and so forth. The major repository for such material is Widener Library, Harvard University, which has complete collections of this type of material for many schools. The library of Teachers College, Columbia University, also has less extensive, but significant, collections of printed materials, particularly long runs of school catalogues. Most valuable in the preparation of this study were manuscript and archival collections. The major ones consulted were:

George Bancroft MSS: American Antiquarian Society, Worcester, Mass.
About three dozen illuminating letters from the young Bancroft to various members of his family, many relating to Round Hill.

George Bancroft MSS: Massachusetts Historical Society, Boston, Mass.
The major collection of Bancroft materials, indispensable for an understanding of Round Hill and Harvard in the 1810s and 1820s.

George Bancroft MSS: New York Public Library, New York City
Many letters relating to Bancroft's Round Hill years, material on the elusive Joseph Green Cogswell, and Bancroft's important unpublished essay, "Of the Liberal Education of Boys."

Joseph H. Choate MSS: Manuscript Division, Library of Congress, Washington, D.C.

Unfortunately, Joseph was rather disdainful of his brother William, founder of the Choate School—but there are a few revealing items relating to the school in his correspondence.

The Choate School: Archives and Collections, Administrative Offices and Andrew Mellon Library, Wallingford, Conn.

In 1963, when my research there was carried on, Choate had only just begun to organize its archives. Among the MS sources examined, though not for the most part used in the present study, were: the MS Scholarship Records, 1925–1940; the MS Alumni Records, 1900–1940; the MS Admission Applications, 1918–1935, and the MS Minutes of the Board of Trustees, 1930–1940.

Aside from the annual *Catalogue,* the most valuable printed sources were the student magazine, *The Choate School Brief,* and *The Choate Alumni Bulletin.* The material for a full-scale history of the school is readily available; one is promised in time for the school's seventy-fifth anniversary in 1971.

Jeremiah Day MSS: Beinecke Library, Yale University, New Haven, Conn.

Several important letters regarding Round Hill and its problems from Joseph Green Cogswell and George Bancroft.

Charles W. Eliot MSS: Harvard University Archives, Widener Library, Cambridge, Mass.

Eliot was the single most important figure in late nineteenth-century American education; his interests and influence touched every aspect of the field. His papers are indispensable for an understanding of American secondary and higher education.

William C. Endicott MSS: Massachusetts Historical Society

A disappointingly few letters from Endicott Peabody to Groton's influential treasurer.

Samuel A. Green MSS: Massachusetts Historical Society

A few letters from Endicott Peabody requesting support in founding Groton.

Harvard College Admission Books: Harvard University Archives, Widener Library

The four MS Admission Books, covering the period from the 1830s to the 1880s, illustrate well the difficulties involved in trying to determine the manner in which students prepared for college in the nineteenth century. The books record the student's name, date of admission, age, and the *individual* presenting the boy for admission. Not until the late 1870s are *institutions* listed. In other words, one has no way (unless one has an encyclopedic knowledge of nineteenth-century schoolmen) of determining whether or not the youth was prepared at an institution, or by a private individual.

Harvard College Papers: Harvard University Archives, Widener Library

Several documents and letters relating to the Round Hill School.

[*Harvard University*] *Schools Examination Board Reports and Papers:* Harvard University Archives, Widener Library

A treasure-trove of opinion and information on American secondary schools in the 1890s. Between 1892 and 1894 many of the most illustrious members of the Harvard faculty investigated and reported on eleven different secondary schools: Milton Academy, Peekskill Military Academy, Groton, Phillips Exeter Academy, Roxbury Latin School, Salem High School, Watertown (Mass.) High School, St. Mark's, Mt. Hermon School, Clinton (N.H.) High School, and Newton (Mass.) High School. Their voluminous reports not only give an excellent picture of practices and conditions at the schools, but implicitly reflect their authors' assumptions about the nature of the emerging academic profession. They might constitute the base for an extremely interesting and revealing monograph.

Lawrenceville School: Archives and Collections, John Dixon Library, Lawrenceville, New Jersey

The Archives Room of the Dixon Library contains a great deal of valuable manuscript material, especially various reports on the condition and future of the school prepared at different times. There is also a considerable amount of material relating to the headmastership of James Mackenzie, and a special folder relating to Mackenzie's work on the Committee of Ten. The basement of the administration building houses masses of uncatalogued materials.

Among printed sources the most useful are the annual catalogue (*The Register*), two student publications, *The Olla Pod* and the *Lawrence,* and the *Lawrenceville Alumni Magazine*.

Endicott Peabody MSS: Houghton Library, Harvard University

Though strictly speaking a collection of private papers, in fact the Peabody MSS constitute a school archive of 160 boxes of miscellaneous materials. About 2,000 letters (largely those received by Peabody) have been catalogued, but these only begin to indicate the richness of this collection. Although Frank Ashburn's *Peabody of Groton* (1944) is an excellent example of the Mark Howe school of biography, Peabody should have a full, professional "life." Consider his position in the late 1930s: his cousin Billy Endicott's grandson, Neville Chamberlain, was in residence at 10 Downing Street; his cousin Eleanor Roosevelt's husband, Franklin, was in residence at 1600 Pennsylvania Avenue; Peabody could provide the fulcrum for a provocative study of Anglo-American relations in the late nineteenth and early twentieth centuries.

Among printed sources, the annual *Catalogue* of the Groton School is valuable, as are the student magazine, *The Grotonian,* and *The Groton School Quarterly,* the most sophisticated of preparatory school publications.

Phillips Exeter Academy: Archives and Collections, Administrative Offices and Davis Library, Exeter, N.H.

More than at most schools, Exeter's library and administrative staffs are conscious of the school's historical importance and of the value of their records. However, the records are scattered from one end of the Academy to the other and are, with some notable exceptions, quite incomplete due to the several disastrous fires Exeter has suffered in the past 170 years.

The most valuable single source is the MS Records of the Board of Trustees, 1783–1934. More than simply minutes of meetings, they include reports of committees on various aspects of the Academy, annual budgets, many copies of important incoming and outgoing letters and other items. Valuable too—and a distressing tribute to the invention of the typewriter—is the MS Principals' Administrative Correspondence, 1903–23, consisting of about 30,000 outgoing letters which touch on every aspect of the Academy's affairs. In 1964 they were housed under the eaves in the attic of Jeremiah Smith Hall; Exeter is planning a new library with a special Archives Room, which may be completed by the time this book appears.

Among printed sources the most useful are the annual *Catalogue of the Phillips Exeter Academy, The Phillips Exeter Monthly,* and *The Phillips Exeter Bulletin. The Pean,* the student yearbook, is particularly valuable: only with the introduction of class photographs in the 1890s did I realize that there were black students at Exeter; I have not been able to determine whether or not any attended the Academy in earlier years.

Jacob A. Riis MSS: Library of Congress

Disappointingly thin, considering Riis's extensive acquaintance among educators and experience with preparatory schools—only a couple of items.

Theodore Roosevelt MSS: Library of Congress

Many letters from and to Endicott Peabody, extremely illuminating.

College and Grammar School of St. James: Maryland Diocesan [Episcopal] MSS, Rare Book and Manuscript Room, Peabody Institute Library, Baltimore, Maryland.

The papers of the Maryland Episcopal Diocese contain a great deal of material relating to the College and Grammar School of St. James: correspondence, financial records, trustees' records, newspaper clippings, programs, student lists, circulars, and so forth. They also contain almost all of J. B. Kerfoot's correspondence with Bishop Whittingham and the original manuscript of Hall Harrison's *Life of Kerfoot.* A history of St. James would be a substantial contribution to our knowledge of *ante bellum* southern educational, religious, and social history. In June 1966, the Peabody Institute Library was merged with Baltimore's Pratt Free Library; the future location of the Diocesan Papers was undecided.

St. Paul's School: Archives and Collections, Administrative Offices and Sheldon Library, Concord, N.H.

During my two months at St. Paul's, I was able only to skim the surface of its extensive records. Particularly valuable were the copies of MS letters relating to the founding of the school. The MS autograph collections are large and include many valuable letters, diaries of students, and diaries of faculty members, like that of Willard Scudder. The MS Minutes of the Board of Trustees, 1911–1941 (no one knew where the pre-1911 Minutes were) are enlightening on St. Paul's history for that period, but were barely utilized in this study. Especially useful was the MS "Rural Record," six folio volumes of day-by-day happenings at the school kept by various hands from 1856 to 1902. The MS records of student literary, social, and athletic organizations, enormous in extent, were examined. They did not prove particularly useful in this study; however, they could provide in themselves the basis for an interesting study of student life. The archives contain too a large an amount of miscellaneous manuscript material—letters, reports, and so forth.

Printed school publications were particularly helpful. Most useful in tracing enrollment, curriculum, etc., was the *Annual Statement of St. Paul's School,* 1858–1914. *The Horae Scholasticae,* 1860– , the student magazine, is a mine of interesting material, as are the *Annual Report of the Rector to the Corporation,* 1907– , and the *Alumni Horae,* 1921–

Shattuck Family MSS: Massachusetts Historical Society

Another enormous collection, extending from the eighteenth to the twentieth centuries. Valuable material on Round Hill and on the background of St. Paul's. Apparently, Round Hill's lessons in penmanship did not endure: aside from Henry Cabot Lodge, the second George Shattuck's script is the most difficult to decipher of any nineteenth-century American that I have encountered. Even more than the Warrens of Boston, the Shattuck medical dynasty deserves a "family biography."

Benjamin Silliman, Sr., MSS: Beinecke Library, Yale University

A few items relating to Round Hill.

William Howard Taft MSS: Library of Congress
Unlike the Choate brothers, William and his brother Horace Dutton were close friends. The Taft MSS contain many revealing letters from Horace to his brother, not for the most part utilized in this study; they will be indispensable if a history of the Taft School is ever written.

Ward Family MSS: Manuscript Division, New York Public Library
Several letters from Bancroft and Cogswell relating to the Round Hill School; better than any other source I know, the letters of Henry, Samuel, and Marion Ward to their parents convey the "feel" of Round Hill.

Warren Family MSS: Massachusetts Historical Society
One interesting letter from Endicott Peabody to Dr. J. C. Warren.

Thomas Kelah Wharton, MS Journal: Manuscript Division, New York Public Library
An intimate and charming picture of life at the Flushing Institute, and the only source that ties Muhlenberg's practices directly to those of Fellenberg's Hofwyl.

Yale University: Miscellaneous Corporation Papers, Beinecke Library
Jeremiah Day's important report on the college in 1818, the forerunner of the famous Report of 1828.

Index